CASS SERIES: STUDI
(Series Editor: Se

AIR POWER HISTORY

CASS SERIES: STUDIES IN AIR POWER

(Series Editor: Sebastian Cox)

ISSN 1368-5597

AIR POWER HISTORY

TURNING POINTS FROM KITTY HAWK TO KOSOVO

Edited by
SEBASTIAN COX
Head of Air Historical Branch, Ministry of Defence
and
PETER GRAY
Director of Defence Studies, Royal Air Force

With an Introduction by
RICHARD OVERY

FRANK CASS
LONDON • PORTLAND, OR

First published in 2002 in Great Britain by
FRANK CASS PUBLISHERS
2 Park Square, Milton Park, Abingdon,
Oxon, OX14 4RN

and in the United States of America by
FRANK CASS PUBLISHERS
270 Madison Ave,
New York NY 10016

Transferred to Digital Printing 2005

Website: www.frankcass.com

British Library Cataloguing in Publication Data

Air power history: turning points from Kitty Hawk to Kosovo / edited by Sebastian Cox
and Peter Gray with a foreword by Richard Overy.
    p.   cm. – (Cass series–studies in air power, ISSN 1368-5597; 13)
    Includes bibliographical references and index.
    ISBN 0-7146-5291-1 (cloth) – ISBN 0-7146-8257-8 (paper)
    1. Air power–History. 2. Air warfare–History. 3. Aeronautics, Military. I. Cox,
Sebastian. II. Gray, Peter, 1953 June 13. III. Series.

UG630 .A38257 2002
358.4'009–dc21   2002025987

ISBN 0-7146-5291-1 (cloth)
ISBN 0-7146-8257-8 (paper)
ISSN 1368-5597

Library of Congress Cataloging-in-Publication Data

Air power history: turning points from Kitty Hawk to
    Kosovo. – (Cass series. Studies in air power; no. 13)
    1. Air power – History 2. Air warfare – History
    I. Cox, Sebastian II. Gray, Peter, 1949–
    358.4'009

Typeset in 11/12 Monotype Imprint by Vitaset, Paddock Wood, Kent

Printed and bound by Antony Rowe Ltd, Eastbourne

Contents

Editors' Preface

This book comprises papers presented at a conference held at the Royal Air Force Museum at Hendon on 10–11 July 2001. The Conference was organized jointly by the Air Historical Branch, the Museum and the Royal Air Force Director of Defence Studies.

The aim of the conference was to examine the events and experiences, from the First World War to Kosovo, which have shaped present-day thinking on the use of air power and the evolution of modern doctrine. This book is intended to bring the topics covered to a wider audience, albeit without the discussions that took place in the main forum and in the margins. A brief glance at the contents page will show that we were able to bring together many leading air power specialists from academia and the services.

Airmen the world over are at their happiest talking tactics or technology. For many, history was a school subject to be abandoned at the earliest opportunity along with its lists of kings, presidents and prime ministers. For some, the accumulation of knowledge extends no further back than the debrief points from the last flight. Yet at least one current definition of doctrine cites the accumulation of knowledge and experience as the seed corn of conceptual thinking; in other words, doctrine is what has worked best in the past. Yet gleaning relevant experience from history is no easy task. It requires thought, analysis and a knowledge of the context far beyond the straight narrative that used to be the standard fare of old. History, if it is to provide guidance for doctrine writers and, more importantly, for practitioners must be shorn of its myths, fables and legends. We hope that the ensuing chapters will allow the reader to look at the span of aviation history and decide for him or herself what constitutes a turning point and wherein lies the enduring elements of air power. The chapters follow a broad chronological order with self-evident titles. The erudition of the authors is such that any attempt to summarize, or paraphrase their work would be a nugatory effort on our part.

We are particularly grateful to all of those who took part in the conference – the speakers who have taken time to update their papers in the light of the subsequent discussion, the delegates whose participation ensured that the proceedings were lively and productive, the panel chairmen and the Museum staff who provided such excellent facilities. No conference, and ensuing publication, is possible without considerable hard work and we are most grateful to Wing Commanders Roger Marsh, Philip Greville, Squadron Leader Tim Mason and Ms Jane Curtis who ensured that the necessary detail was seen to in immaculate style and with considerable good humour. Thanks also go to the staff at Frank Cass Publishers and to the wider staffs of all three organizations for their unfailing support – repercussions from planning and running conferences spread far and wide!

Sebastian Cox
Peter Gray

Introduction

Richard Overy

Powered flight is a century old. Air power – the application of aircraft in military conflict – is younger still. It might be dated from the moment when two Italian aviators decided to throw shells from their reconnaissance aircraft on to their Turkish enemy in the Italo-Turkish war of 1911, but as a serious element in combat air power emerged slowly during the course of the First World War.[1] Even then air power theory ran well ahead of the technical capability of aircraft to transform theory into practice. The popular imagination was also well in advance of reality. Fears about the extraordinary destructive power of the aeroplane flourished between the wars, even though all the practical evidence – the partial destruction of the Spanish city of Guernica in 1937 being the best-known example, indeed almost the only example – came from very small-scale attacks, whose impact was anything but decisive. Air power emerged as a major strategic element during the course of the Second World War and for the rest of the twentieth century remained so. Recent conflict, from the Gulf War to Afghanistan, has seen air power come of age. Its development has been linear or evolutionary in character, but, like modern versions of Darwin's theory, the course of air power history has been punctuated by sudden periods of accelerated change.

Air power history has also come of age. For much of the last century the focus of this history was on air combat and aircraft technology, often divorced from the wider history of warfare, or from the history of scientific and technical development. Aircraft generated a glamorous drama that made them the stuff of endless war novels and feature films. Air fighting generated its own historical myths and legends. Yet the serious business of defeating the enemy was still seen as the function of surface forces. Air power faded away in accounts of the invasion of Hitler's Europe on all fronts, or of the defeat of Japan in the Pacific. Aircraft have always been regarded as ancillary to the story of army against army in the First World War. Even the obvious exception – the bombing of Germany between 1940 and 1945 – was popularly regarded as a waste of strategic effort, which might more usefully have been devoted to producing ships and tanks to speed up the defeat of German submarines and the formidable German Army.

Over the past quarter century or so much of this has changed. Air power history has become respectable. There is now a large body of scholarly academic literature, which has not only succeeded in placing air power in its proper historical context, but in pushing the subject beyond the fighting front to embrace a whole range of different historical issues and approaches. There is now an extensive intellectual history of air power that focuses on the development of doctrine in many differing contexts, thanks in no small part to the interest of air force history offices in understanding the historical roots of current air power thinking. The evolution of air power theory is no longer regarded as a single story. Where American and British thinkers concentrated on defining the nature and objectives of long-range bombing as the principal function of air power, German, French and Soviet air power theorists were more concerned with the strategic gains to be made by using aircraft in optimal ways at the battlefront, in support of ground forces.[2] The reasons for these differences in the approach to air doctrine are to be found not simply in the influence of prominent individuals, but arose from differing perceptions about the nature of modern warfare, or from the differing balance of political power among army, navy and air force, or differences derived from cultural or social diversity. Air power doctrine cannot be understood apart from the intellectual, cultural and political context in which it has been generated, and it is from this perspective that much recent writing on doctrine has proceeded.[3]

The economic history of air power is also now well developed. Aircraft production and development form a central part of the story of air power, which can be told in its own right rather than as a footnote to air combat. Aircraft production was an important test of fundamental questions of economic and technical modernity. Small powers could produce as much air power theory as they liked, but effective air power could be exercised only by states with the technical and resource capability to produce aircraft of advanced design and in large quantities. The accelerating cost of aviation development and procurement since the 1950s has, if anything, made this gap wider. As economic history, aircraft production raises questions that are quite distinct from air power history in a narrow sense. Corelli Barnett's *Audit of War*, a challenging indictment of British technical capability in the Second World War, rested on comparisons between British, German and American aircraft factories, in which British performance was deemed to be less productive and technically adept. This thesis has not gone unchallenged, but above all it has encouraged economic historians to think more carefully about comparative industrial performance and differences in labour practices and managerial cultures.[4]

It is only in this way that some large questions about aircraft production can be answered. How, for example, did Britain succeed in outproducing Germany in 1940 during the critical months of the Battle of Britain, despite the fact that Germany had more aluminium, more machine-tools and a larger aircraft industry labour force? When US air intelligence assessed German capabilities in 1939 and 1940, based on what was known of German factory capacity and on generous assumptions about German technical competence, it was estimated that Germany could produce between 32,000 and 48,000 aircraft a year, making it overwhelmingly more powerful in the air than the RAF.[5] Instead, Britain produced 50 per cent more aircraft than Germany during that critical year, and 100 per cent more in 1941. Actual German production was 10,000 in 1940 and 11,000 the following year.

The explanations for this are complex. The two sides were working under different pressures – German intelligence greatly underestimated the capacity of British aircraft production, British intelligence greatly inflated German capabilities – but there were other contrasts that mattered. In Germany the technical requirements were set very high, and were constantly changed by the air force in response to short-run tactical requirements. High standards meant a high skill ratio in the workforce, and work practices that militated against faster output. Managers had little incentive to produce other than a high-cost product, since that was what the air force wanted. The result was an individual aircraft of a very high standard and quality of finish, but too few to meet current strategic needs. British construction was better planned, less subject to short-term interruption and better adapted to lower-cost quantity production, even if, as German test pilots argued, the end product was less technically sophisticated than German models.[6] Similar questions might be asked of Soviet production in the 1930s and 1940s, where inherited technical backwardness had to be overcome very quickly to generate the robust generation of high-performance aircraft produced between 1942 and 1945. Aircraft production exposed the strengths and weaknesses of planning and production processes up to the point in the 1960s where the technology became so complex and expensive that aircraft were produced in multiples of ten rather than thousands, and marginal costs mattered less than technical sophistication.

The most distinctive aspect of the new air power history is the growing emphasis on the social, cultural and political dimensions of the subject. Air forces have their own social history separate from, if related to, the nature of combat. The sociological analysis of air force personnel is still in its infancy. The nature of recruitment, the social

origins of recruits, their educational and cultural outlook, are all issues
that deserve more scholarly attention. Some aspects have already been
tackled. The role of women aviators in the Soviet Air Force during the
Second World War has raised important questions about patterns of
sexual recruitment and discrimination in modern air forces.[7] The role
of black aviators in the United States Air Forces has at last been
recognized.[8] The social history of air force life has been explored less.
The pioneering study of air force morale in the Second World War by
Mark Wells demonstrates a great deal about the social character of the
two bomber forces he examines, while it also analyses issues of psychological health, courage and discipline that ought to form an essential
part of any air force history.[9]

The social and cultural history of air power has an external dimension as well. During the inter-war years there developed what in Britain
was called 'air-mindedness', a widespread and popular interest in air
power, air travel and aeronautical culture. This was an international
phenomenon. Uri Bialer's seminal study of British attitudes to air power
can now be read together with Peter Fritzsche's account of popular
aviation culture in Germany.[10] The cultural history of air power goes
back to the late nineteenth century, when popular literature began
to explore air wars of the future well before powered flight had been
achieved. By the period following the First World War, air power culture
was well established. Thousands of young Europeans and Americans
were fascinated by aircraft. In the USSR the Society for Promoting
Aviation and Chemical Defence (*Osaviakhim*) could boast 13 million
members by the mid-1930s, thousands of whom later went on to
become pilots in the Second World War. During the years of enforced
disarmament in the 1920s, young Germans fascinated by aviation set up
aero-model clubs or learned gliding.[11] The combat airmen of the
Second World War were mainly volunteers, seduced by the excitement
and modernity of air power. In the popular imagination, aircraft
produced a fundamental turning point in human conflict.

Air power also critically affected, and still affects, the societies and
political systems subject to air attack. Sometimes the impact can be
dramatic: Taliban fundamentalism brutally transformed Afghan society,
but its defeat under the impact of heavy air attack has just as rapidly
reshaped Afghan politics and social possibilities. During the Second
World War, air power produced widespread social distortions, dis-
placing populations, compelling evacuation and the dispersal of the
workplace, disrupting patterns of family life, education and welfare.
The mass destruction of German and Japanese cities engendered
profound changes in the landscape constructed after 1945, as well
as profound psychological trauma, whose consequences have scarcely
been studied.[12] The social and moral impact of air attack has received

less attention than the economic or political effects and consequences, yet in terms of the current exercise of air power it is a dimension that needs to be understood more fully, not least to ensure that the consequences of air attack are fully understood when making judgements about its desirability as an instrument of coercion.

The many ways in which air power is now understood historically have produced a fuller and more comprehensible narrative of the century of air power. The story is continuous and evolutionary, but there were evident turning points, when the process of change and development was accelerated, or in some cases forced along different paths. Some dramatic events in air power history turn out to be a less of a turning point than they seemed at the time. The Battle of Britain was certainly vital for the short-term survival of Britain in 1940, but the air power developments that made the battle and its outcome possible would have evolved in any case. The fast fighters and radar screens were part of the general programme of vanguard research and development in the 1930s, whether war had come or not. Many turning points lacked real drama, but were of decisive significance. A good case might be made for the day in February 1935 when it was finally demonstrated that radio pulses could detect oncoming aircraft. This was a turning point – and not just in air power history – that had profound implications for the combat performance of all three services in the future. There have been periods of accelerated technical change (radar, jet engines, rockets, nuclear weapons all appeared in one decade) that self-evidently transformed air power. There have been longer periods of quieter evolution. Turning points of any real historical significance have been less common, often unpredictable and subject to regular historical reevaluation. The essays in this book indicate how wide-ranging and historically diverse the idea of turning point can be.

On one conclusion there must be general agreement: the greatest turning point in air power history came with the Second World War. This was the hinge of air power, closing the door on the early, tentative history of simple, lightly-armed bi-planes, and opening a new one on the world of fast monoplane fighters, high-performance bombers, modern armament and equipment that has been sustained for the half-century thereafter with few fundamental discontinuities. The Second World War saw the introduction of large-scale long-range bombardment, whose effects, though hotly debated still, were infinitely greater than the impact of bombing at any point earlier in the century.[13] The war also launched the effective use of tactical aircraft working closely with mobile ground forces. The rocket-firing, high-speed fighter bomber of the last years of the war is recognizable still in the aircraft operating in Afghanistan or Kosovo, but it is incomparably different from the tiny low-powered biplanes of the Great War.[14] The super-bombers of the

late war period – the German Arado 234, or the Boeing B-29 – were the
direct ancestors of the B-52s, still in action as large level-flying bombers
60 years later. A great many other technical and organizational innovations cut off the wartime experience from the pre-war age. Above all,
the Second World War generated the rockets and nuclear warheads that
would become the standard armoury of the Cold War and post-Cold War
superpowers, changing the nature of air power beyond recognition.

The war represented a turning point in another less evident sense. In
the 1920s and 1930s, there was a widespread, if irrational, belief that
air war in the future would bring about apocalyptic destruction and the
end of civilization. Governments gloomily surveyed the prospects of
surviving beyond the nightmare of massive air attack. Air power was
believed to be unstoppable, in some sense beyond mere human agency.
In H. G. Wells's *The War in the Air,* first written in 1908, but widely
reprinted and read in the inter-war years, his characters reflect in an
epilogue on the reasons why their world was destroyed by air war:

> 'But why did they start the War?'
> 'They couldn't stop themselves. 'Aving them airships made 'em.'
> 'And 'ow did the War end?'
> 'Lord knows if it's ended, boy,' said old Tom. 'Lord knows if it's
> ended.' ...
> 'But why didn't they end the War?'
> 'Obstinacy. Everybody was getting 'urt, but everybody was 'urtin and
> everybody was 'igh-spirited and patriotic, and so they smeshed up things
> instead. They jes' went on smeshin'. And afterwards they jes' got desp'rite
> and savige.'[15]

As real war came closer in the 1930s there was a fatalistic fear that air
warfare, using bombs, gas or biological weapons, would scarcely be survivable. During the winter 'Blitz' on London of 1940–41, German
leaders waited for the bombing to create so much panic and social crisis
that the British would sue for peace rather than endure it further.[16]

In reality, air warfare, even the Combined Bomber Offensive and the
atomic attacks on Japan, was 'survivable' for those who were not its
victims. Civilization did not perish under bomb attack; instead, both
Japan and Germany rapidly revived as major industrial societies, enjoying exceptional standards of living. Since 1945, and the onset of the
nuclear age, there has been a growing sense that air power is control-
lable by human agency; indeed, the prospect of a mutual nuclear
exchange places a high premium on the need to control their use, and
to minimize any danger that their employment might be triggered by
technical or organizational imperatives that decision-makers would
find very difficult to resist. This was a slow development. It could well
be argued that the bombing of Vietnam was carried out because of just

such imperatives, in the uncritical belief that once again, as in the Second World War, massive bombing would solve a strategic problem by making life unendurable for the North Vietnamese and warfare unsustainable by the Viet Cong. The failure of bombing on this occasion coincided with a technical revolution that was making it possible for air power and its effects to be controlled very closely by the use of sophisticated new systems for identifying and destroying precise targets, with weapons of sufficient rather than overwhelming power. While city-busting nuclear missiles and level-flying super-bombers have survived to this day, the main focus of air power development since the 1970s has been on missiles and aircraft capable of destruction with a high degree of accuracy. The current armoury of stand-off weapons, computer-directed battlefields and air drones has brought air power enhanced lethality, but at the same time the means to closely control its employment.

For all the massive destruction wrought by aircraft in the Second World War, the vision of the end of the world peddled by pre-war popular writing was confounded. After 1945 anti-aircraft defences and civil defence preparation became more sophisticated, eliminating any prospect of conventional air attack of devastating effect between major states. But the effects of bombing during the war created a different turning point. By the war's end, there was already a popular backlash against bombing on moral grounds. For the past half-century there has been a continuous debate on the legitimacy of air attack where there is a strong likelihood of civilian casualties.[17] There is an explicit assumption that bombing can now be directed at precise targets with few civilian casualties; why, then, did the wars of the twentieth century kill so many civilians from the air?

There were two ways in which such casualties could have been avoided or minimized. One was to increase accuracy to an exceptional degree. Great efforts were made to do so, but even the US Air Forces, whose doctrine was predicated on accurate daytime bombing, found that in practice most bombs missed the target by a wide margin and killed Germans instead.[18] The second path was self-restraint. This was the position of the major powers at the onset of the Second World War: targets which carried the risk of civilian casualty should be avoided.[19] The escalation of the bombing war was partly a consequence of the prevailing idea of total war. It was widely assumed that war would be directed at whole populations through blockade, bombing and other forms of economic and psychological warfare. The Western states expected the worst of Germany, whose system of government was likely, it was believed, to endorse the most extreme forms of air warfare. According to one contemporary volume, entitled *Air Power and Civilization,* bombing and dictatorship went hand-in-hand:

The outstanding feature of the Second World War is, of course, its extreme totalitarian character, brought about by intensive development of the military aeroplane, the devising of new techniques for its use in battle, and, above all, its less discriminate employment against civil populations. The whole is the product of a system of authoritative government described as totalitarian ...[20]

Under these conditions, self-restraint was believed to open Western, non-totalitarian states to forms of military pressure that would lead to defeat unless they adopted the same values of 'total war'. When Germany bombed Rotterdam in May 1940, the British government ordered bombing of German targets; self-restraint was abandoned. The logic of total war became self-fulfilling. It ended with the destruction of Hiroshima and Nagasaki in August 1945, when in the face of what was perceived to be yet another fanatical, totalitarian system, restraint was lifted on the most destructive weapon of all.[21]

   Since 1945, there have been two distinct but related developments. The nuclear attacks on Japan ushered in an age in which the superpowers were capable of destroying each other utterly and most of the world's ecosystem at the same time. The prospect of mutual destruction, dangerous though it appeared to the post-war generation that had experienced 'total war' in raw reality, in fact produced a mutual restraint that survived the entire Cold War period. H. G. Wells's vision of the prospective end of civilization did not materialize once weapons were developed that were unmistakably capable of achieving it. Total war thus declined as an idea, and by the 1960s was no longer part of the popular discourse as it had been in the 1930s. On the other hand, a great deal of research effort went into developing weapons that could increase accuracy a great deal, and remove the objections to the morally questionable and militarily inefficient forms of long-range air power used in Korea and Vietnam. The end point came in the military intervention in Kosovo in 1999, where NATO suffered no combat casualties, while Serbian civilian losses were kept to a minimum. The nuclear attacks of 1945 had the long-term effect of reducing the possibility of total war with nuclear weapons, while encouraging the development of conventional weapons whose destructive power and utility would at last achieve what the target planners of the Second World War would have liked to have done.

   Victory in 1945 was achieved by all three armed services, but airmen were tempted to argue that this had really been a vindication of air power. When Lord Tedder, the British air marshal who had been Eisenhower's deputy in the invasion of Europe, gave the Lees-Knowles lectures at Cambridge in 1947 he told his audience that the 'vital lesson' of the Second World War was that 'air power is the dominant factor in this modern world and that ... it will remain the dominant factor so long as power determines the fate of nations'.[22] It might well be argued that what the war demonstrated was the opposite, that the services operating in close collaboration together achieved victory. Air power was complementary to ground power on both the western and eastern fronts in the defeat of Hitler's Germany. Air power operated with surface forces in the Pacific to achieve the defeat of Japan. Collaboration did not eliminate often bitter arguments between the services about strategic objectives or outcomes, but the war made clear that pre-war fantasies about air power superseding other forms of combat were unfounded. Of course, victory would have been unlikely without air power; German defeat would have been less certain if the German Air Force had fulfilled its very great potential. But these conclusions do not imply that air power was the decisive element on its own. After the war the US Air Forces, given independence from the Army and reorganized in 1946 as the Strategic Air Command, certainly assumed that air power was the senior partner in future war. None the less, the lessons of the Second World War all pointed in the direction of combined operations. Despite persistent inter-service jealousies and serious arguments about doctrine, in practice 'jointery' evolved continuously, if very unevenly, out of the experience of fighting between 1939 and 1945. The arguments of the Italian air strategist, Giulio Douhet, or the American airman, Billy Mitchell, that air power rendered other forms of fighting redundant, have had few champions since 1945. The realization that air power cannot be exercised in isolation, except under the most exceptional of circumstances, has been a turning point that has contributed to the high level of inter-service collaboration and doctrinal convergence of the past ten years.

The history of air power has had its turning points. Air power reached its zenith in terms of its scale and destructiveness, and the popular culture of aviation, between 1914 and 1945. Since 1945, air power has lost much of the mystique that surrounded it for the generation before 1939. The air ace has disappeared as the schoolboy hero; the great triumphs of air exploration and navigation now seem quaint in the days of supersonic travel. Air war as science fiction has been replaced by more modest and functional images. Air power has been tamed; apocalypse has receded as a metaphor. Air forces are made up of ordinary men and women, not knights of the sky. Air power in the modern age has become one element in a sophisticated and professional defence establishment, not the destructive, unpredictable demon it once seemed. This is a real and necessary turning point.

NOTES

1. R. Hallion, *Strike from the Sky: The History of Battlefield Air Attack 1911–1945* (Washington, DC: Smithsonian Institute Press, 1989), p. 11.
2. See, for example, P. le Goyet, 'Evolution de la doctrine d'emploi de l'aviation française êntre 1919 et 1939', *Revue d'histoire de la Deuxième Guerre Mondiale*, 19 (1969); P. Vennesson, 'Institution and Air Power: The Making of the French Air Force', in J. Gooch (ed.), *Airpower: Theory and Practice* (London: Frank Cass, 1995), pp. 36–67; on the USSR, K. R. Whiting, 'Soviet Aviation and Air Power under Stalin 1928–1941', in R. Higham and J. Kipp (eds), *Soviet Aviation and Air Power: A Historical View* (London: Westview Press, 1978), pp. 50–7, or more recently R. Pennington, 'From Chaos to the Eve of the Great Patriotic War 1922–41', in R. Higham, J. T. Greenwood and Von Hardesty (eds), *Russian Aviation and Air Power in the Twentieth Century* (London: Frank Cass, 1998), pp. 37–61.
3. See the excellent study by T. D. Biddle, *Rhetoric and Reality in Air Warfare: the Evolution of British and American Ideas about Strategic Bombing, 1914–1945* (Princeton, NJ: Princeton University Press, 2002); M. Sherry, *The Rise of American Air Power: the Creation of Armageddon* (New Haven, CT: Yale University Press, 1987) is a classic study of the evolution of air power doctrine in a particular social and cultural milieu.
4. C. Barnett, *The Audit of War: the Illusion and Reality of Britain as a Great Nation* (London: Macmillan, 1986); for a more benign view of British performance see S. Ritchie, *Industry and Air Power: the Expansion of British Aircraft Production 1935–1941* (London: Frank Cass, 1997).
5. Library of Congress, Washington DC, Arnold Papers, Box 246, memorandum for Chief of Intelligence, G-2, 'Estimates of German Air Strength, Jan. 21 1941', and enclosure 'Germany, Domestic Production, Capacity and Sources of Aviation Equipment', pp. 1–8.
6. On German performance see L. Budrass, *Flugzeugindustrie und Luftrustung in Deutschland 1918–1945* (Dusseldorf, 1998), esp. Ch V. See, too, the article by J. Zeitlin, 'Flexibility and Mass Production in War: Aircraft Manufacture in Britain, the United States and Germany, 1939–1945', *Technology and Culture*, 36 (1995), pp. 46–79.
7. R. Pennington, *Wings, Women and Warfare: Soviet Airwomen in World War II Combat* (Lawrence, KS: University of Kansas Press, 2001).
8. S. Sandler, *Segregated Skies: All-Black Combat Squadrons of World War II* (Washington, DC: Smithsonian Institute Press, 1992).
9. M. Wells, *Courage and Air Warfare: The Allied Aircrew Experience in the Second World War* (London: Frank Cass, 1995).
10. U. Bialer, *The Shadow of the Bomber: The Fear of Air Attack and British Politics, 1936–1939* (London: Royal Historical Society, 1980); P. Fritzsche, *A Nation of Flyers: German Aviation and the Popular Imagination* (Cambridge, MA: Harvard University Press, 1992).
11. Details on USSR from W. Chamberlin, *Russia's Iron Age* (London, 1934), p. 200.
12. The best books are E. Beck, *Under the Bombs: The German Home Front 1942–1945* (Lexington, KY: University Press of Kentucky, 1986); O. Groehler, *Bombenkrieggegen Deutschland* (Berlin, 1990), pp. 230–320. The classic study remains F. C. Iklé, *The Social Impact of Bomb Destruction* (Norman, OK: University of Oklahoma Press, 1958).
13. See two differing views on bombing in J. McCarthy, 'Did the Bomber Always Get Through? The Control of Strategic Air Space 1939–1945' and R. J. Overy, 'World War II: the Bombing of Germany', both in A. Stephens (ed.), *The War in the Air 1914–1994* (Canberra, 1994), pp. 69–84, 107–42.

14. B. F. Cooling (ed.), *Case Studies in the Development of Close Air Support* (Washington, DC: US Government Printing Office, 1990) for a comprehensive overview of the period from 1914 to the 1960s.
15. H. G. Wells, *The War in the Air* (London, 1908), pp. 374–5.
16. For example, E. Fröhlich (ed.), *Die Tagebücher von Joseph Goebbels: sämtliche Fragmente* (4 vols, Munich, 1987), III, pp. 410, 420, 429: 'When will Churchill capitulate?' or 'so it must go on until England is on her knees, begging for peace' or 'England is isolated, will bit by bit be driven to the ground'.
17. For example, S. Garrett, *Ethics and Air Power in World War II: The British Bombing of German Cities* (New York: Palgrave Macmillan, 1993). See too J. Glover, *Humanity: A Moral History of the Twentieth Century* (London: Yale University Press, 1998), pp. 69–88. See too P. Johnson, *The Withered Garland: Reflections and Doubts of a Bomber* (London: New European Publications, 1995).
18. W. H. Park, '"Precision" and "Area" Bombing: Who Did Which, and When?', in Gooch, *Air Power*, pp. 145–74.
19. See R. J. Overy, 'Strategic Bombardment before 1939', in R. C. Hall (ed.), *Case Studies in Strategic Bombardment* (Washington, DC: Brassey's, 1998), pp. 37–8, 68–9.
20. M. J. B. Davy, *Air Power and Civilization* (London, 1941), p.147.
21. See for example M. J. Sherwin, A *World Destroyed: The Atomic Bomb and the Grand Alliance* (Stanford, CA: Stanford University Press, 2001).
22. Lord Tedder, *Air Power in War* (London: Greenwood, 1948), p. 123.

PART I:

THE FIRST WORLD WAR AND THE INTER-WAR YEARS

1

Learning in Real Time: The Development and Implementation of Air Power in the First World War

Tami Biddle

In terms of air power history, the First World War has been over-shadowed by the Second World War. But the war of 1914–18 is in fact the mother-lode for air power historians. Indeed, virtually every important manifestation of twentieth-century air power was envisioned and worked out in at least rudimentary form between 1914 and 1918. Those who want to understand the role of aircraft in subsequent con-flicts do well to turn back to the experience of the Great War precisely because all the roots of modern practice are there to be explored. Both official and unofficial interpretations of the events of the First World War had a strong influence throughout the inter-war years. In this short essay I can draw attention only to some of the highlights. I shall try to explain, concisely, what happened during the war, how it was under-stood, and how realities and interpretations sometimes conflicted. The essay will examine both tactical and strategic aviation, placing a slight emphasis on the latter. Throughout I shall focus mainly but not exclusively on the British experience.

The First World War brought to the battlefield an intimidating array of new tools for combat; not only did the 1914 generation of military leaders have to equip, organize, train, and direct million-man armies over extended battle fronts, they also had to assimilate and integrate potent new technologies. One of these – the aeroplane – had been anticipated in the popular literature for a long time.[1] There was no consensus on the role that aeroplanes would play in a coming war. High expectations in some circles were juxtaposed against the reality that the war had begun only 11 years after the Wright Brothers' success at Kitty Hawk. Early aeroplanes were experimental, unreliable craft whose military advantages remained speculative; indeed one American aviator called the early First World War aeroplane a 'little, flimsy spider-work of wood and linen'.[2]

As is always the case in war, however, progress was telescoped: by 1918 the Germans had a four-engine bomber with a wingspan just shy of a Second World War B-29, and the British were closing in fast. In a sense, both the visionaries and the conservatives were right: the war foreshadowed what was to come in the realm of air power, and saw accelerated development of most of the roles we now associate with combat aircraft. But aviation remained on the periphery of a war dominated by colossal campaigns of attrition on the ground.

The First World War tested theory and became the anvil on which new aerial missions were forged. As was true of land warfare, however, the task of developing doctrine, missions and suitable weapons types for modern warfighting proved to be complex and difficult; it demanded technological and managerial prowess at the national level, insight and flexibility at the operational and tactical levels, and skill and courage at the individual level. No nation managed to achieve all of these simultaneously and consistently throughout the war. Every nation using air power had to wrestle with a wide array of challenges, including building an adequate production base, responding to the technological innovations of the enemy, developing organizational and bureaucratic structures to support and define the use of air power, and finding ways to integrate air and ground operations successfully.

At the outset of the war, all of the European powers were in the midst of working out the competing aviation interests of their armies and navies. In no state had an ideal organizational solution been found, and service rivalries and jealousies persisted throughout the war. Perhaps the biggest challenge of all, though, was for leaders to perceive and understand the roles of aircraft in war even as they watched them develop for the first time. Errors, problems and shortfalls were paid for all too often with the lives of young men who had to entrust themselves to imperfect machines operating on the basis of flawed premises in very difficult tactical conditions.

OBSERVATION AND RECONNAISSANCE

Even those possessed of limited imagination could accept the idea that an aerial perspective would change the nature of warfighting in some fundamental ways. Aircraft, acting as observers and scouts, would be a powerful adjunct to cavalry in the reconnaissance mission. In the event, access to an aerial panorama did prove valuable – indeed, the point was made early and dramatically at both the Marne and Tannenberg.[3] Observers were called upon to locate troops, railheads, aerodromes, camps and supply dumps. Reconnaissance information, initially conveyed by notes and hand-drawn sketches, was soon gathered by aeroplane-mounted cameras. As photographic technology improved throughout the war, so did the quality of information provided to commanders; photographs became the basis of highly detailed maps, which could be widely distributed – and which would remain accurate for some time due to the static nature of the war in the west.[4]

Artillery spotting became particularly important because of the central role artillery came to play in the war. Communication posed obstacles, however, and made the process of air-artillery co-operation difficult, especially early in the war. Initially, only a very small number of planes were equipped with wireless telegraphy, and these sets were so large and clumsy that their utility was greatly compromised; other aircraft used Very lights and electric lanterns to signal back to batteries. By 1916, more and more planes were being fitted with wireless sets, but this communication went only one way – from air to ground. Troops wanting to get information back to aircraft had to rely on awkward cloth ground markers, or signal lanterns. Over time, aerial photographs came to be relied on heavily for counter-battery work.[5]

Many observer aircraft were light, unstable and possessed of unreliable, vibrating engines. They were vulnerable due to their flight altitudes and slow speeds. Observer training was spotty, and even the trained often had difficulty making out features on the ground, especially in bad weather or under fire.[6] The wireless sets of artillery spotters were subject to background noise and other types of interference, and only a limited number of aircraft could operate in a given area and frequency band. Observation for counter-battery work was painstakingly slow: engaging just one target usually took an hour's effort. And communication broke down simply because spotters were often inadequately indoctrinated in the work of the artillery arm, and thus not in a good position to intuit the kind of information required by its members. One British document on artillery spotting observed laconically, 'One of the principal factors necessary to enable successful work with the artillery is a slight knowledge of gunnery on the part of the observer.'[7]

Despite the problems, the information provided by aircraft proved enormously valuable. The inevitable result was the development of anti-aircraft techniques, air-to-air combat, and purpose-built aircraft designed to gain control of enemy airspace and protect those doing observation and artillery spotting. Airspace had become a crucial commodity and, as such, would be hotly contested.

FIGHTERS AND THEIR PILOTS

The evolution of aerial combat is a well-known story; it commences with opposing pilots firing pot shots at one another with pistols and carbines, and moves on to sophisticated dog-fighting techniques with specialized airplanes carrying fixed, forward-firing machine-guns.[8] The intense competition for advantage in the air led to a self-generating, spiralling quest for new and better fighter technology. Innovative, energetic and immensely brave individual pilots made their own unique contributions in this realm. Pilots such as Georges Guynemer, Albert Ball, Manfred von Richthofen and Oswald Boelke discovered the performance envelopes of their machines, came to grips with the physics of flying, and caused the tactical manuals to be revised and rewritten every few months.[9]

There is, of course, a fascinating social and cultural story about the fighter pilots. Heralded as heroes, and offered up as a source of glamour in an otherwise bleak war of masses, these men and their stories were publicized to help maintain morale on the home front and in the trenches.[10] Glorified as individualistic 'knights of the air', they were frequently contrasted to the war's faceless armies and massed artillery. But though some of the most talented pilots continued to favour lone-wolf tactics over formations, the growing lethality of aerial combat forced the refinement of mutual support among fighting and bombing aircraft. The technology and tactics employed by fighter escadrilles grew more sophisticated throughout the war. Despite the glamorous images perpetrated by a press desperate for tales of glory, the real lives of fighter pilots were dangerous, physically and emotionally gruelling – and short. Those who beat the fearsome odds of being killed flew exhausted and under constant strain. French ace Charles Nungesser, who was wounded 17 times during the course of the war, was so weakened during the Battle of Verdun that he had to be lifted bodily into the cockpit and could use only one leg on the rudder controls.[11]

CONTACT PATROL, GROUND ATTACK AND INTERDICTION BOMBING

Infantry contact patrol (monitoring the progress of friendly troops) and ground attack of enemy troops developed during the course of the First World War as well. To be accurate, ground attack had to be low. This meant it was dangerous – and often costly. The costs would be emphasized during the inter-war years by air organizations, like the Royal Air Force, which were trying to de-emphasize ground war-oriented operations. But the fact was (and the Germans well understood it) that, under the right circumstances, ground attack could have potent effects.[12]

Under the heading of 'tactical bombing' one can place not only bombing in direct support of troops engaged in ground battle, but also aerial interdiction meant to isolate the battlefield and deny one's enemy the ability to supply and manoeuvre his forces. The potential value of aerial interdiction was grasped quickly. In a war that relied heavily on railways to bring forward the masses of men and materiel needed for battle, it made sense to try to interrupt rail traffic by any means available. Writing during the war, aviation author Charles C. Turner remarked that, 'From the military point of view, perhaps, the most important of all the bearings of aircraft ... concerns the vulnerability of railways to attack from above.'[13] The problem was that bombing by aeroplane was a haphazard and inefficient business: getting bombs on target reliably was far harder than anyone had anticipated. Historian Basil Collier has pointed out that an analysis of all-day bombing done by Allied aircraft between 1 March and 20 June 1915 revealed that only three out of 141 attempts to bomb railway stations were known to have succeeded.[14]

British battle plans for the Somme, commencing in July 1916, involved tactical bombing aimed at German communications, including railway lines, railway stations, bridges and command headquarters. Despite British efforts to provide for communication between different units and arms operating at the Somme, the fog of war intruded on the opening stages of the assault, and air squadrons had to muddle through as best they could on a chaotic battlefield. Complicated systems of signalling between flyers and ground troops were undermined by mist, and swirling clouds of dust and smoke. In general, the opening phase of the battle revealed the persistent difficulty of co-ordination in modern, industrialized warfare and the enduring complexities of communication between the ground and the air. Major-General Sir Hugh Trenchard, head of the Royal Flying Corps (RFC), used tactical bombing not only to attempt to damage enemy targets, but also to draw off enemy fighters, which would be forced to attack bombers and thus unavailable to harass aircraft working over the battlefield. Following the lead of the French at Verdun, Trenchard also had his pilots fly aggressive patrols designed to win freedom of manoeuvre for British reconnaissance, artillery and other ground support aircraft, and to deny such freedom to the enemy. In September 1916 Trenchard issued an important (and later much-quoted) memorandum which asserted that at the Somme British air policy had been one of 'relentless and incessant offensive', which, he argued 'had the effect so far on the enemy of compelling him to keep back or to detail portions of his forces in the air for defensive purposes'.[15] If Trenchard's tactics gave the Germans pause, they were

costly to the British. Believing he had little choice but to continue to
press his offensive, Trenchard sent novices – many of had whom only
the minimum 15 hours' flying time – into combat. The price was high:
210 planes written off from all causes in July 1916, with 97 lost to
enemy action. This daunting ratio of accidents to combat losses would
persist through the war.[16]

LONG RANGE BOMBING

If the Royal Flying Corps kept its attention squarely on the ground
war, the Royal Naval Air Service (RNAS) took an interest in both pre-
emptive attacks on enemy aircraft, and the long-range bombardment of
enemy resources. The French also took an interest in long-range or
'strategic' bombing, adopting a pragmatic approach that sought to
attack those industries most vital to the German war effort. But both
the RNAS and French efforts were hindered by shortages of funding
and resources.[17] Field Marshal Sir Douglas Haig's doubts about the
usefulness of the work of the RNAS's No. 3 Naval Wing caused that
operation to wind down in April 1917. This was only one manifestation
of ongoing troubles in Britain over air organization, and the issues of
long-range bombing and home defence.

These issues would be sorely tested by the German bomber campaign against Britain, commencing in the spring of 1917. In launching
this strategic air campaign (in concert with unrestricted submarine
warfare), the Germans figured that they might damage British war
resources and deal a fatal blow to British morale. Proponents of strategic
bombing (in Germany and elsewhere) believed it might be revolutionary in its effects because it would enable a new type of warfighting
that went right over the heads of armies and navies, and directly to the
sources of a nation's strength in its urban-industrial centres. Bomber
aircraft might – quickly and single-handedly – collapse the war-fighting
infrastructure and the popular will of an enemy state.[18]

The prospect was both alluring and terrifying. Popular speculation
about the potential effectiveness of such bombing worked hand in hand
with the idea that if war bypassed armies and was instead taken directly
to civilians, those civilians might not be able to endure its demands and
deprivations. In Britain, civil strife and industrial crises in the decades
leading up to the First World War had raised the concerns of planners
and policymakers: How would industrial labour be carried out? How
would order be maintained among populations already hard pressed by
long hours of work and poor living conditions in crowded, congested
cities?[19] Government officials already worried about the loyalty and
stability of their working classes had now to ponder the possibility that

aerial bombardment of the home front might help trigger social upheaval. Military authorities expressed such concerns as well.[20] Some commentators on the subject expressed the hope that the laws of war, which had been outlined during international conferences at the Hague in 1899 and 1907, and the attempts to stigmatize the bombing of 'open cities' from the air, might provide a check on the use of aircraft in war. But such hopes had proven over-optimistic.[21]

The German bombing campaign was not the first air campaign the Germans had waged against the British in the course of the war. In early 1915 they had commenced Zeppelin attacks that ranged widely over Britain. There was considerable popular enthusiasm in Germany for the use of these weapons, which had come to represent in the public mind the technological prowess and great-power status of the German nation. The Kaiser was conservative at first, wary of dropping bombs on the heads of his relatives in Buckingham Palace; over time, however, the official constraints were lifted. The Germans did well at first – scoring a number of lucky early raids, notably against Central London, Greenwich and Hull. The raids, flown mainly at night, and inhibited by weather, bomb-load limits and service rivalry in Germany, caused only limited physical damage. But they provoked disruption and drew personnel and resources away from the Western Front. Indeed, a Zeppelin attack set fire to the heart of London on 8 September 1915. During that month thousands flocked to the Underground stations for shelter.[22]

Early British attempts at air defence were Keystone Cops affairs, exacerbated by service rivalry and the limitations of early British aircraft engines, which did not have the power to take defenders to altitude quickly. The poor early record of the defenders tended to convey the impression that little could be done to keep aircraft from flying overhead at will. But if air defence seemed inept at first, it improved quickly and dramatically. Specialized weapons, improved climb speeds for engines, and increasingly sophisticated communications systems made the life of the Zeppelin pilot increasingly difficult.[23] Though Zeppelin raids continued through the war, by late 1916 they were no longer a serious threat to Britain.

In 1917, the Germans gambled that heavier-than-air craft might break the war's deadlock; though the new planes (Gothas and Giant bombers) could carry only a fraction of a Zeppelin's bomb-load, they were faster, more manoeuvrable, and able to attack in daylight – at least initially. German bomber raids on Britain commenced in late May 1917 against Folkestone and Shorncliffe, followed by attacks on London on 13 June and 7 July. The London raids were carried out in broad daylight by a handful of bombers flying taking advantage of full surprise,[24] killing 227 persons and injuring 677. Some of the bombs hit an infants' school in the East End, causing intense grief and indignation. Despite the large numbers of British aircraft attempting to intercept, only one Gotha was destroyed. The impotence of the defenders caused the public to recall the failure against the early Zeppelin raids.[25]

The Times's description of the 13 June raid pointed out that the German attack had 'made London quiver, not with fear, but with sorrow and anger'.[26] On 15 June, the *Daily Mail* published photographs of the child victims of the first raid, along with a 'Reprisal Map' of German towns.[27] Well-attended public meetings at Tower Hill and the London Opera House debated air defence and air reprisals.[28] The 7 July 1917 raid caused a more dramatic, sustained reaction in the press. In an outpouring of description, commentary and debate that continued for days, the pages of *The Times* were full of the air raid. Letters to editors called for defence restructuring, including the creation of a separate air force responsible for both air defence and reprisal raids.[29]

The home front population, disappointed and angered, had sought a voice in the prosecution of modern conflict, and the government had been forced to take notice. This represented the beginning of a trend many had feared. Some military officials, unsurprisingly, looked with trepidation on the implications arising from the public's new place in the line of fire and its new voice in matters of war. Strategy and wartime decision-making, once the preserve of a small, insulated elite, was now subjected to the broader influence of the domestic polity, including the working classes.

The Lloyd George government was deeply concerned about the public reaction at the time, and many historians have portrayed it in dark tones. Looking back carefully at these events, however, we can take a more optimistic view. In light of all that happened over British skies between 1915 and 1918, the British public held up quite well. Certainly, they were angry and indignant about the poor state of their defences, and outraged in general that their government initially seemed so inept at the business of air defence, but there is little evidence of persistent or widespread panic over the air raids. Panic and anger are two different reactions, and ought not to be conflated.

The British population wanted a say in the prosecution of the war, and this was a new and uncomfortable development for policy elites. Understanding the concerns of those elites means understanding the context in which they lived and worked. The Edwardians were an anxious people. Early twentieth-century Britain was a vigorous, dynamic society, brimming with the products of modern science and technology: electric power, automobiles, photography, telephones, cheap newspapers, the cinema.[30] But it was also a society adjusting to modernity and the effects of large-scale industrialization. The growth of industry had concentrated working populations in congested, polluted cities. For government officials, concerns over sanitation and public health were unavoidable, along with worries about the political stability of vast populations forced to endure long hours of labour and stressful living conditions.

The urban poor were, as scholar Samuel Hynes has explained, 'a mysterious and frightening new force' inhabiting the nation's cities and towns.[31] Would the home front hold? In 1917, right in the midst of the harrowing furore over the Russian revolution, this was the question of the hour. In his memoirs, Lloyd George would later write: 'Of all the problems which Governments had to handle during the Great War, the most delicate and probably the most perilous were those arising on the home front ... the contentment and co-operation of the wage earners was our vital concern, and industrial unrest spelt a graver menace to our endurance and ultimate victory than even the military strength of Germany.'[32]

The Gotha raids provoked several important official responses. After the attacks on London, the government requested that General Haig send fighter squadrons from the front line back home to help defend Britain; he reluctantly complied.[33] The War Cabinet mandated that aircraft production should be given priority over other forms of weapon production. Forty new squadrons were to be devoted to reprisals against Germany.[34] On 11 July, the War Cabinet began serious discussion of reforming air organization. This led to two reports, one on air defence and one on retaliation.[35] The first insured that British air defences would once again rise to the challenge posed by the Germans. The second, articulating a futurist vision of the yet unrealized potential of air war, argued for a drastic change in British aviation organization: the creation of a separate, independent air arm to better defend the nation *and* to conduct a counter-offensive through long-range bombing.[36] To restructure national defences in the midst of a war is both a radical and uncomfortable step for a nation to take, and yet the British took it. The Air Force Constitution Bill was passed in November 1917, and in January 1918 an Air Council was constituted and charged with overseeing the administration of an independent 'Royal Air Force' (RAF), which came into existence in April 1918.[37] Ironically, the British were taking steps to establish a long-range bombing force just as the Germans were becoming frustrated with the limited results of their own strategic air campaign.

The newly minted RAF commenced its own long-range air campaign in the spring of 1918 with what was then called the 'Independent Force' (IF). A flurry of intellectual activity surrounded this development. The range, quality and sophistication of the young Air Staff's thinking about strategic bombing in 1918 was remarkable: in a few short months they worked out very nearly every important idea about strategic bombing that would be developed during the twentieth century – including theories about striking 'bottleneck' targets in the enemy war economy that the Americans would claim, later on, to have invented entirely themselves in the 1930s.[38]

But, in 1918, the gap was great between ideas and the ability to implement them. Although the hopes and plans for the Independent Force had been impressive, the reality was rather less so. At inception, it had only five squadrons of the much larger force envisioned, and its total strength would never amount to more than 10 per cent of the total British air strength in France.[39] Target finding and bomb-sighting capabilities were very crude, and pilots had only a random chance of hitting their intended targets.[40]

Trenchard, who through a strange set of twists and turns had found himself – reluctantly – at the helm of this British strategic force, once again pushed his pilots hard, causing sometimes staggeringly high accident rates. Because the IF's scattered attacks lacked impact, they did little real damage to German industrial output. One scholar of German aviation concluded that, 'The expense of the RAF's destroyed aircraft exceeded the cost of the damage it inflicted on Germany.'[41] Also, German defenders (paralleling the British experience) took an increasingly heavy toll on invading British bombers. Trenchard, who in fact spent a great deal of his time attacking tactical targets, none the less felt compelled to meet high public and governmental expectations surrounding the strategic campaign; he thus launched a public-relations campaign that belied the IF's meagre results. He argued that even a limited aerial assault had an impact on the enemy. Keeping German towns under constant apprehension about being bombed, he asserted, made unremitting demands on the enemy's defences. Even bombers on their way to other targets would trigger air raid alerts:

> Every big German town hit at once screams for assistance. In this way hundreds of guns, searchlights, planes, and thousands of men have been drawn away from the front to meet the occasional attacks of a comparatively small number of assailants. It would be no exaggeration to say that every unit of the Independent Force immobilizes at least 50 times its fighting value from the ranks of the enemy.[42]

Trenchard's mathematics were not based upon any rational calculation or operational observation, but were intended instead to satisfy public opinion as well as the demands of politicians and the civilian leaders of the young RAF, who were often strident and vengeful in their desire for reprisal raids.[43] As the post-war Chief of Air Staff, Trenchard maintained and stressed these arguments – not only to justify the existence and expense of the IF, but also to help maintain the post-war independence of the RAF, which did not have a guaranteed future after the war as a separate service. This was not purely cynical and bureaucratic, however; Trenchard believed in the 'moral' effect of bombing, which stressed in particular the indirect effects of aerial bombardment campaigns, including the disruption and production loss caused by frequent air-raid warnings. But this particular interpretation – and the circumstances surrounding it – would have the effect of taking Trenchard and his service away from a rigorous investigation of either the wartime experience, or the future requirements of effective long-range bombing.

Trenchard's assumptions reflected not only what he believed took place in Germany, but also what he extracted from the British domestic experience. He had been impressed by the role that the public had played in shaping important wartime policy decisions. The need to pay increasing attention to home air defence had been a cause of deep consternation for British policymakers generally, especially since resources were always stretched thin in a war effort that had seemingly insatiable demands. After the war, RAF analyses and staff college lectures devoted much attention to the fact that the German strategic-bombing offensives ultimately had demanded a significant defensive response. For instance, the first commandant of the RAF Staff College, pointed out in his lectures that in order to meet a German offensive, which at no time consisted of more than 50 machines, the British had to employ over 270 airplanes and 13,000 men.[44]

The implication that much larger raids in the future would divert a comparably disproportionate effort from defenders was problematical, however. Such implicit linear extrapolation from limited experience ignored the possibility that the number of defenders needed per attacker might decline as the number of attackers increased, and subsequent experience (in the Second World War) would show exactly this. The commandant's numbers, interpreted as they were, helped fuel the idea that the cost of defending against a relatively small enemy offensive could become fatally high. Indeed, Trenchard ultimately used this notion as the main driver in his post-war rhetoric, arguing that, in the event of war, the key would be to undertake an immediate, relentless aerial offensive which would cause enemy production losses and would create overwhelming public demands for protection. Once forced onto the defensive, the enemy would find itself on a slippery slope from which he would have no hope of recovery.[45]

This assertive declaratory policy did not keep Trenchard's RAF from making important strides in air defence – in essence, the service hedged its bets against its own public declarations. During the inter-war years members of the RAF followed up on the lessons they had learned about fighters and air defence. By the autumn of 1918, the British air-defence net was able to collect information from thousands of observers (within a 90-second period) and use it to direct fighter aircraft to specific targets at 20,000 feet.[46] This network, into which radar was placed in the 1930s, would serve the British well, once again, in the crucial days of 1940. But the powerful appeal of bombers, both for deterrence and for warfighting if deterrence failed, grew stronger than ever in the 1920s and 1930s. Right up to his retirement in 1929, Trenchard continued to focus his service on the 'moral effect' of bombing. Indeed, when he was called back to an Air Staff meeting to tender his advice on bombing in 1941, he stayed true to his convictions, making largely the same claims about strategic bombing and its 'moral effect' as he had made during and after the First World War.[47]

Trenchard's public declarations about the 'incessant offensive' and the 'moral effect' had consequences: they helped set up a pattern of claims which, while helping the RAF in its inter-war bureaucratic dogfights, nonetheless underscored and promoted high expectations for long-range bombing, and helped place Britain in a position where it might, itself, one day be 'self-deterred' in part by the rhetoric of her own service.

At the end of the Great War no consensus on the record and the future of strategic bombing emerged; none the less, it had won a set of adherents – including Trenchard, Giulio Douhet and Billy Mitchell – who would, in the inter-war years, warn repeatedly of its power and insist that their own nations maintain air-striking forces that would give them crucial advantages over their enemies. These advocates found an audience among a generation of people who had witnessed the catastrophic impact of industrialized warfare and who looked forward with awe and trepidation to a future in which bombers would become larger, faster and more capable of dropping increasingly devastating weapons.[48]

CONCLUSION

Assessing the impact of aircraft in the First World War is more complex than it might at first appear. Observation aircraft offered a useful perspective of the battlefield and beyond, and helped to provide badly needed fire direction to artillery crews. Ground-attack aircraft sought to demoralize enemy troops, and bombers disrupted enemy operations behind the lines, incidentally drawing enemy fighter aircraft away from their primary duties. The air war demanded specialization and constant technological innovation, portending a bleak pattern for the future barring disarmament or arms control. But the embryonic nature of aerial operations in 1914–18 ensured that they were only partly effective at best, and in no case had a decisive impact on the outcome of the war. Airplanes created a need for other airplanes, and this self-replicating helix eventually made for a kind of aerial Brownian motion over the skies of the Western Front. But if Royal Flying Corps casualties raised the question of whether airplanes were worth the cost, the experience of the war made it clear that no power could dispense with them; to do so would be to make one's self fatally vulnerable to an enemy who did possess them. This instrument, heavy with foreboding and promise alike, could not be un-invented.

Perhaps the ambiguity of results aggravated the inter-war schism between those who believed that the future of war lay with aviation, and those who did not. Field Marshal Haig, who had come to appreciate the fact that airplanes could aid his effort in certain ways, none the less said little about aviation in his personal draft for a final dispatch, concluding simply: 'Though aircraft and tanks proved of enormous value, their true value is as ancillaries of infantry, artillery, and cavalry.'[49] Similarly, Marshal Ferdinand Foch and General John J. Pershing were adamant in viewing aviation as a support arm.

If the ground warriors tended to interpret the war conservatively and to assess the role of aviation in terms of its ability to aid the infantry and artillery, a new group of commentators and theorists took a very different approach. Aviation proponents were prepared to argue that, in the future, aircraft would decide the outcomes of wars. Many of them gravitated towards placing their emphasis on the most dramatic manifestation of air war: long-range bombing aimed at quickly collapsing economies and societies in a single blow.[50] They focused overwhelmingly on the offensive power of bombing aircraft, forgetting that much of the experience of the Great War had taught harsh lessons about the toll that could be taken by defenders. Increasingly, their voices were heard by politicians and national publics both captivated and concerned by the future of the air weapon, and by what they understood to be the vulnerability of modern societies and economies.

NOTES

1. On speculation about the potential uses of aircraft prior to 1914, see Michael Paris, *Winged Warfare: The Literature and Theory of Aerial Warfare in Britain, 1859–1917* (Manchester: Manchester University Press, 1992); Robert Wohl, *A Passion for Wings: Aviation and the Western Imagination, 1908–1918* (New Haven, CT: Yale University Press, 1994); and John Gooch, 'The Bolt from the Blue' and 'Attitudes to War in Late Victorian and Edwardian England', in *The Prospect of War* (London: Frank Cass, 1981).

2. Harold Porter, *Aerial Observation* (New York: Harper Brothers, 1921), p. 8.

3. The role of reconnaissance in these battles is frequently noted. A concise overview can be found in Lee Kennett, *The First Air War* (New York: The Free Press, 1991), pp. 31–2. See also Charles C. Turner, *Aircraft of Today* (London: Seeley, Service and Co., 1917), pp. 244–7; and, on the Marne, Sir Walter Raleigh, *The War in the Air*, Vol. I (Oxford: Clarendon Press, 1922), pp. 330–8.

4. See Kennett, *The First Air War*, pp. 35–8; and Raleigh,*The War in the Air*, pp. 338–9.
5. On aerial co-operation with artillery see *A Short History of the Royal Air Force*, Air Ministry Publication 125 (London: Air Ministry, 1929), pp. 28, 33, 51–2, and 75; and Peter Mead, *The Eye in the Air* (London: HMSO, 1983), pp. 51–110. Another account, written by a major in the US Air Service, is Harold E. Porter, *Aerial Observation* (New York: Harper Bros, 1921). Porter's volume was written in order to raise the profile of observers among the American public. For a description of the functioning of aerial artillery spotting written during the First World War, see *Cooperation of Aircraft with Artillery*, Air Ministry Publication 155 (London: Air Ministry, 1917). The Air Ministry publications are available at the RAF Museum, Hendon, UK.
6. See Mead, *The Eye in the Air*, pp. 57–8. On training see 'Training of Observers, Royal Air Force, 1915–1918' by J. A. Chamier, in AIR 1/161/15/123/15, PRO, London. For a discussion of the lack of respect and attention accorded to observers, see Porter, *Aerial Observation*, pp. 8–15 and 36–9.
7. See 'Duties of Air Craft in the Field', No. 1 School of Aeronautics, RAF, 1918, in AIR 1/161/15/123/14, Public Record Office, London. See in general, Mead, *The Eye in the Air*, pp. 99–109. On the issue of inadequate exposure of air observers to the work of artillery batteries, he writes: '... no member of the battery would carry out a shoot until he had served an apprenticeship on the guns, in the battery command post and as a signaller and knew what it was all about ... But the air observer, supplied with inferior communications and a number of functions unrelated to observation, was entrusted with this most important link in the battery's battle function without any but the most superficial knowledge of the remaining links' (p. 107); also Porter, *Aerial Observation*, esp. pp. 53–216. On artillery cooperation and the utility of aerial photographs, see Air Publication 155 (AP 155), *Cooperation of Aircraft with Artillery* (December 1917), RAF Museum, Hendon. Its authors stated: 'Photography is the basis of good artillery work, especially counter-battery work, and photographs must be very carefully studied for indications of new work and fresh dispositions' (p. 13); also, Paddy Griffith, *Battle Tactics of the Western Front* (New Haven, CT: Yale University Press, 1994), pp. 152–3.
8. See, generally, Richard Hallion, *The Rise of the Fighter Aircraft, 1914–1918* (Baltimore, MD: Nautical and Aviation Press, 1984).
9. Aerial tactics were under development throughout the war, and manuals had to be continually revised and rewritten to take account of new information. There is, for instance, an ongoing increase in sophistication in the information contained in the subsequent editions of the British manual for fighter pilots, Air Publication 302, *Fighting in the Air*, which can be found at the RAF Museum, Hendon. See also AP 38, *Notes on Aerial Fighting*, July 1918.
10. Robert Wohl has written of Georges Guynemer, 'Not one to hide his many honours and decorations, Guynemer was often to be seen on leave in Paris where his mere appearance at a restaurant was enough to inspire a standing ovation and a stampede of women determined to touch or kiss his heavily bemedalled tunic.' See 'The Bards of Aviation: Flight and French Culture, 1909–1939', *Michigan Quarterly Review*, Vol. XXIX, No. 3 (Summer 1990), p. 308. Not all the aces were so outgoing however; Albert Ball, for all his audacity in the air, was rather distant and introspective. See Denis Winter, *The First of the Few: Fighter Pilots of the First World War* (Athens, GA: University of Georgia Press, 1982), pp. 133–4.
11. Alistair Horne, *The Price of Glory* (London: Macmillan, 1962), pp. 203–4. Horne offers an evocative glimpse into the lives of some of the famous French aces. On combat pilots and their memory generally, see Robert Wohl, *A Passion for Wings:*

Aviation and the Western Imagination, 1908–1918 (London/New Haven, CT: Yale University Press, 1994), pp. 203–50; and George Mosse, 'The Knights of the Sky and the Myth of the War Experience', in Robert Hinde and Helen Watson, eds, *War: A Cruel Necessity?* (London: I. B. Tauris, 1995), pp. 132–42. See also John H. Morrow, Jr, *The Great War in the Air* (Washington, DC: Smithsonian Institution Press, 1993), pp. 202–4 and 315.

12. See Kennett, *The First Air War*, p. 211, and also 'Developments to 1939', in *Case Studies in the Development of Close Air Support* (Washington, DC: Office of Air Force History, 1990), pp. 13–27. See also Richard Hallion, *Strike from the Sky: The History of Battlefield Air Attack, 1911–1945* (Washington, DC: Smithsonian Institution Press, 1989), pp. 19–20.

13. Charles C. Turner, *Aircraft of Today* (London: Seeley, Service and Co., 1917), p. 249.

14. See Basil Collier, *A History of Air Power* (London: Weidenfeld & Nicolson, 1974), p. 53.

15. On the RFC at the Somme, see Robin Higham, *The Military Intellectuals in Britain: 1918–1939* (New Brunswick, NJ: Rutgers University Press, 1966), pp. 132–59, and Appendix B, which reprints Trenchard's order to the RFC of September 1916. See also S. F. Wise, *Canadian Airmen and the First World War* (Toronto: University of Toronto Press, 1980), pp. 358–92, especially pp. 362 and 366. Wise's book, which is the first volume of the official history of the Royal Canadian Air Force, sets the history of the RCAF into the rich context of all aviation in the First World War. Based on a wide range of sources, it offers the reader one of the best treatments available of air power in the Great War. Documents revealing Trenchard's thinking at the time can be found in AIR 1/522/16/12/5, Public Record Office, London.

16. See Morrow, *The Great War in the Air*, pp. 167–9; and Wise, *Canadian Airmen*, pp. 364–5. On the British offensive policy generally, see H. A. Jones, *The War in the Air*, Vol. II (Oxford: Clarendon Press, Jones's Vols II to VI of the British official history were published 1928–37), pp. 164–8.

17. On the RNAS and French bombing programmes see George K. Williams, 'Statistics and Strategic Bombardment: Operations and Records of the British Long-Range Bombing Force During World War I and Their Implications for the Development of the Post-War Royal Air Force, 1917–1923', D.Phil. thesis, Oxford University, 1987. This work has recently been published, in slightly abridged form, by the Air University Press (1999), under the title *Biplanes and Bombsights: British Bombing in World War I*. See also Morrow, *The Great War in the Air*, pp. 94–103, and (on the RNAS) Christina J. M. Goulter, *A Forgotten Offensive: Royal Air Force Coastal Command's Anti-Shipping Campaign, 1940–1945* (London: Frank Cass, 1995), pp. 1–33.

18. On early ideas about strategic bombing see generally, Tami Davis Biddle, *Rhetoric and Reality in Air Warfare: The Evolution of British and American Ideas about Strategic Bombing, 1914–1945* (Princeton, NJ: Princeton University Press, 2002).

19. In his 1908 book *The War in the Air*, H. G. Wells had helped to foster such speculation when he argued that urban populations, already weakened by the dislocations of war would, upon the appearance of an air fleet, fall victim to 'civil conflict and passionate disorder'. See Wells quoted in T. H. E. Travers, 'Future Warfare: H. G. Wells and British Military Theory, 1865–1916', in Brian Bond and Ian Roy, eds, *War and Society: A Yearbook of Military History* (New York: Holmes & Meier, 1975), p. 75. On the industrial crisis in Britain prior to the war, see Allen Hutt, *The Postwar History of the British Working Class* (New York: Coward-McCann, 1938), and Paul Addison, 'Winston Churchill and the Working Class,

1900–1914', in Jay Winter, ed., *The Working Class in Modern British History* (Cambridge: Cambridge University Press, 1983), pp. 43–64.

20. In a 1913 lecture to the Royal United Services Institute, for instance, Maj. Stewart L. Murray speculated that a major war might see 'the explosion of those volcanic forces which underlie every modern democracy', and he urged that 'unless steps are taken to prevent the hardships of war pressing intolerably upon the new working classed, the whole organized political power of labour may be used to demand the cessation of the war, even at the price of submission to our enemies'. See Maj. Stewart L. Murray, 'Internal Condition of Great Britain During a Great War', *Journal of the Royal United Services Institute*, Vol. 57, No. 430 (Dec. 1913), pp. 1564, 1566, 1587–8.

21. On air power and the law of war see: D. C. Watt, 'Restraints on War in the Air Before 1945', in Michael Howard, ed., *Restraints on War: Studies in the Limitation of Armed Conflict* (New York: Oxford University Press, 1979), pp. 57–77; Geoffrey Best, *Humanity in Warfare* (New York: Columbia University Press, 1980), pp. 262–85; W. Hays Parks, 'Air War and the Law of War', *Air Force Law Review*, Vol. 32, No. 1 (1990), pp. 1–225; and Tami Davis Biddle, 'Air Power', in Michael Howard, George Andreopoulos and Mark Shulman, eds, *The Laws of War* (New Haven, CT: Yale University Press, 1994), pp. 140–59.

22. Wise, *Canadian Airmen and the First World War*, pp. 234–5. On the Zeppelin programme generally, see Peter Fritzsche, *A Nation of Flyers* (Cambridge, MA: Harvard University Press, 1992); Douglas Robinson, *The Zeppelin in Combat, 1912 to 1918* (London: G. T. Foulis & Co., 1962); and Marian C. McKenna, 'The Development of Air Raid Precautions in World War I', in Timothy Travers and Christon Archer, eds, *Men at War* (Chicago, IL: Precedent Publishing, 1982), pp. 173–95. On British air organization and its problems see Alfred Gollin, *The Impact of Air Power* (London: Macmillan, 1989), pp. 159–290; Barry Powers, *Strategy Without Slide Rule* (London: Croom Helm, 1976), pp. 15–17; David Edgerton, *England and the Aeroplane* (London: Macmillan, 1991), pp. 9–10; Sir Walter Raleigh, *The War in the Air*, Vol. I, pp. 357–409; and 'Memorandum on the Organization of the Air Services' by Lt-Gen. Sir David Henderson, July 1917, reprinted in H. A. Jones, *The War in the Air*, Appendices (Nashville, TN: The Battery Press, 1997; reprint of 1937 original), pp. 1–8.

23. See John R. Ferris, 'Airbandit: C3I and Strategic Air Defence during the First Battle of Britain, 1915–1918', in Michael Dockrill and David French, eds, *Strategy and Intelligence: British Policy during the First World War* (London: The Hambledon Press, 1996), pp. 23–66; 'Fighter Defence before Fighter Command: The Rise of Strategic Air Defence in Great Britain', *Journal of Military History*, Vol. 63, No. 4, pp. 845–84, esp. 853. See also, generally, AIR 9/69, Public Record Office, London, which contains plentiful evidence of rapid improvements in wartime air defence.

24. Signals intelligence had not, in this case, helped the British to predict the arrival of the aircraft. See Ferris, 'Airbandit', pp. 41–2.

25. On the London raids see Sir Charles Webster and Noble Frankland, *The Strategic Air Offensive against Germany*, Vol. I (London: HMSO, 1961), p. 35; and, generally, Raymond Fredette, *The Sky on Fire: The First Battle of Britain, 1917–1918* (New York: Harcourt, Brace & Jovanovich, 1966). For the War Cabinet responses to the raids of June and July, see CAB 23/3/163 (163rd meeting, War Cabinet), and CAB 23/3/178 (178th meeting, War Cabinet), Public Record Office, London.

26. 'The Air Attack on London', *The Times* (London), 14 June 1917, p. 7; 'Story of the Raid', *The Times*, 14 June 1917, p. 7.

27. See Powers, *Strategy without Slide Rule*, p. 55.

28. 'Air Raid Warnings for the City', *The Times*, 18 June 1917, p. 8.

29. See, for instance, the letters printed under the heading 'The Air Raid: Lessons of Saturday's Attack', *The Times*, 10 July 1917, p. 5; 'Air Raid Disorders', *The Times*, 10 July 1917, p. 3, and 'Anti-German Disturbances', *The Times*, 11 July 1917, p. 3.

30. See Edgerton, *England and the Aeroplane*, pp. 12–13

31. Samuel Hynes, *The Edwardian Turn of Mind* (Princeton, NJ: Princeton University Press, 1968), pp. 21–2, 54–5 and 63. See also, generally, Gareth Stedman Jones, *Outcast London* (New York: Pantheon, 1984, originally published in 1971); and Geoffrey Barraclough, *An Introduction to Contemporary History* (London: C. A. Watts, 1964).

32. David Lloyd George, *War Memoirs*, Vol. IV (London: Ivor Nicholson & Watson, 1934), p. 1925. See also pp. 1960–1.

33. Jones, *The War in the Air*, Vol. IV, pp. 152–3. Because the second raid had taken place immediately after the fighter squadrons (sent home after the first raid) had returned to France, the War Cabinet suspected 'effective German espionage'. See CAB 23/3/178.

34. On these events, see: Sir Frederick Sykes, *From Many Angles* (London: Harrap, 1942), pp. 215–24; Wise, *Canadian Airmen*, pp. 278–80; Neville Jones, *The Origins of Strategic Bombing* (London: William Kimber, 1973), pp. 130–9; J. M. Spaight, *The Beginnings of Organized Air Power* (London: Longmans, Green and Co., 1927), pp. 126–30; and Sir Charles Webster and Noble Frankland, *The Strategic Air Offensive against Germany*, 4 vols (London: HMSO, 1961), Vol. I, p. 37.

35. See W. K. Hancock, *Smuts: The Sanguine Years, 1870–1919* (Cambridge: Cambridge University Press, 1962), pp. 438–42; Lloyd George, *War Memoirs*, Vol. IV, pp. 1844–70; and Malcolm Cooper, *The Birth of Independent Air Power* (London: Allen & Unwin, 1986), pp. 97–107.

36. See 'Second Report of the Prime Minister's Committee on Air Organization and Home Defence against Air Raids, 17 August 1917' reprinted in Jones, *Appendices*, Appendix II, pp. 8–14.

37. See Lloyd George, *War Memoirs*, Vol. IV, p. 1875.

38. For excellent, detailed coverage of this topic, see George K. Williams, 'The Shank of the Drill: Americans and Strategical Aviation in the Great War', *Journal of Strategic Studies*, Vol. 19, No. 3 (Sept. 1996), pp. 381–431.

39. On the number of planes originally envisioned for the force, see Jones, *The War in the Air*, Vol. VI, p. 173. On the actual strength of the IF, see Jones, *Appendices*, Appendix XII, 'Statistics of Work of Squadrons of the Independent Force, Including Wastage, June–November 1918'.

40. On these problems, see Trenchard's report on July operations in AIR 1/2000/204/273/275. See also Squadron Leader J. C. Quinnell, 'Experiences with a Day Bombing Squadron in the Independent Force, 1918' in 'A Selection of Lectures and Essays from the Work of Officers Attending the Second Course at the Royal Air Force Staff College (Andover), 1923–1924' (London: Air Ministry, 1924). Formerly in the library of the Royal Air Force Staff College, Bracknell, Berkshire, United Kingdom.

41. James Corum, *The Luftwaffe* (Lawrence, KS: University of Kansas Press, 1997), p. 40.

42. 'Huns Raid Panic' in the *Daily Mail*, 21 September 1918, copy in AIR 462/15/312/116.

43. In response to a toast in his honour in December 1917, Secretary of State for Air Lord Rothermere said: 'It is our duty to avenge the murder of innocent women and children. As the enemy elects, so it will be the case of 'eye for an eye, and a tooth

for a tooth,' and in this respect we shall slave for complete and satisfying retaliation'. Rothermere quoted in Williams, 'Statistics and Strategic Bombardment', p. 203. On 25 March 1918 MP Sir Henry Norman drew up an elaborate bombing scheme: 'the future of our race and empire may depend on whether or not we rise now – though it be at the eleventh hour – to this conception'. He envisioned a force that would deliver twenty tons of bombs hourly for ten consecutive hours, so as to bring victory 'in sight' in a month. He was, however, a bit out of step with reality as it had taken the 41st Wing five months to drop 48 tons of bombs on German targets. Williams, 'Statistics and Strategic Bombardment', pp. 199–203.

44. Commandant's lecture (1924), 'Air Warfare', RAF Staff College, in AIR 1/2385/228/10, p. 71

45. This argument is articulated in the 1928 RAF Manual, Part I, Operations, Ministry of Defence, London (copy at Air Historical Branch, RAF, London).

46. See Ferris, 'Airbandit', p. 24.

47. See Tami Davis Biddle, 'British and American Approaches to Strategic Bombing: Their Origins and Implementation in the World War II Combined Bomber Offensive', *Journal of Strategic Studies*, Vol. 18, No. 1 (March 1995), p. 116.

48. The degree to which politicians in Britain were influenced by concerns about strategic bombing is striking. In the 1930s Winston Churchill, Sir John Simon, Clement Attlee, and Stanley Baldwin (one of the twentieth century's greatest prophets of gloom) all evoked frightening images of what air war of the future would look like. As their speeches and writings garnered a large audience, they could not help but influence public views and expectations. On this see Tom Harrison and Charles Madge, eds, *War Begins at Home* (the reports of Mass Observation) (London: Chatto & Windus, 1940), pp. 38–42.

49. Haig quoted in Denis Winter, *The First of the Few*, p. 11.

50. Many authors have examined aspects of the development of air power theory in the inter-war years. See, for instance, Higham, *The Military Intellectuals in Britain*, pp. 119–205; Richard Overy, 'Air Power and the Origins of Deterrence Theory before 1939', *Journal of Strategic Studies*, Vol. 15, No. 1 (March 1992); Brian Bond, *War and Society in Europe, 1870–1970* (New York: Oxford University Press, 1986), pp. 135–67; Malcolm Smith, *British Air Strategy between the Wars* (Oxford: Clarendon, 1984).

2

Achieving Air Ascendancy: Challenge and Response in British Strategic Air Defence, 1915–40

John Ferris

'The success of Home Defence is the result of interception, whatever the means employed to secure this object. Thus if we always maintain our fighter equipment superior to that of the enemy bomber, in flying performance and in hitting power, we shall be able to inflict such casualties on him that he will lose his morale. His pilots will tend to drop their bombs anywhere rather than seek their way through to the vital objectives. While 100% interception must be our first aim, a lesser percentage, if combined with heavy casualties to raids intercepted, will achieve air ascendancy. On the other hand if our fighters are not superior to the enemy bombers, the most perfect system of intelligence and interception will fail, and so would the air defence of the country against air attack. The sole purpose of the interception system is to concentrate in time and place, and to achieve local air superiority by the most economical method.'

Air Chief Marshal Dowding, 1938[1]

Conventionally, the inter-war RAF is thought to have been unenthusiastic about air defence. Before 1934, it ignored the matter; thereafter it moved with reluctance. Fighter Command's problems in 1940 are taken to prove inadequacy of action at the Air Ministry; the successes of air defence are credited to a handful of heroes – the gallant Few, the boffins, Hugh Dowding, even Thomas Inskip. Many scholars recognize that the Air Ministry took air defence seriously during 1934–39, but others seem to think that everyone but that body deserves credit for victory in the Battle of Britain; these attitudes are widespread among non-specialist historians and the general public. This victory often is used to attack the Air Ministry. By denying it responsibility for the only success of British air power in the early stages of the Second World War that cannot be explained away, critics strengthen their arguments for the case that everything it wanted turned to dust. Underlying this is a deeper tendency: that of reading the policy of the Royal Air Force (RAF) between 1918 and 1939 in a simplistic way. Assumptions about doctrine create presumptions about action – thus, scholars argue, ideas on strategic bombing shaped all RAF policies and led straight toward specific forms of force structure and war planning. RAF doctrine denigrated air defence and shaped policy: as one official history of Allied air power puts it, until 1934, 'captivated by the strategic bombing doctrine enshrined in the concept of an "independent" air force, the Royal Air Force paid scant attention to the question of air defence'.[2] These views are wrong. They reflect a form of idealism common in the study of military doctrine – the assumption that ideas produce things, leading to the notion that we can understand things simply by studying ideas about them. The relationship between things and ideas about them, however, is more complicated than this, nor is effect produced solely by intent. Between 1921 and 1939 the RAF, an institution which wanted to establish a strategic bombing force, instead created a fighter defence system, because this was faster and cheaper to build; and it devoted no more attention to strategic air warfare than to replacing soldiers or warships in conventional roles. RAF thinking about strategic bombing was not a 'doctrine', with a close relationship among ideas, policies, strategies and forces – rather, it was a particular theory regarding how bombing would affect the will and economies of peoples, contained within a larger theory that air power was producing a revolution in military affairs.[3] It is too easy to conflate evidence on these two theories and so misconstrue them both. RAF policy did indeed stem from theory; just not only from one about strategic bombing.

The RAF was created in 1917 to pursue a revolution in military affairs (RMA), though, characteristically, it was not given the resources to do so. Officers, extrapolating from trends in technology, held that power was being transformed. As the first Chief of the Air Staff (CAS), Frederick Sykes, wrote in 1918,

> In future the existence of any nation will depend primarily upon its Air Power ... The Royal Air Force will in future be the first line of defence and offence of the British Empire. It is to her Air Fleet that Britain must look to safeguard herself and her Dominions. Aviation enables us to think and act in the third dimension. In peace, the nation or nations which exploit this most fully will gain great advantages over those still thinking in two. In war the nation which is already in possession of this facility will obtain a transcendental if not decisive lead.

Air forces would strike 'the armies and navies of the opponent, his population as a whole, his national moral [*sic*], and his industries, without which he cannot wage war', and it would win independent of support from the other services.[4]

Faith in an RMA underlay all RAF policy; thus a small institution reached for the sky. This faith had flaws – it was driven by technological determinism, assumed extrapolated trends would never end, and exaggerated the speed and the result of this revolution. It led the RAF to pursue the technical and tactical possibilities likely to produce the most revolutionary results – but only if an uncertain number of uncertainties, 'known unknowns' and 'unknown unknowns' alike, could be overcome. The development of air power was bound to be complicated. The RAF did it the hard way, rejecting a conservative approach, which would have produced important results – even some revolutionary ones – because it faced fewer uncertainties, mostly 'known unknowns'. The experiments in strategic air warfare produced much fruit, expected and unexpected but, given the limits to RAF resources, only at the cost of developments in ground and maritime support. Meanwhile, the RAF had not merely to attack, but to defend. Its main objective was to survive as an independent service in control of all British air power; to defend its autonomy and to strengthen its budgets. It was an institution with a vision looking for a role, which the government would fund, so that it could repeat the process until it reached the millennium. The RAF always aimed to replace the Army and Navy and become the dominant military institution on earth, but there was no direct route to this objective. So vast a theory and distant an aim could not guide immediate action; instead, opportunistic politics did so. At any point, the RAF emphasized one of its many aims over the rest simply because that object seemed easier to sell, and its leaders contemplated many different futures. They aimed no more at strategic bombing than at entirely replacing the older services in their conventional roles. Precisely their failure to achieve the latter aim increased their focus on strategic bombing.

Several axioms underlay the RAF's views on strategic bombing. The natural condition of maritime and land operations was costly stalemate. Such operations might be unavoidable, in which case air power would be their most important tool; aircraft, however, could sidestep this process and win a war by themselves. They would do so not through the classical means of engaging an enemy's forces, but by directly attacking the sources of its war power, civilian morale and industrial capacity. The 'Trenchard doctrine', emphasizing 'moral' factors as the true target of air power, dominated RAF discussions about the mechanics and the aim of a bombing offensive.[5] When hostilities opened, the belligerents would launch an all-out knockout blow by air, aiming to shatter an enemy's will to fight, rather than its industrial capacity. RAF officers did not make a radical distinction in targeting between morale and matériel. They always assumed morale could not be struck without hitting matériel, and vice-versa; even Trenchard held that only attacks on matériel targets could damage morale, thereby demonstrating one's superiority:

> What is required is to bring the greatest moral effect on the maximum number of people. For instance, knocking out a boat factory in the heart of Paris would have greater moral effect than the bombing of an Aircraft Factory 50 or 60 miles from Paris. The moral effect of the bombing of a boat factory in Paris would have a direct moral effect on a considerable number of people whereas if they read of the bombing of an Aircraft factory in the country it would produce only very limited moral effect.
> Given that the Aircraft factory and the Boat Factory were both in the heart of Paris the bombing of the former would produce the better result as it would have equal moral effect but a greater material effect. Generally speaking the material effect of bombing aircraft was small compared with its moral effect.[6]

These aims could best be achieved by keeping air forces concentrated, by striking immediately and with full force at the outbreak of war, and by pounding targets unrelentingly. This might break a people and their government, but air defence and accident would inflict heavy losses. If victory did not occur within a month, the weight of bombing would decline until new pilots and aircraft enabled a renewed effort. Air warfare could become spasmodic and last for a year or more, but always, as one Air Minister, Lord Swinton, noted in 1937, 'success will go to the nation which can most quickly overcome the will of his opponent to continue the fight'.[7]

Central to these views was the idea that air warfare fundamentally embodied a struggle between the will of air forces and of peoples, with the concept of 'moral' factors (meaning both 'morale' and 'psychology') generalized to refer to national or class characteristics. Debate on air defence focused less on how it would destroy enemy aircraft than the morale of aircrew. In 1923, Trenchard held that combat losses 'would have a greater effect on the morale of the French pilots then it would on ours. Casualties affect the French more than they did the British.' A decade later, discussions on the effect of air combat between fighters and bombers tended to discuss material matters in terms of their effect on psychology – high losses would wreck morale, the provision of armour would give aircrew 'great moral support'.[8] Again, though the RAF distorted the precision and effect of the bombing of industrial targets, its argument was less that bombing was strong, than that will was weak. Making crude assumptions about the collective character of peoples and crowds, especially of the working classes in urban centres, RAF officers held bombing would spark upheaval among 'volatile' peoples such as the Jews in London's East End or Frenchmen everywhere (which helps to explain the pessimism regarding bombing of the Germans, whose morale was assumed to be rather British). Trenchard, like J. F. C. Fuller and other military theorists who combined reactionary politics with technological determinism and faith in dominant weapons, promoted not total war but a mixture of medieval and futuristic conflict – one of champions, fought between small elites of technologically trained members of the upper classes, with the attacker throwing its will against the crowd below, winning by the demonstration of superiority rather than destruction – an image reflected in the post-war image of the social origins of fighter pilots during the battle of Britain.[9] Characteristically, in 1926, when his staff claimed nine months was needed to train new aircrew in a major war, Trenchard cut that figure to six: 'the best type would be those coming forward at once ... The type would be that of the young masters at Eton and other Schools and they had been used to guns and rifles all of their lives.'[10]

There were some odd characteristics to RAF thinking about strategic bombing. It often drifted toward the idea that merely to show the ability to bomb would be enough to win, and perhaps to deter war; since one could win by demonstration, why think of damage and, therefore, why plan for war? As the CAS Charles Ellington said in 1934, the RAF had to rely on 'pure guess-work' and 'arbitrary assumptions' about every detail of strategic air warfare, 'as we have no practical experience of air warfare on a major scale under modern conditions to provide us with definite conclusions capable of mathematical expression'.[11] Detailed war planning must be speculative, hence pointless. Given the political-psychological considerations in British thinking about grand strategy and air power theory, discussions on how strategic bombers would fight a war easily slipped into one about how they would deter war. Meanwhile, the need for detailed planning was sapped by the concept that bombing would win quickly and through metaphysical means, by wrecking the 'morale' of a 'nation'. The RAF never formed a coherent case about how bombing would affect morale, no doubt because it declined, for obvious political reasons, to espouse the most obvious means to do so – a naked policy of terror bombing against civilians. As one Air Staff officer noted, bombing could affect morale only through a policy of terror, adding, with a touch of prophecy, that 'no doubt with our usual skill at putting our enemies in the wrong in the eyes of the world, we shall see to it that the enemy is the first to transgress international laws'.[12] The need to avoid this political danger twisted the logic of strategy. Trenchard held that a bombing campaign against economic targets need not be 'indiscriminate' even if 98 per cent of bombs missed their targets and hit civilians, so long as the heart was pure; scarcely the means to foster serious debate.[13] In 1941, the RAF was happy when

2 per cent of its bombs landed within ten miles of their target. Yet the oddities in RAF thinking about strategic bombing had at least one positive consequence. If air warfare centred on struggles between national and military morale, then attack was better than defence, though some defence was essential. Even those who most disparaged the matter agreed that only the sight of stiff upper lips above could stiffen the nerve of the *hoi polloi* below.

This phenomenon emerged with force, as did a characteristic pattern in RAF decision-making, when the Air Ministry first turned its ideas on strategic air warfare into a system, with the authorization of the 52 Squadron Home Defence Air Force (HDAF) programme in 1923.[14] During the inter-war years, RAF officers were few in number, shared remarkably similar professional backgrounds and formulated policy in a consensual fashion, whereby junior officers had opportunity to influence high policy – a pattern unlike those in the Army and Navy or in most contemporary military institutions. Despite his reputation for intolerance, Trenchard was willing to listen to his subordinates, and to let them change his mind. In 1924, when the RAF considered major changes in the organization of carrier-borne aviation, it immediately solicited the views not just of all commanding officers but of every naval aviation pilot![15] Again, RAF exercises were open ended – the rules were not rigged, either side could lose, and in fact the theory favoured by the institution was judged to have lost more often than not.[16] In 1923, frank and wide-ranging discussions between senior members of the RAF, the most important ever held on the theory of air warfare in Britain, produced a consensus. The main aim, in Trenchard's words, was to go 'straight at its main objective, the destruction of the enemy's will power'.[17] On issues of the attack, he did represent the general views of RAF officers, but in the broader sense of a theory of air warfare he and a few others formed a tiny minority. They saw strategic air defence as impossible, though a few fighter squadrons must be assigned to assuage public fears. Against this, a large minority of RAF officers had great faith in strategic air defence, while most fell between the two schools, believing a tolerably effective defence system was possible. On these issues, Trenchard could express his views but could not make them prevail. The debates of 1923–24 assigned great power to the defensive, which became the real centre of controversy, in a surprising and overlooked fashion. Virtually alone, Trenchard argued that effective air defence was impossible. Almost every other discussant assumed that air defence could be made effective and the HDAF must do so as a first priority, equalling the development of a bomber force. Some officers went even further, especially T. C. R. Higgins, a senior staff officer, commander of air forces in home defence during 1918 and the RAF's recognized expert on the topic, and the respected Air Officer

Commanding (AOC) India, J. A. Chamier. They asserted that developments in fighter aircraft, radio-telephones (R/T) for ground-to-air communications and early-warning systems would let aircraft routinely force each other into air combat.[18] These comments challenged a central element in the emerging orthodoxy of RAF thought – they implied that strategic bombing must fail until enemy air forces were defeated through pitched battles. The Air Member for Supply and Research (AMSR) and future CAS, Geoffrey Salmond, held precisely this view: 'in air warfare, as on land, enemy air forces should be the primary objective', while 'developments in R/T should make it feasible for all (fighter) machines in the air to concentrate at whatever height the enemy's formations are found within two or three minutes'.[19] Higgins, too, rejected the idea that air forces could never be forced into battle. Britain must develop long-distance fighter escorts to enter the enemy's defences and provoke (in what became his standard formula) 'daily, and even nightly, battles between opposing formations of fighters. As a result of these battles, one side would probably in time obtain a fighting superiority, which would carry with it a concomitant bombing superiority.'[20]

These statements of principle were far-seeing, and they illuminate the actions of two figures, Higgins and Salmond, who played central roles in creating effective air defence between 1921 and 1934. Still, their prescience should not be exaggerated. These men believed developments in R/T and sound locators would make air defence effective, but not that it could achieve a high level of efficiency, economy or concentration of force. Higgins doubted that fighters could reach bombers at 20,000 feet, certainly not if they took off only 'when Sound Locators on the coast reported them to be coming over, as it is reasonable to suppose that no Fighter could be designed with the necessary climb performance'. Hence, home defence would have to rely on a variant of its inefficient wartime procedures, 'continuous high patrol(s)' of fighters, perhaps directed to targets by 'AA Smoke Shells fired by AA guns directed by Sound Locators'.[21] The exponents of air defence thought that it would inflict a slow and low, if continuous, rate of attrition rather than catastrophic losses on an attacker. This would grind down any bombing offensive, but on its own could not break a determined one. None the less, all these comments horrified Trenchard:

> The matter was being looked at from the wrong point of view, and ... the defence of this country was being reckoned with without taking account the offence against the enemy ... it is easy to lose sight of the effect one is making on the enemy if one is too anxious to safeguard oneself from attack. What often happened was that the enemy suddenly collapsed, just as the people at home were beginning to lose heart. Our people would undoubtedly squeal if they were bombed, but we should find, if we bombed the enemy enough, that he would collapse before we did.[22]

On this issue the Trenchardians, the bomber purists, were a tiny minority and ultimately a defeated one, but the nature of this defeat and of the debate must be qualified. Trenchard could not convince his colleagues on this issue. For example, Christopher Bullock, the dominant civilian figure within the Air Ministry and significant in the debate over the theory of air warfare, held that Trenchard and his allies underestimated air defence because they viewed it through the prism of their own experiences of operations on the narrow Western Front. In his polemic against his foes, the CAS claimed that the RAF was divided between 'defensive' as against 'offensive' schools. To this Bullock retorted that all 'are "offensives"; everybody wants to get a maximum into the offensive, and a minimum into the defensive. The only difference of opinion is as to what constitutes the minimum which can be usefully employed in the defensive.'[23] This doctrine was incorporated into official RAF theory and embodied through the use of marginal utility. As the young Charles Portal noted, 'there must be a line somewhere where the greatest effect could be obtained, and where the proportion between bombing and defence squadrons could be found'.[24] According to one Air Staff assessment, this proportion could be determined through one of two approaches: 'So many fighters are necessary for adequate defence; that will leave us so many bombers', or 'We require so many bombers to form an adequate striking force; that will leave us so many fighters': 'One School of thought suggested 20 fighters to 32 bombers. The other 13 fighters to 39 bombers.'[25] The RAF split the difference between these two methods and their conclusions. Most commanding officers, the Air Staff and the Staff College wanted between 14 and 20 fighter squadrons; Trenchard eight or ten. Ultimately, all compromised on a figure of 17, or 33 per cent of the HDAF programme, which figure was formally adopted.[26] The HDAF contained twice as many fighters as Trenchard preferred, at the cost of having 20 per cent fewer bombers, and he bowed to majority opinion.

This was among the most important and revealing decisions on the organization of the HDAF programme. It demonstrates that, from the start, defence held a major place in the RAF's strategic air forces and its theory of air warfare. Anyone arguing that RAF doctrine opposed air defence must address two facts: first, that so many senior RAF figures could put forward such heretical views, and, second, that the rest could accept that these might be right, despite Trenchard's ferocious opposition. The RAF's dominant figures did not fully understand air defence, but they listened to their experts, and the latter understood their craft. Mainstream RAF opinion believed fighter defence could be effective, and would cripple attackers, and must be developed as a great priority. The Air Staff's doctrinal 'principle' of 1924 'that the bombing squadrons should be as numerous as possible and the fighters as few as popular opinion and the necessity for defending vital objectives will permit',[27] is sometimes read to mean that, ideally, the RAF would have had no fighter squadrons at all. In fact, this statement meant exactly what it said. The RAF decided that it absolutely needed the number of fighter squadrons which its technical experts thought necessary to defend Britain. Moreover, though air-defence units did not break from conventional RAF opinions regarding the air offensive, they did share the views expressed by Higgins, Chamier and Salmond, and thus followed a distinct variant of RAF doctrine, one which regarded effective air defence as a possibility which could and should be achieved. The effect of this decision was even greater in practice. It ensured air defence would be a major priority in Britain, and receive far more attention and funding than anywhere else – that Britain would create both the world's first strategic bombing and its first strategic air defence force, and link the two. Without Bomber Command, there could have been no Fighter Command. Another irony emerged through the distinction between intention and effect in air expansion. Though fighter squadrons were supposed to represent just 33 per cent of the HDAF, they proved far easier to construct than bombers. Between 1924 and 1927 the HDAF had more fighter than bomber squadrons, which still made up 40 per cent of its strength even in 1934 – and retained that proportion throughout the rearmament programme. Between 1926 and 1939, home-defence fighter squadrons consistently made up 20 per cent of the RAF's total strength and were its second-largest component.

All these characteristics remained in RAF thinking throughout the rearmament period. In 1937, Swinton thus defined the policy of 'air parity' for the Cabinet.

> We are determined that we will not be inferior in air strength at home to any country within striking distance of our shores. This implies:
>
> (i) That we should build and maintain a defensive force adequate to meet any anticipated scale of attack.
>
> (ii) That we should build and maintain a counter-offensive force not inferior in power and efficiency to the offensive force of a foreign Power/German offensive force.[28]

The Air Ministry insisted that defence was essential but attack fundamental, doubly so from late 1937 when the Treasury and politicians used the prospect of defence as a tool to pare offence. 'It would be an illusion to suppose that we have a sure means of defence', Swinton told the Minister for Defence Co-ordination, Inskip; 'a vast amount remains to be done here both in development and application. Counter-attack still remains the chief deterrent and defence'; 'the bomber force is fundamentally the basis of all air strategy', wrote the Air Staff. Still, Swinton rightly emphasized, the RAF supported air defence. 'We have mobilised every asset that science can give us, and not only the Air Staff but the Commander-in-Chief and the whole Fighter Command are concentrating whole-heartedly on applying the scientific results. But we must not exaggerate the possibilities.'[29] In 1934, the Air Staff refused to increase the number of fighters in the HDAF programme at the expense of bombers, but did include 'a minimum' of eight new fighter squadrons (for total of 25) in the expanded 'Metropolitan Air Force' (MAF). Ellington increased that level to 30 squadrons of a 100 squadron MAF, just a marginal decline from the proportion of 1923.[30] In subsequent air programmes, fighter squadrons declined in planned proportion to bomber but rose in absolute number – by 1937 the Air Staff wanted 500 per cent more than Trenchard had requested in 1923. The abortive Scheme J of 1938 advocated an MAF of 38 fighter and 90 bomber squadrons; after the Inskip report the Air Ministry pursued 45 fighter and 86 bomber squadrons.[31] Even more striking than the RAF's requests were what it received, because of the ease of creating fighters. The MAF always contained a higher proportion of fighter squadrons than was intended, the same share as it had in 1934. In September 1938, it had 29 of the 30 fighter squadrons that were supposed to exist at that time, but just 42 of 68 bombers squadrons; four fighters to six bombers.[32] The number of home-defence fighter squadrons increased by over 250 per cent between 1932 and 1938, while an even more striking subterranean change occurred. Since the strength of pilots per squadron rose by 33 per cent during the rearmament era, their numbers in air defence increased by 325 per cent; meanwhile, the Air Ministry poured a remarkable amount of its technical and scientific resources and funding into related equipment. Anyone arguing that the Air Ministry denigrated air defence might consider these facts. Throughout the inter-war years, air defence was treated seriously; it received ample resources; it was left in the hands of the experts; it was developed with skill and power; and the Air Ministry intended all the developments which produced victory in 1940.

During the First World War, in response to raids by German airships and aircraft, Britain developed a sophisticated air-defence system. It had an effective means of early warning, signals intelligence, while ground-based observers provided decent tactical information. Ground commanders could not communicate with aeroplanes in the air, which precluded effective and economical operations or guided interceptions. Instead, aircraft constantly flew along patrol lines, staggered at different altitudes, hoping that by chance one would sight an intruder. Interception rates were low – only 3 per cent of fighters despatched on a given mission struck an enemy, only 10 per cent of intruders were hit. Once intercepted, German bombers outgunned and often outnumbered home-defence fighters. Even so, after failures in each case, in 1916 this system wrecked the Zeppelin onslaught; in 1917, it smashed daylight Gotha attacks; and in 1918, it broke German night raids.[33] Air defence demonstrated a remarkable ability to recalibrate in response to new challenges, and to develop advanced information processing, and command, control, communication and intelligence (C3I) systems. The main air defence force of 1918, the London Air Defence Area (LADA), was a cybernetic structure, featuring what its commander called 'a highly centralized intelligence and command system'. Within one minute LADA could receive and process reports from thousands of observers over a 10,000 square mile area, place them before commanders, let them despatch orders to aircraft standing ready on the runway, which were in the air within two-and-a-half to five minutes. Some 286 guns and 200 aircraft could act within two minutes on the report of one observer 50 miles away. At a moment's notice, each unit could switch from independent operations to fighting under LADA's order and back again. By the end of the war, with R/T provided to some squadrons, this system was on the technical verge of being able to conduct ground directed interception of enemy bombers at 20,000 feet. The basic structure of Fighter Command in 1940 was not new.

Between 1923 and 1934, the RAF developed a new air-defence system, modelled on LADA, especially in C3I. It centred on a cordon-defence system, the 'Aircraft Fighting Zone' (AFZ), with sectors, defended by aircraft stationed sufficiently back from the coast 'to receive the necessary warning of attack and reach their fighting height' before the enemy arrived. Zone-fighter squadrons, supposed to defend only the rectangle in which they were stationed, were augmented by a few interception squadrons to strike day bombers and break their formations before they reached London, to add depth and the possibility of mass, to provide a freely deployable reserve for any squadron under attack, and to hunt the foe as it ran for home, all backed by anti-aircraft forces and searchlights. Ground-to-air R/T multiplied the effect of the system, letting aircraft in the sky use the knowledge available on the ground. In order to provide such material, FAHQ developed LADA's two best intelligence sources, which also proved useful during the Second World War, the Observer Corps and signals intelligence. Fighting Area Headquarters (FAHQ), a command under Air Defence Great Britain (ADGB) controlled all fighters and ground forces in the AFZ and issued operational orders directly to squadrons or sector commands. This decision surpassed in significance the establishment of Fighter Command. It was in 1924, not 1936, that a headquarters first was ordered to solve the task of air defence and nothing else, and given complete control over the development of strategic air defence and the use of its resources. Home-defence fighters, under a specialized command, formed a critical mass well suited for development and innovation. Over the next decade, FAHQ established and trained powerful forces for these purposes and achieved great successes in communications, matériel, organization and intelligence.

Until 1930, FAHQ essentially just re-established the air defence system of 1918, improving its communications and squadron performance. Then it began systematically to improve that system, through twice-yearly exercises pitting all fighter squadrons against bombers, war games, the issuing and regular updating of Battle Orders, continual improvement of all aspects of C3I and tactics. In the process, FAHQ began to break from the system of cordon defence. FAHQ developed drills for effective sector patrol but even more: to maximize the opportunities to operate on interior lines and to concentrate superior numbers against the attackers and to defeat it in detail. By the early 1930s, in exercises FAHQ routinely intercepted day bombers with entire fighter squadrons, and achieved effective individual strikes on night bombers. Operating on the expectation of a high level of tactical intelligence and communication, FAHQ trained its forces in a striking direction: to achieve ground-directed concentrations of force against precise targets. When FAHQ received information that enemies were coming, sector commanders were ordered to place aircraft at an altitude slightly above that at which the intruders were reported, and to patrol a certain area or line which the enemy was expected to pass, and then strike, guided either by their own vision or intelligence from the ground. These interceptions were less precise than those of 1940, but still guided and still ground directed. This major development in tactics and command occurred in a sporadic process long before Dowding or radar were on the scene.

FAHQ was driven to pursue innovation because its tasks were regarded as demanding. As C.-in-C. ADGB, Geoffrey Salmond stated 'the main problem of the defence of London is time'.[34] His predecessor and brother, John Salmond, saw an 'unenviable position'. Despite 'the highest speed and most clockwork regularity ... in all the functions of communication and execution up to the moment of our Squadrons leaving the ground', on an 'optimistic calculation' interception would require 32 minutes from first warning of the enemy, ten in preparing for take-off, 22 in flying to 17,000 feet.[35] Until 1935, the RAF assumed enemy aircraft would cross the coast at 15–20,000 feet with an airspeed between 100 and 150 miles per hour, and fly 30–50 miles toward London and back again, spending perhaps 20–60 minutes over Britain. Under these conditions, aircraft on the ground would have to move with lightning speed – to lose a minute might be to lose an interception. The aim was to move aircraft from hangars to runways in four minutes after warning, to warm engines within another three, to take off within another two minutes and to reach their operating altitude within nine minutes after take-off.[36] An aircraft in a state of 'Readiness' (engines running on the ground, increasing the rate of mechanical casualties) should be airborne within two minutes, one at 'Stand-By' (on the field but with engines off) within five.

Home-defence squadrons met these standards, aided by technical developments. In particular, rates of climb for fighters rose dramatically throughout this period – whereas Snipes (1918) took 10.5 minutes to reach 10,000 feet, Siskin 111s (1925) reached 15,000 feet in the same time, while Bulldogs (1929) reached 20,000 feet in 14.5 minutes and Fury 1s (1931) in 7 minutes 37 seconds. In the 1927 exercises, fighters left the ground on average within 3.9 minutes after receiving an alarm. By 1931, the system was sufficiently taut that some squadrons took off within 80 seconds of receiving a warning, and reached 15,000 feet within eight minutes. These figures were achieved under special circumstances, with pilots permanently sitting in their cockpits. Under more realistic conditions in 1935, with pilots resting away from their machines, aircraft still took off three to five minutes after receiving warning. In 1933, fighters landed and were rearmed, refuelled and ready for takeoff within 10 minutes; within 12 minutes in 1935.[37] FAHQ developed an elaborate system of tactics suited to these circumstances, in which fighters armed only with two .303 machine-guns and 600 rounds could reach bombers midway through the AFZ but then stay with them for long periods. Three to nine fighters conducted intricate manoeuvres against bomber formations for several minutes, each firing simultaneously at its own individual target, hoping gradually to whittle the force and its formation away, aiming not to kill, to throw one fighter on to one bomber for two seconds of murder, but to choreograph a ballet.

By 1934, the 'unenviable position' described by John Salmond seemed to be worsening. A German threat by air seemed possible. The general rise in airspeeds and the expectation that fighters soon would lose their edge over bombers in this sphere, reinforced by exercise data, indicated interception might be impossible until the enemy was over London. Defenders might have just a few seconds to fire on their targets, able to succeed only if their killing was quick. This situation sometimes is described as a crisis of confidence in air defence; in fact, there was more confidence in that power than the historiography indicates, and no more doubts than had been usual since 1919. There were few pessimists and many optimists, including even some who later described themselves as having been pessimists. The RAF's scientists were the largest group of pessimists, and their views have dominated the historiography precisely because their fears sparked the search which led to radar. Yet Britain did not need radar to master the threat of 1934. It was essential for that of 1940, though far from sufficient for victory. Because RAF scientists viewed the problems of air defence as fundamental, however, and because they underestimated the quality of the air-defence system of 1934, they developed a new intelligence source which met their concern. Bomber advocates and scientists thought that within five years air defence might collapse; the Air Staff and ADGB merely that the situation was changing. Problems confronted air defence; so did opportunities. As the C.-in-C. of ADGB during 1934–35, Robert Brooke-Popham, noted:

> The defence is being driven backwards through the increasing speed of the bombers ... It is not merely a problem of relative speeds but of absolute factors, some of which are invariable. The speed of the bombers is steadily increasing; on the other hand two other factors remain constant; firstly, the distance of LONDON from the coast and secondly, the time that must elapse between the aircraft being seen by observers and the defending aeroplanes leaving the ground.

Brooke-Popham did not believe air defence was doomed, simply that one means of forcing the enemy to fight through a deep AFZ was failing. Another set might achieve that aim. Though Interceptor squadrons usually could not strike incoming enemy raids, they often struck their prey as it flew for home, and were amply justified on that account alone. If 'the present method of keeping squadrons on the ground until the enemy are reported is giving increasingly poor results as regards the interception of enemy bombers before they reach their target', a better one might lie in permanent squadron patrols, directed on to the enemy by R/T. That is, Brooke-Popham, advocated precisely the correct way for FAHQ to improve its operations. When this approach was tested during the 1935 exercises it worked well. Still, he questioned the efficacy of this system without assured means of good intelligence, since in exercises the FAHQ 'knows to within an hour or two at the most when he may anticipate enemy activity'. FAHQ required 'information 20–30 miles out to sea so that (it) is able to rely on early warning of enemy activity and thereby conserve his force'.[38]

There was no sense of crisis about air defence because there was no crisis. In 1934–35 British air defence was the best on earth and achieving new levels of performance. FAHQ did face challenges, but these were not of a fundamental nature in the short run, and, ultimately, all they did was to make the snake shed its skin – to abandon one form of air defence without destroying the underlying structure. Authorities demanded that the air-defence system be reconsidered, and recalibrated to deal with a new set of conditions and that the result might make it less powerful against threats by 1939, or more so. The base for these actions was FAHQ and the lessons it had learned over the past decade – both, fortunately, sound. By 1934 its ideas of what to do were five years ahead of the curve. From these different perceptions of challenge stemmed various responses, which, united, could not be defeated.

In 1934–35, the Air Staff, ADGB and FAHQ reconsidered air defence to account for the new German threat and the lessons learned in exercises. By 1938, 820 first-line German aircraft (including fighters), which had risen 1,230 by 1942, could strike at Britain from across the North Sea or, perhaps, from the Low Countries. Against this threat Britain needed two loci of air defence: the old one around London, and a new one in the Midlands, with 'a minimum', respectively, of 16 and nine fighter squadrons.[39] ADGB and the Air Staff agreed the potential power of bombers was rising, but so was that of air defence. With early warning through sound mirrors, and R/T to pass intelligence and orders, permanent combat air patrols or even squadrons on the ground probably could 'intercept incoming raids at the earliest possible moment', perhaps on the coast. Complex practical problems had to be overcome to achieve these results, but they could be overcome. 'It is not at present advisable to advance the forward line of the aircraft zone, but the organization should be speeded up generally, so as to bring about interception on the front line of the zone. This will require the despatch of fighters as early as possible after receipt of the first reliable raid warning.' The Air Staff agreed that with early-warning systems and R/T perhaps 50 per cent of enemy raids could be intercepted 'quite near the coast, by fighters held in readiness on the ground', or possibly through combat air patrols. Though they spent much time tinkering with the AFZ defined in 1923, ADGB and the Air Staff aimed at greater ends, and through developments in communication and intelligence systems. New equipment and procedures eased communication between ground and air, and opened wider opportunities: the head of FAHQ literally could control any action in the AFZ, rendering possible fundamental changes in the command system. These prospects might overload commands and aircraft. Brooke-Popham noted that R/T allowed the Air Officer Commanding (AOC) FAHQ to 'give the necessary orders to his squadrons in the air in the event of unexpected action on the part of the enemy and to receive the reports of his squadrons about what they had carried out', but the greater ease of communication might cause FAHQ and sector headquarters to clash over executive decisions. One Air Staff officer recommended the retention of the present balance of responsibility between AOC and subordinate areas; 'A visit to Fighting Area Operations Room, when as few as ten bomber and ten fighter squadrons only are operating and only half the present fighter front is in use, is convincing evidence that the task of controlling

the whole front in face of a strong and intelligence enemy may prove
too much for one man.' These authorities also held, however, that if
properly handled, those developments in C3I might transform 'the
present rigid sector organization' and unify all the divisions within
the AFZ – a crucial move toward the air-defence system of 1940, by
which time in effect all fighters could operate under ground control in
every part of the AFZ they could reach.[40] Furthermore, the system was
redesigned on the assumption sound mirrors would do what RDF did
do – that is, the tactical system was preparing to incorporate radar
before it existed! In any case, RDF was not the foundation of the
system of air defence, but its capstone. Between 1934 and 1940 there
were no fundamental changes in the organization of air defence, rather
a series of minor alterations, as in Operations Rooms or the rise of the
Filtering Room; the most significant changes of this sort – the transformation of C3I and of the nature of sector commands to allow
ground-directed interceptions by squadrons at the coast – were
precisely the reforms FAHQ had recommended. Equipment changed
radically but then was plugged into a pre-existing system. The story of
air defence is usually told from the perspective of one or another of
these radical technological changes: the real point was organizational
continuity. Meanwhile, lessons learned from exercises continued to be
refined and tested again. In the 1935 exercises, FAHQ practised interception from the air, with ground controllers guiding combat air patrols
on to incoming raids; interception rates were impressive (71 per cent of
day raids, 42 per cent of night raids).[41]

Where ADGB and FAHQ thought the structure of air defence
sound, and capable of greater power through reforms they advocated a
revolution in tactics. Interception would be harder than before, and
briefer. Fighters must abandon 'ponderous manoeuvre for combined
attack' and aim for 'almost complete annihilation on the occasions when
they effectively intercept'. Joubert de la Ferté, the AOC Fighting Area,
commented that even simplified combat drills were 'still too complicated to allow for decisive fire by individual aircraft. In future
attacks, concentration should be attempted by obtaining the maximum
volume of accurate fire in the minimum time rather than by throwing
large numbers of aircraft into the attack at the same time. This method
of concentration would favour the present policy of increasing the
number of guns in SS Fighters.' ADGB advocated a 'policy of annihilation'; fighter formations must seek to destroy every enemy they
engaged, even if that meant letting other forces pass unscathed (i.e. as
deliberate policy, interception rates would decline so to increase concentration of force against those formations which were struck): 'if an
Air Force learns that some of its formations are completely wiped out,
then all sorts of alarmist rumours are sure to start and every pilot will

think he is being sent to meet some new and dreadful form of fright-
fulness'.[42] This approach broke with the assumptions of Higgins and
Geoffrey Salmond in 1923, marking even greater optimism about the
power of air defence. So to achieve these results, in 1934–35 FAHQ
developed tactics 'simple and easy to carry out', of a 'continuous
nature', involving the rapid 'concentration of superior numbers against
the enemy' – aiming to concentrate fire rather than fighters. 'With the
high speeds of modern aircraft and the small margin of speed between
fighters and day bombers, simplified attacks of this nature could be
launched with less delay, as attacks in which more manoeuvre is
required necessitate an appreciable loss of time in gaining and regaining the position from which to attack.' These tactics were successfully
tested at the 1935 exercises.[43] In reality, they were five years ahead of the
aircraft able to apply them; thus, much of this promise could not bloom
before battle.

The revolution in tactics was paralleled by others in technology. By
1931, RAF technical authorities were thinking of new fighter aircraft
with four machine-guns, the 'highest possible' rate of climb and
airspeed (around 200 mph at 15,000 feet) and a service ceiling of 28,000
feet. Air authorities were impressed by the industry's response to these
demands; the 'comparative predicted performances' of models submitted to the F7/30 competition ranged from 240 to 261 mph at 15,000
feet, a 7.8–8.6-minute climb to 20,000 feet and a 35,400–38,000-foot
ceiling, well above the best performance of the day. Gunnery experts
then increased this already long list of demands. They thought interceptors could engage their targets for just a few moments, but large
concentrations of fire could demolish the structure of an aircraft;
hence, the next generation of fighters must be able to deliver a lethal
density of fire (defined as 256 rounds at 200 metres in a two-second
burst). Such aircraft must carry eight machine-guns with 1,000 rounds
of ammunition, though experts debated whether to replace these
weapons with rapid-firing small cannon. In either case, this armament
required a different housing than before, in an aircraft's wings; that
component must meet the demands both of flying and of firing.
Operational authorities feared these technical demands were so high as
to cripple development of the next generation of aircraft. Brooke-
Popham thought 'eight guns is going a bit too far and we should be
content with four' – even so, such an aircraft would not be available
until 1941. He was no reactionary – experience at ADGB and as the
RAF's Director of Research had taught him much about research and
development; as events proved, he was no more pessimistic than air
gunners were optimistic. In any case, the RAF chose to leap as far as
possible in one jump. Its competition for a new model fighter, F5/34 of
16.11.34, began thus: 'The speed excess of a modern fighter over that

of a contemporary bomber has so reduced the chance of repeated attacks by the same fighter(s) that it becomes essential to obtain decisive results in the short space of time offered for one attack only.' It offered remarkably open-ended specifications, which emphasized the 'primary importance' of 'maximum hitting power' and 'speed in overtaking an enemy at 15,000 feet, combined with rapid climb to this height'.[44] From this competition sprang the Hurricane and Spitfire. Nor did this step satisfy the RAF's ambitions – in 1935, precisely when it approved the production of these fighters, it defined specifications for the next generation, cannon-armed, of a performance matching that of the Spitfire IX model, of 400 mph airspeed and a ceiling of 39,000 feet; soon, the RAF had far more first-rate fighter prototypes than it needed. By 1939, it planned to equip all MAF fighter squadrons with Spitfires and Hurricanes, but also to begin replacing them with improved aircraft – Tornadoes, Whirlwinds, Beaufighters – quickly phasing out the Hurricane and retaining the Spitfire for only 25 per cent of Fighter Command, or ten squadrons.[45]

By 1935, radical changes were occurring simultaneously in every sphere of air defence, tactics, technology, command, intelligence, organization; fortunately, the RAF gave responsibility for these issues to three bodies which integrated each concern with the others, with science, technology and experience. The process showed the RAF system at its best: technical practitioners pursued the paths likely to produce the most revolutionary results, 'unknown unknowns' be damned, guided by a flexible organization which harnessed their power to a sound system. Without knowing it, the RAF began to develop unmatched strength in matters which affected air warfare much as the General Staff system had done land warfare between 1866 and 1871. From a close and fruitful link between scientists, engineers, firms and commanders stemmed key successes like radar and scientific air intelligence. The RAF pioneered a new form of learning and of command, control, communications and intelligence, which spread from air defence through every branch during 1934–41. Through the 'Air Fighting Committee' (AFC) and the developers of radar, the RAF was the first military service on earth to develop Operations Research, mathematically based assessments of force structures and tactics, linked to practice with Operational Development Units, with the resulting praxis incorporated into all elements of planning. Not that mathematics were applied universally well; as one staff officer wrote in 1937, 'our present wastage rates are not, as I had thought, based on the experience of the last war. They are really based on nothing at all.'[46] This was the root for the RAF's extraordinary learning curve during the Second World War, its unparalleled ability to improve its performance, once it had hard facts. The record was less remarkable during the pioneering years of this process, when the institution revolutionized military method without knowing that it was doing so – before 1940, Fighter Command did more for these procedures than they for it. In 1940, there were flaws in its tactics, which every squadron solved on its own, without attempt at cross-fertilization or learning from best experience. None the less, no other military institution of the inter-war years handled so well any matter of equal complexity.

Radar emerged from the RAF's relationship with British scientists. These ties began before 1914, grew during the First World War, and remained powerful thereafter. The RN, and foreign-armed services heavily reliant on technology, maintained close ties with military-industrial and scientific communities, but the RAF's links with such groups were particularly profound, largely because of air defence. From the 1920s, the RAF's scientific advisor, H. E. Wimperis, was key to policy on issues linked to technical matters, such as the 'bomber versus battleships' campaign, while the Air Ministry brought leading scientists, like J. B. S. Haldane, to address air defence. Though the 'sound mirror' project failed, it showed a willingness to apply science to air defence. All the matters which sparked Britain's development of radar – Wimperis's proposal of 1934 that the RAF pursue scientific assistance to solve the looming problems in air defence; the Air Ministry's willingness to act on this idea; its ability to gain co-operation from leading university-based figures; and the key work of scientists working for a civilian agency of the state – were systematic, not accidental. Between 1934 and 1939, scientific authorities conceived of and oversaw the development of radar, enthusiastically supported by the Air Ministry, taking care to acquire military expertise. As soon as their equipment was proven, scientists tested how to apply radar to interception with fighters and FAHQ – officers experienced from years of exercises worked out how to connect dots on a screen to directions in the sky; later, FAHQ's expert on Operations Rooms organized these for radar. The latter was absorbed into a C3I system pre-adapted to its characteristics – aiming at ground-directed interceptions by squadrons on the enemy as it crossed the coast, at the centralized but flexible co-ordination of all home forces. Ultimately, these scientists became a branch of the Air Ministry.[47]

Meanwhile, the AFC, a high-level working body chaired by the Deputy Chief of the Air Staff (DCAS), linked the commands and the Air Ministry branches concerned with aerial combat. It was established in 1934 'to provide a more rapid means of co-ordination between tactical and technical development work in connection with air fighting'.[48] Technical experts led the AFC, though all of its members could link these matters to broader ones, and worked in a thorough and objective fashion. They did not debate whether the bomber would always get through, but whether machine-guns or cannon were better airborne ordnance, or armour essential for aircraft. They integrated theory and practice, and science, technology, tactics and military forces. Fighter Command controlled and the AFC directed the Air Fighting Development Establishment (AFDE), with two fighter squadrons on establishment and the frequent loan of bomber flights, 'for the principal purpose of studying tactics, with the idea of evolving equipment to suit those tactics'. The ability to test theory when and as the AFC wished was vital: the 'Bombing Committee' suffered because it had no equivalent 'Bombing Development Unit'. Praxis was powerful; the AFC was able to test in wind tunnels the effect of a bomber's slipstream on a fighter's ability to attack, and to have scientists assess AFDE reports; conversely, the radical changes in tactics studied at the AFDE in 1934 were applied in the 1935 air exercises. Hugh Dowding noted 'how valuable these practical experiments are and how misleading arguments can be when they are based on theory alone'.[49]

These technical bodies generated many innovations and some revolutions. FAHQ, an able but junior organization, would have found it hard to integrate them into a defence system which itself simultaneously was being revised. Fortunately, this task of co-ordination was assigned to a body with more resources and standing. When Bomber Command and Fighter Command replaced ADGB, the status of both attack and defence in strategic air warfare rose. ADGB had been effective, even-handed towards its wings (thus annoying bomber advocates), the most prestigious of RAF headquarters, but now two commands responsible for strategic air warfare stood at the top of the totem pole, with Fighter Command number two – no mean location. Its first head was a respected and senior officer. Dowding had just completed six years as AMSR, the second position in the Air Ministry after the CAS, acquiring ample experience in the technical issues he would have to integrate into the structure bequeathed by FAHQ. He was put at Fighter Command because he was a big man for a big job – the creation of that headquarters and his appointment to it show the Air Ministry took air defence seriously. Dowding has been the subject of mythologization and self-mythologization; any objective account, no matter how sympathetic, must cut him down to size, but the remains are large. He had little impact on the design and procurement of new equipment, nor did he single-handedly create air defence. That structure remained that of LADA and FAHQ; his deputy, Keith Park, reshaped it as much as Dowding. The latter, however, did oversee the greatest recalibration in British strategic air defence between 1915 and 1950. He achieved the radical overhaul in C3I and structure which FAHQ had conceptualized, and made its organization, sketchy in parts, such as Operations Room, into flesh. He retooled the engine of strategic air defence, placed an integrated and centralized C3I system at the wheel and expanded the war machine they served six times in size, making it stronger, better, unbeatable. He made mistakes, yet most of his decisions were good; and he effectively defended his command in Whitehall (though the Air Ministry was sympathetic, not hostile, contrary to myth). Dowding was not a great captain, but he was a great airman.

Together, these three bodies ensured that in 1940 air defence functioned with the same cohesion as in 1934, but more power. This is a success story, but with failings – in 1938–39, parts key to the machine of 1940 did not function. At the outbreak of war, radar reports often were inaccurate for reasons of both omission and commission, with reports of intruders wrong by thousands of feet in altitude and dozens of aircraft in strength, so Fighter Command had to inform its personnel when it realized they, in Park's words, thought radar 'black magic'.[50] These problems had one basic cause: a revolution was in progress. Many different technical matters were changing at once, each had to be tested in isolation rather than in context, the whole remained unclear, and hard opportunities to prove the system and to acquire accurate data were rare. Theory could not be tested with modern fighters until mid-1938, which proved what some technical authorities had suspected since 1936, that a two second burst of machine-gun fire could deliver lethal densities at 600 yards. These lessons had consequences for the power of fighters and vulnerability of bombers (including British ones); they came too late to be applied perfectly in 1940. The Manual of Air Tactics insisted that pilots not fire at targets beyond 400 yards, even though this was feasible.[51] Meanwhile, the only air exercise after 1935 was the least useful of the inter-war years. The 1938 exercises were intended largely to test the value of radar for detection and interception; this aim failed, because personnel inexperienced with the use of radar sets or the interpretation of the results were observing bombers on cramped flight paths, where aircraft flew out as 'neutral' and suddenly returned as 'enemy', and launched few large attacks.[52] Again, combat against the *Luftwaffe* was uncommon before April 1940, slowing any opportunity to learn lessons (although this experience was important in the calibration of radar and ground directed interception). The old rigidities of command over squadron and sectors were reduced, but new problems arose in the relations between the largest components of air defence – Fighter Command and Nos 11 and 12 Groups. These circumstances produced problems in air defence; their nature and causes merit consideration.

The RAF always recognized night bombing as a problem, and aimed to solve it, including tests with searchlights, radar and modern aircraft in 1938; it found no solution because the problem was hard, and the kit unavailable until late in the day.[53] Other difficulties were not solved because they were not seen as such. In 1940, for example, the 'vic' formation of British fighters was inferior to the German 'finger-four' system. This failure was produced by theory just as surely as were those with British bombers. During 1923–25 senior officers working with air defence recognized that fighter escorts might accompany bombers in attacks over London; a decade later, the authorities reconsidered the matter but deemed it unworkable, a view with some force, given German experiences during the Battle of Britain. They also discussed, inconclusively, whether the tactics for air defence and air superiority were identical, which Dowding asserted was the case. British fighter tactics were created not to achieve air superiority against other fighters, but to intercept bomber groups, against which the 'vic' was useful and tight formations seen as essential. So powerful were these preconceptions that the RAF could not even recognize its error without costly experience. In early 1940, the Air Tactics branch interpreted reports of the 'finger-four' formation as indicating that the *Luftwaffe* fought in a 'section of two fighter aircraft', possibly the 'logical outcome' of a German variant of the British 'two fighters to one bomber theory' in air defence; but it was not. Similarly, during the Battle of Britain some fighter pilots interpreted German groups of two or four aircraft as being in 'vics' of three.[54] British concepts of aerial combat had problems, largely stemming from the rigid assumption that in strategic air warfare, bombers attacked cities and fighters attacked bombers. However, the RAF got the main thing right for 1940 – how to smash mass daylight raids; it adjusted to ancillary aspects of that issue, fighter escorts and the 'finger four', though with more pain than necessary. The problem it found most difficult to overcome, night raids by individual aircraft, was nuisance not menace. These failures were minor compared with those of the *Luftwaffe* – it should have done so badly – and Britain suffered most for them in 1941, as it struggled to develop new tactics for air superiority and to attack with air defence fighters.

In 1940, however, Fighter Command did suffer from two grave weaknesses. Though the most fundamental components of its C3I system were protected, key parts – radar sets, sector headquarters, the airlines over which much communication passed – were desperately vulnerable to attack. The German failure to exploit this weakness, to strike the senses and nerves of British air defence instead of hurling itself on fist and flesh, was the turning point in the Battle of Britain, not the *Luftwaffe*'s move from attacking Biggin Hill to London. Fighter Command was beyond German comprehension; they did not understand its weaknesses because they misunderstood its nature – they were whipped from the start. Britain exposed this needless weakness because air defence planned for a bad case but not the worst case; against an enemy flying across the North Sea, rather than one based across the

Channel. This same problem shaped the second great weakness in Fighter Command during 1940, the shortage of pilots trained with modern fighters. Inter-war RAF planning paid careful attention to wastage and training. It assumed home-defence fighter squadrons would suffer losses second to none, and at worst might be outnumbered by two, perhaps three, to one, from across the North Sea. In the summer of 1940, Fighter Command confronted four times its strength, next door. Meanwhile, few pilots were trained on modern fighters because such aircraft had only just become available. In the summer of 1940, Fighter Command confronted four times its strength across the Channel, including superior numbers of first-class fighters engaged in a high-intensity struggle for air supremacy. This was perhaps the RAF's worst problem; it certainly magnified many others.

By 1940, Britain possessed fighter aircraft better than or equal to German ones; in every design category, the Hurricane matched and the Spitfire exceeded the RAF's expectations of 1934. These aircraft can be criticized – they were slow to mount rapid-firing cannon – but equal criticisms can be made of every air force in 1940. Neither quality nor quantity of fighter aircraft troubled the RAF during the Battle of Britain. It was, however, crippled by their halting production during 1935–40. Technical staffs of the 1920s emphasized that the aircraft industry must match foreign developments, so RAF policy 'will not be deflected out of its way by some single advance', while a regular programme of orders ensured that at any time most British aircraft were good, the remainder being obsolescent or excellent.[55] Unfortunately, by 1934, Britain did lag in one advance, which rendered all its aircraft obsolete all at once. The British aircraft industry fell 18 months behind Germany and the United States in the monoplane wing – key to the development of speed, range and firepower – which caused a cascading series of problems. Britain had no modern aircraft between 1936 and 1938, fatal to a policy based on 'pure guesswork' and little fact. Between the wars, the RAF had a good long-term policy for procurement and development which failed just once, in 1936–39; that moment when success was most essential. In 1933–34, at about the same time as the *Luftwaffe*, the RAF accepted the need for monoplane fighters of new design, quickly placed orders for Hurricanes and Spitfires and expected to have many of them by late 1937, assuming that design, development and production would take no longer than had been normal for fighter models over the past decade. In fact, few Hurricanes and no Spitfires were available until 1939, 18 months after the *Luftwaffe* received its first models of the Bf 109. That aircraft was not the ME 109 E, but in September 1938 Fighter Command still had just 24 squadrons of biplanes and five of monoplanes (three with Hurricanes and one partly equipped with Spitfires).

   This problem affected the production of all British aircraft but it was most pronounced with the most significant of its fighters, the Spitfire. Supermarine – a technically innovative firm with little experience in big orders – attempted to design and manufacture an aircraft which jumped as far in one leap as Hawkers, a firm more experienced with fighters, production and development, aimed to do with two generations of aircraft. The die was cast in mid-1935, when the Air Ministry and Supermarine assumed the Spitfire could easily be modified to meet all of the RAF's desiderata, by having the firm 'design and manufacture ... a new set of wings' to carry eight .303 machine-guns.[56] This process proved more complex than anyone expected, largely because R. J. Mitchell's design for the wing was so advanced, compared with that for the Hurricane. Supermarine, without experience in large production or the normal process of subcontracting parts, had 500 employees and a contract for 310 aircraft. The Air Ministry made its first production order for 310 Spitfire 1s in July 1936. On past experience, it probably expected the first models to begin reaching squadrons within a year – by which time Supermarine had barely given its subcontractors specifications for the wings they were to construct. For several months, the RAF considered abandoning the project. Finally, it solved the problem by merging the managerial and financial capabilities of Messrs Vickers and Lord Nuffield with the technical expertise of Supermarine, and by establishing an entirely new plant at Castle Bromwich to manufacture Spitfires on lines of mass production.[57] Supermarine was criticized bitterly far into the war: in June 1941, despite a recognition that 'quality is all important in fighter aircraft, and ... quantity in production must if necessary to sacrificed to some extent in order to obtain quality'; the C.-in-C. of Fighter Command, William Sholto Douglas, complained that 'time slips by and very little seems to happen' regarding modifications in the Spitfire.[58] Ultimately, the RAF made the Spitfire its standard fighter between 1940 and 1945 almost by accident, because that aircraft could incorporate the characteristics desired from the next generation without the confusion caused by switching production to untried models. Meanwhile, the slow pace of production discouraged further orders. Only 49 Spitfires were delivered to squadrons in 1938, with another 58 by March 1939; only 510 by March 1940 (though, fortunately, substantial numbers began to appear from the next month). No Spitfires ordered after August 1939 entered squadron service until after the Battle of Britain; not until 1940 were large orders constantly placed for Spitfires, and not until January 1942 did supply begin to reach demand.

   This delay in the availability of modern aircraft had widespread and unfortunate effects on British air power and the British Empire. It produced an odd phenomenon for air power in 1939–41: steadily rising superiority in those areas the RAF deemed most significant, coupled with disastrous weakness in all others. Since few first-class fighters were available during 1940–41, tight rationing was unavoidable, forcing third-class models on second-class theatres. Had the RAF begun to receive high-performance fighters and bombers 18 months before it did, arguably it would have avoided most of its failures of 1940–41. Instead, the need to replace every RAF aircraft at once created knock on problems for those fields or areas receiving the lowest priorities, producing misfortune for ground support and in the Middle East, and disaster at Singapore and for carrier borne aviation. This matter also damaged the bomber offensive. From 1934, the Air Staff accepted that bombers must match the rise in fighter weaponry, forcing 'a consider-able increase in defensive armament'. The RAF was divided over the consequences. Some held that,

> The fighter, strictly specialized in design for this duty can, in equal numbers, develop a much higher firepower in attack than the bomber. The bomber for defence requires all-round fire which entails the distri-bution of the available firepower into two, three of four gun positions, according to the design and class of the bomber. A bomber carrying eight guns in four positions might have an all-round fire power between two and four guns only, whereas the single-seat fighter, carrying weight guns, would be able to bring all eight to bear in the direction of attack.[59]

John Slessor, conversely, envisaged a bomber 'so heavily armed that it will be a very unpleasant object to attack', able to operate individually over enemy airspace and to fight through a defensive system by itself. FAHQ held 'the safest course for bombers to pursue when attacked is to fly fast, keep closely together and shoot straight', which, combined with manoeuvres by aircraft or formation, would give them real power in air combat; fighter tactics assumed bomber formations were hard to destroy.[60] In the absence of proof, faith had free rein. Such optimism began to wane by mid-1938, with the tests of the Hispano-Suiza 20mm cannon, and of the Hurricane against all-British bomber models. The latter tests reversed every expectation which had caused concern for air defence in 1934. The AFDE concluded that modern fighters possessed devastating firepower (lethal fire could be delivered at 200 yards in 0.5 seconds – 400 per cent better than the standard of 1934 – and at 800 yards in 2.4 seconds) and an unprecedented advantage in speed over bombers; fighters had a better chance to intercept than before, and more time on station and more firepower when that occurred. Most defensive techniques of bomber formations collapsed, sapping the basis for British fighters tactics to boot. The AFC began to read the writing on the wall as, with less enthusiasm, did the Air Staff. By December 1938 it noted that existing bombers were 'very seriously handicapped' against modern fighters, especially those mounting cannon. The CAS, Cyril Newall, wished to add cannon to existing bombers, because of '(a) the doubtful efficacy of .303 guns as shown by experiments on new type aircraft, and (b) to meet enemy aircraft armed with cannons', but rejected the idea as it would force a complete redesign of existing models. Just after the outbreak of war, Bomber Command reversed its attitudes toward air combat, holding all bombers needed more firepower, including tail turrets. These changes in attitude came too late to affect bomber defences during 1939–42; doubly so, because the most devastating of the AFDE's trials came just before and after the outbreak of war, when Spitfires devoured an English breakfast of bombers, including one fabled as fleety, the Blenheim.[61]

Between 1914 and 1940, Britain created, maintained and refined the world's first strategic air defence system, and the only effective one. The RAF learned all the right lessons of the Great War; it was always able to handle any and every strategic bombing force which might have attacked Britain, whether in 1926, 1934 or 1938. Fighter Command in 1940 was not the product of heroes or of rebels but of the system – of the institutional decision of the RAF over a 15-year period to develop air defence through regular and sizeable investments.[62] The Battle of Britain was a walkover, one of the most one-sided victories in military history. This is a success story; credit for it must go to the RAF.

NOTES

1. Report on the 1938 Air Exercises, Fighter Command, 8.11.38, AIR 20/470. All material from files in the AIR and CAB series are held at the Public Records Office, Kew Garden, and are cited by permission of the Controller of Her Majesty's Stationary Office. I am grateful to Sebastian Cox for many conversations about air defence, and for not complaining too much when I steal his ideas.
2. Brereton Greenhous, Stephen J. Harris, William C. Johnston and William G. P. Rawling, *The Crucible of War, 1939–1945, The Official History of the Royal Canadian Air Force*, Volume III (Toronto, University of Toronto Press, 1994), p. 164. The milk of this doctrine flows pure in the works tending toward hagiography of Lord Dowding, e.g. Robert Wright, *Dowding and the Battle of Britain* (London, MacDonald, 1969), and its influence is widespread in the standard literature, see H. Montgomery Hyde, *British Air Policy between the Wars, 1918–1939* (London, Heinemann, 1976), pp. 322–3, John Terraine, *The Right of the Line: The Royal Air Force in the European War, 1939–1945* (London, Hodder & Stoughton, 1985), pp. 20–1; Malcolm Smith, *British Air Strategy between the Wars* (Oxford, Clarendon, 1984), p. 79. Three accounts of air defence share these general views, though each remains useful and readable; the Air Historical Branch, 'RAF Narrative, The Origins and Pre-War Growth of Fighter Command', AIR 20/393, Norman Franks, *RAF Fighter Command* (Sparkford, Patrick Stephens, 1992) and Peter Wykeham, *Fighter Command: A Study of Air Defence, 1914–1960*

(London, Putnam, 1960). Against this tide of opinion, students of air defence during 1917–18, and from a more technical viewpoint, maintain that the roots of effective air defence begin during the First World War: see Barry Powers, *Strategy without Slide Rule* (London, Croom Helm, 1974), p. 74, and Michael J. Gething, *Sky Guardians: Britain's Air Defence 1919–1993* (London, Arms & Armour, 1993), pp. 22–7. The brief but informative and perceptive account in R. J. Overy, *The Air War, 1939–1945* (London, Europa, 1980), pp. 14–16, *passim*, avoids most of these mistakes.

3. For a discussion of these points, see John Ferris, 'The Air Force Brats' View of History: Recent Writings on the Royal Air Force, 1918–1960', *International History Review*, XX, 1 (Jan. 1998), pp. 118–43.

4. Memorandum by Sykes, 21.10.18, AIR 2/71 A. 6446.

5. This matter is complex: one must distinguish (a) the loose and general consensus of RAF officers about strategic air warfare from (b) one (if the most influential) variant of them, the views of Lord Trenchard, the first CAS, and (c) the opinions cited in official air theory – which often directly contradicted Trenchard's views, and (d) the subsequent critical literature on the matter, which sometimes conflates (a) (b) and (c). For important discussions of these issues see Michael Paris, *Winged Warfare: The Literature and Theory of Aerial Warfare in Britain, 1859–1917* (Manchester, Manchester University Press, 1992), Tami Davis Biddle, *Rhetoric and Reality in Air Warfare: The Evolution of British and American Ideas about Strategic Bombing, 1917–1945* (Princeton, NJ: Princeton University Press, 2002); Robertson, *RAF Strategic Bombing Doctrine*; Powers, *Strategy without Slide Rule*; Smith, *British Air Strategy between the Wars*; Allen D. English, 'The RAF Staff College and the Evolution of RAF Strategic Bombing Policy, 1922–9', *Journal of Strategic Studies*, 16 (1993), pp. 401–31. David Edgerton, *England and the Aeroplane: An Essay on a Militant and Technological Nation* (London, Macmillan, 1991), offers penetrating comments on the socio-cultural roots of the RAF and its theories of air warfare.

6. Briefing by Trenchard for lecture by Brooke-Popham, undated, circa December 1923 by internal evidence, AIR 5/328.

7. Swinton to Inskip, 4.11.37, AIR 2/226.

8. Minutes of meeting in CAS's Room, 19.7.23, AIR 19/92; AFC 2, AFC 51, Air Fighting Committee, copy, Air Historical Branch.

9. Edgerton, *England and the Aeroplane.*

10. 'Minutes of Meeting in CAS's Room', 25.1.26, AIR 2/301 S. 25566.

11. COS 553, CAB 53/30; 125th COS meeting, 4.5.34, CAB 53/4.

12. Minutes by Higgins, July 1923, and Chamier, 10.1.24, AIR 5/328.

13. 70th COS meeting, 30.5.28, CAB 53/2.

14. John Ferris, 'The Theory of a "French Air Menace", Anglo-French Relations and the British Home Defence Air Force Programmes of 1921–1925', *Journal of Strategic Studies*, 10 (1987), pp. 62–83.

15. Minute by Trenchard, 6.11.24, *passim*, AIR 5/387.

16. Ferris, 'Fighter Defence Before Fighter Command: The Rise of Strategic Air Defence in Great Britain, 1917–1934', *Journal of Military History*, Vol. 63 (October 1999), pp. 845–84.

17. Briefing by CAS for Brooke-Popham, 15.12.23, AIR 5/328.

18. Minutes of meeting in CAS's Room, 26.7.23, AIR 19/92; Chamier to Steel, 10.1.24, AIR 5/328.

19. Meeting in CAS's Room, 26.7.23, AIR 19/92.

20. Minute by Higgins, undated but July 1923; Higgins to DCAS, 12.6.23, AIR 5/328;

Higgins to AMSR, 25.1.24, and memorandum, undated, 'Lecture to RAF Staff College', AIR 5/954.

21. Untitled memorandum, but by Higgins according to other information in the file, 'Considerations Governing the Design of Home Defence Heavy Day Bombers and Day Fighters', 5.12.23, AIR 5/954.

22. Minutes of meeting in CAS's Room, 10.7.23, AIR 19/92.

23. Undated and unsigned memorandum, but by Bullock and July 1923 by internal evidence, AIR 19/92.

24. Minutes of meeting in CAS's Room, 10.7.23, 13.7.23, AIR 19/92.

25. Air Staff, July 1923, 'The proportion of fighters to bombers, and of day to night bombers, in the Home Defence Air Force', AIR 9/69.

26. Minutes of meeting in CAS's Room, 10.7.23, AIR 19/92; CID Memorandum 120-A, CAB 3/4.

27. Air Staff Memorandum No. 11A, February 1924, AIR 5/328.

28. CP 27 (37), Swinton, 22.1.37, AIR 8/227.

29. 'Note by the Air Staff on Sir T. Inskip's Queries regarding Scheme 'J', 24.11.37. Swinton to Inskip, 4.11.37, 26.11.37, AIR 2/226.

30. Minutes by Ellington, 16.2.34, 27.2.34, 22.3.24, AIR 2/907. This figure included 5 fighter squadrons with the task of defending any strategic bombers deployed on the continent. Later Air Ministry figures for the total number of fighters in the United Kingdom included some which, in formal terms, might also serve with an army on the continent, though it always privately regarded strategic air defence as their main task. This double ear-marking of squadrons produced some trauma in 1940.

31. Air Staff, 'Note on Air Parity', 20.5.38: AIR 8/227.

32. E.P.M. 155 (38), 140th Progress Meeting, 25.10.38, 'Air Ministry Report on the Lessons of the September, 1938, Emergency', AIR 6/55.

33. John Ferris, '"Airbandit!": C3I and Strategic Air Defence during the First Battle of Britain, 1915–18', in Michael Dockrill and David French (eds), *Strategy and Intelligence: British Policy during the First World War* (London, Hambledon, 1995).

34. 'Air Staff Requirements in Aircraft', undated and unsigned memorandum, but lecture notes for speech by Geoffrey Salmond, *c*. 1927–28, according to internal evidence, AIR 9/37, Warrant Officer R. W. Woodly, 'The Growth and Progress of Operations Rooms in Fighting Area (Now No. 11 (Fighter) Group) and Associated sectors, 1929–37', AIR 20/2069.

35. ADGB to Air Ministry, 19.5.25, AIR 5/410. For lengthy expositions on air defence between 1923–34, see John Ferris, 'Fighter Defence'.

36. Lecture by DCAS, 10.3.24, AIR 9/69.

37. 'ADGB Exercises – July 1927', AIR 9/69; *The Times*, 19.7.32, 'Air Exercises, Arduous Task of the Defence'; ADGB 30.10.33, 'Report on the Air Exercises 1933', Brooke-Popham, AIR 20/185; 'Report on Air Defence of Great Britain Command Exercise 1935', AIR 20/470.

38. Ferris, 'Fighter Defence', pp. 863–83.

39. 'Estimate of the Requirements for the Security of Great Britain against Air Attack from Germany', AS, 29.5.34 AIR 9/69; The Re-Orientation of the Air Defence System, 1934', AM, 30.7.34, AIR 2/697.

40. FO 1 to DDOI, 17.3.34, Air Ministry Conference to Review the System of Home Defence, 13.12.33, Air Commodore Gossage, 3.34, ADGB, 'Appreciation of the situation ...', AIR 2/907; AIR 9/69, *passim;* Report on the Air Exercises, 1933, AIR 20/185.

41. ADGB 25.11.35, 'Report on the Air Exercises, 1935', AIR 20/470.

42. Memorandum by ADGB 25.11.35, 'Report on the Air Exercises, 1935', AIR 20/470. 'Day Fighting in Home Defence', *Royal Air Force Quarterly*, 5/1, 1934 – an unsigned article in a demi-official journal which reflected contemporary FAHQ and ADGB views.
43. AFC 2, AHB; ADGB 25.11.35, 'Report on the Air Exercises, 1935', AIR 20/470.
44. Two useful technical works on these broad topics are G. F. Wallace, *The Guns of the Royal Air Force 1939–1945* (London, Wallace, 1970) and Eric B. Morgan and Edward Shacklady, *Spitfire, The History* (Stanford, CA, Key Publishing, 2000). Important discussions on the armament and tactical issues are contained in the files of the Air Fighting Committee.
45. Secretary of State's Progress Meetings, 1.12.38, 2.12.38, E.P.M. 175 (38) and 176 (38), AIR 6/55.
46. Minute by F.O. 1, 22.6.37, AIR 5/1124.
47. David Zimmerman, *Britain's Shield: Radar and the Defeat of the Luftwaffe* (Stroud, Sutton, 2001); Alan Beyerchen, 'From Radio to Radar: Interwar Military Adaptation to Technological Change in Germany, the United Kingdom, and the United States', in Williamson Murray and Alan Millett (eds), *Military Innovation in the Interwar Period* (Cambridge, Cambridge University Press, 1996); Air Historical Branch, *Signals*, Volume IV, *Radar in Raid Reporting* (London, 1950) and Volume V, *Fighter Control and Interception* (London, 1952), *The Second World War, 1939–1945, Royal Air Force*.
48. First Interim Report of the Work of the Bombing and Air Fighting Committees', 9.36, *passim*, AIR 5/1143.
49. AFC 27, AFC 34, AFC 52; ADGB 25.11.35, 'Report on the Air Exercises, 1935', AIR 20/470.
50. Minute by Park, 27.11.39, AIR 16/19.
51. AFC 6, AFC 15, AFC 17; Fourth Interim Report of the Work of the Bombing and Air Fighting Committees', 2.39, AIR 5/1143.
52. Report on the 1938 Air Exercises, Fighter Command, 8.11.38, AIR 20/470.
53. AFC 57, 64,66; Ferris, 'Fighter Defence'.
54. ADGB to Air Ministry, 19.5.25, AIR 5/410; AFC 32, 73, 81, 84, Air Fighting Committee; Third Interim Report of the Work of the Bombing and Air Fighting Committees, 5.38, AIR 5/1143. Franks, *RAF Fighter Command*, pp. 15–103, offers useful data and analysis regarding issues of fighter tactics, 1934–40.
55. Minute by Geoffrey Salmond, 18.4.25, AIR 5/406.
56. DTD to Director of Contracts, 28.5.35, AIR 2/2824.
57. Morgan and Shacklady, *Spitfire*, has useful details on the issue of Supermarine and Spitfires; Sebastian Ritchie, *Industry and Air Power: The Expansion of British Aircraft Production, 1935–1941* (London, Frank Cass, 1997), offers a powerful analysis of the military-industrial base of British air power in this period.
58. Fighter Command to Air Ministry, FC/S.22754, 18.6.41, AIR 2/2824.
59. Memoranda by Plans, 12.34, 'Notes on Certain Factors Influencing Air Staff Requirements in Bomber Aircraft', by Air Staff 8.35.
60. 'The Influence of Tactics Upon Design of Bombers for the Air Defence of Great Britain', Slessor, DD Plans, Minute to DDOR, 20.7.37, AIR 9/37; AFC 2, AHB. Contemporary views in the demi-official literature also varied widely; see *Royal Air Force Quarterly*, 'Format', 'The Defensive Powers of Bomber Aircraft', Vol. 4/4 (10.33), pp. 400–6, J. A. Chamier, 'The Heavy Fighting Aeroplane', 11/3 (1931), pp 422–6; 'Day Fighting in Home Defence', 5/1 (1934), p. 3, 'Bomber Formations', pp. 214–21, 8/1 (1.36), G. C. Pattinson, 'Renewed Reflections on Day-Bomber Formations, 1918', 11/4 (10.31), pp. 586–90.

61. AFC 55, 58, 65, 67, 70, 83, 82, Air Fighting Committee; 'Air Staff Notes on the Size of Bomber Aircraft'; 22.12.38, AIR 9/37, Memorandum by Newall, CAS, to DGRD/DGP/DCAS/ACAS, 5.12.38, 'Orders for New Types', AIR 6/55; 'Fourth Interim Report of the Work of the Bombing and Air Fighting Committees', 2.39, AIR 5/1143.
62. Ferris, 'Fighter Defence'.

3

The Royal Naval Air Service:
A Very Modern Force

Christina J. M. Goulter

When reflecting on air power history, it is difficult to discern marked watersheds, with the exception, perhaps, of the introduction of the aircraft carrier and the jet engine. But, equally, it would be wrong to view the development of air power as a steady evolutionary process. Its growth was episodic, spurred on, as one would expect, by war, and often retarded during peacetime when there was budgetary constraint on research and development. One of the values of reflecting on air power history is that it offers insight into what can happen if we fail to nurture military capability during periods of peace, at the very least in a doctrinal sense, and it also highlights the dangers of forgetting the important lessons of the last war. For these reasons, one of the most interesting periods is that of the First World War and the decades that followed. Many important lessons were learned about the nature of military aviation between 1914 and 1918, but most of those lessons were neatly filed away and forgotten during the inter-war years, only to be painfully relearned by the next generation of airmen. There were many reasons for this, including the appearance of a doctrine of air power which was more of an article of faith than any real reflection of military capability.[1] The consequences were extremely serious. In this business, reinventing the wheel means lives lost unnecessarily and certainly much wasted treasure.

At the forefront of aeronautical science and its military application during the First World War was the Royal Naval Air Service (RNAS), and between 1914 and 1918 it made enormous strides, especially in relation to Anti-Submarine Warfare (ASW) and strategic bombing. One of the main reasons it made such progress was that the RNAS was very good at identifying and investigating operational problems. Not only was the Admiralty quick to adopt aircraft as a new technology, but its extensive research and development facilities were tasked with solving the problems associated with long-range navigation, air-to-ground communications, bomb aiming and weapons performance. In so doing, the RNAS developed Operational Research techniques which we usually associate with the Second World War. But what is particularly striking about the RNAS was its ability to think about air power in a conceptual way, from a very early date. Throughout the First World War, the air power roles to develop most rapidly in conceptual and doctrinal terms were those practised by the Naval Air Service.[2]

In view of just how young aeronautical science was by 1914, it is surprising to see how quickly air power roles developed. But, while it is true to say that virtually all the air power roles with which we are now familiar had made an appearance by 1915, not all of these roles were fully thought through in conceptual terms. It is important to make this point, because there is a tendency sometimes to overstate the extent of advances in military aeronautics in the First World War. Nor should we be too critical of the lengthy time it took for certain roles to develop. Aviation was a new science, and, as with most technologies that make a difference, conceptualizing and building new doctrine takes a while. A good example of this was the counter-air role. The Royal Flying Corps (RFC), under Trenchard, fell into the trap of defining offensive counter-air in terms of the extent to which his aircraft managed to penetrate German air space. For him, penetrating German airspace by ten miles was offensive; 20 miles was even more offensive. The problem with this, of course, is that aircraft could not hold ground, so using the extent to which you penetrate the enemy's airspace as a yardstick of success became very dangerous. It was Trenchard's dogged pursuit of this notion of offensive counter-air that led to the rapid escalation of losses. The more losses he had, the greater the pressure on the training organization, which, to meet the demands of the Western Front, was shortening courses, and the greater the inexperience of the pilot arriving on a squadron, the quicker he was lost! As in any war, you must choose your yardsticks of success very carefully.[3]

But while the Royal Flying Corps was grappling with the counter-air concept, other elements of British military aviation were forging ahead. Some roles developed conceptually and doctrinally very quickly, and this is particularly so in the maritime sphere. Even before the First World War, the Royal Navy seemed to be anxious to adopt the new aviation technology, in spite of the fact that aircraft had yet to prove themselves in the military sphere. The issue of technology acceptance is an interesting one. General Haig was widely criticized for being less than enthusiastic about aviation at the start of the war, but, given the state of aviation technology at the time, he was perfectly correct to have his reservations. Aircraft were not robust enough to carry much ordnance, but Haig was to change his mind by the end of 1914, after he had seen the valuable reconnaissance work done by the Royal Flying Corps during the battle for the Marne. The Royal Navy, in the meantime, had wasted little time investigating the possibilities that aviation offered. As early as 1911, the Admiralty raised the possibility of flying an aircraft off a ship's deck, and the first such flight was performed in December of that year. The language they used at the time demonstrated that they understood this would represent a Revolution in Military Affairs, even if they did not express it in these terms. Here was the ability, potentially, to fly to the heart of an enemy fleet and destroy it, without having to engage surface fleets.[4]

This led to other discussions about the potential utility of aircraft in an anti-submarine role, not only in detecting but attacking submarines. In January 1912, the Admiralty was circulating a paper which pointed to the advantages of having an aircraft carry out both scouting and attacking functions. Three months later, the Admiralty conducted its first bomb-dropping experiments. More rigorous experimentation in 1913 pointed to the problem of bomb aiming, and so the Admiralty created a section in one of its research and development sections devoted entirely to the production of a bombsight. Other experimentation in 1912–13 aimed at the application of radio and wireless telegraphy to improve communications between ship and aircraft, and by the time war broke out the Navy had a functioning torpedo aircraft.[5]

The point of this detail is to demonstrate just how proactive the Navy was in developing aviation science, even before 1914. They had identified aircraft as a force multiplier at sea, as something that would not only aid patrol work but could also be used to attack the enemy. As one might expect, the research and development tempo increased after the war broke out. In August 1914, the Royal Naval Air Service was assigned two principal functions: co-operation with the Navy and air defence of Great Britain (as part of a general naval undertaking to protect the British Isles). The former involved acting as the 'eyes' of the Fleet and performing anti-submarine and anti-shipping attacks; the latter aimed at protecting British cities, dockyards and other military installations from Zeppelin or aeroplane attack. It was in performing these various roles that the RNAS leapt to the forefront of aviation science, and much was learned about the nature of maritime aviation and strategic bombing.[6]

Of greatest concern, very early on, was the submarine threat, especially when the Germans launched an organized submarine campaign at the start of 1915. What is remarkable, given the infancy of both the aircraft and the submarine as weapons of war, is just how quickly the Admiralty set about developing tactical doctrine for use of aircraft against submarines. One of the Navy's departments, which had been created in December 1913 for the purpose of investigating aeronautical and related inventions, was entrusted with finding out what type of ordnance and what forms of attack would be best suited to anti-submarine warfare. Drawing on both operational experience to date and experimentation, it was discovered that a method of 'straddling' bombs across a submarine was the best method of attack, and that surprise could be achieved if the aircraft took advantage of certain conditions, such as coming out of the sun or maintaining a reasonably high altitude until the last minute. As the Germans expanded their submarine campaign in 1916, the Admiralty's operational research sections were also focused on finding the most effective patrol patterns. What they came up with included the famous 'Spider's Web' configuration, which enabled a single aircraft to cover some 4,000 square miles of sea. Someone came up with the idea that much valuable time could be saved if the anti-submarine squadrons used reconnaissance aircraft to locate submarines, and then the main force would be vectored onto the target. This idea of using a scouting aircraft ahead of a strike force pre-dated by 29 years the introduction in Coastal Command of 'outriders', reconnaissance aircraft sent ahead of a strike wing to find 'chance' targets or re-locate shipping previously reported by agents or photo reconnaissance. Thus, we see the Admiralty attempting to solve one of the greatest operational problems in Anti-Submarine Warfare: the need to economize on effort in the face of a massive operational task.[7]

The Admiralty sought other force multipliers in this first Battle of the Atlantic, including intelligence, and it was during the First World War, rather than, as some people suppose, during the Second World War, that we see the first use of intelligence as a means of tracking U-boats. Building on the classic use of naval attachés, the Admiralty's Naval Intelligence Division (NID) developed a network of agents reporting on enemy submarine movements in and out of their home ports. In addition, the NID also established a chain of listening stations along the English and French coastlines to pick up both radio and Wireless Telegraphy signals. Armed with this intelligence, aircraft could be sent to patrol in the area identified, and this would have the dual benefit of economizing on effort and also sanitizing the intelligence sources by making the Germans think that their submarine had been located by aircraft patrol work rather than by any other means.[8]

The problems of measurement of success in war have already been noted. As early as 1916, the Navy acknowledged that submarine kills were only one indicator of success. Just as important was the effect of keeping submarines submerged, and, therefore, unable to fire their torpedoes. This is why near continuous air patrolling in the Channel was considered so important. The importance of air patrols in keeping U-boats submerged was discussed in Operational Research papers in 1941 and 1942, and just as the biggest impetus behind the development of Operational Research in the Second World War was the desperate need to beat the U-boat menace, so the RNAS's greatest operational analysis during 1915–16 was devoted to ASW.[9]

The technical developments and operational research performed between 1915 and 1918 were intended for use largely in the anti-submarine war, but they also had wider application, including anti-surface operations. For example, it was proposed that relative immunity from enemy fire could be obtained if aircraft attacked in force, and this was adopted against both submarines and surface vessels whenever possible from 1916 onwards. Not until 1942 did Coastal Command adopt Strike Wing tactics, involving 30 or more aircraft against one objective. It was thought then that the idea of saturating enemy defences in this way was completely revolutionary.[10]

There were many other technological and doctrinal developments in the maritime sphere, which had to be thought through again at the start of the Second World War, especially the use of aircraft against surface shipping, either against major naval units or in a blockade role against sea trade. Blockading was done successfully in the Mediterranean, against Turkish merchant-men in 1915, and blockade became a hot topic for the Navy's Air Department. Pre-dating by some 24 years Coastal Command's anti-shipping campaign against German imports of Swedish iron ore, the Navy spoke of the possibility of launching a joint surface–air action against German sea trade. What they were talking about was Germany's coastal trade, for the most part. But, from a doctrinal point of view, what makes the Admiralty's air-blockade concept particularly interesting is not only the Jointery aspects, but that they spoke about such action having important strategic implications for Germany, by affecting its industrial production. In other words, this was strategic air power. In the years that followed the First World War, the only strategic air power acknowledged was strategic bombing, and, sadly, this remains to a large extent true today.[11]

For those who have ventured back to look at the RNAS in the First World War, undoubtedly one of the most exciting facets was the 1916 proposal to launch a massed torpedo attack on the German High Seas Fleet at Wilhemshaven. Coupled with such a strong tradition in research and development, one of the Admiralty's greatest assets during this period was the calibre of its naval staff. Perhaps it is no surprise that some of the most far-sighted individuals were those attracted to the new air service in the Navy. A key figure was undoubtedly Captain (later Rear-Admiral) Murray Sueter, who was the first Director of the Navy's Air Department, and who had been the Inspector of Airships after serving in the Department of Naval Ordnance and Torpedoes. Towards the end of 1916, he was hatching plans for the attack on the German High Seas Fleet at Wilhemshaven and the Austrian Fleet in the Adriatic harbours. Both plans stalled during the early part of 1917. The attack on the Austrian Fleet was deferred after technical problems with the seaplanes sent out to the Mediterranean, and the Wilhemshaven attack was considered to be too risky because of the weight of German defences around the base. Nevertheless, the Wilhemshaven plan was resuscitated in the middle of the year by the Commander-in-Chief of the Grand Fleet, Admiral Sir David Beatty.

Beatty championed the idea because he believed that the only way to defeat the U-boat threat was to put out of commission the submarine bases along the German coast, and the only way this could be done was to first remove the German High Seas Fleet. He was a convert to carrier-borne operations, and advocated using a massed torpedo attack involving upwards of 121 aircraft. However, Beatty was overruled by First Sea Lord, Jellicoe, who was far less enthusiastic about carrier aviation. At Jutland, Jellicoe had sent back to base the carrier HMS *Campania*, in large part because he lacked confidence in her usefulness, but he was also an over-cautious man. In response to Beatty's proposal, he said that the risks of a massed torpedo attack far outweighed the benefits. The risks were undoubtedly great, and it is debatable whether the Navy possessed a sufficient number of aircraft capable of performing such an operation at that point in the war. Purpose-built torpedo aircraft (the Sopwith Cuckoo) did not enter front-line service with the Navy until October 1918, and the first flush-decked aircraft carrier, HMS *Argus*, the same month. But the plan developed by Sueter and championed by Beatty was still visionary, and received ultimate vindication a generation later at Taranto in November 1940 and Pearl Harbor in December 1941.[12]

In many respects, however, it was in performing its second chief role of defending Great Britain, that the Naval Air Service demonstrated its greatest ability to 'think outside the box'. At first, the RNAS instituted coastal patrols, but it was soon realized that defending against Zeppelin attacks was difficult. Therefore, the Admiralty, with First Lord Churchill at the forefront, was anxious to take the war to the enemy, and aircraft were positioned on the French coast around Dunkirk, not only in order to prevent the Germans from using the area for Zeppelin basing, but also to attack Zeppelin installations inside Germany. At the end of September 1914, the RNAS launched attacks on Zeppelin sheds in Cologne and Dusseldorf. Then the fall of Belgium in October 1914 created enormous problems for Britain. If Britain had been concerned earlier about how the advent of air power was reducing its strategic depth, it now came sharply into focus. Not only could the Germans use the Belgian ports to stage attacks on Allied shipping, but Belgium could now be used as a major basing area for Zeppelin and fixed-wing attacks on mainland Britain. The RNAS was very robust in its response to this development, and stepped up its campaign by increasing the number of Zeppelin installations it targeted, and such attacks continued into 1915. This was not all. The Admiralty set about developing its intelligence sources on the Continent, with the objective of picking up German efforts to establish bases in Belgium. Not content that these measures were sufficient defence against Zeppelin attacks, the Admiralty also positioned three squadrons of home-defence aircraft around London, in case any Zeppelins succeeded in getting across the Channel. This looked much like our conception of 'layered defence', and the way it was basing its aircraft forward on the Continent might also take modern doctrinalists by surprise, as this was 'expeditionary warfare' at its best.[13]

But, for our purposes, what is most interesting is the way in which the Navy started to think about finding a cure, rather than treating the symptoms. Throughout 1915, the Admiralty had been thinking about the feasibility of attacking industrial targets in mainland Germany. By the New Year, the Navy's resolve had hardened, and the Admiralty placed strategic bombing of German industrial targets at the top of its list of priorities, sharing equal billing with attacks on the enemy Fleet and dockyards. At the forefront of this line of thought was First Lord, Winston Churchill, who, in April 1915, proposed that the RNAS should develop 'a very large fleet of aircraft, capable of delivering a sustained series of "smashing blows" on the enemy; more in the nature of a "bombardment" by ships than the present isolated "dashing exploits" of individual or two or three aeroplanes dropping a few bombs only'.[14] He went on to say: 'The object to aim at was so to harass the enemy and destroy his works as to effect very materially his ability to continue the war.'[15] If this had been General Billy Mitchell speaking in 1925, we would not have been surprised, but this was the First Lord speaking ten years earlier, saying that the best way to undermine an enemy's war effort was to attack its industrial foundations.[16]

Such discussions in the Admiralty coincided with the promise of aircraft capable of longer range bombing operations, manufactured by the Shorts and Sopwith companies, which the RNAS had sought since the start of the war. Again, the First Lord was at the forefront of those championing the development of aircraft capable of carrying heavier loads over longer distances, but a number of other individuals who would later rise to prominence were also involved. One such was Commander Arthur Longmore, who would later become Air Officer Commanding-in-Chief (AOC-in-C) of Coastal Command in the mid-1930s and AOC-in-C, Middle East, until 1941. Longmore sat on a number of procurement committees during the First World War, and appears to have been behind the decision to develop a heavy bomber capable of carrying at least 500 lb of bombs over a distance of 150 miles.[17]

However, this was the point in the war when the Admiralty's farsightedness slammed into a brick wall of inter-Service rivalry, caused largely by resource-allocation issues, and the start of long-range bombing operations against strategic targets in Germany was delayed by at least six months. In the closing stages of 1915, tensions arose between the Navy and the War Office over the issue of London's defence, which had been a naval responsibility, but one which the Navy handed over to the Army. The Army saw this as a major inconvenience, at a time when it had no aircraft to spare, as the campaign on the Western Front seemed to be making increasing demands on the Army. This prompted discussions over whether the Services needed to be reorganized, and, in the meantime, a Joint War Air Committee was established to investigate the best use to which Britain's air assets could be put. Any question over the future organization of the air services was inseparably linked with the question of which Service should carry out long-range bombing operations. This was because whoever was made responsible for such operations would need to have first call on large aircraft and powerful engines, of which there was an acute shortage. The Navy put forward a well-reasoned case that it should perform long-range bombing, as it had the most experience to date, but the War Office felt that the bombing of inland targets should be their responsibility. In its eagerness to commence bombing attacks on mainland Germany, having said that 'a defensive policy limited to our own shores cannot compare with a vigorous offensive', the RNAS pressed ahead without any agreement having been made.[18]

In the spring, the Admiralty made a direct approach to the French, asking them whether they were prepared to sanction the establishment of a bombing wing. The French responded warmly, and the RNAS No. 3 Wing was formed at Luxeuil in June, with the objective of attacking German industry in cities such as Freiburg. However, when the War Office found out about this initiative, they were, quite understandably, piqued. Politically, the Admiralty's decision not 'to say anything on this side but to make an arrangement with the French' proved to be a very serious mistake.[19] If the Army had been lukewarm about long-range bombing operations before, it was now openly hostile, and the consequences of this were seen first in the middle of 1916, when the Somme began to place a serious strain on the Royal Flying Corp's resources. Trenchard's offensive policy meant that the RFC was running out of both trained pilots and aircraft, and he saw the Admiralty's plan to undertake long-range bombing operations as a serious threat to his supply of new aircraft. Therefore, he used his influence with Haig to prevent the latest aircraft production going into equipping the RNAS, and the planned output of bombers was put on hold.[20]

However, some bombing operations were undertaken in the summer of 1916 from bases at Dunkirk and near Nancy. But the main bombing effort from Luxeuil did not commence until October. These operations starting in October were directed against chemical factories and blast furnaces, with munitions factories next in line of priority, and most of the objectives were concentrated in the Saar, Lorraine and Luxembourg. The decision to go after industry in this sector was based on two principal considerations. First, objectives were well within range of the aircraft then available, and this was an important operational consideration. Second, although, as recent scholarship has shown, the domestic steel product was of a relatively low quality, it supplied nearly half of Germany's total steel requirements. This assessment was based on intelligence analysis produced by the War Trade Intelligence Department (whose work laid the foundation for the Industrial Intelligence Centre in the 1930s and, later, the Ministry of Economic Warfare in the Second World War). Further, there were indications that the Germans were having difficulty meeting all their steel needs. So, it was argued that a concerted attack on these steel plants would completely undermine Germany's war effort. This analysis was largely correct, as the Germans were consuming steel in a hand-to-mouth fashion. From a doctrinal point of view, what makes this particularly interesting is the fact that the RNAS planners were clearly thinking in terms of attacking the heart of German strength. They were seeking a Centre of Gravity. A paper written by Rear-Admiral C. L. Vaughn-Lee, the Admiralty's Director of Air Services, in February 1916 spoke of attacking German 'centres of production' so as to affect the enemy's 'productive capacity as a whole'.[21]

The efficacy of the RNAS attacks on German industry, which continued until the spring of 1917, is difficult to discern at this distance. Evidence is extremely fragmentary, because many records were destroyed in the Second World War. The problem for the researcher is exacerbated by the decentralized nature of the German federal system at the time, there being no centralized statistics gathering bodies. However, there is some evidence to suggest that some industries were affected, not so much by the physical impact of bombing as by the interruptions to production caused by air raid alarms. As the Allies were to find in the Second World War, heavy industries, especially steel plants, were not ideal targets because they could withstand even direct hits with high-explosive bombs. But interruptions to production, as workers sought shelter from the bombing, were serious enough for the president of one large steelworks in Dusseldorf to write on 18 November 1916:

> At a meeting of the Board of Administration held today, reference was made by the steel works on the Western Front to the serious dislocation of work caused by air raids. The perpetually increasing curtailment of

night work due to these raids not only results in an average decease of thirty per cent of the steel works' output, but it is feared that night work may soon have to be entirely suspended. Since, in order to carry out the vast programme, we are instructed to increase production at these very works on the Western Front, we consider that better protection is absolutely necessary.[22]

Reports such as this, and civilian casualties caused mainly by the French bombing, compelled the Germans to investigate air-defence possibilities, and fighter aircraft were diverted from the front lines to cover the principal industrial cities within range of the Allied bases. German civilian morale was said to have been badly shaken by the bombing raids, especially those carried out at night, and the German High Command understood the morale effect of building up anti-aircraft defences.[23]

This was a very promising start to the naval bombing operations, and more was promised in the New Year with the arrival of a night-bomber squadron equipped with the latest bombing aircraft, the Handley Page 0/100, which had been built to an Admiralty specification. However, the Admiralty was compelled to back down in their debate with the War Office over the employment of long-range bombers in the RNAS, and the 'offending' bombing wing at Luxeuil was disbanded in March 1917.

Nevertheless, what had been gained by the RNAS was a real understanding of strategic bombing. Even if they did not use today's language of 'nodal analysis', they understood the need to identify correctly the targets that would have a decisive impact on the enemy war effort. They understood that this required a fundamental understanding of the nature of the enemy, and this is why the Admiralty placed heavy emphasis on intelligence. They also understood that targeting for strategic effect demanded a close examination of many operational problems; you might have identified an enemy Centre of Gravity, but unless you had the *means* to find and attack it accurately, it was a pointless exercise. It is not an exaggeration to say that virtually all the operational problems associated with long-range flying and targeting had either been solved or at least investigated by the RNAS by 1918. Much of the work done for maritime operations had direct read over to strategic bombing operations. This is particularly true of research into aids to navigation. By 1917, the RNAS squadrons had all the basic instruments found in the Second World War aircraft: protractors, drift indicators, but, most important, Direction Finding Wireless Telegraphy. No more work was done in this important area until just prior to the Second World War, when the RAF experimented with radio beams based on the same 'dot-dash and steady signal' principle. Also high on the RNAS's list of technical problems to be solved was that of bomb aiming. Until 1917, the bombsights available required the pilot to fly a steady course either up or down wind. Further experimentation by the Naval Air Department produced the so-called Course Setting Bombsight, which allowed an aircraft to attack from any angle, irrespective of the wind direction, and this bombsight remained in service until two years into the Second World War.[24]

These examples demonstrate to what extent the RNAS was at the forefront of aviation science. This became very apparent when the RAF was created in April 1918, by amalgamating the RNAS and the Royal Flying Corps. The new Service was closer in character and outlook to the Royal Flying Corps, simply because the Flying Corps had been much larger than the Naval Air Service, providing over 200,000 men, as compared with 55,000. But, more seriously, there was less than proportionate old naval air representation on the Air Staff of the new Service. As a result, the Admiralty's influence on British aviation diminished, and this was to have far-reaching consequences. It was felt immediately when the RAF commenced its own strategic bombing operations in earnest in June 1918, with the creation of the so-called Independent Bombing Force. There was a heavy reliance on any former RNAS bombsights, other instruments and tactical manuals, because the Royal Flying Corps had comparatively little experience in longer-range bombing operations (only since the end of 1917). A number of writers (and the author does not exclude herself from this) have been over-critical of the Royal Flying Corps' comparatively late venture into strategic bombing, or, at least, long-range bombing. But, leaving aside the fact that the RFC needed to do more in the way of battlefield air interdiction, the RFC's focus, quite rightly, lay elsewhere: immediate battlefield support and the air superiority battle.[25]

But, the new Service could live off the fat provided by the Naval Air Service for only so long. The ever-decreasing influence of the RNAS was felt even before the end of the war in terms of research and development. There was nothing to replace the Navy's strong R&D tradition. Again, even before the war was out, the Admiralty was complaining that the RAF was not paying sufficient attention to maritime aviation. It was to get much, much worse. Those who are familiar with the present author's earlier work will know what arguments have been put forward to explain why both maritime and support aviation dropped off the plot during the inter-war years; suffice it to say that the pre-eminence given to strategic bombing theory had almost everything to do with it. If a bomber could fly to the enemy heartland, and deliver the 'knock-out blow', then there was no need for support aviation, or, indeed, the traditional Services. The Air Staff of the late 1930s claimed that 'in the unlikely event' of the RAF having to take action against surface forces, then this could be done with a minimal diversion of bomber assets away from the main strategic bombing force. It was the 'one-size-fits-all' philosophy, or maybe the 'silver-bullet solution', in our parlance. But, coupled with financial stringency and more than a little complacency, this faith in the bomber was really faith without good works, and had as much of a deleterious effect on Britain's strategic-bombing capability at the start of the Second World War as it did on the other branches of the RAF. The period 1939–40 saw much reinvention of the wheel, resulting in unnecessary loss of life and much lost treasure.[26]

The intention here has been to highlight the fact that maritime aviation and strategic bombing, and, indeed, aviation in general, got off to such a strong start under the auspices of the Royal Naval Air Service. However, this is not to suggest that the interests of maritime aviation and strategic bombing would have been better served had the RAF not been created. It is merely regrettable that a confluence of factors pushed strategic-bombing doctrine over the line into the realm of dogma. But, it is interesting to see that the areas in which Bomber Command and the RAF was weakest at the start of the Second World War were Naval Air Service strengths: operational and nodal analysis, not to mention ASW and anti-surface unit warfare. What is particularly impressive is just how quickly the RNAS (or Admiralty) identified problems and set about solving them, and this applies to all the levels of war, from strategic down to tactical. Within weeks of the First World War breaking out, they recognized that they had to engage in expeditionary warfare in order to beat the Zeppelin threat; it was not sufficient to do localized Defensive Counter Air – they had to do Offensive Counter Air. This was never a feature of the early RAF doctrine, and it required the US Army Air Forces' experience in the Second World War to underscore its importance. Realizing that its Offensive Counter Air operations were only addressing the symptoms, the RNAS sought to find the German Centre of Gravity, which they identified as the industrial machine feeding the front lines. In many ways, the RNAS proved itself better than some modern air forces at thinking about air power in the round. Its interest in using aircraft for blockading purposes demonstrated that the RNAS understood that strategic effect air power was more than just strategic bombing. The Admiralty's use of intelligence, its close liaison with aircraft and related industries, and interest in supporting technologies showed that the Navy had grasped an important doctrinal point, namely, that air power constitutes far more than the delivery systems. Air power capability is dependent on a broad base of factors, including manpower, industry, science, technology, intelligence and doctrine, and that doctrine must be evolutionary rather than static. The RNAS's ability to 'think outside the box' and to conceptualize air power was, perhaps, its greatest asset, and it did these things during peacetime, not only during the war. After the First

World War, air power thinking stalled; doctrine became dogma, and gone was the frank approach to operational problems. It required close on two years' bitter experience at the start of the Second World War for the RAF to get close to the levels of operational analysis reached by the RNAS, and when the RAF achieved a marriage of science, technology and air power in something like the Battle of the Atlantic, they thought then that this was revolutionary.

NOTES

1. For a full discussion of the inter-war years, see H. M. Hyde, *British Air Policy between the Wars, 1918–1939* (Heinemann, London, 1976); C. J. M. Goulter, *A Forgotten Offensive: Royal Air Force Coastal Command's Anti-Shipping Campaign, 1939–1945* (Frank Cass, London, 1995), esp. Chs 1–3; C. Webster, and N. Frankland, *The Strategic Air Offensive Against Germany, 1939–45* (HMSO, London, 1961), Vol. I; M. Smith, *British Air Strategy between the Wars* (Clarendon Press, Oxford, 1984); D. Omissi, *Air Power and Colonial Control: the Royal Air Force, 1919–1939* (Manchester University Press, Manchester, 1991).
2. Goulter, *A Forgotten Offensive*, Ch. 1 generally.
3. H. A. Jones, *The War in the Air*, Vol. II (Clarendon Press, Oxford, 1928), Ch. 3.
4. S. W. Roskill (ed.), *Documents Relating to the Naval Air Service*, Vol. I, 1908–1918 (Navy Records Society, London, 1968), Letter from Rear-Admiral Sir Charles Ottley to Admiral Prince Louis of Battenberg, 1st Sea Lord, dd. 16 Jan. 1912; W. Raleigh, *The War in the Air*, Vol. I (Oxford University Press, Oxford, 1922), pp. 185, 334–5; C. F. S. Gamble, *The Story of a North Sea Air Station* (Oxford University Press, London, 1928), p. 13.
5. AIR 1/626, 17/88. Paper on aeroplanes for Naval Service, Part III, by Lt H. Williamson, pp. 1–8; covering note by Vice-Admiral E. Charlton, ADT, dd. 22 Feb. 1912; Letter to Commander-in-Chief, HM Ships and Vessels, The Nore, from Captain HMS ACTEON, dd. 27 Feb. 1912; Letter from Admiralty to C.-in-C., HM Ships and Vessels, dd. 27 May 1912.
6. Roskill, *Documents Relating*. Extracts from 'Report on the subject of defence of London against aerial attack', by Capt Murray Sueter, Dir. of Air Dept., dd. 16 Oct. 1916. See also Goulter, *A Forgotten Offensive*, p. 9.
7. Goulter, *A Forgotten Offensive*, pp. 10–12.
8. Ibid. See also Jones, *War in the Air*, Vol. IV, pp. 48–9.
9. AIR 1/675,21/13/1385. Paper entitled: 'The Anti-Submarine Campaign, 1914–1917', pp. 1–2, 4–7, 27; Roskill, *Documents Relating*. Extracts from paper by Sueter, dd. 29 Aug. 1912; Extracts of Conference held in Admiralty on 3 April 1915; AIR 1/308,15/226/191. 'Appreciation of British Naval Effort', pp. 1–2; AIR 1/2323,223/41/1515(7). 'Serial History of Technical Problems Dealt with by Admiralty Departments', by Anti-Submarine Division of Naval Staff; Table 12, 'Enemy Submarine Losses', p. 63; AIR 1/2393,228/13/1. 'Anti-Submarine Operations (Aircraft versus Submarine)', paper by Flt Lt Coleman, n.d.; Gamble, *The Story of a North Sea Air Station*, pp. 305–6; Jones, *War in the Air*, Vol. II, pp 354–6; ADM 1/8408. Admiralty Weekly Order, No. 1204/15, dd. 29 July 1915; AIR 1/672,17/134/39. Notes on Bomb Dropping, by Cdr C. R. Samson, OOIC, Dunkirk, dd. 2 March 1915; 'Development of Bomb-dropping', n.d. [circa March 1915], pp. 1–11; A. Gayer, *Die deutschen U-Boote im ihrer Kriegsfuhrung*,

1914–1918, Vol. II (Berlin, 1920), p. 53; AHB IIH/68. 'Coastal Command Review'. See esp Vol. I, 1942. See also Goulter, *A Forgotten Offensive*, pp. 10–12.

10. AIR 1/672,17/134/39. 'Development of Bomb-dropping', pp. 1–2. See also Goulter, *A Forgotten Offensive*, Chs 5–6.

11. AIR 1/713,27/16. Air Ministry 'History of the Development of Torpedo Aircraft', dd. Feb. 1916, p. 79, and Appendix X, Paper by Lt Hyde-Thompson, 6 Sept. 1915; AIR 1/305,15/226/161. Seaplane carrying flotilla (*Engadine, Ben-my-Chree, Empress*), correspondence 20 Nov. 1914–April 1916; Roskill, *Documents Relating*. Extracts from Minutes of Conference held in Admiralty, 14 Aug. 1915; Joint War Air Committee, extracts from Paper Air 4, dd. 3 March 1916; AIR 1/2393,238/1. Reports on seaplane torpedo attacks on enemy shipping in Dardanelles, 12–17 Aug. 1915. See also Goulter, *A Forgotten Offensive*, pp. 11–14; P. Kemp (ed.), *The Papers of Admiral Sir John Fisher* (Ballantyne, for Navy Records Society, London, 1968), Vol. II, pp. 315f.; and ADM 116/1233 generally.

12. Roskill, *Documents Relating*. Memorandum by Sueter, 'Policy to be followed as regards development and use of torpedo carrying seaplanes', dd. 20 Dec. 1916; Extracts from letter of 11 Sept. 1917 from Admiral Sir David Beatty, C.-in-C., Grand Fleet, 'Considerations of an attack by torpedo planes on the High Sea[s] Fleet'; AIR 1/713,27/16. 'History of the Development of Torpedo Aircraft', pp. 31–2; H. Newbolt, *Naval Operations* (Longmans, London, 1931), p. 83; R. Hough, *The Great War at Sea, 1914–1918* (Oxford University Press, Oxford, 1986), p. 194.

13. Roskill, *Documents Relating*. Extracts from 'Report on the subject of defence of London against aerial attack', by Sueter, Dir. Air Dept., dd. 16 Oct. 1914; 'Report from Commander Spenser D. A. Grey to the Director of the Air Department, Admiralty, on the raid on Cologne and Dusseldorf, dd. 17 Oct. 1914; Memorandum on 'Aerial Defence', by Churchill, dd. 22 Oct. 1914; Extracts from 'Secretary's Notes of a Meeting of a War Council', dd. 7 Jan. 1915.

14. Roskill, *Documents Relating*. Extracts from Minutes of a Conference held in the Admiralty on 3 April 1915, p. 199. See also p. 195.

15. Ibid.

16. For a discussion of Mitchell's ideas, see M. Clodfelter, 'Molding Airpower Convictions: Development and Legacy of William Mitchell's Strategic Thought', in P. Meilinger (ed.), *The Paths of Heaven: The Evolution of Airpower Theory* (Air University Press, Maxwell AFB, AL, 1997), pp. 79–114.

17. Roskill, *Documents Relating*. Extracts from Minutes of a Conference held in the Admiralty on 3 April 1915, pp. 195–8; Minute to War Council by First Lord, Churchill, dd. 3 April 1915, p. 200. See also pp. 33f. and 589f.

18. Roskill, *Documents Relating*. Memorandum by Rear-Admiral C. L. Vaughn-Lee, Director of Air Services, dd. 4 April 1916, p. 344. See also: Extract from 'Secretary's Notes of a Meeting of the War Committee', held on 26 Jan. 1916, pp. 283–5; Extract from Proceedings of 71st Meeting of the War Committee held on 15 Feb. 1916, pp. 302–4. See also p. 269.

19. Roskill, *Documents Relating*. Minute by Vice-Admiral Sir Henry Oliver, Chief of the War Staff, dd. 5 April 1916, p. 344. See also p. 272.

20. Roskill, *Documents Relating*. Joint War Air Committee, Extracts from Paper Air 4, dd. 3 March 1916, pp. 309–10; War Office Letter to Admiralty, dd. 25 May 1916, pp. 364–6; Letter from Secretary Air Board to Secretary Admiralty, dd. 23 June 1916, pp. 366–7. See also Extracts from Letter from General Haig to War Office, dd. 1 Nov. 1916; War Office letter to Admiralty, dd. 10 Nov. 1916, pp. 405–12.

21. Ibid. Draft paper by Rear-Admiral Vaughn-Lee, dd. 28 Feb. 1916, and presented to the Joint War Air Committee, p. 310. See also N. Jones, *The Origins of Strategic*

Bombing: A Study of the Development of British Air Strategic Thought and Practice up to 1918 (William Kimber, London 1973), pp. 107–10. See also Goulter, *A Forgotten Offensive*, esp. Chs 4–9.

22. Jones, *War in the Air*, Vol. VI, p. 118.
23. Ibid. pp. 130–3.
24. Goulter, *A Forgotten Offensive*, esp. Chs 1–5.
25. Ibid. See Chs 1 and 2, esp.
26. Ibid. Chs 1–3.

4

The *Luftwaffe* and Lessons Learned in the Spanish Civil War

James S. Corum

The Spanish Civil War was, by any reckoning, the most important single military air power event in the period between the world wars. Although air power has been used in numerous conflicts, the Spanish War saw large-scale sustained air operations with the latest military aircraft for three years (July 1936–March 1939). Spain was the first major operation of the reborn German *Luftwaffe* and has often been referred to as the *Luftwaffe*'s 'testing ground' for equipment and tactics. This is an apt description of the *Luftwaffe*'s experience in Spain. During three years of war the *Luftwaffe* developed the tactics and evaluated the equipment it would use in the first years of the Second World War. Much of the its success from 1939 to 1942, and some of its failures, can be traced to lessons that were learned, or not learned, during the Spanish Civil War.

GERMAN INVOLVEMENT IN SPAIN

The Spanish Civil War began on 17 July 1936 as a coup by rightist generals, supported by conservative forces, against a leftist republic.[1] The coup failed to seize control of Spain's largest cities, Madrid and Barcelona, when the government armed the workers' unions and leftist parties to oppose the military. However, in other regions the coup succeeded. Most importantly for the Nationalists, the Army in Spain's North African colony of Morocco declared themselves for the coup leaders. The North African Army was composed of 30,000 of Spain's best-trained and toughest troops, many of them veterans of bloody colonial campaigns. These troops were more than a match for the generally poorly trained and equipped units of the Army in mainland Spain, supported by the untrained leftist militias that had rallied to the Republic. The first problem was to transport these troops to the Spanish mainland, as most of the Spanish Navy had declared for the Republic and blocked any sea movement from North Africa.

On 25 July, a week into the uprising, a German businessman representing General Franco approached Hitler with a request for aid for the Nationalist cause, especially aircraft to ferry troops from North Africa, as well as other military supplies. Without much thought or discussion, Hitler ordered his *Luftwaffe* to send aircraft and support to the Spanish Nationalists. Lieutenant-General Helmuth Wilberg, a highly experienced *Luftwaffe* staff officer, was given the task of organizing this. Within two days, a staff was put together, plans made and orders issued. By 31 July, Ju 52 transports were on their way to Spanish Morocco to airlift Franco's superb African Army to mainland Spain. The same day a ship carrying 600 *Luftwaffe* personnel, a small fighter detachment, equipped with six Heinkel He 51 fighters, 20 flak guns and other equipment to support the Nationalists, departed for Spain.[2] Mussolini's Italy also saw an opportunity to expand its influence in the Mediterranean and dispatched aircraft and supplies to the Nationalists.

The airlift by the German and Italian transports, as well as commercial transports that the Spanish had assembled, worked brilliantly. Between 31 July and 11 October 1936, by which time the Nationalists had air superiority over the straits of Gibraltar and could ship men and matériel by sea, over 20,000 Nationalist troops and 270,199 kilos of arms, ammunition and equipment had been airlifted from Morocco to southern Spain. The German transports had carried approximately two-thirds of the load, with the Italians taking the rest.[3] The airlift had been a model operation carried out under arduous conditions with the loss of only one aircraft.[4] The Nationalist coup, whose momentum had stalled, was reinvigorated by the influx of hardened, veteran troops and swept forward on the offensive, overrunning much of southern and western Spain. It is no exaggeration to say that the airlift saved the Nationalist cause in the summer of 1936. The airlift was notable as the largest military air-transport operation conducted up to that time and as the first example of an air force playing a truly decisive role in the success of a campaign and of a war. Nationalist troops quickly secured their base in southern Spain and advanced north to link up with the Nationalist areas of northern Spain. In September and October the Nationalist forces, led by the African Army units and supported by the small *Luftwaffe* fighter unit and Ju 52 transports serving as bombers, advanced on Madrid.[5] It appeared that the war would soon conclude with the fall of Madrid and a Nationalist victory.

Yet Madrid would not fall for another two-and-a-half years. Noting German and Italian intervention in support of the Nationalists, the Soviet Union, also playing a political influence game, threw its support behind the Republic in the form of large arms shipments, which included the latest tanks and aircraft. Hundreds of Soviet advisors and personnel to man the tanks and fly the planes also arrived.[6] The Soviet T-26 tanks that supported the Republican counter-attacks around Madrid in October came as a shock to the Nationalists, as they outclassed anything the Nationalists had on the battlefield. Another shock was the arrival of Soviet SB-2 bombers and I-15 and I-16 fighters, which were far superior to the Ju 52 improvised bombers and He 51 fighters of the Germans and Fiat biplane fighters of the Italians. By November, the Russian-piloted aircraft had given the Republicans air superiority over the Madrid front.[7] The influx of Soviet equipment as well as the international brigades' planes halted the Nationalist offensive in late October, and by November 1936 the war had reached a stalemate, with each side holding roughly half of the country and neither having any military advantage.

In November both sides and their foreign backers reconsidered their respective positions on the Spanish War. The Soviets would continue to sell arms and munitions to the Republic and provide a significant air force, manned mostly by Russian pilots.[8] The Germans decided to step up their support for the Nationalists by sending a force of a few hundred army trainers, an armoured battalion and an air force of approximately 100 aircraft organized into fighter, reconnaissance, ground-support and bomber squadrons. The strength of the *Luftwaffe*'s composite force in Spain, called the 'Condor Legion', would be set at about 5,000 men (officially all 'volunteers' wearing Spanish uniforms) and included signals units, ground staff and a large flak battalion. The German force in Spain was carefully limited to 100–120 aircraft in order to avoid provoking a major reaction from France, which would have considered intervention if a large German ground and air force showed up on its southern border. Since the war would apparently be protracted, the *Luftwaffe* decided to use the conflict as a testing ground for new aircraft, equipment and tactics. It would eventually send 22 different aircraft types to Spain (not including several different models of the Bf 109 fighter and He 111 bomber), as well as a variety of flak guns, munitions and radios for use under real combat conditions.[9] Moreover, the Spanish Civil War offered an opportunity for thousands of German soldiers and aircrew to get some war experience.

Under the Versailles Treaty, Germany had been forbidden to have an air force. However, the German Army continued to maintain a small secret air force led by a cadre of veterans of the *Luftstreitkräfte* (Imperial Air Service) and developed and tested aircraft during the 1920s and 1930s. When Hitler came to power in 1933, this small air force was quickly expanded under the cover of civil aviation. In March 1935 Hitler publicly renounced the disarmament provisions of

Versailles and publicly revealed the existence of a sizeable and rapidly expanding *Luftwaffe*, which already had a strength of over 18,000 men and a much larger budget than the British and French Air Forces combined.[10] By the outbreak of the war in Spain in 1936, the new *Luftwaffe* was in a phase of rapid expansion and had already fielded well-trained fighter, bomber and reconnaissance groups equipped with aircraft developed during the early 1930s. The first generation of the *Luftwaffe*'s aircraft, such as the Ju 52 transports modified as bombers and the Heinkel He 45 and He 46 reconnaissance planes, were already obsolescent but they served to equip the air force in its early organizational and training phases. However, superior new aircraft such as the Bf 109 fighter and He 111 bomber were ready for mass production along with new flak guns, and state-of-the-art communications gear. A new operational doctrine had been published in 1935 and combat tactics were already being tested in wargames and large-scale manoeuvres. Basically, the Spanish Civil War came at exactly the right moment of the *Luftwaffe*'s development of equipment and doctrine. If the war had come a year earlier, the *Luftwaffe* would have been in no position to intervene in the conflict. If the war had come a year later, the *Luftwaffe* would have already made numerous decisions on equipment without the benefit of combat testing.

The *Luftwaffe* aircraft first committed to Spain, the Ju 52 bombers, He 45 and He 46 bomber/light reconnaissance planes, He 51 fighters and He 59 seaplanes, were unimpressive in performance but still fairly capable aircraft for the day. Their deployment made an enormous difference on the battlefield for the Nationalists. However, the equation quickly changed in the late autumn of 1936 as the Condor Legion, the Italian Air Force and the small Nationalist air force faced a formidable new foe in the form of the Republican air force, newly equipped with Soviet fighters and bombers piloted by experienced Soviet airmen. From October 1936 to early 1939 the Soviet Union sent over 700 aircraft to the Spanish Republic, and provided several hundred experienced pilots to the Republican air force. The Russian I-15 biplane fighter and I-16 all-metal monoplane fighters were among the best fighter planes in the world when they arrived in Spain in 1936. The Soviet SB-2 bomber sent to Spain was also one of the best light bombers of the era.[11] When introduced to combat, in November 1936, the Soviet-supplied fighters clearly outclassed the Heinkel 51s of the Condor Legion and the Republic achieved air superiority over Madrid. Although the Condor Legion and Nationalist coalition would regain air superiority in 1937 and generally hold it to the end of the war, the Condor Legion would continue to face a tough and very capable aerial opponent up to the final battles in 1939.

During the winter of 1936–37, both sides built up their forces for the prospect of a long war. The Condor Legion rapidly expanded and began to receive the latest equipment from Germany for combat testing. The first available pre-production models of the Bf 109 arrived at the end of 1936, and by early 1937 the new He 111 bombers began to arrive. In November 1936 Major-General Hugo Sperrle, a veteran of the *Luft-streitkräfte* and one of Germany's most experienced air commanders, assumed command of the Condor Legion. His chief of staff was the brilliant Lieutenant-Colonel Wolfram von Richthofen, a First World War fighter pilot who had earned an engineering degree after the war and been a senior officer in the technical office of the *Luftwaffe*. Both men were not only well suited to lead an air war; they were also especially qualified to carry out the mission of evaluating *Luftwaffe* tactics and equipment.

THE TACTICAL/TECHNICAL LESSONS

The most important tactical development to come out of the Spanish Civil War was the revolution in squadron fighter tactics. Up through the 1930s every major air force used a system of squadron battle formations that had been developed during the First World War. The basic formation was a flight of three aircraft, usually flying in a 'V'. Three or four flights would constitute a squadron, which would fly into battle in a series of fairly complex large formations.

During the course of the war in Spain the Condor Legion evolved a system of new squadron fighter tactics. Captain Werner Mölders, one of Germany's top fighter pilots, took command of the Bf 109 squadron of the Condor Legion in January 1938 and is credited with formally instituting a new tactical system based on pairs of aircraft instead of threes.[12] Two aircraft made up the basic fighter formation ('Rotte'), with one pilot flying slightly behind and to the side of his wingman. Two 'Rottes' would constitute a 'Schwarm' with four aircraft spread out in the 'finger four' formation. Squadrons would fly as a group of 'Schwarms'. It was a more open and more flexible formation than the tight squadron formations previously used and, by basing tactics on pairs, each pilot could concentrate on covering and supporting just one wingman rather than two.

The new tactical system proved its worth in Spain. With superior aircraft and tactics, the Condor Legion won clear air superiority in early 1937 and never lost it. The Condor Legion shot down 327 Republican aircraft in air-to-air combat for 72 combat losses. After shooting down 14 enemy aircraft in Spain, Mölders was brought back to Germany in late 1938 and set to work by the Air Staff writing a new fighter tactics manual and making the tactics proven effective in Spain standard throughout the *Luftwaffe*.[13]

Another important tactical lesson was the importance of night and poor-weather flying. In contrast to the low losses of aircraft to combat, the losses due to operational (i.e. non-combat) accidents was relatively high. The Condor Legion lost 160 aircraft in Spain to flying accidents, many of these through crashes at night or in poor weather. When the Germans intervened in Spain's civil war, the *Luftwaffe* pilots and navigators were as well trained as the pilots of any of the major air forces. *Luftwaffe* pilot and navigator instruction included instrument flying and German civil aviation, which provided pilots and training to the new *Luftwaffe*, had been a world leader in developing instrument flight systems as early as the 1920s. Yet this was not enough for flying in combat conditions. One of the most important lessons from the first part of the war in Spain was the need to improve night and instrument flying in the *Luftwaffe*. General Sperrle, upon his return to Germany in November 1937, took over the air units in southern Germany that would become the Third Air Fleet. One of his first orders to the command was to increase the amount and intensity of instrument flying.[14] In the next two years, instrument flying received much more emphasis throughout the *Luftwaffe*.

Important lessons concerning the equipment and aircraft were learned in Spain. The latest aircraft guns, bombs, fuses, anti-aircraft guns and radios were all used and reports on the performance of specific items of equipment are found in most of the reports the Condor Legion sent back to Berlin.[15] The war in Spain pointed out the strengths and weaknesses of the *Luftwaffe*'s latest fighter aircraft. The He 51 biplane, the main fighter of the *Luftwaffe* in 1936 and that which first equipped the fighter squadrons of the Condor Legion, proved a real dud as a combat airplane. The He 51 handled badly, was prone to landing accidents and was generally disliked by the men that flew it. By contrast, the Bf 109 proved to be the star aircraft of the war. It outflew all the Republican aircraft, including the excellent Soviet I-16 fighter, and gave the Nationalist air force a clear margin of performance superiority from its introduction into combat in early 1937. As a result of the combat evaluations, the He 51 was taken out of the *Luftwaffe*'s aircraft inventory ahead of schedule and the production of the Bf 109 as the main fighter aircraft of the *Luftwaffe* was speeded up.[16]

Testing new bombers in combat was an important mission of the Condor Legion. The Dornier Do 17 appeared in Spain in 1937 and performed creditably as a fast, light bomber. The *Luftwaffe* also sent several Ju 86 bombers to Spain for combat testing. In the mid-1930s, the Ju 86 had been placed into production to be one of the primary bombers of the *Luftwaffe*, but during the Spanish War the Ju 86 demonstrated mediocre performance and was soon taken out of the bomber units.[17] The primary German bomber in Spain was the Heinkel

He 111, probably the best medium bomber in the world when it was introduced into Spain in 1937. It was relatively fast, reliable and carried an adequate bombload of two tons. It provided sterling service to the Nationalists throughout the war while bombing a great variety of targets. However, the greatest weakness of the He 111, a defensive armament of only three light machine-guns, was not noted during the Spanish War, thanks to the success of the Bf 109 fighter. Since Bf 109s provided effective escort for the He 111s and were usually able to sweep the skies of Republican opposition during bomber missions, the weak protective armament of the bomber was not noted and nothing was done to improve the defences of the aircraft.

As a result, during the Battle of Britain, when the He 111 flew without escort (as in the one major raid of the Fifth Air Fleet bombers from Norway) or when the British fighters fought through the escorting Bf 109s, the He 111 proved to be easy prey for any RAF fighter.

OPERATIONAL LESSONS

In Spain the *Luftwaffe* gained an enormous amount of practical experience at the operational level of war. The first lesson, one that was dramatically illustrated, was the importance of air transport in modern war. At the beginning of the conflict it was proven that large forces could be moved by air with dramatic effect. Before this time little thought had been given in any of the major air forces to moving and supplying large ground forces by air. Because air transport proved successful in Spain, the *Luftwaffe* now had a use for its large force of Ju 52 transport. The Ju 52 predated the Nazi regime and had gone into production as a civil transport in 1932. It was a remarkably successful transport aircraft. When the Nazis came to power and needed to build an air force quickly, Ju 52s were obtained and easily converted into improvised bombers. As a bomber, the Ju 52 was a poor improvisation. However, it was good enough for bomber units to train with until modern purpose-built bombers like the He 111 came on line. By 1937, the He 111 and Do 17 were in full production and bomber units were being rapidly re-equipped. The experience of Spain solved the problem of what to do with several hundred Ju 52 improvised bombers. Ju 52s could be easily reconverted for transport duties and the *Luftwaffe* found itself with a transport force of several wings.[18] This force was available to support the operations of the newly formed paratroop force, and could also airlift supplies and material to forward airfields in wartime, thereby giving the *Luftwaffe* a tremendous increase in its logistical capability in a *Blitzkrieg* war.

The *Luftwaffe* provided the Condor Legion with a reinforced flak battalion, consisting of four batteries of heavy 88mm guns and two batteries of 20mm light flak guns. In the First World War the German Air Service had employed a large flak force and *Luftwaffe* doctrine emphasized anti-aircraft artillery as a primary means of air defence. The Condor Legion's airfields, certainly a major target for the Republican air force, were well defended with both heavy and light flak guns. At times Condor Legion flak operated at the front to cover vital points in the line.

The airfield defence system of the Condor Legion proved to be quite successful. Condor Legion airfields were subjected to several attacks by Republican fighters and bombers without causing heavy damage. Passive and active measures were taken to protect the airfields. The Condor Legion deployed decoy aircraft to attract Republican bombs while attacking aircraft faced a heavy flak barrage. During the course of the war, the German flak force proved its effectiveness by shooting down 59 Republican aircraft.[19]

Another important use for the flak force in Spain was in direct fire support of the ground troops. In the early part of the war, the Nationalist artillery arm was very weak and the Condor Legion flak force represented a significant reinforcement for the ground forces. When deployed to the northern front in early 1937, the Condor Legion faced little aerial opposition. With little threat to the airfields, the Legion's flak guns were deployed to the front to bolster the Nationalist artillery force. The flak guns proved to be superb weapons in the ground role. For instance, the 88mm heavy flak gun, with its flat trajectory and high velocity, proved to be an ideal weapon for destroying enemy bunkers and defensive positions. During the course of the war it became normal procedure for the Condor Legion to deploy part of its light and heavy flak forces to the 'Schwerpunkt' (point of main effort) of the Nationalist forces on the defence or offence. The importance of the flak gun support to the ground battle was noted in numerous detailed reports the Condor Legion sent back to Berlin and the use of flak in the ground battle became part of the *Luftwaffe*'s standard doctrine.[20]

The Condor Legion conducted almost every type of major operation in Spain. On occasion, the Condor Legion carried out strategic strikes on vital Republican industrial targets. Interdiction of ports, rail and logistics lines were an important part of Condor Legion operations. The Condor Legion also carried out air superiority campaigns, attacking Republican airfields and engaging Republican aircraft over the front. The transport operations of the Condor Legion have already been noted. However, owing to the nature of the war, close air support of the Nationalist Army became the primary mission of the Condor Legion throughout the war.

The Condor Legion first conducted close support operations on a large scale in the campaign in the north in 1937. Virtually the whole Condor Legion was deployed from the stalemated Madrid front to northern Spain to support the Nationalist Army offensive against the Basque state. The Basques were tough and capable fighters, and occupied ideal defensive ground in their mountainous region, and breaking through their defence lines required a lot of firepower. The Nationalist commander General Mola had a severe shortage of artillery and needed the Condor Legion to provide the heavy firepower to break the Basque defences.

Close support of the ground forces was already part of *Luftwaffe*'s doctrine. The imperial *Luftstreitkräfte* had employed specialized ground-attack squadrons on the battlefield in 1917–18 with some success. Starting in 1935 a course had been set up to train some *Luftwaffe* officers to carry out liaison between ground forces' headquarters and supporting air commands. However, close support of ground troops is one of the most complicated missions for an air force and, by 1937, precise procedures for working out air/ground co-ordination had not been worked out. Furthermore, no one had any clear idea just how difficult close air support could be. The first close-support missions for the Nationalist army exposed a lot of problems in effectively co-ordinating air strikes. Communications were the first major problem to overcome. Although most Condor Legion aircraft had radios, the planes could only communicate with each other and their home base; there was no effective radio communication from the front lines to the aircraft. A system of ground signals had to be quickly worked out. In one expedient the Condor Legion commander, General Sperrle, set up command posts on hilltops overlooking the point of a planned air strike and ground attack. He was linked by ground telephone to the aircraft home base, which could then relay messages from the ground commander to aircraft by radio. Needless to say, it was an awkward system, but it worked.

A big part of the problem lay in the poor training of the Nationalist Army in 1937. The Nationalist Army had relatively few well-trained commanders and staff officers and was still in the process of learning how to fight a modern war. On several occasions in the early stages of the offensive in March–April 1937, air strikes on Basque positions would be carried out on schedule as planned. Yet the effort was wasted, because the follow-up ground attack by the Nationalist army was delayed owing to poor staff work.[21]

Despite all its teething problems, the Condor Legion was soon capable of planning and co-ordinating large-scale ground-support operations with the Nationalist Army. The Nationalists were able to advance slowly on the major Basque city of Bilbao, largely due to the impressive fire support provided by the Condor Legion. In June 1937, the Nationalist Army reached the final Basque defence line, a 35-kilometre-long line of well-sited concrete bunkers and trenches dug in on the hilltops and ridgelines before Bilbao. Between 12 and 14 June, the Condor Legion made some of its heaviest attacks of the war, saturating sections of the 'Iron Belt' defence line with high explosives and enabling the Nationalist Army, after several days of desperate fighting, to break the line and crush the final Basque resistance.[22]

The Germans learned that the biggest problem with conducting close air support was in co-ordinating air action with the Spanish ground commanders. Each operation had to be carefully planned between the German and Spanish staffs at the top level. At the lower levels of command, the *Luftwaffe* assigned liaison and communications teams to the Nationalist Army units to ensure effective co-ordination between the *Luftwaffe* and the Army.[23] With more attention paid to communications, the co-ordination of the air and ground forces improved markedly through the first half of 1937.[24] However, considerable friction still remained with the communications and signal system, and there were several instances of German and Italian aircraft accidentally bombing Nationalist infantry units in April 1937.[25]

Although the *Luftwaffe* doctrine of the period emphasized using air power in mass to achieve maximum shock effect, one tactic that was found to be very successful in Spain was the shuttle attack. The Condor Legion would send one flight of aircraft at a time to bomb enemy front-line positions. After the strike, the flight would return to base to rearm and refuel for the next attack while the next flight in the squadron bombed the position. Because the Condor Legion air bases were usually close to the front lines, aircraft could fly three or more sorties a day against the same target. This tactic of shuttle bombing kept the enemy under continuous attack for hours on end, which dramatically increased the psychological stress of the defenders and lowered their morale. Sometimes Republican morale would break under air attack and allow the Nationalist Army to overrun strong positions with few casualties.[26]

The Condor Legion was employed extensively in close support operations for the rest of the war and, by all accounts, became very good at the job. The close air support provided by the Condor Legion played a major role in the success of the Nationalist Army in its major defensive battles, such as Brunete in July–August 1937 and the Ebro campaign in July 1938. When the Republican forces conducted major offensives, the Condor Legion put enemy command posts, supply points, troop columns and artillery under continuous attack. It became difficult for the Republican forces to move in daylight and to maintain the momentum of their attacks when their logistics and artillery were under constant air attack. When the Nationalists went on the offensive, the Condor Legion blasted holes through Republican front-line positions and targeted Republican forces assembling for counter-attacks. The Ju 87 (Stuka) dive bombers, first deployed to Spain in January 1938, proved to be ideal in the close support role as the Stukas were able to drop large bombs (500 kg) with great accuracy upon enemy strong-points. The Condor Legion's effective close air support can be credited with a considerable part of the Nationalist success on the battlefield. While the Republican air force also carried out strikes in support of its ground troops, the Republican attacks were never as well planned or effective as the Condor Legion's. Close air support gave the Nationalists a decided advantage on the battlefield.

NAVAL AIR OPERATIONS

When the *Luftwaffe* was officially created in 1935 it formally established a naval air arm that would be part of the *Luftwaffe* but under the operational command of the navy. Before the *Luftwaffe* was formally created, the Navy had fought to have its own naval air arm on the model of its air arm of the First World War, which had won air superiority over the English Channel and had carried out numerous successful anti-shipping strikes in 1917–18. Hermann Goering, however, was jealous of his power as Chief of the *Luftwaffe* and insisted that 'everything that flies belongs to me'. Such was his position in the Third Reich that he generally got his way. The small air force Goering allocated to the Navy consisted of a small number of flying boats and seaplanes to carry out long-range scouting and patrol for the fleet.

When the Condor Legion was committed to Spain, a naval air squadron of eight Heinkel He 60 and nine He 59 seaplanes was also deployed.[27] The naval air unit served apart from the rest of the Condor Legion and operated closely with the Nationalist and Italian seaplane units, first based at Malaga, and then from 1937 to 1939 on the island of Mallorca. The mission of the naval air units in Spain was to patrol the coastal waters and monitor shipping into Republican ports. The naval air units were also given free rein to attack Republican shipping close to the coast or in harbour.

The He 60 was a two-seat, single-engine biplane that was primarily a reconnaissance craft as it could carry no more than 120 kilograms of bombs. The He 59 was a large, slow twin-engine biplane with a crew of four that verged on obsolescence. However, it was relatively heavily armed, able to carry a 20mm cannon and two machine-guns as well as 2,000 lb of bombs or torpedoes.

The Spanish, German and Italian units that formed the seaplane force of the Nationalist coalition, although equipped with obsolete aircraft, proved to be remarkably successful. During the war, the Republicans lost 554 ships, 144 to German and Italian action.[28] Of these, the Condor Legion's seaplane squadron claimed a total of 52 Republican ships sunk and many others damaged. The Stuka detachment of the Condor Legion claimed a further eight ships.[29] Although naval forces were also involved in blockading Republican Spain, air action sank the major proportion of the Republican ships.[30] The Condor Legion's naval air arm progressed from conducting reconnaissance missions to bombing Republican ports and attacking ships at sea.[31] By 1938, the He 59 unit had become proficient in attacking shipping inside ports. Attacks were carried out by day and night, but the preferred time of attack was at night, owing to the slow speed of the He 59s. The He 59s developed a tactic of approaching at medium altitude, cutting their engines and quietly gliding in to attack and dropping flares to illuminate the bomb run. After the bomb release, the pilot would give the plane full throttle and fly back to sea.[32] The standard tactic for attacking Republican merchant vessels at sea was a low-level approach with 250 kg bombs.[33]

During the war, the naval air arm of the Condor Legion developed a cadre of capable airmen with considerable expertise in anti-shipping operations. The most successful period of the German naval air squadron was in 1938, when Captain Martin Harlinghausen commanded the force. Harlinghausen would go on to become the *Luftwaffe*'s leading ship-killer of the Second World War, with the sinking of 22 enemy ships personally credited to him.[34]

OPERATIONAL MOBILITY

German doctrine emphasized the ability to deploy quickly and operate air units from rough airfields close to the front. Usually operating at short range, the *Luftwaffe* had the advantage of a high aircraft sortie rate – sometimes three or more sorties per day. To gain this advantage, however, the *Luftwaffe* had to deploy a large force of ground personnel to set up and man the forward airfields and the logistics units had to be fully motorized with enough vehicles to bring up fuel, ammunition and spare parts. In Spain, the *Luftwaffe*'s mobile ground organization was tested under tough conditions.

On 6 July 1937, the Republicans began one of their biggest offensives of the war, when the best Republican divisions, well-supported with tanks, artillery and 400 Russian aircraft, broke through the thinly held Nationalist lines at Brunete, a small town west of Madrid, with the objective of breaking the siege of Madrid and cutting off a large Nationalist force. It was one of the high points of the Republican Army's operations and one of the best chances the Republic had of inflicting a major defeat on Franco's forces. At this time, the Condor Legion and the best Nationalist divisions were in northern Spain, mopping up the last of the Republican resistance in Asturias. With a crisis at hand, the Condor Legion was immediately pulled out of operations in the north, and two of its squadrons were redeployed near Madrid on the second day of the Republican offensive and commenced operations. The rest of the squadrons followed within days and the Condor Legion head-quarters was given command of all the Italian and Nationalist air units (more than 200 aircraft in total) on the threatened front as well. A highly mobile headquarters and logistics system enabled the Condor Legion immediately to counter the Republicans in the air. During the first half of July, the Nationalist air forces won air superiority and Nationalist troops, with effective German, Italian and Spanish air support, counter-attacked on 24 July 1937 and won a major victory.[35] The German logistics stood up well to the test. The Brunete campaign was one of the toughest air campaigns of the war. The Condor Legion bombers and fighters normally flew several sorties a day to interdict Republican reinforcements and provide close support for the Nationalist Army.[36] During it all, the forward maintenance and supply units kept the Condor Legion at a high operational rate.

During several crises – such as the winter of 1937, when the Republic attacked at Teruel, and July 1938, when the Republic launched its last grand offensive on the Ebro River – the Condor Legion was able to redeploy and respond to the enemy action immediately. In July 1938, when the Republic put 100,000 men supported by tanks, artillery and aircraft across the Ebro, the Condor Legion was in southern Spain supporting a Nationalist offensive. Within two days of the start of the Republican offensive, the Condor Legion was transferred to Catalonia and had begun a massive interdiction effort against the Republican Army's lines of communication. Largely due to the rapid response of the Condor Legion, the Republican offensive soon got bogged down.[37] The *Luftwaffe*'s highly mobile ground logistics and support system had again proven its worth.

STRATEGIC LESSONS

One of the most prevalent myths of the Spanish Civil War is that the lack of any serious strategic bombing campaign taught the *Luftwaffe* the wrong lessons and the nature of the air war over-emphasized air power in support of the ground war. Supposedly, as a result of the Spanish War, the *Luftwaffe* ignored strategic bombing doctrine and heavy bombers, and concentrated its efforts solely upon service as a short-range army support force.[38] This argument ignores the fact that the *Luftwaffe* in Spain was, in fact, heavily engaged in bombing strategic industrial targets and enemy cities and learned some important lessons about the potential for strategic bombing.

In the early months of the war, both sides carried out some relatively minor raids against each other's cities, primarily with the intent of demoralizing the enemy populace.[39] By the end of October 1936, the Condor Legion made its first bombing attacks upon the Republican capital and stronghold of Madrid.[40] As the battle around Madrid reached a climax in late November and the city looked likely to fall, General Franco directed the German, Italian and Nationalist bomber units to carry out a concerted campaign against Madrid.[41] Franco ordered the bombing with the goal of demoralizing the populace and breaking the stalemate, although he also insisted that the bombing should not be indiscriminate and that a bomb-safety zone be established in order to limit civilian casualties. The resulting civilian casualties were minor by the standards of the Second World War, but were considered shockingly heavy at the time. On 30 November 1936, the Nationalist coalition bombers killed 244 Madrid civilians and wounded another 875.[42] However, the raids against Madrid were soon called off as a wasted effort. Not only did bombing fail to break civilian morale but the new Russian fighters over the city made Madrid far too uncomfortable for bombers without heavy fighter escort.

Although most of the bombing operations of the Condor Legion, and Italian and Nationalist air forces were close to the front (Guernica, for example, was a village only six miles from the front line and was considered to be a tactical operation), there were many instances of the Condor Legion bombers attacking strategic industrial targets deep behind the enemy lines. On 19 January 1938 Condor Legion bombers along with Nationalist and Italian aircraft made a co-ordinated attack on the power station near Tremp, which supplied the war industries of Barcelona. The attack was repeated later that month.[43] As the Condor Legion became fully equipped with modern medium bombers, such as the He 111 and Do 17, the German airmen became eager to attack a variety of the Republic's industrial installations. In March 1938 the Condor Legion bomber force attacked the Puebla de Hijar railyard and a munitions factory located nearby.[44] Even when the Condor Legion was heavily involved in supporting ground operations it could often find enough bombers to raid the Republic's ports and munitions factories.[45]

Although the Condor Legion amassed some experience in strategic bombing in Spain, the German commanders came to regard indiscriminate city bombing as a waste of effort and probably counter-productive. However, the Italians had different views on strategic bombing and tried them out in Spain. In March 1938, while the Republican Army on the Aragon front was in headlong retreat, the *Regia Aeronautica*, on the orders of Benito Mussolini himself, launched a three-day series of massive bombing raids directed against Barcelona. As with the bombing of Madrid in November 1936, the objective was to break the faltering morale of the Republic's citizens. Unlike the bombing of Madrid, however, there was no attempt to limit civilian casualties. The target was Barcelona's civilian populace and Italian air theorist Giulio Douhet's theory of aerial warfare was finally to be given a true test.

The attack on Barcelona, the heaviest air attack of the inter-war period, caused approximately 1,300 deaths and wounded another 2,000.[46] At first the bombing demoralized the populace but it also seemed to anger more people than it terrified. There are accounts of wounded civilians in Barcelona who raised their arms in the communist clenched fist salute and exhorted other civilians to fight on as they were carried away.[47] After the bombing, morale in Barcelona remained strong and the Republican forces soon stopped their retreat and dug in to hold off the Nationalist offensive.

The German commanders in Spain saw the bombing of Barcelona as essentially counter-productive. The German ambassador to the Nationalists reported the Condor Legion's assessment of the Barcelona bombing in a message to Berlin: 'Destructive bombardments without clear military targets are, in a civil war like Spain's, not likely to bring about the desired moral results – instead, it makes for a more dangerous future.'[48] German officers realized that bombing cities might even serve to increase enemy morale and strengthen the will to resist.[49]

At the conclusion of the war in March 1939 the *Luftwaffe* carried out a thorough study of the civil defence programme carried out by the Republicans to protect the populations of Madrid and Barcelona from Nationalist coalition bombing. The *Luftwaffe* noted that civil-defence shelters using sandbag and timber-reinforced basements along with underground shelters dug in parks had generally been effective in protecting people from all but a direct hit by a heavy bomb. The *Luftwaffe* also noted that a shelter-building programme combined with civil-defence training for the population had been effective in maintaining the morale of the populace in the face of aerial bombardment.[50] In short, the experience in Spain had upheld the usefulness of strategic attack against industries and transportation centres but had also provided strong evidence that terror bombing was unlikely seriously to demoralize a population provided with adequate civil-defence shelters and training.

LESSONS OF A COALITION WAR

For the whole period of the war in Spain, all German military operations had to be planned and conducted in co-ordination with the Nationalist leaders and the large Italian air and ground forces in Spain.

Although German commanders Sperrle, Volkmann and von Richthofen and their staffs could never be described as having 'diplomatic personalities', the Germans were able to function fairly effectively in a coalition environment. Of course, there were numerous causes of serious friction in the Nationalist alliance. The German relationship with the Italians was often poor, owing to the tendency of the Italians to conduct operations on their own without informing their German and Nationalist allies. On the Nationalist side, many of the senior Army officers who rallied to the cause at the start of the revolt were old and poorly trained men who had risen to high rank due to seniority and politics rather than from merit. The German commanders found many of the senior Nationalist officers to be simply incompetent with little understanding of modern warfare, a not unjustified judgement.[51]

On the German side, Hitler's government was also quite capable of promoting unnecessary friction in the coalition. In November 1936, the German government appointed a retired, Spanish-speaking general, Wilhelm Faupel, as ambassador to Franco's government. Faupel, who was appointed to the post mostly because of his long membership in the Nazi Party, immediately offended Franco by arguing that Franco needed to reorganize the Falange Party in the image of the Nazi Party. This policy ran counter to Franco's attempt to build a political coalition of businessmen, monarchists and conservative Catholics as well as fascists. Faupel also managed to put himself in the bad graces of the Condor Legion commanders by trying to insert himself as Franco's senior military advisor, a mission for which he was specifically not authorized by the Nazi foreign ministry. After managing to offend virtually everyone in the senior leadership of the Nationalist coalition, Faupel was recalled in July 1937 and replaced with an experienced diplomat, who left the military operations to the soldiers and ended the attempt to pressure Franco to accept Nazi ideology. German–Spanish relations immediately improved.[52]

The Germans learned to overcome many of the frictions and coalition disputes and managed to work effectively in a coalition environment throughout the war. While the relationship between the Germans and Franco was never warm, and the Germans often disagreed with Franco on strategic issues, the German commanders and Franco respected each other as military professionals. When Franco set the strategy, the Germans would often disagree, but then loyally carry out orders as soon as the plan was set. The Germans overcame the problem of incompetent and superannuated Spanish officers at the higher levels of command by a common-sense approach. They identified the most capable Nationalist General Staff officers, such as General Juan Vigon (who became Franco's Chief of Staff), and worked through the difficult planning and co-ordination issues with them.[53]

At several times during the war the Condor Legion was given command of all Nationalist and Italian air units on a front. During the offensive in the north in the spring of 1937, the best Nationalist coalition forces assembled to overrun the Basque state and the Condor Legion assumed command of all air units on the front. Using the Germans as operational air commanders for all coalition units apparently worked well. In the summer of 1937, when the Republicans began their major offensive at Brunete, the Nationalist and Italian squadrons were again placed under Condor Legion command. Throughout the war, the *Luftwaffe* in Spain co-ordinated its bombing and ground-support operations with its allied air forces and routinely flew missions with the Spaniards and Italians.

The Germans, along with the Italians, worked to build up the small Nationalist air force that, at the outset of the war, was equipped with a motley collection of obsolete military and civilian aircraft. In the first months of the war the Germans provided the Spanish with their older equipment, such as He 51 fighters and He 45 light bombers. However, by 1938, the Germans were shipping the Nationalists first-rate new aircraft such as the He 112 monoplane fighter and the He 111 medium bomber. The Germans initiated training programmes for Spanish pilots and incorporated Spanish He 111 squadrons into the Condor Legion. German instructors were pleased with the competence of the Nationalist pilots and regarded them as worthy allies.[54] The Nationalists and Germans commonly flew combined missions and many *Luftwaffe* personnel developed a very friendly relationship with their Spanish allies. German junior and senior officers also formed close bonds with the Spanish Army units they often supported and visited them at the front.[55]

Despite the numerous issues of friction inevitable in a coalition war, the Germans demonstrated a solid ability to wage an aerial war with allies and to train and support a weaker partner. By the end of the war in 1939, the Nationalist air force was a fairly well-trained and equipped force, largely due to German efforts and matériel. Shortly after the end of the war in March 1939 the Germans and Spanish concluded a long-term programme to re-equip the Spanish Air Force with modern German aircraft. The Nationalists signed contracts to buy from Germany, or build under licence, 175 Bücker Bu 131 and Gotha 145 trainers, 200 Heinkel He 111 bombers, 100 Junkers Ju 52 transports and 200 Me 109 fighters.[56] With German financial and technical assistance, the Spanish were able to revive a small and war-torn aircraft industry and maintain a small but capable air force.

In terms of training, the *Luftwaffe*'s Spanish Civil War experience gave it a tremendous advantage at the start of the Second World War. Between 1936 and 1939, approximately 20,000 *Luftwaffe* personnel served in Spain on tours lasting between six and 12 months. The Spanish experience was especially pertinent to the *Luftwaffe* as the Condor Legion had conducted almost every kind of air operation during the war from troop transport to strategic bombing to close support of ground troops. As *Luftwaffe* personnel returned from Spain they were posted to operational units, often as commanders or instructors, where they shared their combat experience. Many of Germany's leading fighter aces and bomber commanders of the Second World War, such as Adolf Galland, Martin Harlinghausen and Werner Mölders, got their first taste of aerial combat over Spain. Condor Legion commanders and staff officers had fought in numerous major operations employing large air forces. For example, during the Brunete campaign in 1937 the Condor Legion had command of over 200 Nationalist coalition aircraft. Moreover, the combat experience was gained under tough conditions against a very capable enemy. When the war began, the *Luftwaffe* had been a small force with a minimum of training. By the end of the war, the *Luftwaffe* had more vastly more experience in conducting a modern air war than any opponents they would be likely to face. In short, the *Luftwaffe*'s participation in the Spanish Civil War was a central factor in the effectiveness of the force and provided the *Luftwaffe* with an advantage over their Polish, French and British enemies in 1939–40.

In Spain the *Luftwaffe* proved that it was very good at learning tactical lessons. Going to war in 1939, the *Luftwaffe* could be confident in its aircraft, guns, radios and munitions that had been recently tested in combat. The new fighter tactics developed in Spain gave the Germans a significant advantage in air-to-air combat against French and British fighters in 1940 that were still wedded to less effective squadron formations.[57] The increase in night and instrument training initiated due to the high accident rate in Spain made the *Luftwaffe* a much more formidable force in 1940. As the devastating night attack on Coventry in November 1940 proved, the *Luftwaffe* was the only major air force in 1940 that was even moderately effective in conducting night operations. The one major tactical lesson not learned was the weakness of the German bomber defensive armament. To survive in day operations, German bombers needed heavy escort. When a fighter escort was unavailable German bombers were easy prey for fighters – as the disastrous raid by the Fifth Air Fleet bombers against northern England on 15 August 1940 showed.

In the case of operational lessons, *Luftwaffe* doctrine, tactics and organization was greatly improved by the Spanish experience. Probably the most important single lesson to come out of Spain was the importance of, and difficulty of, conducting close air support of ground troops. As a direct result of Spain, in the summer of 1939 the *Luftwaffe* formed the 'Special Purpose Force', an air division composed of four Stuka groups, one attack group, one reconnaissance squadron and two fighter groups (for escort). This new force, under the command of Major-General Wolfram von Richthofen, who had served as the Condor Legion's last commander, was organized and trained specifically for the close support for ground forces.[58] This force and other bomber units in the army support role performed very effectively in the Polish campaign, and the ability of the *Luftwaffe* to effectively support ground forces in France 1940 was a key element of the overwhelming German victory. From 1939 through the campaign in Russia in 1941, the *Luftwaffe*'s ability to provide effective air support for the army served to ensure rapid German victories on every battlefield.

The *Luftwaffe* used its flak guns in Poland, as it had in Spain, to smash enemy fortifications. The flak force again proved its effectiveness in this role and the *Luftwaffe* organized two flak corps to support the advance of the German armies in France and the Low Countries.[59] In the 1940 campaign the flak guns serving in the front lines proved to be among the deadliest and most effective weapons on the battlefield in the anti-tank role, a mission that the flak force would excel in throughout the war. Another valuable operational lesson was the importance of air transport. The success of the *Luftwaffe*'s airlift of Franco's North African army dramatically demonstrated a major new role for an air force and the *Luftwaffe* built up a large air transport force. The transport units played a central role in German successes in the early campaigns of the Second World War, especially in Norway, where the German invasion would have probably failed without the reinforcements and supplies flown in by transport. The Spanish War also illustrated the importance of highly mobile airfield companies and supply units that could deploy and support combat air units from front line airfields. When the Second World War began, the *Luftwaffe* had a large force of mobile airfield units and supply columns that enabled the *Luftwaffe* fighter, bomber and Stuka units to move close behind the Army and provide close support for ground troops. The ability to quickly redeploy and operate close to the front was essential in giving the *Luftwaffe* a high sortie rate during the 1939 and 1940 campaigns.

The *Luftwaffe*'s one notable failure to learn an operational lesson was that of not building a true maritime strike force specially trained and equipped for the anti-shipping role. The great success of the *Luftwaffe*'s small and obsolete naval air arm in Spain clearly demonstrated the potential of such a force. Several of the *Luftwaffe*'s leading generals, including General Helmuth Felmy, commander of the Second Air Fleet, as well as Grossadmiral Raeder, Commander-in-Chief of the Navy, urged Hermann Goering to create a land-based naval air arm equipped with modern long-range bombers such as the Ju 88.[60] Goering brusquely refused the plan for a modern naval air arm because of inter-service rivalry and his own concept of power. Goering insisted that, as a matter of principle, everything that flew ought to belong to 'his' *Luftwaffe*. Since a naval air arm would be under the operational command of the Navy, and not his own ministry, the Navy would not be allowed to have any true aerial strike force of its own.

At the outbreak of the Second World War the naval air arm was a small force of 240 mostly obsolete flying boats and seaplanes capable only of reconnaissance. What a well-equipped and well-trained aerial strike force might have done to Britain in the fateful summer of 1940 was demonstrated by a handful of FW 200 Condor airliners, hastily converted into a long-range naval strike unit in the summer of 1940. The FW 200s could operate over the Atlantic, far out of range of Britain's fighter planes, and intercept the merchant ships that sustained the British war effort. In August and September 1940 the unit of 16 FW 200s, with usually only four planes operational, sank an impressive total of 90,000 tons of British merchant shipping.[61] One shudders to think of what a force of 100–200 Ju 88s, trained and equipped for over-water operations, might have accomplished against Britain's merchant shipping along with the U-boat offensive in the summer of 1940. However, the *Luftwaffe* would not field a true long-range naval strike force until 1942. It was a major missed opportunity.

STRATEGIC LESSONS NOT LEARNED

In contrast to generally drawing appropriate tactical and operational lessons from the Spanish War, the senior leadership of the *Luftwaffe* proved quite inept at learning strategic lessons. The Germans had gained valuable experience in conducting coalition operations in Spain and for three years had co-ordinated operations with the Italian Air Force. The Germans had also shown themselves capable of equipping and training the Nationalist air force and assisting the Spanish aviation industry. Yet during the Second World War the Germans were generally ineffective in conducting coalition operations with the Italians and in providing similar support to the Italian Air Force. When Italy entered the war as Germany's ally in June 1940 it had a fairly large (over 3,000 planes) air force and aircraft industry. The *Regia Aeronautica* had a corps of trained combat pilots and competent air commanders thanks to its involvement in Spain. Italy's greatest weakness was the lack of up-to-date technology and industrial capacity. Italy's aircraft were mostly obsolete, generally inferior to modern British aircraft, and its aircraft engine industry was incapable of building more than a handful of the large, efficient engines required for combat planes.

While the Germans were fully aware of Italy's technological weakness in the air there was surprisingly little interest among the senior *Luftwaffe* leadership in helping the Italians build up and modernize their air force.[62] The *Regia Aeronautica*, with inferior aircraft and an aircraft industry incapable of replacing losses, fought valiantly in North Africa and over the Mediterranean from 1940 to 1943. However, it remained a secondary player in the air war. If the German Air Ministry had undertaken a moderate programme to assist the Italian Air Force and aircraft industry in 1940 Italy could have been much more effective in the Mediterranean air war. Indeed, assistance to Italy in 1940 would have transformed the air war in 1941–42, when the British were barely able to hold on against a fairly small *Luftwaffe* force in the theatre. It was well within Germany's capability to supply Italy with a few hundred modern aircraft as well as significant financial and technical assistance to the Italian aircraft industry. However, the German leadership expressed little interest in bolstering their ally and took few measures to improve the capability of the *Regia Aeronautica* and thus threw away a major strategic opportunity.

In the matter of strategic bombing, the *Luftwaffe* senior leadership again ignored clear lessons from Spain. The Germans had carefully studied the effect of German and Italian bombing of Republican cities and concluded that bombing civilian populations was not likely to break enemy morale. Yet, in September 1940, Hitler, joined by his *Luftwaffe* commander Goering and the Chief of the *Luftwaffe* General Staff, Hans Jeschonnek, ordered the bombing of London with the expectation that British civilian morale would break under the strain. As one could have predicted, the Britons held up to the bombing as well as the Spaniards had done. The decision to turn away from attacks on RAF airfields and bomb London was another of the grand strategic mistakes of the Second World War.

The Spanish experience provides a useful case study in the ability to learn, or not learn, lessons from military operations. In Spain, as throughout the Second World War, the *Luftwaffe* officer corps generally demonstrated a high level of professionalism and competence at the tactical and operational levels of command. After each major campaign, operations were carefully scrutinized at every level of command in order to improve tactics, operational method and equipment. As a result, the *Luftwaffe* proved effective in learning lessons from combat. However, at the strategic level of command, the Germans consistently exhibited an inability to learn practical lessons and instead relied more upon the *Fuehrer*'s instincts or Nazi ideology to guide decision-making. In short, the Nazi regime became less rational the higher one went. The decision to bomb London in September 1940 was made more in accordance with the Nazi belief that democracies bred weak and spineless people than with any realistic assessment of the British will to fight. The lack of interest that Goering and senior *Luftwaffe* officers such as Field Marshal Milch and General Hans Jeschonnek had in assisting their Italian allies lies partly in Nazi racial prejudice, which convinced them that Italians were inferior and not capable of using German technology.[63] This prejudice, coupled with the belief at the top levels that the war would be short and that aiding Italy would be a wasted effort, served to ensure the loss of North Africa to the Axis.

NOTES

1. The best general work in English on the Spanish Civil War is Hugh Thomas, *The Spanish Civil War* (New York: Harper & Row, 1961).
2. The best account of the *Luftwaffe*'s operations in Spain is Raymond Proctor, *Hitler's Luftwaffe in the Spanish Civil War* (Westport, CT: Greenwood Press, 1983). On the origin of Germany's involvement in Spain see pp. 1–23. Another excellent general history of the *Luftwaffe* in Spain is Karl Ries and Hans Ring, *The Legion Condor: A History of the Luftwaffe in the Spanish Civil War, 1936–1939* (West Chester, PA: Schiffer Military History, 1992).
3. Thomas, *Spanish Civil War*, p. 244. See also Proctor, *Hitler's Luftwaffe*, pp. 21–6.
4. Proctor, *Hitler's Luftwaffe*, p. 31.
5. By the end of September, the *Luftwaffe* had 20 Ju 52 transports/bombers, 24 Heinkel He 51 fighters and 29 He 46 reconnaissance planes in Spain. See Gerald Howson, *Aircraft of the Spanish Civil War* (Washington, DC: Smithsonian Institution Press, 1990), p. 26.
6. On the Soviet support for the Republic see Thomas, *Spanish Civil War*, pp. 292–306.
7. Jesus Salas Larrazabal, *Air War over Spain* (London: Ian Allan, 1969), pp. 95, 103–8; see also Proctor, *Hitler's Luftwaffe*, p. 64.
8. On the Soviet support for the Republic see Thomas, *Spanish Civil War*, pp. 292–306.
9. German aircraft employed in Spain included the Bf 109, He 112 and Ar 68 fighters, the Ju 87 and Hs 123 dive bombers, the Ju 86, He 111 and Do 17 bombers, the Hs 126 reconnaissance plane and Fiesler 156 'Storch' light liaison plane. For the best overview of the aircraft flown in the Spanish War see Howson, *Aircraft of the Spanish Civil War*.
10. Olaf Groehler, *Geschichte des Luftkrieges* (Berlin: Militaerverlag der DDR, 1981), pp. 204, 220.
11. The most detailed account of the Soviet arms sent to the Spanish Republic is Gerald Howson, *Arms for Spain* (New York: St Martin's Press, 1998). On aircraft see pp. 136–7, 302.
12. Mölders probably formalized a tactical system that had already been used for some time in Spain. Supposedly, when the first BF 109s became available there were only

six for bomber escort. Normally bombers would be escorted by three groups of three fighters covering the bomber formation from three sides. With only six fighters available, the bombers could only be escorted by three flights of two aircraft. This expedient soon proved to be superior and was adopted as normal tactics.

13. Ernst Obermaier and Werner Held, *Jagdflieger Oberst Werner Mölders* (Stuttgart: Motorbuch Verlag, 1986), p. 14.
14. Headquarters, Luftwaffenkommando 5, Directive 8, 8 Oct. 1937, in Bundesarchiv/Militärarchiv Freiburg (henceforth BA/MA), BA/MA RL 4/15.
15. Von Richthofen's major comment on the bombing of Guernica was 'complete technical success of the 250 kg EC.B.1 bomb'. See Report of 30 April 1937 in BA/MA N/671/2.
16. William Green, *Warplanes of the Third Reich* (New York: Galahad Books, 1970), pp. 272–3.
17. Ibid., p. 416.
18. Ibid., p. 408.
19. Proctor, *Hitler's Luftwaffe*, p. 253.
20. Von Richthofen's reports repeatedly noted the usefulness of the flak in supporting the ground forces. See Von Richthofen report in BA/MA N/671/2, 1 April 1937.
21. Report of von Richthofen 1 April 1937, in BA/MA N/671/2.
22. General der Flieger Karl Drum, 'Die deutsche Luftwaffe im spanischen Bürgerkrieg', USAF HRA Karlsruhe Collection, Doc. K113-106-150, pp. 183–4. See also Proctor, *Hitler's Luftwaffe*, pp. 138–41.
23. Drum, 'Die deutsche Luftwaffe', p. 199.
24. Proctor, *Hitler's Luftwaffe*, pp. 122–3.
25. Ibid., p. 126.
26. Von Richthofen report of 3 April 1937, in BA/MA N/671/2. See also Proctor, *Hitler's Luftwaffe*, p. 156.
27. Ries and Ring, *The Legion Condor*, p. 83.
28. Stanley Payne, *The Franco Regime, 1936–1975* (Madison, WI: University of Wisconsin Press, 1987), p. 154.
29. Proctor, *Hitler's Luftwaffe*, p. 167.
30. Drum, 'Die deutsche Luftwaffe', pp. 218–26.
31. BA/MA RM 7/168 and RM 7/69 contain reports on the early naval air operations of the Condor Legion.
32. Ries and Ring, *The Legion Condor*, p. 207. See also *Deutsche Kämpfen in Spanien* (Berlin: Wilhelm Limpert Verlag, 1939), pp. 86–8.
33. *Deutsche Kämpfen in Spanien*, pp. 83–5.
34. Proctor, *Hitler's Luftwaffe*, p. 260.
35. Ries and Ring, 'Die deutsche Luftwaffe', pp. 68–72, Howson, *Aircraft of the Spanish Civil War*, pp. 19, 22.
36. Von Richthofen report of 18 July 1937, in BA/MA N/671/2.
37. Report by General Volkmann, 28 July 1938. Condor Legion Lageberichte BA/MA RL 35/4. See also Condor Legion Report, letter from Capt Christ, 11 Dec. 1938 in BA/MA RL 35/3, p. 3.
38. See Samuel Mitcham, *Men of the Luftwaffe* (Novato, CA: Presidio Press, 1988), p. 51 and Proctor, *Hitler's Luftwaffe*, p. 259.
39. In July and August the Nationalists bombed Málaga and Bádajoz. At the same time the Republic bombed Seville, Saragossa, Cordoba and Oviedo. See Jesus Larrazabal, *La Guerra de España desde el aire* (Barcelona: Ediciones Ariel, 1969), p. 499.
40. Ries and Ring, 'Die deutsche Luftwaffe', p. 28.
41. Herbert Mathews, *Half of Spain Died* (New York: Charles Scribner's Sons, 1973) p. 152.

42. Proctor, *Hitler's Luftwaffe*, pp. 66–7.
43. Ries and Ring, 'Die deutsche Luftwaffe', pp. 118–19.
44. Ibid., p. 128, the reports noted that although the bomb pattern was poor, the factory was still destroyed.
45. According to von Richthofen's report of 9 April 1937, German bombers accompanied by Italian bombers attacked a Republican munitions factory in Northern Spain. See BA/MA N 671/2.
46. Thomas, *Spanish Civil War*, p. 523.
47. Ibid., p. 524.
48. Ambassador Stohrer, Report to the Foreign Ministry (23 March 1938) from *Akten xur Deutschen Auswärtigen Politik 1918–1945, Serie D, Band III*, AKT 550.
49. Ibid.
50. *Luftwaffe* chef des Ausbildungswesen, 'Folgerungen aus dem rotspanischer Luftschutz', Sept. 1939. In NARA File T-321, roll 90.
51. For example, von Richthofen's reports referred to General Kindelan, chief of the Nationalist Air Force, to be an 'old, used-up fellow'. See von Richthofen's diary entry of 20 Jan. 1937 and 2 March 1937 in BA/MA N/71/1. Criticisms of the incompetence of many Spanish staff officers and commanders are common in the Condor Legion reports sent to Berlin.
52. For a full account of the German coalition operations in Spain see James Corum, 'The *Luftwaffe* and the Coalition Air War in Spain, 1936–1939', in John Gooch (ed.), *Airpower: Theory and Practice* (London: Frank Cass, 1995), pp. 68–90. On Faupel, see pp. 75–6.
53. Ibid., p. 74.
54. Condor Legion Reports, Lageberichte of 6 Sept. 1938, in BA/MA BL 35/4.
55. Ernst Obermaier and Werner Held, *Jagdflieger Oberst Werner Mölders*, p. 79.
56. Jesus Salas Larrazabal, *From Fabric to Titanium* (Madrid: Espasa-Calpes, 1983), pp. 146–55.
57. Richard Bickers, *The Battle of Britain: The Greatest Battle in the History of Air Warfare* (London: Salamander Books, 1999), pp. 127–8.
58. Hans von Rohden (ed.), *Luftkrieg: Heft 5: Die Planung und Vorbereitung des Luftkriegs gegen Polen 1939*, MS in Air University Library, Nov. 1946, p. II.
59. Horst-Adalbert Koch, *Die Geschichte der deutschen Flakartillerie 1933–1945* (Bad Nauheim: Verlag Hans-Henning, 1955), pp. 35–6.
60. On Raeder's plan for a modern naval air strike force see letter, Grossadmiral Raeder to Reichsmarschall Goering, 31 Oct. 1939, in BA/MA RM 7/168.
61. Green, *Warplanes of the Third Reich*, pp. 224–7.
62. On the German relations with their allies in coalition war see Richard DiNardo and Daniel Hughes, 'Germany and Coalition Warfare in the World Wars: A Comparative Study', *War in History*, Vol. 8, No. 2 (April 2001), pp. 166–90.
63. Ibid., pp. 187–90.

PART II:

THE SECOND WORLD WAR

5

The Second World War as a Turning Point in Air Power

Richard P. Hallion

Air power has been a factor in military operations since the battles of Revolutionary France in 1794, when balloons were first used in a role remarkably similar to that of the J-STARS (Joint Surveillance Target Attack Radar System) today. It may be said that we have gone through two eras in air power and are now entering a third in aerospace power. First, two centuries ago, we had the problem of fully integrating an intelligence, surveillance and reconnaissance system into the military, namely the balloon. Second, a century ago, we had that same problem but now involving the aeroplane. Third, today, we confront it again, as we move to integrate space fully into our operations. I would aver that orbital manned and unmanned spacecraft today bear the same relationship to military aviation and surface warfare as the aeroplane did to the balloon and surface forces a century ago, and as the balloon did to cavalry and surface forces two centuries ago.

In 1892, the French War Ministry contracted with Clément Ader to build a combat aeroplane capable of dropping explosives on a foe. While this resulted in failure (despite his airplane, the steam-powered *Avion III* being preserved in Paris's Conservatoire national des arts et métiers), it indicates just how early people thought of using aircraft in an offensive military role. While Ader was notably unsuccessful as an aeronautical inventor, he was far more perceptive as an air power prophet, noting, in one of his writings, that 'Military aviation shall become all powerful, and control the destiny of nations.'[1]

The Wright brothers completed the first successful flight of an aeroplane in December 1903, and refined their basic concept over the next two years. Then, in 1906, Alberto Santos-Dumont first flew in France. The world reaction was immediate. When the *Daily Mail*, Britain's most widely read newspaper (with an average daily circulation of more than 500,000 copies), reported the flight in a brief notice, Lord

Northcliffe, the newspaper's founder and the first (and one of the greatest) of all press magnates, quickly informed his editors that the story was not that an aeroplane had flown over 700 feet, but that England was no longer an island. 'Let me tell you', he thundered into a telephone, 'there will be no more sleeping safely behind the wooden walls of old England with the Channel as our safety moat. If war comes, the aerial chariots of the enemy will descend on British soil.' (A decade later, they would, in the form of the first Zeppelin and Gotha bombers raiding British cities.) The next day the *Daily Mail* opined, 'They are not mere dreamers who hold that the time is at hand when air power will be an even more important thing than sea power.'[2]

Not all this struck too many people as making a great deal of sense. In 1910, the French General Ferdinand Foch attended the *Circuit de l'Est*, a ten-day aerial tour sponsored by the French newspaper *Le Matin*, watched the sputtering aeroplanes, and remarked dismissively 'That's good sport, but for the Army the plane is of no use.'[3] Four years later, with Britain, France, Germany, Italy and Russia all fielding growing numbers of military aircraft for scouting and observation purposes, and the outbreak of the First World War just weeks away, British General Sir Douglas Haig lectured the officers at the British Army's Staff College, 'I hope none of you gentlemen is so foolish as to think that aeroplanes will be usefully employed for reconnaissance from the air. There is only one way for a commander to get information by reconnaissance and that is by the use of cavalry.'[4]

But within a few years, all of this had changed. Just weeks after the outbreak of the First World War, the reconnaissance aeroplane proved so valuable as to force a new struggle for control of the air to deny the enemy access to one's sky. After Germany's stunning victory at Tannenberg, Field Marshal Paul von Hindenberg stated 'Without airmen, no Tannenberg!'[5] By mid-1915, at the battle of Neuve Chapelle, Haig was berating artillery officers who underestimated or failed to take fullest advantage of aerial reconnaissance for their 'early Victorian methods'.[6] By late November 1916, Foch would issue an order stating 'Only superiority in aviation permits the superiority in artillery that is indispensable for having superiority in the actual battle', adding in his own hand, 'Victory in the air is the preliminary to victory on land, which is forfeit by itself.'[7] A year later, Haig himself would complain to the Chief of the Imperial General Staff that his armies were 'very far short of their requirements' for aircraft and aviators.[8] In the 1930s, reflecting on the development of military aviation in the 'Great War', Major-General Heinz Guderian, the great advocate of armoured warfare and one of the key fathers of the *Blitzkrieg* notion of war would write, 'Aircraft became an offensive weapon of the first order, distinguished by their great speed, range, and effect on target. If their initial development experienced a check when hostilities came to an end in 1918, they had already shown their potential clearly enough to those who were on the receiving end.'[9]

That potential was built upon over the next 20 years. In 1940, Britain would gain its salvation from Hitler through a battle fought exclusively in the air. At Normandy in 1944, General Dwight Eisenhower would tell his son 'If I didn't have air supremacy, I wouldn't be here', and his opposite number, Field Marshal Erwin Rommel, would confide in his diary that 'The enemy's air superiority has a very grave effect on our movements. There's simply no answer to it.'[10] Eight months later, scant weeks before taking their own lives in the *Führerbunker*, Nazi propagandist Josef Goebbels would confide in his diary that he had met with Adolf Hitler and that 'Again and again we return to the starting-point of our conversation. *Our whole military predicament is due to enemy air superiority*.'[11] I will discuss the Second World War in more detail shortly.

In the post-war world, the entire framework of the 40-year Cold War that would culminate in the fall of the Berlin Wall in 1989 revolved around developing, deploying, controlling and (ultimately) limiting strategic weaponry; the weaponry – planes, missiles, bombs and rockets – of the aerospace revolution. The impact of that weaponry was most dramatically illustrated by the events of the 1990s: first, the destruction of Iraq's military machine and Saddam Hussein's ambitions in the Gulf War of 1991, and, most recently, in the Balkans. It is perhaps fitting at this time to remind ourselves of John Keegan's considered judgement:

> There are certain dates in the history of warfare that mark real turning points ... Now there is a new turning point to fix on the calendar: June 3, 1999, when the capitulation of President Milosevic proved that a war can be won by air power alone ... The air forces have won a triumph, are entitled to every plaudit they will receive and can look forward to enjoying a transformed status in the strategic community, one they have earned by their single-handed efforts. All this can be said without reservation, and should be conceded by the doubters, of whom I was one, with generosity. Already some of the critics of the war are indulging in ungracious revisionism, suggesting that we have not witnessed a strategic revolution and that Milosevic was humbled by the threat to deploy ground troops or by the processes of traditional diplomacy ... The revisionists are wrong. This was a victory through air power.[12]

So, to those who would suggest today that air power is still unproven or still only some sort of supporting arm to traditional surface forces, I would only point to those who can speak most persuasively of its effects: Hitler, Tojo, Saddam and Slobodan Milosevic.

The experience of the Second World War offers numerous clear examples of the impact of air power upon the conduct of military operations. I have selected just four on which to comment, and address these in the 'theatre' order in which they took place, first Europe and then the Pacific. The examples selected are:

1. the Battle of Britain;
2. maritime air warfare in the European theatre;
3. *Overlord* and the Bulge; and
4. the air campaign against Imperial Japan.

Each of these are singular events, but also illustrate some of the key mission areas air power has fulfilled since its invention: air superiority, sea control, interdiction and battlefield air support, and strategic bombardment. Of course, these episodes took place within a much larger overall context of military operations and grand strategy. I will try, as much as possible to place these in a larger air power context as well.

THE BATTLE OF BRITAIN: SALVATION THROUGH AIR SUPERIORITY

Not surprisingly, the literature on the Battle of Britain is voluminous. I strongly recommend a short recent summary of the battle by Richard Overy, which cuts right to the heart of many issues in the battle.[13] Quite simply, the battle, as I alluded to earlier, saved Britain. It did not guarantee victory in the war, but it did forestall defeat and absolutely stopped in its tracks a rampaging *Wehrmacht* that had, up to that point, been extraordinarily successful in overrunning the Continent. Was that significant? As Overy has stated, 'The cost of losing the battle would have spelt national disaster.'[14] Most significantly, the Battle of Britain forced Hitler to delay, and then finally cancel, the planned invasion of Great Britain, a decision that brought critical breathing space for both Britain and the United States.[15] Britain gained time to train, rearm, and re-equip. The United States gained time to conclude its debate over isolationism, undertake needed strategic planning, and begin its own program of organizing, training and equipping.[16]

While due attention has been paid to command, control and intelligence issues, not enough has yet been paid to the other aspect of the battle, namely the strikes against German ports and amphibious forces.[17] British air attack on Channel ports forced the Germans to redeploy their small craft all along the North Sea and Channel coastline, greatly diminishing their utility. Further, without air superiority, such an invasion was clearly doomed to defeat – and so the projected German invasion of Britain died. The Battle of Britain was, like

Waterloo, a 'close-run thing'; indeed, it was perhaps even closer than might first be apparent. The battle was won by the creation of the Royal Air Force (RAF) as an independent service. It is likely that the subsequent Battle of Britain would have been lost had Great Britain still possessed a 'Royal Flying Corps' rather than an independent air arm at the time of the Battle of France. Air Chief Marshal Sir Hugh 'Stuffy' Dowding would not have been free to withhold fighters to protect Britain, and the Spitfire and Hurricane squadrons would have been thrown away piece-meal in the French cauldron. As a result, when Germany turned its attention to Britain, there would have been, in all likelihood, a savage and very short air war, followed quickly by amphibious landings on the southern coast.

The implications of a loss of Britain would have been profound. Britain could not have served as a launching point for an invasion of the continent, or as a 'national aircraft carrier' from which to project the Allied air attacks against the Reich that, in effect, constituted a 'second front' from 1941 until the invasion in 1944. The war in Europe would have thus been lengthened appreciably, the Holocaust and other horrors would have been left to run their course, Germany would have been free to apply greater power against the Soviet Union, and, worse, would have had more time to overcome the serious weaknesses in their atomic science and technology efforts and would perhaps have developed a deliverable atomic bomb. From the US standpoint, the B-36 at last might have had an opportunity to go to war, and the post-war nuclear standoff might have been between a nuclear-armed Germany and a nuclear-armed United States.

In hindsight, the winning of the Battle of Britain fatally undermined the ambitions of the Third Reich and set the stage for the combined bomber offensive. This RAF–USAAF (United States Army Air Forces) offensive forced Germany into a defensive acquisition and deployment posture, though at terrible cost to Allied airmen. The offensive disrupted and seriously delayed the German V-weapon campaign, hindered production of German submarines (about the only significant strategic weapon the Nazis possessed), severely limited the ability of Germany to transport materials and ship finished weapons and forces to the front lines, and denied to these forces the lubricants and fuels needed to function. The payoff of that effort came in the early hours of 6 June 1944, when Allied forces stormed ashore at Normandy.[18]

The significance of the Battle of Britain beyond Europe, particularly for Asia and the Pacific, and the United States as well, should not be neglected. Over the spring and summer of 1940, in addition to the crisis in Europe, Asia demanded growing attention from both the United States and Great Britain. A British defeat in 1940 would clearly have accelerated the pace of Japanese aggression in the Pacific, as Japanese militants sought to exploit it in much the same fashion as they had capitalized in Indochina upon the Nazi defeat of France, and the danger of this was uppermost in the minds of Roosevelt's US national-security team. Cordell Hull recollected after the war: 'Those were months when it seemed to me Western civilization hung in the balance. Night after night I tossed in bed, pondering the effect on this country if Hitler should conquer Britain.'[19] Fortunately, such never came to pass, but it is likely a Nazi victory over the Royal Air Force in the Battle of Britain would have led to an even earlier outbreak of the Japanese–American Pacific war.

To the head of plans for the Royal Air Force, Air Commodore John Slessor, 'The crux of the whole matter was air superiority';[20] France's collapse had given an impression of an invincible Wehrmacht, but in reality that impression masked serious problems afflicting the *Luftwaffe*.[21] These included: steady losses in earlier campaigns prior to confronting a tenacious, highly motivated, and well-trained opponent; an inadequate industrial base insufficient to make up for losses; a smaller available fighter-pilot pool than the RAF; poor intelligence organization, collection, interpretation and analysis; mission-compromising aircraft deficiencies in both its fighters and bombers; inferior doctrine that emphasized tactical support of the army; and, most serious of all, amateurishness and favouritism among its air leadership. In short, as one German officer wrote after the war, 'It can therefore be said without exaggeration that the operational arm of the German Air Force was "burnt out" at the end of the 1940 offensive in the West.'[22]

To knowledgeable foreign observers, such as the American Carl Spaatz, the weaknesses of the *Luftwaffe* were quickly apparent once the Battle broke out.[23] By 19 September – four days after the climactic fighting of 15 September – he was writing, 'English have developed real air power whereas Germans so far appear to have developed a mass of air geared to the Army and lost when confronted with properly applied air effort.'[24]

The key lesson, as Slessor had realized at the outset of the battle, was retention of air superiority. For that, the Allies could thank the fighter pilots, aircraft maintainers, and intelligence and communications personnel of the Royal Air Force – and, of course, in particular, 'Stuffy' Dowding.[25] There were other lessons as well. Perhaps the most glaring is the doctrinal bankruptcy of the *Luftwaffe*, which led it to emphasize battlefield air support to the detriment of more significant strategic air power operations, together with its failure to develop an adequate force structure, acquisition system and training apparatus to ensure that it got the right weapons and the right people in sufficient numbers to do the job. Another doctrinal shortcoming was the underestimation of how demanding the air combat environment would be in a future war of national survival. The need for hard-manoeuvring, powerful, long-range, well-armed fighters, and high-capacity, fast, long-range, well-armed bombers for both defensive and offensive operations was not intuitively evident in the 1930s on both sides of the Atlantic. If one thinks of the kinds of aircraft entering service or on design boards in the midst of the Second World War, and then mentally compares them to the design standard for fighters and bombers in the mid-1930s, the extraordinary nature of the change will be immediately evident.

But Spaatz and other American air leaders, together with the US political leadership learned another vitally important lesson: the importance of a powerful, independent air force not limited by doctrinal bonds to merely supporting the activities of a surface army. The outcome of the Battle of Britain immeasurably strengthened the hand of wartime Army Air Forces chief General Hap Arnold, just as it strengthened the case for the creation of a post-war independent United States Air Force (USAF). That outcome, if immaterial to the men and women of the Royal Air Force in 1940, was nevertheless to have the profoundest of consequences for the West in the long watch of the Cold War in the years after 1945, and, indeed, continues to do so today, in the unsettled post-Cold War era.

MARITIME AIR WARFARE IN THE EUROPEAN THEATRE: DOMINATION OF THE SEA

The twentieth century witnessed the development of two military technologies that rapidly transformed maritime affairs, the submarine and the airship/aeroplane. These acted in concert to overturn over two millennia of previous naval practice characterized by the decisiveness of surface combat. Now surface forces increasingly found themselves in thrall to what was happening above and below the surface. It marked the beginning of true three-dimensional warfare.

The naval air war in the Pacific is well known, and has been extensively studied. But before Pearl Harbor and the opening of the great Pacific war, maritime air operations profoundly influenced both European and Mediterranean sea–land warfare, foreshadowing the far more extensive naval air war that would occur subsequently halfway around the world. In the disastrous Norwegian campaign of April–June 1940, air power first showed its mastery in a maritime environment. A Royal Navy after action study stated bluntly that 'the German mastery in the air gained the day for them'.[26] Later, as John Keegan has written, 'Hostile aircraft terrified the seamen of the Atlantic battle, those of the convoys as much as the U-boat crews who were their enemy.'[27] Of course, it was the Fleet Air Arm attack on Taranto that, together with lessons learned by Japan's naval air attaché, Commander Minoru Genda, in London during the Battle of Britain, shaped the thought that evolved into the Japanese air attack on Pearl Harbor that effectively brought the era of battleship-dominant fleets to an end.[28]

Overall, European and Mediterranean operations confirmed the emergence of three-dimensional attack – attack from above and below the ocean's surface – as the greatest threat to ships at sea. The airplane and the submarine in concert produced a synergy of effects: the aeroplane with its speed and quick reach, and the submarine with its stealthiness.

In the Mediterranean theatre, for example, Italy lost 1,324 ships (totalling 2,106,521 tons) to Allied action. Of these, only 59 (4 per cent) were lost to surface ships. The vast majority was lost to submarines and aircraft.[29] Admiral Friedrich Ruge, the former German Senior Naval Officer in Italy, recollected: 'The mere presence of enemy aircraft was itself sufficient to scare the Italian convoy traffic into making wide diversions from the direct route. This caused them and their escorts to consume more fuel and to be exposed for longer periods to attacks by submarines and surface craft. Time and again [Malta's] striking forces caused shortages in fuel, ammunition, weapons, and equipment at a critical stage of the Axis operations in Africa.'[30]

The record of the Royal Air Force in Northern European and Atlantic maritime operations is noteworthy, and has been thoroughly examined in a notable study by Christina Goulter.[31] Post-war analysis of German coastal traffic from the Bay of Biscay to the North Cape over the time period September 1939–January 1945 concluded that direct air attack and mining claimed 77.3 per cent of sinkings, submarines and surface vessels being responsible for the remaining 22.7 per cent.[32] Air attack was deadly against the submarine, particularly after the appearance of long-range maritime patrol aircraft over the mid-Atlantic gap and the introduction of the Mk 24 acoustic homing torpedo by the RAF in 1943. Exact numbers of U-boats destroyed by air attack vary, but all authorities accept without question that the primary tool of U-boat destruction – well over 50 per cent – was the land-or-sea-based airplane. Naval historian Clay Blair has noted that once they were equipped with radar, 'aircraft vaulted to top rank as U-boat killers'.[33] Beyond direct destruction of U-boats, one of air power's most significant attributes was simply in forcing U-boats to remain submerged, hindering their mobility and time at sea.[34]

Mining proved over five times more productive than other forms of air attack; for approximately every 26 mine-dropping sorties flown, the RAF could claim an enemy ship sunk, while it took approximately 148 sorties to generate a sinking by direct air attack. In no small measure, the mining campaign's success stemmed from strong and constant support by the chief of RAF Bomber Command, Air Chief Marshal Arthur T. 'Bomber' Harris. In fact, before the war, as an Air Ministry staff officer, he had successfully pressed for the production of air-dropped magnetic sea mines. Thus, when war broke out, the RAF already possessed a leader and a weapon suitable for sea-denial operations. Mining proved so devastating that Nazi shipping authorities immediately clamoured for strengthened nightfighter forces operating along threatened coasts, but to its dismay, the *Luftwaffe* found it could only harass and not prevent British mining sorties.[35] Direct air attacks and mining together sapped the German maritime war effort, delayed and disrupted logistical flow, and disheartened the German military leadership. For example, between 1943 and 1944, transit times to German ports from Trondheim, Norway, more than doubled, from 14 to 31 days. Northerly voyages in 1944 took an additional 24 days on average over 1943 figures.[36]

RAF operations effectively held the German navy's major combatants in check throughout the war, as feared by Admiral Karl Doenitz, chief of Hitler's U-boat fleet, at the time of the execution of the Z Plan in January 1939.[37] The RAF threat to the battlecruisers *Scharnhorst* and *Gneisenau*, and the heavy cruiser *Prinz Eugen*, forced the Nazi naval leadership to order the three ships on a risky dash through the English Channel to safety in German ports. So urgent was this need – *Gneisenau* had been hit by an aerial torpedo and four bombs while in harbour – that (over Doenitz's protestations) dockyard workers supporting U-boat operations were taken off their tasks and put to work readying the endangered ships so that they could put to sea. This decision, as Doenitz recollected, 'reduced very considerably our sinking potential and resulted generally in very solid advantages to the enemy'.[38] Heavily protected by the *Luftwaffe*, the three ships and their consorts did escape, though both *Scharnhorst* and *Gneisenau* struck magnetic mines dropped previously by Bomber Command and suffered damage that necessitated long repairs. *Scharnhorst* returned to service in 1943, remaining primarily fjord-bound until trapped off North Cape and sunk by British surface forces. *Gneisenau*, while undergoing repairs, sustained three subsequent British air raids that broke her back, destroyed her upperworks, and left her a shattered hulk. *Prinz Eugen* impotently finished its days in the Baltic before serving as an atomic bomb target in the Bikini atoll post-war tests.[39]

Clearly, then, air power had a profound effect on the war at sea, whether in turning the tide in the Battle of the Atlantic, strangling German supply lines, or preventing any productive operations by German surface vessels. The same, on an even grander scale, was true of the war in the Pacific, as shall be discussed subsequently.

By the end of the Second World War, then, air power (and the submarine as well) had radically transformed naval warfare, utterly changing an evolved pattern of warfare that had emphasized purely surface combat for over two millennia.

OVERLORD AND THE BULGE: EXPLOITING AIR SUPREMACY TO GENERATE LAND SUPREMACY

The invasion of Normandy undoubtedly constituted the single most daunting moment that the Allies faced throughout the entire Second World War. It built upon the success of previous campaigns, including the strategic bombing campaign and the steady growth of superior Allied air power, the latter a constant source of frustration to the Nazi military leadership.[40] The roots of Normandy's success dated back more than two years, to fighting in the Western Desert. There, air operations had played an important role in the defeat of Germany's legendary 'Desert Fox', Field Marshal Erwin Rommel, and was, in Rommel's own view, of decisive importance. On land, British battle-field air attacks decided the pivotal battle of Alam Halfa in August 1942, preventing Rommel from once again returning to his offensive operations in North Africa. Reflecting on the battle, he complained that the German attack had to be broken off 'because of the superiority of the enemy air force – although victory was otherwise ours' and that RAF air attacks 'had pinned my army to the ground'; he noted 'the paralysing effect which air activity on such a scale had on motorized forces' and 'above all the serious damage which had been caused to our units by area bombing', concluding that '*In every battle to come the strength of the Anglo-American air force was to be the deciding factor.*'[41]

While the Italian campaign was quickly overshadowed by events in Normandy, some aspects of it foreshadowed the kind of transportation havoc the Allied air campaign would inflict on Rommel during Operation *Overlord*. Italy is best remembered for Operation *Strangle*, an interdiction campaign of mixed results. But while it was accepted for years that *Strangle* inflicted little, if any, significant level of supply denial of German forces, more recent detailed examination of surviving German Army records indicates that, in fact, the air-interdiction campaign *did* have a serious impact on German-resupply efforts, particularly upon two German armies south of Rome, even though it came at a time when there was little fighting actually taking place.[42] *Strangle* undoubtedly achieved its greatest success in denying mobility to German forces; one historian has written that Allied air attacks 'drove German convoys from the road by day while crippling the railroads of central Italy with a newly intensive effort against bridges and other engineering features. The demands on German motor transport soon soared to impossible levels.'[43] Limited to moving only by night, the commander of the XIV Panzer Corps, Major-General Frido von Senger und Etterlin, compared his position to that of a chess player who could make only one move to an opponent's three.[44]

The Normandy invasion and its aftermath offer multiple examples of air power's decisiveness, beginning with the issue of air superiority. The Allied air-superiority campaign in early 1944 essentially gutted the *Luftwaffe*; 25 per cent of Germany's total fighter-pilot force (an average of approximately 2,300 at this time) perished in May 1944 alone, and in each of three successive months, March, April and May 1944, an average of 50 per cent of the available German fighters that month were lost.[45] The achievement of not merely air *superiority* but genuine air *supremacy* gave Allied commanders the confidence and ability to undertake the Normandy landings, and enabled all other subsequent operations. As for whether it was of decisive importance, General Dwight Eisenhower bluntly told his son John slightly over two weeks after the invasion that if he had not had air supremacy, he would not have been there (see p. 95 above).[46]

Eisenhower elaborated on this after the war, stating before the Congress in 1945 (in support of creating a separate United States Air Force) that: 'The Normandy invasion was based on a deep-seated faith in the power of the Air Forces in overwhelming numbers to intervene in the land battle ... making it possible for a small force of land troops to invade a continent ... Without that Air Force, without its independent power, entirely aside from its ability to sweep the enemy air forces out of the sky, without its power to intervene in the ground battle, that invasion would have been fantastic [indeed] it would have been more than fantastic, it would have been criminal.'[47]

Even before the actual invasion, German military leaders had complained about the increasing absence of the *Luftwaffe*; Rommel's naval aide, Vice-Admiral Friedrich Ruge, confided in his diary over a month before D-day that the disparity between the *Luftwaffe* and the allied air forces was 'humiliating'.[48] As a precaution, when the actual invasion began on 6 June 1944, fully 102 squadrons of Allied fighters patrolled the skies above the invasion fleet, the landing area and deep into France to guard against Nazi fighters and bombers. But the *Luftwaffe* was powerless to intervene. General Adolph Galland, the former chief of German fighter forces, wrote after the war that on the morning of the invasion, 'Allied fighters formed a solid air umbrella over the landing sector, and they sent up fighter forces outside the invasion area which closed off the whole zone.' Only in two instances, on the first day of the landing, did German fighter-bombers penetrate the defensive frame and the air umbrella and drop their bombs on the bridgehead. From the very first moment of the invasion the Allies had absolute air supremacy.

Therefore the enemy, our own troops, and the population asked the obvious question, 'Where is the *Luftwaffe?*'[49]

Unprotected from above, German ground commanders discovered immediately what the loss of air control meant for their mobility. With bridges dropped, rail lines cut, and roads constantly patrolled by Allied fighters, many German units were forced to approach the battle area on foot; it was the latter stages of the Western Desert write large. German Lieutenant-General Bodo Zimmerman, the chief operations officer of Army Group D, noted that once a morning fog had dissipated on that fateful day, 'the whole of the area through which the [German] divisions must march was being most intensively patrolled by the Allied air forces. No road movement by day was possible in view of this air umbrella, which reached from Normandy to the Paris area.'[50] Things only became worse over succeeding days. Despite efforts to intervene, the *Luftwaffe* remained on the defensive. Galland recalled that,

> Whenever a fighter plane rolled out of its camouflaged lair, an enemy immediately pounced on it. The danger of being detected and destroyed by the enemy was ever present. At last we retired into the forests. Before and after each sortie the planes were rolled in and out of their leafy protection with great difficulties and much damage ... Fourteen days after the invasion the units had sunk so low in their fighting strength that neither by driving the personnel nor by material replacements could they be put on their legs again.[51]

Rommel subsequently wrote, 'The enemy's air superiority has a very grave effect on our movements. There's simply no answer to it',[52] and his naval aide wrote 'utilization of the Anglo-American air forces is the modern type of warfare, turning the flank not from the side but from above'.[53]

Direct air attack had profound implications, not the least of which was the removal of Rommel himself from the theatre after he was gravely injured (and nearly killed) by a strafing British fighter. On 17 July 1944, a Canadian reconnaissance pilot looking for German road traffic spotted his Horch staff car, and (not knowing the identity of its passenger but realizing that a staff car likely contained an important traveller) reported its movements to 2TAF's (Second Tactical Air Force) air operations centre. The centre called down a section of Spitfires, which strafed it off the road, seriously injuring Rommel and removing him from the war.[54] Field Marshal Hans Guenther von Kluge, the commander-in-chief of Nazi forces in the west, succeeded Rommel as commander of Army Group B following Rommel's injury. Assessing what was happening, he wrote despairingly to Hitler, 'in the face of the total enemy air superiority, we can adopt no tactics to compensate for the annihilating power of air except to retire from the battlefield'.[55] Subsequently, exactly a month after Rommel's crash, von Kluge committed suicide while en route to Germany after being removed from command following his implication in the von Stauffenberg bomb plot against Hitler. His successor as chief of Army Group B was Field Marshal Walter Model. In his post-war assessment Zimmerman wrote that Model 'did not immediately grasp the full gravity of the situation in France and hoped that he might yet restore it. But he was soon to realize the unimaginable effects of the enemy's air supremacy, the massive destruction in the rear areas, the impossibility of travelling along any major road in daylight without great peril, in fact the full significance of the invasion.'[56]

At St Lo, as part of Operation Cobra, battlefield air attacks shattered an emplaced German armoured division, opening the way for the break-out from the beachhead. Though this bombardment was marred by infamous incidents of short bombing that killed just over 100 American soldiers (including Lieutenant-General Lesley J. McNair) and wounded approximately 500 others, it had a profound impact on the Normandy campaign. Lieutenant-General Fritz Bayerlein wrote after the war that it was 'the worst' sight he had seen in his entire war experience, that the bombardment had 'annihilated' the front line, had an 'exterminating morale effect', and that 'The well-dug-in infantry was smashed by the heavy bombs in their foxholes and dugouts or killed and buried by blast ... no human being was alive. Tanks and guns were destroyed and overturned and could not be recovered because all roads and passages were blocked ...'.[57]

Worse was to follow. An attempted German counterattack toward Avranches in early August by eight divisions (five of which were armoured divisions) was halted at Mortain by a day of concentrated RAF Hawker Typhoon fighter-bomber attacks so intense that, in his official after-action report, Eisenhower, while paying tribute to the valour of US ground forces, nevertheless wrote 'The chief credit in smashing the enemy's spearhead, however, must go to the rocket-firing Typhoon planes of the Second Tactical Air Force ... The result of this strafing was that the enemy attack was effectively brought to a halt, and a threat was turned into a great victory.'[58] Decisively halted, German forces now were pummelled by in-place ground forces and continuous air attack before beginning a rapid retreat and joining other German Army units streaming towards the French frontier.[59] Over the next two weeks, in the battle of the Falaise–Argentan Gap, air power again proved its tremendous ability to wreak havoc on surface forces. At Falaise, over 10,000 Nazi soldiers perished, and over 50,000 were taken prisoner; literally hundreds of tanks and artillery pieces were destroyed or abandoned, and other vehicle losses exceeded 2,500.[60] German ground forces were so demoralized that they attempted to surrender to attacking Allied aircraft by displaying white surrender flags.[61] So intense were air attacks that the French dubbed one country road 'Le Couloir de la Mort' ('The Corridor of Death'). Major-General Rudolf-Christoph von Gersdorff, himself wounded by a strafing fighter at Falaise, wrote after the war that 'very strong' air attacks 'caused high losses ... units of the Army were almost entirely destroyed by low flying attacks and artillery'.[62] Touring the area afterwards, Eisenhower likened it to 'scenes that could only be described by Dante'.[63]

Gersdorff's memoir caught the beginning of a dramatic and highly significant shift in warfare that has continued through Korea, Vietnam and on to the post-Gulf War, post-Bosnia era: the primacy of air attack as the *primary* means of inflicting casualties and material destruction upon a foe. After the war, the *Wehrmacht*'s Director of Medical Services, Lieutenant-General (Professor Doctor) Siegfried Handloser stated that, through mid-1943, infantry weapons had caused most German combat casualties, followed by artillery and then air attack. Late in the year, air attack assumed pre-eminence, followed by artillery and then infantry weapons; by 1945, Allied air power was 'far ahead of either artillery or infantry weapons as a cause of casualties in the German armed forces'.[64] Indeed, the ratio of wounded to killed over this time period changed dramatically, a demonstration that air attack was significantly deadlier than conventional infantry and armoured attack: casualties shifted from 8:1 wounded-to-killed at the time of the *Blitzkrieg* in 1940–41, to 5:1 in 1943, and, finally to 3:1 wounded-to-killed in 1945, a transformation which Handloser 'attributed entirely to the devastating effect of aerial warfare'.[65] Further, wounded patients were more seriously injured than earlier in the war, requiring far longer hospitalization, and rendering many unfit for further military service, exacerbating Germany's already severe wartime manpower shortages.

What is more remarkable is that one would expect German casualties to have been *greater* from infantry and armoured fighting vehicle attacks in the 1944–45 period, if for no other reason than Germany was fighting a multi-front land war: in western Europe (after the D-Day and southern France landings), on the Russian front and in Italy, in addition to the steady toll taken by partisans and resistance fighters from Norway through Yugoslavia and Greece. That, even in the face of such constant losses from 'conventional' surface warfare, air was *still* the most significant contributor to German combat casualties is a powerful indicator of the *decisiveness* of air power a mere 40 years after the Wright brothers' first flight at Kitty Hawk.

After Normandy on-call Allied air power (typified by the ubiquitous Republic P-47 Thunderbolts and the rocket-armed Hawker Typhoons roving ahead of Allied armoured columns looking for German armour) remained a defining characteristic of Allied ground operations;

Lieutenant-General George Patton's 3rd Army, for example, relied on Brigadier General Otto P. 'Opie' Weyland's XIX Tactical Air Command to protect his flank as he raced across France. As Patton's biographer Ladislas Farago wrote, 'Knowing how dependent his own success was on air support, Patton shrewdly singled out the airmen for special attention and friendly treatment ... he gave [Weyland] and the whole XIX TAC a feeling of importance and a keen sense of belonging. There was nothing Weyland and his airmen would not have done for Patton in return.'[66]

So accustomed were the US Army's ground forces to having this air power available that it came as a total shock when, in December 1944, under the cover of abysmal weather, the Germans launched a mighty (and last-gasp) counter-offensive, the so-called 'Battle of the Bulge'. In fact, the Germans had chosen the time carefully, specifically so (they hoped) Allied air supremacy would not be a factor; at one point, Hitler remarked to his generals 'The only thing which is not in our favour this time is the air situation. That is why we are now forced to take advantage of the bad winter weather. *The air situation forces us to do so. I cannot wait till the weather gets better. I would be happier if we could somehow hold on till the spring [but] the weather in the spring will give the enemy a decisive advantage.*'[67] So serious did Patton judge his need for air power that he commissioned a weather prayer from his chaplain, so that the airmen could intervene. The weather eventually cleared, and masses of Allied fighter-bombers made short work of the already overstretched and vulnerable German columns.[68] That a committed and dedicated surface warrior such as George Patton could be moved to call upon the Almighty to direct aerial intervention upon his foes, as with the previously cited statistics on German casualties from both Normandy and the Bulge, speaks mightily for the perceived decisiveness of air power in the European theatre by land-war commanders.

In the Bulge operations, air attacks figured prominently both in the defensive 'decisive halt' phase of operations (16 December–27 December), and then in the offensive follow-up. The 12th Army Group commander, General Omar Bradley, stated after the war that, during the defensive phase, 'the greatest benefit derived from the tactical air force *was in the offensive action of the fighter-bomber in blunting the power of the armoured thrust*, and striking specific targets on the front of the ground troops'.[69] The most productive attacks, in the judgement of German forces, were those directed against fuel dumps and fuel trucks, for they produced immediate effects on German mobility. For example, veterans of the 9th SS Panzer, the Hohenstaufen Division, credited the destruction of just one key truck (carrying three tons of gasoline) as the principal reason why they failed to seize Liege, for its loss held up the division's movement for two critical days.[70]

Interrogated after the war, General Bayerlein 'particularly noted the disastrous and calculated selection of fuel tank trucks as fighter-bomber targets. He and others have vivid memories of precious forward gasoline dumps lost through air attack.'[71] Bereft of fuel, Panzer divisions had to abandon increasingly scarce tanks on the side of the road: 53 from the battered Panzer Lehr division, which had been essentially reconstituted after St Lo, and 180 from the 6th SS Panzer Army.[72]

As at Normandy, air attacks denied mobility and forced the Germans to seek safety only in night movement. The Air Effects Committee of General Omar Bradley's 12th Army Group noted after interrogating von Kluge, Bayerlein and Field Marshal Gerd von Rundstedt (the commander of the Bulge offensive) that all three agreed 'that the mass employment of fighter bombers affects command decisions by making troop movements and supply uncertain, thus preventing command from replying with tactical manoeuvre to the moves of the attacker. German commanders agree that a considerable part of the art of war consists of concentrating more force at key points than the enemy; when mobility and manoeuvre are lost, the loss of battles and campaign follows.'[73] Von Rundstedt himself who, after the war, stated 'that the main reason for the failure of the Ardennes offensive was his own lack of fighters and reconnaissance planes the tremendous tactical air power of the Allies', a powerful argument both then and now on the importance of gaining and retaining air superiority, and the decisiveness of air power.[74] At war's end, Bradley and the 12th Army Group Air Effects Committee had no doubt about air power's impact on the *Wehrmacht*: interviews with captured personnel had revealed that 'From the high command to the soldier in the field, German opinion has been agreed that air power was the most striking aspect of allied superiority.'[75]

THE AIR CAMPAIGN AGAINST JAPAN:
THE OBVIATION OF INVASION

The entire Pacific campaign was a struggle to seize bases from which to project three-dimensional power against Japan, the twentieth-century power of the submarine and the aeroplane. As Eliot Cohen has written, 'By the spring of 1945, American army and naval aviators had demolished Japan's civilian and military industries, sunk most of the Japanese fleet, and established a virtual blockade of the Japanese islands (with the aid of US submarines). *Ground and purely naval forces had served mainly to seize and hold forward bases for the projection of air power.*'[76] Indeed, air power became so dominant that one US naval planner plaintively wrote in the midst of the war 'The danger is obvious of our amphibious campaign being turned into one that is auxiliary support to permit the AAF [the United States Army Air Forces] to get into a position to win the war.'[77] In fact, he need not have worried, for historians – rightly – have credited the victory in the Pacific to true joint and coalition warfare. But we should re-examine the purposes behind that joint and coalition warfare, for what becomes glaringly obvious is the conclusion of my first sentence in this section: the purpose of the Pacific campaign was to secure bases ever closer to the Home Islands from which to project the power of the aeroplane and the submarine. If the end goal was to set the stage for an invasion – an invasion that never came, of course – it was a goal to be pursued by means other than the traditional clash of great armies on a field of battle.

In that context, dominating Japan's naval power was paramount, and, in a series of sharp and costly maritime air actions, this was accomplished, starting at Coral Sea, working through the climactic Battle of Midway – truly a turning point – and on to the offensive with the invasion of Guadalcanal and the Solomons, and the beginning of a long campaign through the south and central Pacific that would culminate in the horrific battle for Okinawa. Supporting this were the operations in the China–Burma–India theatre, operations which themselves were critically reliant upon air power, in particular the emerging power of long-range air transportation.[78]

For the Allies, Guadalcanal, a six-month struggle from August 1942 to early February 1943, assumed vital importance. Defeat might have stymied US Pacific strategy for an additional year or two, and allowed Japan the opportunity to rebuild and expand its naval aviation forces devastated by the loss of four carriers at Midway. As with the Battle of Britain, control of the air assumed decisive importance, and, for that matter, the entire campaign was really about securing control over an airfield deemed overwhelmingly significant by both sides.[79] Overall, Japan lost 446 fighters, bombers, and torpedo planes and the United States 264 of its own. But even though this technically gave US airmen 'air superiority', in reality prospects of victory see-sawed for months between the Americans and the Japanese, largely because the United States lacked clear and overwhelming air supremacy that would have greatly eased both air and surface operations. Guadalcanal, in the words of Richard Frank, 'took the aspect of a large-scale attritional battle where the outcome is gauged principally in overall crew and aircraft casualties'.[80]

At the end of the Guadalcanal campaign, the telling advantages the United States would possess over Japan had clearly emerged: newer and better aeroplanes (for example, the AAF P-38 Lightning and the Marine F4U Corsair), massive logistics, better intelligence. All this was soon applied in dramatic fashion against Japanese forces, beginning from the Solomons through New Guinea, particularly in long-range operations. Four particular operations deserve special mention: the air isolation of New Guinea in 1943, naval air operations against Japanese naval forces and merchant shipping, China and Philippine-based air operations against Japanese convoys in the South China Sea, and, finally, the mining campaign against Japan in 1945.

The New Guinea air campaign is a classic of joint and combined operations that has, unfortunately, been too long neglected. Allied defensive air power first saved New Guinea against an abortive Japanese invasion at Milne Bay, in August 1942; failure likely would have left New Guinea in the hands of the Japanese.[81] The Battle of the Bismarck Sea in March 1943, where American and Australian air attacks devastated a Japanese supply convoy, sinking all eight transports and four of eight escorting destroyers, has come to symbolize the productive use of maritime air power. The product of rigorous training, excellent intelligence, imaginative tactics and good leadership, Bismarck Sea essentially led to New Guinea's being placed under an Allied air blockade that remorselessly cut off Japanese forces from any hope of meaningful resupply.[82]

Long-range land-based maritime patrol missions by naval and Army Air Forces airmen were very productive, and, as in the European and Mediterranean theatres, the symbiotic partnership between joint-service carrier planes, landplanes and submarines was a significant one. In February 1944, for example, submarine attack had bottled up Japanese shipping in Truk harbour, permitting two days of carrier raids to sink 186,000 tons of shipping. Navy land-based long-range patrol bombers reconnoitred Singapore harbour, monitoring the progress of repairs on damaged Japanese ships; when the moment was right and the ships left port, submarines promptly sank them. Off the China coast, subs and aircraft worked well together. Marauding submarines forced convoys to sail closer to the China coast; then, alerted by ULTRA and cued by radar-equipped 'snoopers', air attacks by ship-busters took a heavy toll. As a result, Japan's transportation network withered.[83] By the end of 1944, air power (both by land-based and sea-based aircraft) was dominant. In the words of one submariner skipper, 'we had passed the high-water mark of submarine activity. It had become an aviator's, not a submariner's war.'[84] In the summer of 1945, air attacks dominated Japanese ship sinkings; in July 1945, US submarines accounted for 14 ships. But during that same month, aircraft attacks accounted for 129 ships.[85]

For the Allies, the value of air power against Japan's maritime forces was profound, as post-war analysis clearly indicates. The post-war study by a joint US Army and US Navy assessment committee (JANAC) of the maritime war against Japan offers a remarkable look at what air power did in the naval war context, even allowing for its conservative approach to mine casualties. Japan lost a total of 2,728 ships representing 9,736,068 total tonnage. Submarines sank 48 per cent (1,314) of this total and aircraft and aerial mines sank 45 per cent (1,232). Further, in concert with other attackers, aircraft sank an additional 2 per cent (46 ships). Therefore, air power forces, directly, indirectly, or partnered with other attackers, were responsible for 47 per cent of Japan's losses, totalling 4,066,380 tons, and of this total, land-based Army Air Forces aircraft sank fully 46 per cent – 567 ships representing 1,282,192 tons.[86]

By late 1944, US forces were at last in a position to bring to bear strategic air power against Japan's Home Islands. As with the bombing campaign in Europe, there was a 'ramping up' aspect to this campaign, as commanders found what worked and what did not, and the full fury of the assault did not come until the spring of 1945, particularly after (as is well known) the switch from a campaign based in China to a campaign based in the Marianas islands, and from high-altitude to low-altitude operations. Additionally, by mid-1945, Japan was under assault from attackers based in Okinawa and other bases, and from carrier task forces raiding from the sea. In short, the full-fledged air assault that had previously been directed at the outposts of the Japanese empire was now focused on the Home Islands themselves.[87]

From its pre-war origins, the B-29 had been developed specifically to strike at Japan. That the United States could undertake a strategic bombing offensive against Japan was a direct result of Franklin Roosevelt's own attitudes. Roosevelt saw bombing as a very important means of coming to grips with the Axis; in one notable Congressional address he stated that the foes of democracy would be bombed 'heavily and relentlessly', and that they had 'asked for it and they are going to get it'.[88] Indeed, in early 1940, he had participated in discussions about possibly transferring B-17 bombers to China for use against Japan.[89]

The first B-29 combat operations began on 5 June 1944, when XX Bomber Command sent 98 Superfortresses against a railway centre in Thailand. On 14 June, it made its first appearance over Japan, in a disappointing raid against the Yawata steelworks. It should not be surprising that the problems of operating a token force of bombers from China, demanding that the bombers do their own logistical support as well, and then flying them into a heavily defended country, led to mediocre results. By January 1945, the XX Bomber Command had dropped about 800 tons of bombs on the Home Islands, but then, the XXI Bomber Command was ready to begin its own campaign from the Marianas.[90]

As early as the battle for the Marianas – seized to serve as bases for B-29 bomber operations against the Home Islands – Japan's wartime leaders had recognized that Japan was doomed once the very-long-range B-29 Superfortress strategic bomber entered combat. From that point on, Japan's leadership pinned their hopes on inflicting increasingly severe losses on the Allies, so as to win an accommodating peace rather than having to face a disastrous and ignominious surrender. B-29 operations were far from trouble-free: the plane had numerous teething problems, crews needed greater training, doctrinal differences abounded, and operational circumstances (including day bombing from high altitude, the problems of flying in the jet stream, and weather in general) all posed serious challenges to success. In time, it became a fearsome weapon, a low-altitude destroyer of cities and industry, credited by Japan's senior wartime leaders as the decisive threat that forced their surrender in August 1945, before any hostile troops arrived on Japan's shores.[91] For example, Japanese Prince Fumimaro Konoye stated after the war that 'the thing that brought about the determination to make peace was the prolonged bombing by the B-29s', and his colleague Premier Kantaro Suzuki elaborated upon this, stating morosely that 'It seemed to me unavoidable that in the long run Japan would be almost destroyed by air attack so that *merely on the basis of the B-29's alone* I was convinced that Japan should sue for peace. On top of the B-29 raids came the atomic bomb ... which was just one additional reason for giving in ... I myself, on the basis of the B-29 raids, felt that the cause was hopeless.'[92]

There is another aspect to the B-29 story, one that is particularly significant: the B-29 mining campaign in 1945.[93] This was a classic joint-service campaign, with the US Navy offering its mine expertise, and the US Army Air Forces (USAAF) providing the delivery tool. Shipping in the coastal waters of Japan constituted a lucrative target for the B-29, as Japan was heavily dependent upon coastal traffic for its survival; for example, during 1944, 80 per cent of all oil supplies, 80 per cent of all iron, 24 per cent of all coal, and 20 per cent of all food travelled by water.[94] Much of this traffic could not be targeted by marauding submarines, or, if it could, constituted a serious risk for the bold submariners. Mining constituted a potentially productive and safer alternative. Pacific mine-laying distinguished between an 'Outer Zone' (consisting of the south Pacific, south-west Pacific, central Pacific, and the China–Burma–India theatre) and an 'Inner Zone', which consisted of Japan's home waters. Allied aircraft, ships and submarines laid a grand total of 24,876 mines in Japanese waters. Land-based aircraft of the USAAF were responsible for dropping 14,969 mines, representing 70 per cent of the total of 21,389 aerial mines dropped against Japan. Flying primarily at night, B-29s of the XXI Bomber Command dropped all 12,135 mines deployed in Inner Zone attacks, drawn from five different kinds of magnetic, acoustic and pressure-sensitive weapons.[95]

After the war, the Navy subsequently credited B-29 mining with fully 60 per cent of all Japanese shipping losses between March and August 1945. Ship movements through the all-important Shimonoseki Straits decreased from 70,000 tons per day in March, to 35,000 tons in April, plunged to 7,500 tons in May, to 1,750 tons in June, staggered up to 8,000 tons in July, and finally dropped to only 1,500 tons of shipping per day in August.[96] Analysis indicated B-29-laid mines exploded under 606 Japanese ships, sinking 283 (46.7 per cent), damaging 137 (22.6 per cent) so severely that they could not return to service, and damaging the remaining 186 (30.7 per cent), but not fatally so.[97] Further, those ships that were damaged found no easy repairs: no less than 19 of 22 repair yards (86 per cent) were themselves closed from the mine 'blockade'.[98] (Overall, Allied mining accounted for a total of 961 Japanese vessels sunk or damaged during the Second World War.[99])

While it might have been expected that B-29 commanders – particularly General Curtis E. LeMay – would have resented the 'distraction' that mining offered away from attacks against the Japanese mainland, quite the opposite was true; one mine expert wrote 'It was the firm belief in and support of the mining effort by General LeMay himself that made the successful campaign possible at all.' It is striking that LeMay (like the RAF's 'Bomber' Harris before him) intuitively recognized the importance and value of the mining campaign as an integral part of his comprehensive strategic air effort against the enemy.[100]

The success of the B-29 in the strangling of Japan raises interesting questions regarding the relative effectiveness of aircraft versus submarine attack against Japanese shipping. Both aircraft and submarines were decisive in their own way, and both, as discussed earlier, claimed a nearly equal total of Japanese military and commercial shipping. Thus, there is credit enough to go around, and it is worth noting that, in any case, both were three-dimensional attackers striking at a two-dimensionally constrained surface opponent. But it is also worth noting that, at war's end, while 38 (81 per cent) of Japan's 47 separate convoy routes had been closed down, only 4 (9 per cent) of these were due to submarine threat, while 13 (28 per cent) were from the depredations of aircraft. (The remainder stemmed primarily from actual or threatened territorial loss.[101]) Further, B-29 mining operations were safer, more productive, and less costly than those of the submarine force.[102]

One can appreciate why the analysts of the post-war US Strategic Bombing Survey (USSBS) wrote that: 'The war against shipping was perhaps the most decisive single factor in the collapse of the Japanese economy and the logistic support of Japanese military and naval power … It is believed that [the B-29 mining] campaign, begun earlier and laid on with greater weight, would have reduced effective shipping nearly to the vanishing point. It would have produced a condition of crisis in Japan sooner than actually occurred.'[103]

Given the intransigence of the Japanese in the face of overwhelming Allied power of all forms, the dropping of the atomic bombs in 1945 must be seen not as necessary to win the war, but rather as necessary to win the war *quickly*: with far fewer Allied casualties – and certainly far fewer Japanese casualties – than would have otherwise accompanied an invasion of the Home Islands. The atomic attacks of 1945 were decisive in the sense that they forced, ultimately, even the most recalcitrant of Japanese militants to recognize the war was lost; from 6 August 1945 onwards, the only hope of the hard-core in Japan was that, somehow, the nation would choose to perish in some form of national ritual suicide. Fortunately (despite a coup attempt) cooler heads prevailed; if for no other reason, as indicated by the Emperor Hirohito's own proclamation to his people announcing the surrender of Japan, the atomic bombings had given an excuse to do something previously unthinkable in the history of the country: capitulate to foreign invaders. But as many recognized at the time, whether their interest was land-based or naval aviation, Japan had in any sense been mortally wounded by a variety of aerial attacks that had robbed it of its fleet, denied it the fruits of its industry, destroyed its cities and industrial areas, savaged its military installations, shot its air forces from the skies, and, ultimately, killed tens of thousands of its soldiers, sailors, airmen, war workers and civilians. Understandably, then, the authors of the post-war United States Strategic Bombing Survey concluded that the Pacific war record 'supports the findings in Germany that no nation can long survive the free exploitation of air weapons over its homeland. For the future it is important fully to grasp the fact that enemy planes enjoying control of the sky over one's head can be as disastrous to one's country as its occupation by physical invasion.'[104]

CONCLUSION

Over 60 years have passed since Nazi tanks raced across the Polish frontier while bombers streamed overhead, and we are approaching 70 since Japanese forces unleashed a war in China from which would spring the Pacific conflagration. As time goes on, mercifully, the baser passions that accompanied those times tend to cool. But there are some things that are well worth remembering about that conflict that time must not dim, that must not cool. We were in a momentous struggle and, yes, it was between the forces of good and the forces of evil. Certainly, with what we now know, it is hard to imagine two more monstrous states than Nazi Germany and Imperial Japan. And in that conflict, thank God, we had the joint and coalition air power that made *the* critical difference in the war. That, especially, must never be forgotten, particularly today as we see some who should know better argue in our various nations for the primacy of what are by now clearly outdated strategies and forces that emphasize victory through the close and costly fight. If there is one significant lesson from the Second World War, it is that there is nothing noble in the close fight. We should not, via bankrupt strategy and poor thought, make it a necessity; and we certainly should not make it a virtue.

Nearly a decade ago, the historian John Terraine offered some thoughts at a Royal Air Force Historical Society gathering in response to a question about lessons learned and lessons forgotten:

> One thing that frightens me most today, every time I open my newspaper, is the parallel between today and the attitudes of the 20s, and while we are talking about doctrine and dogma let us not leave out the 'anti-war' dogma. There is that extraordinary alliance between economists, pacifists, internationalists, and various other kinds of people who created the 'political correctness' of the 20s which astonishingly resembles the political correctness of today. And that absolutely frightens the daylights out of me. And where history *ought* to come in, if it is allowed half a chance is to enable people to spot these alarming resemblances, to realize what may be in store for them if they don't do something about it.[105]

As we face the uncertain and challenging world of the twenty-first century, let us not minimize or worse, forget, the contributions of air power that got us safely through the twentieth.

NOTES

1. See Clément Ader, *L'Aviation militaire* (Paris: Berger-Levrault Éditeurs, 1911), pp. 2–32. I thank Lt-Col. Steven Rinaldi, USAF, for bringing this work to my attention, which was reprinted and reissued by the Service historique de l'armée de l'Air, Paris, in 1990. See also Pierre Lissarrague, *Clément Ader: Inventeur d'Avions* (Toulouse: Bibliothèque Historique Privat, 1990), pp. 240–3.
2. Northcliffe quotes from Curtis Prendergast, *The First Aviators*, a volume in the Time-Life *Epic of Flight* series (Alexandria, VA: Time-Life Books, 1980), p. 27. See also Alfred Gollin, *No Longer an Island: Britain and the Wright Brothers, 1902–1909* (Stanford, CA: Stanford University Press, 1984), pp. 186–93; the *Daily Mail* air power quote is from page 194.
3. Michael Dewar, ed., *An Anthology of Military Quotations* (London: Robert Hale, 1990), p. 25; Henry Serrano Villard, *Contact! The Story of the Early Birds* (New York: Thomas Y. Crowell, 1968), p. 98.
4. Quoted in Maj.-Gen. A. S. H. Irwin and Lt-Col. D. C. Eccles, 'How Close Are We to the Long-Awaited Demise of the Main Battle Tank?', *British Army Review: The House Journal of the Army*, No. 117 (Dec. 1997), p. 3.
5. Quoted in John R. Cuneo, *The Air Weapon, 1914–1916*, Vol. II of *Winged Mars*

(Harrisburg, PA: Military Service Publishing, 1947), p. 128; see also Lee Kennett, *The First Air War, 1914–1918* (New York: The Free Press, 1991), p. 31.

6. Quoted in David Jordan, 'The Battle for the Skies: Sir Hugh Trenchard as Commander of the Royal Flying Corps', in Matthew Hughes and Matthew Seligmann, eds, *Leadership in Conflict, 1914–1918* (London: Leo Cooper, 2000). I thank Brigadier Jonathan Bailey, Director Royal Artillery, for bringing this to my attention.

7. Foch to Commander 3e Bureau, no. 6145, 23 Nov. 1916, reprinted in Bernard Pujo, 'L'evolution de la pensée du général Foch sur l'emploi de l'aviation en 1915–1916', in Institute d'histoire des conflits contemporains, Service historique de l'armée de l'air, et Fondation pour les etudes de defense nationale, *Colloque Air 1984* (Paris: École Militaire, Sept. 1984), p. 221.

8. Haig to CIGS, 15 Sep. 1917, in H. A. Jones, *The War in the Air: Being the Story of the Part Played in the Great War by the Royal Air Force* (Oxford: Clarendon Press, 1937), Appendix III, 'Sir Douglas Haig's Views on a Separate Air Service', p. 16.

9. Maj.-Gen. Heinz Guderian, *'Achtung – Panzer!' The Development of Armoured Forces, Their Tactics and Operational Potential* (London: Arms & Armour Press, 1996 edn.), p. 128.

10. John S. D. Eisenhower, *Strictly Personal* (Garden City, NY: Doubleday, 1974), p. 72; B. H. Liddell Hart, ed., with the assistance of Lucie-Maria Rommel, Manfred Rommel, and General Fritz Bayerlein, *The Rommel Papers* (New York: Harcourt, Brace, 1953), p. 491.

11. Goebbels Diary, 21 March 1945. Emphasis added.

12. *Daily Telegraph* (London), 6 June 1999.

13. Richard Overy, *The Battle of Britain: The Myth and the Reality* (New York: W. W. Norton, 2001).

14. Ibid., p. 134.

15. See Hitler War Directives 16, 17 and 18, and editor's commentary, in H. R. Trevor-Roper, ed., *Blitzkrieg to Defeat: Hitler's War Directives, 1939–1945* (New York: Holt, Rinehart & Winston, 1971 edn.), pp. 33–43.

16. For example, Franklin Roosevelt's 702nd Press Conference (17 Dec. 1940), and his famed 'Arsenal of Democracy' speech (29 Dec. 1940), reprinted in Franklin D. Roosevelt, *The Public Papers and Addresses of Franklin D. Roosevelt, 1940 Volume: War and Aid to Democracies* (New York: Macmillan, 1941); see particularly pp. 606–8, and 640; Langer and Gleason, *Undeclared War*, p. 175.

17. A notable exception – and the best short account – is John Terraine's masterful *A Time for Courage: The Royal Air Force in the European War, 1939–1945* (New York: Macmillan, 1985), published in Great Britain under the title *The Right of the Line*, which incorporates later analysis, interpretation and available materials than earlier (though still useful) accounts. Numerous fine pilot memoirs exist, from both sides.

18. There is a voluminous body of literature on the combined bomber offensive; the best source on the US campaign is Richard G. Davis's *Carl A. Spaatz and the Air War in Europe* (Washington, DC: Air Force History and Museums Program, 1993). For the British air campaign, see Denis Richards, *The Hardest Victory: RAF Bomber Command in the Second World War* (London: Hodder & Stoughton, 1995), and Derek Wood, ed., *Reaping the Whirlwind: A Symposium on the Strategic Bomber Offensive, 1939–45*, Bracknell Paper No. 4 (Bracknell: Royal Air Force Historical Society and the Royal Air Force Staff College, 26 March 1993).

19. Cordell Hull, *The Memoirs of Cordell Hull*, Vol. I (New York: Macmillan, 1948), p. 863. Churchill to Roosevelt, 15 May 1940, in Loewenheim, Harold D. Langley

and Manfred Jonas, eds, *Roosevelt and Churchill: Their Secret Wartime Correspondence* (New York: Saturday Review Press/E. P. Dutton & Co, 1975), p. 95; See also William L. Langer and S. Everitt Gleason, *The Challenge of Isolation: The Undeclared War, 1940–41* (New York: Harper, 1953), p. 18.

20. Marshal of the Royal Air Force Sir John Slessor, *The Central Blue: The Autobiography of Sir John Slessor, Marshal of the Royal Air Force* (New York: Frederick A. Praeger, 1957), pp. 298–9.

21. See Richard P. Hallion, 'The Luftwaffe in Poland and the West, 1939–1940', a paper presented at the Annual Meeting of the American Military Institute, Crystal City, Virginia, 29–31 March 1990. The *Luftwaffe* has been the subject of a great number of works, among the better of which are Edward L. Homze, *Arming the Luftwaffe: The Reich Air Ministry and the German Aircraft Industry, 1919–1939* (Lincoln, NE: University of Nebraska Press, 1976) an excellent study of its industrial and technological development; James S. Corum, *The Luftwaffe: Creating the Operational Air War, 1918–1940* (Lawrence, KS: University Press of Kansas, 1997), which examines its doctrinal underpinnings; Raymond L. Proctor, *Hitler's Luftwaffe in the Spanish Civil War* (Westport, CT: Greenwood Press, 1983), an excellent survey of its first combat experience; and Williamson Murray, *Strategy for Defeat: The Luftwaffe, 1933–1945* (Maxwell AFB, AL: Airpower Research Institute and Air University Press, Jan. 1983), the best and most comprehensive combat history of Hitler's air arm, subsequently commercially published as *Luftwaffe* (Baltimore, MD: The Nautical & Aviation Publishing Company of America, 1985), which complements W. H. Tantum IV and E. J. Hoffschmidt's *The Rise and Fall of the German Air Force* (Old Greenwich, CT: W. E. Inc., 1969), a reprint of a classic RAF Air Historical Branch study.

22. For information on these, see Horst Boog, 'German Air Intelligence in World War II', *Aerospace Historian*, XXXIII, 2 (June 1986), pp. 121–9; F. H. Hinsley, with E. E. Thomas, C. F. G. Ransom and R. C. Knight, *British Intelligence in the Second World War: Its Influence on Strategy and Operations*, Vol. I (London: HMSO, 1979), p. 177; R. J. Overy, *The Air War 1939–1945* (Chelsea, MI: Scarborough House Publishers, 1991 edn), pp. 28–9, 35; Telford Taylor, *The Breaking Wave: The Second World War in the Summer of 1940* (New York: Simon & Schuster, 1967), p. 102; Horst Boog, 'High Command and Leadership in the German Luftwaffe, 1935–1945', in Alfred F. Hurley and Robert C. Ehrhart, eds, *Air Power and Warfare: Proceedings of the 8th Military History Symposium* (Washington, DC: Office of Air Force History, 1979); Stephen L. McFarland and Wesley Phillips Newton, *To Command the Sky: The Battle for Air Superiority Over Germany, 1942–1944* (Washington, DC: Smithsonian Institution Press, 1991), p. 42; Paul Deichmann, *German Air Force Operations in Support of the Army* (Maxwell AFB, AL: Air University Press, June 1962), pp. 153–4; and Wilhelm Speidel's *The Campaign in Western Europe, 1939–1940: The German Air Force in the Polish Campaign of 1939*, manuscript (Maxwell AFB, AL: Air University Press, 1956), copy in the library of the Air Force History Support Office, Bolling AFB, DC (catalog number K113.107-151), Part 4, p. 361; Tantum and Hoffschmidt, *Rise and Fall of German Air Force*, pp. 57–64; Loss data from German Quartermaster records compiled by the RAF Air Historical Branch, and reprinted in Table III of Murray, *Strategy for Defeat*, p. 40; *Luftwaffe* operations staff IC, 'German Intelligence Appreciation of the RAF and Comparison with Current Luftwaffe Strength', *Oberkommando der Luftwaffe*, 16 July 1940, reprinted as Appendix K, in Francis K. Mason, *Battle over Britain* (London: McWhirter Twins, 1969), pp. 612–13, offers a good example of *Luftwaffe* underestimation of the RAF and its capabilities.

23. See Spaatz to General Henry H. Arnold, 31 July 1940, Spaatz Papers, Manuscript Division, Library of Congress, Washington DC (copy in the archives of the Air Force History Support Office, Bolling AFB, DC).

24. Carl Spaatz, 'Leaves from my Battle of Britain Diary', *Air Power Historian*, Vol. 4, No. 2 (April 1957), p. 75.

25. For an excellent survey of issues and questions on the Battle, see Air Commodore Henry Probert, RAF, and Sebastian Cox, eds, *The Battle Re-Thought: A Symposium on the Battle of Britain* (Bracknell: Royal Air Force Historical Society and the Royal Air Force Staff College, 25 June 1990).

26. Introduction to Appendix G, 'Some Extracts of General Auchinleck's Dispatch, Dated 19th June 1940', in Historical Section, Naval Staff, Admiralty, *Naval Operations of the Campaign in Norway, April–June 1940*, Battle Summary No. 17 of the *Naval Staff History Second World War* (London: HMSO, 1950), p. 162. This volume has now been reprinted with new introductions and edited by David Brown under the title *Naval Operations of the Campaign in Norway, April–June 1940* (London: Frank Cass, 2000). I wish to thank Capt. Christopher Page, RN, the Head, Naval Historical Branch, Ministry of Defence, for bringing this to my attention.

27. John Keegan, *The Price of Admiralty: The Evolution of Naval Warfare* (New York: Penguin Books, 1990 edn), p. 284.

28. Minoru Genda with Masataka Chihaya, 'How the Japanese Task Force Idea Materialized', in Donald M. Goldstein and Katherine V. Dillon, eds, *The Pearl Harbor Papers: Inside the Japanese Plans* (Washington, DC: Brassey's US, 1993), pp. 8–9, 11.

29. Marc' Antonio Bragadin, *The Italian Navy in World War II* (Annapolis, MD: US Naval Institute, 1957) p. 366.

30. Vice-Admiral Friedrich Ruge, *Der Seekrieg: The German Navy's Story, 1939–1945* (Annapolis, MD: US Naval Institute, 1957), p. 249.

31. For an excellent (and very welcome) analytical account of the RAF's anti-shipping war, see Christina J. M. Goulter, *A Forgotten Offensive: Royal Air Force Coastal Command's Anti-shipping Campaign, 1940–1945* (London: Frank Cass, 1995).

32. Arthur W. (Lord) Tedder, *Air Power in War* (London: Hodder & Stoughton, 1948), p. 58. A total of 920 coastal vessels were sunk. Across all Nazi vessels, a total of 1,475 enemy surface vessels (representing 1,654,670 tons of shipping) sank at sea or were destroyed in port by RAF attack, constituting 51 per cent of the total enemy losses of 2,885 ships (totalling 4,693,836 tons) destroyed by Allied sea and air action, captured, or scuttled from 1939 through 1945. A total of 437 of these ships (186 of which were warships) sank from direct air attack at sea, while 279 others (of which 152 were warships) were bombed and destroyed in port. Mines laid by Coastal Command and Bomber Command claimed an additional 759 ships, of which 215 were warships. These 759 represented fully 51 per cent of all ships lost to RAF air attack.

33. Clay Blair, *Hitler's U-Boat War*, Vol. II: *The Hunted, 1942–1945* (New York: Random House, 1998), p. 710. From a tabulation of 606 U-boat sinkings, Axel Niestlé credits aircraft with 53 per cent (324), and ships with 47 per cent (282). The official history of the Royal Navy in the war credits air attack with destroying 368 of 785 submarines Germany lost in the Second World War, fully 47 per cent. A further 48 U-boats (6 per cent) fell to combined air and surface ship attack. Thus 416 U-boats – 53 per cent of those lost – fell before air or combined air-and-sea attack. (Statistics are computed on the basis of data from Stephen W. Roskill, *The War at Sea, 1939–45*, Vol. 3 (London: HMSO, 1961), Appendices XX and

Y, Tables III and IV, pp. 457–61, 471–2. One unfortunate torpedo boat was sunk by air attack, salvaged, and bombed and sunk again.) See also Paul Kemp, *U-Boats Destroyed: German Submarine Losses in the World Wars* (Annapolis, MD: Naval Institute Press, 1997) for a boat-by-boat tally.

34. Brian McCue, *U-boats in the Bay of Biscay: An Essay in Operations Analysis* (Washington, DC: National Defense University Press, 1990), esp. pp. 154–6. See also Max Schoenfeld, *Stalking the U-boat: USAAF Offensive Antisubmarine Operations in World War II* (Washington, DC: Smithsonian Institution Press, 1995), esp. pp. 161–79.

35. Richards, *The Hardest Victory*, p. 47. See also Robin Neillands, *The Bomber War: Arthur Harris and the Allied Bomber Offensive, 1939–1945* (London: John Murray, 2001), p. 185; and Hilary St George Saunders, *The Fight is Won*, Vol. 3 of *Royal Air Force, 1939–1945* (London: HMSO, 1954), Appendix VII, p. 405. Data on the German response to the mining campaign are drawn from ACM Sir Arthur Harris's *Dispatch on War Operations: 23rd February, 1942, to 8th May, 1945*, first issued in classified form in October 1945 and recently reissued under the same title, edited by Sebastian Cox with additional material by Horst Boog (London: Frank Cass, 1995), p. 174.

36. Goulter, *A Forgotten Offensive*, p. 294.

37. Grand Admiral Karl Doenitz, *Memoirs: Ten Years and Twenty Days* (New York: Da Capo Press, 1997 edn.), p. 38.

38. Ibid., p. 165.

39. Peter Kemp, *The Escape of the Scharnhorst and Gneisenau* (Annapolis, MD: Naval Institute Press, 1975), pp. 63–72, 78–80; see also Richards, *The Hardest Victory*, *passim*.

40. For example, see General Walter Warlimont, *Inside Hitler's Headquarters, 1939–45* (Novato, CA: Presidio Press, n.d.), p. 228.

41. B. H. Liddell Hart, ed., with Lucie-Maria Rommel, Manfred Rommel and General Fritz Bayerlein, *The Rommel Papers* (New York: Harcourt, Brace, 1953), pp. 282–6. Emphasis added.

42. See Eduard Mark, *Aerial Interdiction in Three Wars* (Washington, DC: Air Force History and Museums Program, 1994), pp. 141–78; for the more traditional view, see F. M. Sallagar, *Operation 'Strangle' (Italy, Spring 1944): A Case Study of Tactical Air Interdiction*, RAND Report R-851-PR (Santa Monica, CA: RAND Corporation, 1972).

43. Mark, *Aerial Interdiction*, p. 141.

44. Maj.-Gen. Frido von Senger und Etterlin, *Neither Fear Nor Hope* (New York: Dutton, 1964), p. 224; the exact quote is 'a chess player who for three moves of his opponent has the right to make only one'.

45. See Williamson Murray, *Luftwaffe* (Baltimore, MD: Nautical & Aviation Publishing, 1985), pp. 223–32, undoubtedly the best survey of the rise and fall of Hitler's air force. The best account of the Allied winning of air superiority prior to D-Day is Stephen L. McFarland and Wesley Phillips Newton's superb *To Command the Sky: The Battle for Air Superiority Over Germany, 1942–1944* (Washington, DC: Smithsonian Institution Press, 1994).

46. See John S. D. Eisenhower, *Strictly Personal*, p. 72.

47. Testimony of General Dwight D. Eisenhower, in US Senate, Committee on Military Affairs, *Department of Armed Forces and Military Security: Hearings on S. 84 and S. 1482* (Washington, DC: 79th Congress, 1st Session, 1945), p. 360.

48. Ruge, *Rommel in Normandy*, p. 15. See also pp. 26, 38, 64–6, 143, 152, 159, 167 and 172.

49. Adolph Galland, *The First and the Last: The Rise and Fall of the German Fighter*

Forces, 1938–1945 (New York: Henry Holt, 1954), p. 274.

50. Bodo Zimmermann, 'France, 1944', in Seymour Freidin and William Richardson, with Werner Kreipe *et al.*, *The Fatal Decisions* (New York: William Sloane Associates, 1956), p. 215.
51. Galland, *The First and the Last*, pp. 280–1.
52. Liddell Hart, *Rommel Papers*, p. 491.
53. Ruge, *Rommel in Normandy*, p. 187.
54. Liddell Hart, *Rommel Papers*, p. 491. There is a small but very informative exhibit on this accompanying a painting in the Royal Air Force Club, London, across from the Members' Bar.
55. Quoted in John S. D. Eisenhower, *The Bitter Woods* (New York: G. P. Putnam's Sons, 1969), p. 40.
56. Zimmermann, 'France, 1944', in Freidin *et al.*, *Fatal Decisions*, p. 227.
57. Gen. Fritz Bayerlein, 'Panzer-Lehr Division (24–25 July 44)', Manuscript A-902 (Historical Division, HQ US Army, Europe, n.d.), copy in the US Army Military History Institute Library, US Army War College, Carlisle Barracks, PA.
58. General Dwight D. Eisenhower, *Supreme Commander's Despatch for Operations in Northwest Europe, 6 June 1944–8 May 1945* (SHAEF, n.d.), pp. 43–4. Document catalogued as D756 A24c c.2, in the US Army Military History Institute Library.
59. For a perspective on Allied air operations at this time, see Thomas Alexander Hughes, *Overlord: General Pete Quesada and the Triumph of Tactical Air Power in World War II* (New York: The Free Press, 1995).
60. For an overview of Falaise, see Max Hasting's *Overlord: D-Day and the Battle for Normandy* (New York: Simon & Schuster, 1984).
61. Hilary St George Saunders, *Royal Air Force 1939–1945*, Vol. III, *The Fight is Won* (London: HMSO, 1954), p. 136.
62. Maj.-Gen. Rudolf-Christoph von Gersdorff, 'Northern France: vol 5 [Fifth Panzer Army (25 Jul–25 Aug 44)]', Manuscript B-726 (Historical Division, HQ US Army, Europe, n.d.), pp. 33–4, and 'The Argentan–Falaise Pocket', Manuscript A-919 (Historical Division, HQ US Army, Europe, 1954), pp. 5–6; copies of both are in the US Army Military History Institute Library.
63. Dwight D. Eisenhower, *Crusade in Europe* (Garden City, NY: Doubleday, 1948), p. 279.
64. Quote is from United States Strategic Bombing Survey (USSBS), *The Impact of the Allied Air Effort on German Logistics* (Washington, DC: USSBS, Military Analysis Division, Jan. 1947 edn.), Ch. VI, and 'Medical', Para. 216, p. 105, on Air Force Historical Research Agency Microfilm Roll A1128, Frame 1099 (call number 137.306-7). For additional material on this, see USSBS Interview #75, 'Interview with Professor Doctor Siegfried Handloser, Lt-Gen., Chief Medical Officer, *OKW* [*Oberkommando der Wehrmacht*, the High Command of the German Armed Forces] by Lt-Col. Richard L. Meiling, MC, Chief, Morale Division, USSBS, on 27 July 1945', reprinted as Appendix 2 of the USSBS, Consolidated Report of the Medical Sciences Branch (Washington, DC: USSBS Morale Division, 1945), available on AFHRA Microfilm Roll A1128, Frames 1974–1985 (call number 137.307-1). See also Group Captain (now Air Commodore) A. P. N. Lambert, RAF, *The Psychology of Air Power*, Royal United Services Institute for Defence Studies Whitehall Paper Series 1994 (London, RUSI, 1995), p. 13. I wish to thank Air Commodore Lambert for bringing this report to my attention.
65. Handloser interview. He further attributed 50 per cent of all German missing in action casualties to air attack. For the record (according to Handloser), Germany had the following medical losses from 1939 to 1945 among the *Wehrmacht*:

2,030,000 killed, 5,000,000 wounded and 2,000,000 missing.

66. Ladislas Farago, *Patton: Ordeal and Triumph* (New York: Dell Publishing, 1970 edn), p. 658. A forthcoming history on the activities of the XIX TAC, *Air Power for Patton's Army* by David Spires, is being prepared for publication by the Air Force History and Museums Program.

67. Quoted in Warlimont, *Inside Hitler's Headquarters*, p. 492. For a perspective on this, see also 'Hitler's Speech to his Generals, 12 December, 1944', and Percy Schramm, 'The Preparations for the German Offensive in the Ardennes', both in Danny S. Parker, ed., *The Battle of the Bulge: The German View – Perspectives from Hitler's High Command* (London: Greenhill Books, 1999), pp. 5, 9–10, 18, 20, 23, 29, 32–4. Schramm, despite his first name, was a Nazi officer in Wehrmacht headquarters, charged with responsibility for keeping the official war diary.

68. Eisenhower, *Bitter Woods*, pp. 337–8; Hughes, *Overlord*, pp. 271–96. Patton was so pleased by the prayer that, when the weather cleared and 3rd Army had 18 groups of fighters and bombers, a division of the 8th AF, and some RAF air strikes all operating in support of it, he called the chaplain to his headquarters and awarded him the Bronze Star.

69. General Omar N. Bradley and the Air Effects Committee of the 12th Army Group, *Effect of Air Power on Military Operations: Western Europe*, a report prepared for the USSBS (HQ 12th Army Group, Air Effects Committee, n.d.), p. 157 (emphasis added). Copy in the US Army Military History Institute Library.

70. Ibid., p. 171.

71. Ibid.

72. Ibid.

73. Ibid., p. 181.

74. Ibid., p. 180.

75. Ibid.

76. Eliot A. Cohen, 'The Unsheltering Sky', *New Republic*, 204, No. 6 (11 Feb. 1991), p. 24. Emphasis added.

77. Quoted in Ronald H. Spector, *Eagle against the Sun: The American War with Japan* (New York: The Free Press, 1985), p. 485.

78. Many detailed accounts of these actions exist. The most useful include the following: Paul S. Dull, *A Battle History of the Imperial Japanese Navy, 1941–1945* (Annapolis, MD: Naval Institute Press, 1978); John B. Lundstrom, *The First Team: Pacific Naval Air Combat From Pearl Harbor to Midway* (Annapolis, MD: Naval Institute Press, 1984); Samuel Eliot Morison, *Coral Sea, Midway and Submarine Actions, May 1942–August 1942, and The Struggle for Guadalcanal, August 1942–February 1943*, Vols 4 and 5 of the *History of United States Naval Operations in World War II* (Boston, MA: Little, Brown, 1949); Walter Lord, *Incredible Victory* (New York: Pocket Books, 1968 edn), a superb narrative of the Battle of Midway; Mitsuo Fuchida and Masatake Okumiya, *Midway: The Battle that Doomed Japan* (Annapolis, MD, United States Naval Institute, 1955), an excellent assessment of Midway from the Japanese perspective; and Clark G. Reynolds, *The Fast Carriers: The Forging of an Air Navy* (Annapolis, MD: Naval Institute Press, 1992 edn), and Richard B. Frank, *Guadalcanal* (New York: Penguin Books, 1992).

79. For example, see Frank, *Guadalcanal*, p. 609.

80. Ibid.

81. Assistant Chief of Air Staff Intelligence – Historical Division, *Army Air Forces in the War Against Japan, 1941–1942*, n. 34 of the *Army Air Force Historical Studies* series (Washington, DC: HQ USAAF, June 1945), pp. 151–3. I have also

drawn from Gary Null's *Weapon of Denial: Air Power and the Battle for New Guinea*, a study in *The US Army Air Forces in World War II* series (Washington, DC: Air Force History and Museums Program, 1995). At least two other examples of air attack defeating amphibious forces exist: the abortive attempt in August 1936 by Loyalists to seize Majorca from the Nationalists during the Spanish Civil War, where Italian bombing of the landing forces precipitated their hasty withdrawal; and the far better known defeat of anti-Castro exile forces by Cuban air force attacks during the Bay of Pigs invasion.

82. There are a number of sources that discuss these matters, including the previously cited Null, *Weapon of Denial*; Lex McAulay, *Battle of the Bismarck Sea* (New York: St Martin's Press, 1991); James T. Murphy with A. B. Feuer, *Skip Bombing* (Westport, CT: Praeger, 1993); and Lawrence Cortesi, *Operation Bismarck Sea* (Canoga Park, CA: Major Books, 1977); see also Steve Birdsall's *Flying Buccaneers: The Illustrated Story of Kenney's Fifth Air Force* (Garden City, NY: Doubleday, 1977), which has an excellent account of the battle from the airmen's perspective. Finally, the command perspective is well covered in George C. Kenney's *General Kenney Reports* (Washington, DC: Office of Air Force History, 1987 edn). For a thorough assessment of Kenney as an air leader, see Herman S. Wolk, 'George C. Kenney: MacArthur's Premier Airman', in William M. Leary, ed., *We Shall Return! MacArthur's Commanders and the Defeat of Japan, 1942–1945* (Lexington, KY: University Press of Kentucky, 1988), pp. 88–114.

83. United States Strategic Bombing Survey, Transportation Division, *The War Against Japanese Transportation, 1941–1945* (Washington, DC: Government Printing Office (GPO), May 1947), p. 50; microfilm copy in the archives of the Air Force History Support Office, Bolling AFB, Washington, DC.

84. I. J. Galantin, *Take Her Deep! A Submarine Against Japan in World War II* (New York: Pocket Books, 1988), p. 256.

85. Ibid., pp. 292–3.

86. JANAC, Table II, p. vii. While some – notably submarine commanders whose wartime tallies were significantly revised downwards – have quibbled over numbers in the JANAC study, it is generally more favourable to the submarine than to other attackers; its multiple categories of data tend to fragment sea-and-land-based air power's contributions, and its first bar chart (p. v) is visually misleading. Additionally, as mentioned earlier, its mine statistics are so much at variance with other sources as to indicate that mining from all forms of minelayers has not been adequately treated. I wish to thank Jacob Neufeld of the Air Force History Support Office for making a copy of the JANAC report available to me.

87. There is a tremendous body of literature on this aspect of the air campaign against Japan, and little agreement among authors as to outcomes, values or ethics. The best analysis of the B-29 campaign against Japan is Kenneth P. Werrell's exhaustive *Blankets of Fire: US Bombers Over Japan During World War II* (Washington, DC: Smithsonian Institution Press, 1996). See also Maj.-Gen. Haywood S. Hansell, Jr, *The Strategic Air War Against Germany and Japan: A Memoir* (Washington, DC: Air Force History and Museums Program, 1986); Michael S. Sherry, *The Rise of American Air Power: The Creation of Armageddon* (New Haven, CT: Yale University Press, 1987); James Lea Cate and Wesley Frank Craven, eds, *The Army Air Forces in World War II*, Vol. 5, *The Pacific: Matterhorn to Nagasaki, June 1944 to August 1945* (Chicago, IL: University of Chicago Press, 1953); USSBS, *Summary Reports (European and Pacific Theaters)* (Maxwell AFB, AL: Air University Press, 1987); USSBS, *The Strategic Air Operation of Very Heavy Bombardment in the War Against Japan (Twentieth AF Final Report)*

(Washington, DC: USSBS, 1946); Ronald Schaffer, *Wings of Judgment: American Bombing in World War II* (New York: Oxford University Press, 1985); Curtis E. LeMay and Bill Yenne, *Superfortress: The B-29 and American Air Power* (New York: McGraw-Hill, 1988); Richard B. Frank, *Downfall: The End of the Imperial Japanese Empire* (New York: Random House, 1999); Daniel Haulman, *Hitting Home: The Air Offensive Against Japan* (Washington, DC: Air Force History and Museums Program, 1999), William M. Leary, 'The Strategic Air War Against Japan', and Theodore H. McNelly, 'The Decision to Drop the Atomic Bomb', in Jacob Neufeld *et al.*, *Pearl to V-J Day: World War II in the Pacific – Proceedings of a Symposium Sponsored by the Air Force History and Museums Program and the Air Force Historical Foundation* (Washington, DC: Air Force History and Museums Program, 2000).

88. Franklin D. Roosevelt, 'Report to Congress, Jan. 7, 1943', reprinted in Executive Office of the President, *The War Messages of Franklin D Roosevelt* (Washington, DC: GPO, 1943), p. 32.

89. Daniel Ford, *Flying Tigers: Claire Chennault and the American Volunteer Group* (Washington, DC: Smithsonian Institution Press, 1991), pp. 46–8.

90. Robert Frank Futrell, *Ideas, Concepts, Doctrine: Basic Thinking in the United States Air Force*, Vol. 1, *1907–1960* (Maxwell AFB, AL: Air University Press, 1989), p. 161; Craven and Cate, *Army Air Forces in World War II*, Vol. 5, pp. 58–91, 131–2.

91. See Werrell, *Blankets of Fire, passim.*

92. Both quotes are from James Lea Cate and Wesley Frank Craven, 'Victory', in *The Pacific: Matterhorn to Nagasaki, June 1944 to August 1945*, Vol. V of *The Army Air Forces in World War II*, ed. Craven and Cate (Chicago, IL: University of Chicago Press, 1953), p. 756.

93. Data in the following discussion are drawn from Ellis A. Johnson and David A. Katcher, *Mines against Japan* (Silver Spring, MD: Naval Ordnance Laboratory, 1973), *passim.* This is an excellent survey, first prepared in 1947 as a classified document. A caution to readers: the mine data in this document is far more favourable to mining as a weapon of war than the JANAC study cited subsequently. On the other hand, the JANAC study has such a questionable interpretation of mining – crediting only two ships sunk to Navy-dropped mines, for example – that I believe it is not reliable on the mine issue. The Johnson and Katcher study is so detailed and so internally consistent that I have accepted it as authoritative on the mining question. JANAC, on the other hand, is more reliable and more detailed on other forms of attack, notably by ships, aircraft and – especially – submarines. I have chosen therefore to rely on Johnson and Katcher on mining and JANAC for general submarine and aircraft data. See also AAF, *Starvation: Phase Analysis of Strategic Mining Blockade of the Japanese Empire* (HQ 20th Air Force A-3, 1945), in the files of the AFHRA (call number 760.491-1); and Major John S. Chilstrom, *Mines Away! The Significance of US Army Air Forces Minelaying in World War II* (Maxwell AFB, AL: School of Advanced Airpower Studies, May 1992).

94. AAF, *Starvation*, p. 4.

95. Johnson and Katcher, *Mines against Japan*, pp. 21–9, esp. Tables 3-1 and 3-3.

96. Ibid., Figure 7-16, pp. 132 and 133.

97. Craven and Cate, 'Victory', pp. 662–74, and Johnson and Katcher, *Mines against Japan*, p. 16.

98. Johnson and Katcher, *Mines against Japan*, p. 133.

99. Ibid., pp. 31–2, Table 3-4, 'Summary of Japanese Ship Casualties to Allied Mines (Based on Japanese Records)'.

100. Ibid., p. ix.

101. USSBS, *The War against Japanese Transportation*, p. 50.
102. Only counting sinkings, B-29 Inner Zone mining cost Japan 283 vessels lost over 4½ months, a monthly average of 63 ships. By comparison, submarine attacks by 190 subs cost Japan 1,314 vessels over 44½ months, a monthly average of 30 ships, thus averaging 6.92 ships sunk per submarine. But the B-29 mining force deployed against Japan was only approximately 40 aircraft, producing an average of 7.08 ships sunk per B-29. Thus, a $639,188 B-29 with a crew of 11 men achieved slightly better results than an approximately $3.6 million submarine with a crew of 85 men. Further, it cost the United States government only $90,281 in B-29 aircraft costs per Japanese ship sunk versus $520,231 in submarine costs per Japanese ship sunk. The overall force economic costs – just looking at the costs of the aircraft and submarines involved – makes for its own interesting comparison: $25,567,520 for the B-29 mining force vs $684,000,000 for the submarine force. The cost differential in human lives is even more sobering. For every airman lost on the Inner Zone mining campaign (a total of 103 men), Japan lost 2.75 ships; for every sailor lost in the submarine campaign (approximately 3,300), Japan only lost 0.40 ships. Additionally, the aircraft dropped a relatively 'stupid' and reasonably cheap weapon – the mine. The submarine fired a far more expensive miniature submersible, the self-propelled torpedo. In the mining campaign, the B-29s dropped 12,135 mines; in the submarine campaign, the Navy fired 14,748 torpedoes. Although fewer torpedoes were expended per sunken Japanese ship than mines (11.22 torpedoes vs 42.88 mines), mines clearly were a cheaper alternative and, more importantly, did not require the characteristically close and dangerous approach to enemy shipping and heavily armed escort vessels necessitated by the torpedo. In sum, then, aerial mining risked fewer lives, used fewer resources, and, proportionally, achieved far more with less than the much-heralded submarine campaign. Further, it is likely that submarine pickings of Japanese shipping over the spring and summer of 1945 were as lean as they were not because so many ships had already been sunk (as submarine adherents have traditionally claimed), but, rather, because so many were bottled up in port by the aerial mining campaign. And, finally, it must be remembered that, in the case of the B-29s, mining was incidental to the fundamental purpose of the airplanes – strategic bombing – whereas, for submarines, torpedo attacks on shipping were their *raison d'être*. See The Joint Army–Navy Assessment Committee, *Japanese Naval and Merchant Shipping Losses during World War II by All Causes* (Washington, DC: GPO, Feb. 1947), Table II, p. vii; Johnson and Katcher, *Mines against Japan*, pp. 17, 129; Clay Blair, Jr, *Silent Victory: The US Submarine War against Japan*, Vol. 2 (Philadelphia, PA: J. B. Lippincott, 1975), p. 853.
103. USSBS, *The War against Japanese Transportation*, pp. 6–8.
104. USSBS, *Summary Reports*, p. 110.
105. Derek Wood, ed., *The End of the Beginning: A Symposium on the Land/Air Co-operation in the Mediterranean War 1940–43* (Bracknell: Royal Air Force Historical Society and the Royal Air Force Staff College, 20 March 1992), p. 64.

6

Maritime Air Power and the Second World War: Britain, the USA and Japan

John Buckley

INTRODUCTION

The Second World War was undoubtedly the defining conflict in the development of maritime air power. Although the roots were firmly bedded in the past, and notably in the First World War, it was the campaigns against the Axis powers between 1939 and 1945 that witnessed the establishment of air power as a crucial and decisive factor in determining the outcome of maritime campaigns. Moreover, in two particular cases maritime air power was critical to the conduct and indeed outcome of the war. Undoubtedly, for both the Allies and the Axis powers, success in anti-submarine warfare was a linchpin of victory. Both the Western Allies, Britain in particular, and Japan were heavily reliant on the use of merchant shipping and maritime lines of communication to feed production and facilitate any expanded war effort, while, conversely, opposing powers saw great opportunity and merit in limiting or closing such maritime lines of supply. For the British, the threat came from German U-boats and surface vessels operating predominantly in the North Atlantic, while for Japan the crucial theatre was to be the maritime network linking the home islands to the resource rich areas of South-east Asia. Air power was a critical factor in respective success and failure in both campaigns.

However, while Japan's economy might be throttled by US submarines, the means of delivering a knock out blow to Japan itself was to become largely reliant on the ability of the US Navy to project US strength across the central Pacific, preparatory to invasion of Japan, or indeed to secure bases for long-range strategic bombing. The development of carrier-based aviation, its rise and fall in the Japanese Navy and ultimately its fulfilment in the US Navy of 1944–45, was the second key role played by maritime air power in the Second World War. Although carrier-based air power did play a role in the European theatre of operations, most obviously in the Battle of the Atlantic, it was in the Pacific in the battles between the US Navy and its Japanese counterpart that carrier aviation came of age. By 1944, the carrier-based task force or battlegroup had become the centrepiece of maritime power projection, clearly supplanting the battleship as the capital ship of future navies.

Moreover, maritime air power forcefully proved why the Allies were much more adept at modern industrial, perhaps total war, than their Axis counterparts, particularly the Japanese. Success in both the Pacific and the Atlantic was founded, in varying degrees, upon clear strategic appreciation, doctrinal flexibility, applied technological capability and considered resource-sensitive planning and production. In all these cases, the Allies proved much more successful than the Axis powers. Such strengths were amplified in the war against the German U-boat and against the Japanese merchant marine, and between the fleets of the Japanese and US Navies. Despite greater long-term preparation for war and in spite of supposed doctrinal superiority in the early stages of the conflict, the requirements of employing or defeating maritime air power confounded both Germany and Japan, though it was in the latter case that it proved most obviously terminal to continued belligerency. The Americans in the Pacific, the US Navy in particular, were able to focus clearly and rapidly on the pivotal role of air power in deciding the fate of Japan, while Britain's need to maintain the Atlantic lifeline was also quickly established as the key to any long-term success against Germany. In both cases, the Allies were willing and able to employ their superior skills to lay the foundations for victory, while simultaneously exposing the deficiencies of their Axis opponents.

AIR POWER AND THE WAR AGAINST THE SUBMARINE

For both Japan and Britain, the importance of defending maritime trade and communications was fundamental to any major war effort. Both were in similar geostrategic positions, being island groups weak in resources and heavily reliant on imports of raw materials. Yet, despite the evidence of 1917–18, on the outbreak of war in 1939 the British were in poor shape to defend their maritime trade routes. Suitable equipment, considered doctrine and appropriate planning were in short supply. Likewise the Japanese in 1941, for they had done little to investigate the lessons of the U-boat offensive in the First World War, and trade defence planning remained very low on the agenda on the outbreak of war.[1] Yet, during the Second World War the British and their Allies adapted to the demands of anti-submarine warfare relatively effectively and prevailed, bringing shipping losses under control and ultimately inflicting heavy casualties on the U-boat fleet. By contrast, the Japanese failed this test of organization, planning and application of resources, thus leaving their merchant marine to wither away, and with it the Japanese economy and war effort.

A simple examination of the losses and sinkings reveals the disparity in performance. The US lost less than one submarine a month in the Pacific to enemy action throughout the war, while the Axis powers suffered losses of over ten per month.[2] Indeed, the US Navy lost only 11 submarines to Japanese aircraft either independently or in combination with surface units, while RAF Coastal Command alone accounted for 191 U-boats.[3] German loss rates of operational U-boats for the war reached a shade under 84 per cent, while similar US losses were less than 16 per cent.[4] In terms of tonnage sunk per submarine lost, the Allied forces suffered the average monthly loss of some 27,000 tons of shipping for each U-boat destroyed and by late 1943 this figure was running at 3,000 tons and remained so for the rest of the war.[5] By contrast, the Japanese lost 150,000 tons of shipping per month throughout the entire war for each US submarine eliminated.[6] Clearly, the Allies proved much more adept at dealing with the exigencies of the anti-submarine war than the Japanese, despite its critical importance for both. It is therefore crucial to examine the degree to which air power resources and doctrine adapted to the needs of national strategy in Britain while it failed palpably to do so in Japan.

Whatever the failings of British anti-submarine air power in 1939, once the problems began to emerge measures were rapidly implemented to right the failings. The British were fortunate that until the late summer of 1940 the German U-boat fleet was incapable of doing much more damage than it did, owing to the small number of available U-boats and the geographical position of their bases. Once France had fallen, however, a major crisis began to emerge and was to last through to the late spring of 1941.

From mid-1940 onwards, the effective employment of aircraft in anti-submarine warfare by both the British and the Japanese would be determined by three key factors: inter-service co-operation, and in the case of the Allies international co-operation; the allocation of appropriate levels of resources concomitant with strategic need; and the development and employment of effective doctrine, to ensure that available resources were utilized to their utmost.

The RAF and the Royal Navy had not enjoyed an always harmonious relationship in the inter-war era, as the latter initially attempted to carve up the former in the 1920s and then endeavoured to retrieve maritime air power from the air force in the 1930s. On the outbreak of war in 1939, however, agreement had been reached between the Air Staff and the Admiralty over the employment of land-based maritime air power, a role centred on naval reconnaissance for the fleet. The Royal Navy believed the U-boat to have been defeated by *asdic* (echo-sounder) and convoy, and that any serious threat to British shipping would come from German surface vessels. The RAF accepted this view, despite reservations over the vulnerability of convoys to air attack. This policy was rapidly exposed in the first few months of the war as U-boats again became a problem, and a reinvention of the employment of air power in the defence of British sea lanes was undertaken with the RAF and the Royal Navy working closely together. RAF Coastal Command's role was recast in early 1940 when the Admiralty and the Air Staff acknowledged that even small numbers of U-boats were inflicting too much damage on Britain's merchant fleet. From that point on, the anti-U-boat war became the priority in Coastal Command. The Admiralty also abandoned its hunter-killer groups centred on fleet aircraft carriers following the loss of HMS *Courageous* and a near miss involving the *Ark Royal*. The efficacy of waiting for the U-boats to come to the convoy was soon once again accepted and understood as it had been previously in 1917.[7]

However, some lingering inter-service issues spilled over into the Second World War, notably the issue of operational control of Coastal Command. It should be noted that after 1937 land-based maritime air power continued to reside in the hands of the RAF, despite the latter's indifference to the duties so involved. However, in November 1940, the Admiralty, greatly concerned over the inadequate resources available to Coastal Command, and with shipping losses soaring out of control began a campaign to elevate the importance of maritime trade defence air power. The crucial nature of long-range air power in particular had been firmly established in the early autumn of 1940 and the Navy's prime concern was to enhance Coastal Command's resources as quickly as possible. The Admiralty issued a memorandum on 4 November 1940 arguing this precise case. Although some 400 aircraft were now available to Coastal Command, the First Lord of the Admiralty, A. V. Alexander, claimed a target of some 1,000 aircraft to be much closer to current needs.[8] The whole issue was discussed at the following day's Cabinet Defence Committee meeting, where Alexander clashed with Archibald Sinclair, the Secretary of State for Air. Lord Beaverbrook then escalated the debate by arguing for Coastal Command to be transferred in its entirety to the Royal Navy. However, the First Sea Lord, Dudley Pound, whilst accepting that such an absorption of Coastal Command was desired in the long term, the middle of a crisis was not the time to attempt it. Sinclair and Chief of the Air Staff, Charles Portal, were, unsurprisingly alarmed about having to squabble over ownership of Coastal Command, especially so when they considered that the Admiralty had effective operational control anyway. However, the genie was out of the lamp and Churchill called for a full investigation.[9]

What had started out as a simple effort to squeeze more resources out of the RAF for Coastal Command had developed into a row fired up by Beaverbrook. Jack Slessor, later an AOC-in-C (Air Officer Commanding-in-Chief), Coastal Command, squarely blamed the whole fracas on 'Beaverbrook's crass ignorance of air or sea warfare [which] was only excelled [*sic*] by the unsoundness of his judgement on anything connected with the conduct of the war.' By contrast, Slessor saw Alexander as being more responsible and focused on the matter in hand, winning the war against the U-boat.[10] Further indicating that the Admiralty was interested in the more pressing matter of resources for Coastal Command, than inter-service bickering, the Naval Staff responded to Churchill's inquiry by arguing against an immediate transfer of Coastal Command to the navy for a variety of logistical and organizational issues.[11] The Air Staff had also cannily agreed with the Admiralty to an expansion of Coastal Command in an effort to stymie the row. It was also agreed in the following month that operational control of Coastal Command was formally to switch to the Admiralty.[12] This in fact was little more than a cosmetic change, for many in the RAF believed that the Admiralty already had effective control of Coastal Command.[13] By early 1941, the shift in control, such as it was had taken place, but more importantly, as far as the Admiralty was concerned, an increase in resources had been agreed at a critical period in the Battle of the Atlantic.

The operational control issue demonstrated that the Navy and the Air Force, despite historical tensions were willing to deal and compromise and not use the war to gain institutional debating points, if wider and greater issues were at stake. For most of the war, the ongoing resource debate aside, the RAF and the Royal Navy co-operated very effectively, with close-knit systems of communications and co-ordination being established that were to bear fruit in the ensuing years. The British had rapidly come to accept that an anti-submarine campaign being fought over the Atlantic required centralized intelligence-driven control to maximize available resources and in the case of air power, to direct specialized units to crucial duties.

This acceptance of a high level of centralized command and co-ordination was to be less apparent when the USA joined the war effort in 1941. Centralized operational control was anathema to US Naval thinking and both the navy and the USAAF were unwilling to co-operate closely with each other, let alone the RAF and the Royal Navy. Getting two services to work together was difficult enough, but doubling the problem and inserting national differences into the equation made close co-operation something of a chimera.

The Americans had particular problems that precluded the always rational employment of air assets to the anti-submarine war, with water-based aircraft being deployed by the navy, and land-based patrol aircraft by the Army Air Force. To compound matters, the headquarters of US Navy and Army anti-submarine branches were situated on the same floor of the same building, but acted totally independently of each other. The British suggested that the United States adopt a unified air command structure, similar to Coastal Command, but the Americans rejected the idea.[14] Rivalry between the US Navy and the USAAF also plagued the allocation of resources to Coastal Command in 1942, resulting in shortages of crucial aircraft.[15]

Nevertheless, despite such problems and others centred on the personality of Admiral Ernest King and his unsympathetic opinion of the British and the Royal Navy, measures were taken to alleviate the difficulties inherent in such a multi-service and multi-national organization. Control of US anti-submarine air power was eventually concentrated in the Navy, which brought the RAF into closer contact with the US Navy, though King never acknowledged the existence of Coastal Command at any point. However, eliminating the USAAF from the loop certainly aided co-operation.

Efforts to create an Atlantic central command for air assets foundered throughout 1942, with Coastal Command's Commander-in-Chief Philip Joubert de la Ferté's initiatives being constantly blocked by the US services.[16] Ultimately, the British backed away from this solution, as they believed that only the Royal Navy had the expertise to direct the anti-U-boat war and that the Americans would never agree to British command.[17] However, the downturn in the Atlantic campaign focused attention, and the Allied services received encouragement from the Casablanca Conference to find a solution to the problem of the Atlantic sea lanes. In March 1943, King organized the Atlantic Convoy Conference, partly in an effort to short-circuit the growing clamour for a centralized command structure. Many anomalies in the existing organization were eliminated, but significant over-arching change was avoided, and in the next few weeks, before the findings of the conference could be properly acted upon, the Battle of the Atlantic turned decisively in favour of the Allies.[18] Nevertheless, the conference and its results did demonstrate that even recalcitrant neighbours such as the RAF and US Navy could resolve differences, if the circumstances dictated, and in late 1942 they did.

Resource allocation was another area in which the British initially and then the Allies proved themselves adaptable and flexible, just. The continuing debate between the Admiralty and the Air Staff over the requirements for Coastal Command persisted throughout the crucial period of the Atlantic campaign. In 1940–41, Coastal Command and the Admiralty were desperate for any aircraft to cover convoys, but by 1942 this had been replaced by specific requirements for long- and then very-long-range aircraft. It was this latter debate in particular that caused problems as such aircraft were those precisely required by the bomber fleets. Despite Churchill's proclamation of the Battle of the Atlantic on 6 March 1941, Coastal Command remained weak in key aircraft, notably those capable of long-range operations and those able to carry ASV (air-to-surface-vessel radar/RDF). The problem of covering convoys close to the British Isles had been successfully solved with the reallocation of a hotch-potch of aircraft types to maritime patrolling over the winter on 1940–41, with the result that U-boats began operating further out into the Atlantic, beyond the range of many of Coastal Command's aircraft.

In February 1941 Bowhill, AOC-in-C, Coastal Command, outlined his command's deficiencies, stating that few aircraft were equipped with LRASV (ASVII, radar with a wavelength of 1.5 metres), he was short of long-range Sunderland flying boats, and that, apart from his understrength Beaufort torpedo-bomber squadrons, he had no specifically designed land-based maritime aircraft. He pointed out that it was asking a good deal of pilots to use aircraft such as the Whitley or the Wellington on long-range maritime operations when pilots were well aware that they could not fly should an engine give out.[19] The allocation of air resources to Coastal Command remained low in key areas, and its commanders had to fight tooth and nail to hold on to what they had, but the Atlantic situation eased in the summer of 1941 and demands for new four-engined bombers to be diverted to maritime operations were shelved.

The crisis re-emerged in the summer of 1942, when U-boats concentrated their efforts in the central Atlantic, away from all but the very-long-range aircraft of Coastal Command. Thus began the most protracted and bitter debate over the allocation of resources to the maritime air war. In early 1942 the Admiralty and Coastal Command, recognizing that the sea lanes were vulnerable in the central Atlantic, requested the allocation of nine squadrons of Flying Fortresses or Liberators to Coastal Command. The Air Staff demurred arguing that Sunderlands, Catalinas and a small number of Fortresses were pencilled in for delivery to Coastal Command from June onwards. The Admiralty was unconvinced and Joubert de la Ferté underpinned this view by pointing out that other deliveries of important aircraft, such as Liberators, were late and there was little sign of them arriving.[20] The debate continued throughout the summer with memoranda, papers and notes circulating between the Admiralty, Coastal Command, the Air

Staff and the Cabinet. In May, Coastal Command was effectively informed that it would have to get by until the Air Ministry's expansion scheme yielded Liberators and Flying Fortresses in early 1943.[21] The Admiralty and Coastal Command were dismayed at this, and there was even brief discussion of mass resignations on the part of the Sea Lords to make the point forcibly.[22] The Air Staff also benefited from the support of Churchill, who, as late as October 1942, just prior to the worst month for Allied shipping losses of the whole war, stated that, 'at present, in spite of U-boat losses [sic], the bomber offensive should have first place our effort'.[23]

However, the following month the crisis escalated and at the second and third meetings of the newly established Anti-U-boat War Committee, Churchill and Portal finally accepted that priority must in the short term be given to the defence of shipping, and importantly to the closing of the mid-Atlantic air gap. Joubert pointed out that 40 VLR Liberator aircraft would have been sufficient to close the air gap and that this would have prevented or at least alleviated the crisis in the first place.[24] However, once the problem had been accepted the Allies worked hard to find the required numbers of Liberators to close the air gap, and though it took until spring 1943 for them so to do, the political decision had been made and the appropriate application of resources made. It was undoubtedly a close-run thing and criticism can be levelled at certain individuals for allowing the crisis to develop to the heights that it did, but the Allies were able, ultimately, to identify the crisis and allocate the resources to deal with the problem.

The British also demonstrated considerable technical and doctrinal flexibility in the anti-submarine war. The role envisaged for Coastal Command in 1939 was one which centred largely on naval co-operation, or acting as the eyes for the fleet when it sallied forth to deal with German surface vessels.[25] Working with convoys or offensive anti-submarine warfare was low on the agenda and prior to the outbreak of war the principal anti-U-boat weapon, the anti-submarine bomb, had not been tested against a submarine, and there had been no significant study of how to attack a U-boat from the air, nor what the consequences of poor visibility or night-time might be for locating targets.

However, over the next three years Coastal Command was to be rapidly transformed into a highly effective anti-submarine force. The emphasis was shifted quickly towards anti-submarine warfare but, two critical issues remained to be solved, beyond acquiring sufficient long-range aircraft. First, although air cover was effective in daylight, at night-time or in poor visibility, the value of air support for convoys waned. Second, Coastal Command aircraft lacked the necessary offensive kit to take a toll of U-boats. Until these problems could be solved aircraft could act only as scarecrows, scaring U-boats off without being able to destroy them. The scarecrow effect should not be downplayed however, as in the first U-boat crisis in 1940–41, air power played a crucial role in helping to bring shipping losses under control, yet proved unable to sink German submarines.

At the beginning of the war, offensive weaponry in Coastal Command had consisted of the anti-submarine bomb, a device that curiously had never been fully tested against a submarine. The inadequacies of this weapon soon became self-evident and as early as November 1939 a programme designed to press depth-charges into use was introduced at the Vernon Torpedo and Mining Establishment in Portsmouth.[26] By the summer of 1940 a modified Mark VII naval depth-charge had been introduced and the lethality of Coastal Command attacks on U-boats became a potential reality, if the U-boats could be located.[27]

It was this point that prompted the most significant re-evaluation of Coastal Command doctrine when the introduction of operational research began in 1941. Such technical and theoretical innovation was a key factor in the creation of an effective and potent anti-submarine air arm in Britain by 1942. It was an approach that emphasized a modern concept of the conduct of war, but one that was to prove crucial to success. Joubert de la Ferté had already been appointed to lead Coastal Command, with the brief to build up the technological side of the force, for it was clear that the integration of LRASV (ASV II) into the aircrews' operating practice was spotty. Indeed, many were simply using the radar equipment as a navigational tool.[28] Yet with the creation of the Operational Research Section at Coastal Command in 1941, change was widespread and profound in its effectiveness. In 1941, the lethality of air attacks on U-boats was around 2–3 per cent, but by 1944 it had been increased to 40 per cent.

The successive introduction of new practices, careful evaluation of operational procedures and the arrival of new equipment, shaped and modified by the scientific analyses of the Operational Research Section (ORS), transformed Coastal Command. In 1942 and 1943 Coastal Command claimed 30 per cent and 35 per cent respectively of the total U-boat kills attributed to Allied action, helping significantly to defeat the U-boat fleet and win the Battle of the Atlantic.[29]

In all three cases of service co-operation, resource allocation and doctrinal innovation and flexibility, the British and the Allies had demonstrated just enough acumen to achieve the necessary aim of survival against the U-boat fleet. For the Japanese and their military and political institutions this proved unattainable. Despite a myriad of difficulties that faced the American submariners, most notably the lack of a reliable torpedo until mid-1943, the Japanese had lost some 50 per cent of their merchant fleet, including replacements and two-thirds of the tanker fleet by the end of 1944.[30] By the end of the war, the combined merchant marine had been cut by 77 per cent with US submarines taking the greatest toll, sinking almost 60 per cent of the total.[31]

The employment of Japanese air units to protect merchant shipping proved wholly inadequate, being poorly planned, inadequately resourced and too inflexible to be responsive to the demands of the US submarine threat. That the crisis emerged quickly is not in doubt, but the Japanese failed to adapt quickly, and rapidly came to pay the price. The unwillingness of the Japanese Navy and the Army to co-operate meaningfully in a whole variety of areas is well documented and it spilled over into the aerial anti-submarine war, with the Army providing escorts only for its own convoys, and then not always. However, even when available it was of little value as the army pilots had no maritime navigational training and their ability to communicate either with merchant vessels or naval escorts was very limited. It was to take until 1944 for the Army to take convoy escorting more seriously, but inter-service bickering persisted and undermined efforts.[32] However, the Army squarely blamed the navy for the mounting shipping losses.[33]

The allocation of air resources to convoy protection was non-existent at the outbreak of war, and the establishment of increased numbers came slowly and ultimately too late and too little. The navy had made four air groups available for escort duties soon after the outbreak of hostilities, but only as a secondary role.[34] This approach was bolstered by the Navy's pre-war estimates of likely shipping losses to enemy action, which were considered well within acceptable limits.[35] However, as the situation deteriorated in 1943, the Navy General Staff set up Grand Escort HQ with the 901st Naval Air Unit attached, the first air unit specifically assigned to maritime escort duties. It consisted of 80 Mitsubishi G4M2 Betty twin-engined bombers and Kawanishi H8K2 Emily flying boats, both types with more than adequate range and payload capabilities, though they were distinctly inferior to an aircraft such as the US B-24.[36] The Japanese aircraft were often deficient in technological aids, with many malfunctioning radios and limited supplies of radar equipment. Although the Japanese produced some 2,000 airborne radar sets during the war, an aircraft actually carrying a set was a rarity before July 1944.[37] Those that were available were often not reliable, and with a range of only ten miles crews often relied on eyesight for detection. Nothing was done to examine the effectiveness of this practice, and this stands in stark contrast to the British approach where the ORS demonstrated that radar equipment could be more appropriate in many operating conditions.

In addition to the land-based air power elements, the Japanese Navy also directed four small aircraft carriers to escort duties, though this was admittedly small fry compared with the 120 commissioned by the US and Royal Navies in the Second World War. In addition, the Japanese carriers required extensive repairs and were not serviceable until mid-1944. Moreover, with inadequately equipped aircraft and poorly trained aircrew, the carriers proved to be little more than liabilities, with three being sunk on their maiden escort voyages in 1944. The fourth never left port.[38] The aircrew who survived these disasters were then transferred back to the main fleet, rather than used to expand the anti-submarine air strength.[39] It is clear that, throughout the campaign, resources allocated by the Japanese armed forces to anti-submarine warfare were hopelessly inadequate for the task confronting them, and the consequences were to be profound for the Japanese State.

The approach to anti-submarine doctrine was also flawed in the Japanese armed services from the off. Staff officers viewed anti-submarine warfare as common sense, requiring only basic organizational skills. This attitude permeated the Navy, where the best officers were focused on preparing and planning for the grand fleet action expected to decide the war. Prior to the establishment of 901st Air Unit in December 1943, there had been no considered investigation into aerial anti-submarine doctrine, and even this newly created unit was thrown into action with woefully inadequate preparation due to the increasing severity of shipping losses.[40] The Navy eventually reacted by setting up the Air Group Anti-Submarine Research Section at Yokosuka, and a specially designed maritime escort and patrol aircraft (Q1W1 Tokai Lorna) was designed and produced in small quantities, though only some 20 saw action before the end of the war.

The Japanese were undoubtedly sluggish in the development of aerial maritime trade defence forces and doctrine, but they were not incapable. Localized units developed effective tactics, occasionally gaining the respect of US submariners, but such efforts were sporadic. Each district often employed very different tactics with varying degrees of success, and the Navy was always desperately short of aircraft and was reduced to sending unarmed training flights over the sea in the hope that this might deter US submarines.

Thus, in the three key areas the Japanese failed. Aerial anti-submarine warfare ranked very low in the priority of Navy and Army planners and strategists, and thus any chance of co-operation was unlikely. Allocation of resources was too late and too little to be effective and the development of appropriate tactics and doctrine was patchy, uncoordinated and driven by anecdotal evidence. The failings of the Japanese war effort were clearly evident in their trade defence policies, but more emphatically so. The British and the Allies demonstrated that errors and mistakes could be overcome, if flexibility and adaptability were maintained, and if the strategic view was sound. Organization, co-operation and planning were the cornerstones of success in the employment of airborne maritime patrol assets, and whereas the Allies adapted quickly enough and employed just enough resources to survive, the Japanese could not, shackled as they were by outdated martial orientated views of war.

CARRIER AVIATION

In the field of carrier aviation, however, Japanese air power seemed in 1941–42 to be much more developed. This was an offensive and battle governed style of war for which the Japanese had been planning and training for years. Yet, even if initial success was based upon high capability and doctrinal superiority, by 1944 the US carrier fleet was clearly in the ascendancy and had adapted cleverly and effectively to the demands made of it by the unfolding war. The Japanese did not. The Imperial Fleet's view of carrier aviation was not so advanced and in some ways was clearly deficient, and the roots of this can be traced back to the pre-war era and the role envisaged for the carrier fleet in Japanese naval strategy.

Although the Japanese created a first-rate carrier strike force by 1941, it was a flawed weapon, and strategic vision and operational art had not adapted to incorporate this new method of fighting properly. Japanese planners had recognized the value of air power to the prosecution of a campaign against the US Navy since the late 1920s, though in a defensive and attritional manner. The defensive plan of luring the US fleet to a place of the Japanese Navy's choosing, wearing it down en route and then winning in a decisive grand-fleet action, had driven Japanese strategy for a decade until the appointment of Admiral Yamamoto in 1939. He recognized the offensive potential of carrier based aviation and swung behind the concept of a surprise air strike against Pearl Harbor, to get in the first blow against the US Navy.[41] It was not a new idea and had been discussed by eager naval students many times in the past, only for them to be castigated for not adhering to Japan's defensive strategy.[42] However, Yamamoto's strategy fused with the emerging operational ideas of Commander Minoru Genda, of creating a concentrated carrier strike force to deliver a knockout blow to the Americans. Genda had supposedly been inspired by the Royal Navy's Taranto raid, but also saw great benefit in concentrating carrier air power, for this would increase the aerial-defensive capability of carriers, whilst requiring proportionally fewer interceptors. In turn, this would allow the carriers to operate more bombers, thus increasing their striking potential.[43]

However, although the basic concept of the value of carrier battle groups had been acknowledged by the Japanese Naval staff, its implications were not fully appreciated. Japanese strategy did not adapt to the new method of fighting, even after the tremendous successes of the first few months of the war. Pre-war planning saw no greater role for the carrier fleet than that of a specialist arm, temporarily useful for knocking out the US fleet, and seizing territory and bases around the Pacific. Naval aviator training in Japan remained elitist and enormously wasteful, demonstrating that a major expansion of naval aviation was not envisaged.[44] Indeed, in spite of Genda's arguments, focus in the Japanese navy remained squarely on the surface fleet, with a grand decisive battle viewed as the natural endgame to any Pacific campaign. At the Battle of Midway, June 1942, Yamamoto effectively used his carriers as bait to lure out the US carriers, rather than placing them at the centre of a vast concentration of force, thus indicating the value placed upon them. The level of resources poured into the construction of the Yamato-class battleships also illustrated the degree of relative value placed on surface vessels and naval aviation. Indeed, the Japanese completed into service only one purpose-built fleet aircraft carrier in the Second World War, the others being conversions from liners and so on, often crude and unwieldy. Compared with the huge expansion of the US carrier fleet, and the corresponding cancellations of significant battleship production in 1942 and 1943, the Japanese production effort, even allowing for the great disparity in available resources demonstrated where their priorities lay.

The Japanese also failed to appreciate the growing importance of concentration of air assets in the Pacific campaign, unlike their US counterparts. Initial carrier doctrine in both navies viewed the operating method of the carrier taskforce as one of surprise and stealth, using the expanses of the Pacific in which to hide. Such a carrier force would launch a stinging attack and then disappear before a counter-blow could be made. The thinking ensured the effective employment of seaborne air power, whilst recognizing the weakness of carrier based aviation compared to its land-based cousin. A one or two carrier task force, once located, proved quite vulnerable either to land-based air attack, or more probably an air strike from a lurking enemy carrier group. Indeed, the worst position to be in was to have shown your hand to the enemy, be under observation, and not know the location of the enemy carrier force.

The first half of the war in the Pacific underpinned this view. Fleeting carrier groups proved vulnerable to surprise attacks and small penny packets of land-based air power. Moreover, co-ordinating air attacks from dispersed carrier groups proved exceptionally difficult. The Coral Sea, Midway and the battles of the South Pacific in late 1942 all witnessed to a greater or lesser degree small carrier groups being ambushed and carriers lost.

Both the US and Japanese navies were confronted with the same problem of how best to adapt carrier air power to these circumstances. The disparity in the respective overarching views of the role of the aircraft carrier and its importance to naval strategy was nowhere best illustrated in the response to this issue. The Japanese, reflecting their continuing predilection for the primacy of the obsolescent battleship, persisted with a cavalier attitude to air power. The available pool of highly trained naval aviators was already small and plans for expansion limited, but air assets continued to be dispersed over a wide area, even when it became clear that such a policy was causing the haemorrhaging of Japanese air power. Naval aviators were even based on land as the carriers were proving vulnerable, and in this manner over two-thirds of Japan's highly trained naval aviators were frittered away.[45] Japan's naval staff also persisted with dispersing carriers. At the Coral Sea, the Japanese had put two valuable fleet carriers at risk in order to support amphibious operations, and both consequently suffered damage and loss, leading to their withdrawal from the Midway operation. Even at Midway, all available air power was not concentrated at the crucial point, leading to the disparity between Japanese and US air strength being small. Yet, in 1944, at the Philippine Sea the Japanese were still dispersing land-based air forces and splitting up their carriers, precipitating disaster. It was in this year that the doctrinal gap opened up significantly and the Americans demonstrated their firmer grasp of the requirements of operating in the Pacific.

US naval and carrier doctrine had gone through a similar painful learning curve to the Japanese in the early months of the war, but by necessity the US Navy had been forced into re-evaluating the role of air power in determining the nature of the Pacific Campaign. A major debate had been ongoing in the US Navy in the late 1930s over the importance and employment of carriers. Like the Japanese, thought had been given to the creation of a six to eight carrier group. In the naval expansion plans of 1940–41, carriers had been given a major boost mirroring the expansion of the battleship force, but on the outbreak of war the debate had not been won over the primacy of air power over the surface vessel.[46] The loss of the battleships at Pearl Harbor, however, forced the Navy's hand and made the adoption of carrier based tactics essential.

However, the vulnerability of fleeting one or two fast carrier groups was illustrated by the actions of 1942. The US Navy lost four fleet carriers in that year, all of them acting in small one or two carrier groups. MacArthur and his staff argued that this proved that the US Navy could not drive the assault across the Pacific as the carrier was too vulnerable. The Navy responded by radically adapting its doctrine to the new strategic situation. The role of Admiral John H. Towers, appointed to command the Air Force Pacific Fleet in October 1942, was crucial as he and his team argued that the carriers should be concentrated into one large fleet which would operate generally as mutually supporting groups, but which could concentrate quickly when threatened. Such a fleet would be able to present such a concentration of air and naval power that surprise would become redundant.[47]

This development marked the transition from the supremacy of land-based air power to the primacy of massed carrier air power in the Pacific. The dispersed air assets of the Japanese could not hope to compete with the concentrated air power of the US Navy and were picked off piecemeal. Prior to the Great Marianas Turkey Shoot in June 1944, the US Navy had eliminated much of Japan's land-based air power in the area, and Japanese carrier strength had been reduced as vulnerable small fleet groups were penetrated by US submarines, an occurrence much more unlikely if forces were concentrated.[48] By 1944, the US Navy had formulated a very specific doctrine for the highly effective employment of air power and demonstrated flexibility firstly in adopting the carrier as the capital ship in 1942 and then developing the use of the weapon to a new level in 1943 and 1944. Such recognition of the primacy of air power greatly overshadowed the Japanese Navy's initial tactical superiority which failed to develop effectively or respond to the environment of the unfolding Pacific War.

CONCLUSIONS

The effective development and employment of maritime air power was fundamental to Allied success in two critical theatres of operations. Air power required a focused and disciplined approach to the conduct of war, not just at the battlefront but in planning and strategy, and in the Battle of the Atlantic the necessity of such thinking was emphasized still further. Co-operation, co-ordination and resource allocation were critical, and the Allies just about managed this most difficult of tasks, whereas the Japanese did not.

Moreover, the Allies demonstrated flexibility and adaptability of doctrine to the unfolding war. In the Battle of the Atlantic, and in the Pacific, the respective British and US maritime air and naval forces began the war with inappropriate doctrine, yet both were able to adapt and mould themselves to the demands of winning the campaigns. By contrast, the Japanese proved much less flexible and persisted with tactics and strategies that had been superseded by the nature of the war.

It should be noted however, that the Pacific theatre threw up a peculiar set of operational and strategical circumstances. Although the US Navy adapted very effectively to the requirements of defeating the Japanese, it could be argued that the campaign led air power up

something of a cul-de-sac. The ability of carrier-based aviation to dominate land-based air power was something of an anomaly specific to the
battles with the Japanese. In the Cold War world the value of the carrier
taskforce was questionable, especially when long-range continental
bombers emerged equipped with nuclear weapons. How useful expensive aircraft carriers would have been in a confrontation with the Soviets
is highly debatable, though one might also argue that since the end of
the Cold War, their value has been enhanced. Therefore, the concept of
adaptability needs to be strongly emphasized as crucial in times of both
peace and war. Indeed, distorting and misreading the meanings of war
for air power has been a consistent failing of the Western democracies
and is a lesson that should not be ignored in the future.

NOTES

1. M. Parillo, *The Japanese Merchant Marine in World War Two* (Annapolis, MD: Naval Institute Press, 1993), Ch. 1 in particular.
2. Naval History Division: Office of the Chief of Naval Operations, *United States Submarine Losses – World War Two* (Washington, DC: Government Printing Office, 1963), pp. 8 and 11.
3. Compiled from John Terraine, *Business in Great Waters: The U-boat Wars 1916–1945* (London: Leo Cooper, 1989), pp. 767–9; N. L. R. Franks, *Search, Find and Kill* (Aston: Bourne End, 1990), pp. 10–11.
4. E. Bagnasco, *Submarines of World War Two* (Annapolis, MD: Naval Institute Press, 1973), pp. 57, 132, 136 and 214; Dan van der Vat, *The Atlantic Campaign* (London: Hodder & Stoughton, 1988), pp. 76–7, 236 and 382.
5. Terraine, *Business in Great Waters*.
6. Bagnasco, *Submarines of World War Two*, p. 56; S. E. Morison, *History of US Naval Operations in World War Two – Volume X* (Boston, MA: Little Brown, 1956/84), pp. 244, 365–6.
7. J. Buckley, 'Failing to Learn from the Past: The RAF and Trade Defence 1917–1943', *War Studies Journal*, Vol. II, No. 1 (1996).
8. AIR 41/73, D. V. Peyton-Ward, *The RAF in the Maritime War – Vol. II: The Atlantic and Home Waters, September 1939 to June 1941* (Air Historical Branch narrative), p. 276.
9. CAB 69/1, Notes from the meeting of the Cabinet Defence Committee, 5/11/40.
10. Slessor Papers, IIF, Air Historical Branch (AHB), Slessor to Hilary St George-Saunders, 22/6/49.
11. AIR 41/73, Admiralty response to PM's questions, 22/11/40.
12. AIR 20/2891, Portal to PM, Coastal Command – Operational Control, 4/12/40.
13. Slessor Papers, AHB, Slessor to Saunders, 22/6/49; W. Sholto Douglas, *Years of Command* (London: Collins, 1966), p. 247.
14. AIR 20/1040, A. V. M. Geoffrey Bromet's trip to the USA and Canada, Jan./Feb. 1942; E. A. Cohen and John Gooch, *Military Misfortunes: The Anatomy of Failure in War* (London: Macmillan, 1990), p. 85.
15. John Buckley, *The RAF and Trade Defence 1919–1945: Constant Endeavour* (Keele: Keele University Press, 1995), pp. 143–7.
16. Slessor Papers, Box II, AHB, note by Peyton-Ward, *Combined Anti-U-boat Command in the Atlantic*; D. Richards and H. St George Saunders, *The Royal Air*

Force 1939–45, Volume III (London: HMSO, 1954), p. 36.

17. ADM 1/12663, Director of Plans to Admiralty and Pound, 15/2/43.
18. AIR 8/1083, Report on the Atlantic Convoy Conference, 1-12/3/43.
19. AIR 15/43, Bowhill to VCAS Freeman, 28/2/41.
20. AIR 20/846, Memo by AV Alexander for War Cabinet Defence Committee, Admiralty requirements, 14/2/42; Notes by the Air Staff on Alexander's memo, 14/2/42.
21. AIR 41/73, Peyton-Ward, *RAF in Maritime War*, p. 14.
22. ADM 234/578, Tovey to Pound, 2/6/42.
23. CAB 66/30, Churchill memo for Cabinet, 24/10/42, WP(42)483.
24. CAB 86/2, Minutes of the Anti-U-boat War Committee, 13 and 18/11/42.
25. AIR 41/73, Peyton-Ward, *RAF in Maritime War*, p. 2.
26. AIR 41/73, Peyton-Ward, *RAF in Maritime War*, p. 51.
27. AIR 15/29, Air Tactics – a/s bombing, 3/1/41.
28. P. B. Joubert de la Ferté, *The Fated Sky* (London: Hutchinson, 1952), p. 208.
29. J. Buckley, *Air Power in the Age of Total War* (London: UCL Press, 1999), p. 137.
30. C. Blair Jnr, *Silent Victory: The US Submarine War against Japan* (Philadelphia, PA: J. B. Lippincott, 1975), p. 792.
31. M. P. Parillo, *The Japanese Merchant Marine in World War Two* (Annapolis, MD: Naval Institute Press, 1993), pp. 243–4.
32. United States Strategic Bombing Survey (USSBS), *Interrogations – II* (Washington, DC: Government Printing Office, no date) (Washington, DC: Government Printing Office, undated), p. 407, interrogation of Colonel Kaneko Rinsuka, 21/11/45; National Archives II, Maryland, USA, Special Research History Report No.101, Seventh Fleet Intelligence Center, *Estimated Disposition of Japanese Fleet, Naval Aircraft and Merchant Shipping, 13/8/44 to 18/4/44*, pp. 5–6.
33. Parillo, *Japanese Merchant Marine*, p. 120.
34. USSBS, *The Campaigns of the Pacific War* (New York: Greenwood, 1969), p. 378.
35. W. J. Holmes, *Undersea Victory: The Influence of Submarine Operations in the Pacific* (New York: Greenwood, 1966), p. 192.
36. USSBS, *Interrogations – II*, p. 309, interrogation of Captain S. Kamide, 12/11/45.
37. Atsushi Oi, *The Maritime Protection War* (Tokyo: Asahi Sonorama, 1983), p. 285.
38. Ibid., pp. 275–7.
39. Atsushi Oi, 'Why Japan's Anti-Submarine Warfare Failed', *United States Naval Institute Proceedings*, Vol. 78, No. 6 (June 1952), p. 595.
40. Oi, *The Maritime Protection War*, pp. 149–51.
41. S. Howarth, 'Isoroku Yamamoto', in S. Howarth, ed., *Men of War: Great Naval Leaders of World War Two* (London: Weidenfeld & Nicolson, 1992), pp. 108–15.
42. Ikuhiko Hata, 'Admiral Yamamoto's Surprise Attack and the Japanese Navy's War Strategy', in S. Dockrill, ed., *From Pearl Harbor to Hiroshima: The Second World War in Asia 1941–45* (London: Macmillan, 1994).
43. C. G. Reynolds, *The Fast Carriers: The Forging of an Air Navy* (New York: McGraw Hill, 1968), pp. 6–9.
44. J. H. and W. M. Belote, *Titans of the Seas* (New York: Harper & Row, 1975), pp. 20–2.
45. I. Masanori and R. Pineau, *The End of the Imperial Japanese Navy* (London: Weidenfeld & Nicolson, 1962), p. 84.
46. Reynolds, *The Fast Carriers*, p. 18.
47. C. G. Reynolds, *Admiral John H. Towers: The Struggle for Naval Air Supremacy* (Annapolis, MD: Naval Institute Press, 1991), Chs 13 and 14.
48. W. T. Y'Blood, *Red Sun Setting: The Battle of the Philippine Sea* (Annapolis, MD: Naval Institute Press, 1981).

7

A Neglected Turning Point in Air Power History: Air Power and the Fall of France

Stuart W. Peach

'The Battle of France demonstrated the importance of air power in modern warfare; it proved that an army can do nothing without the support of an adequate air force.'

Pierre Cot, 1940[1]

INTRODUCTION

The fall of France in 1940, in just a few weeks following the German invasion of May 1940, remains one of the strategic surprises of the Second World War, and the role of air power was significant – on both sides. However, the outcome of the first large-scale tactical air battle between the Allies and Axis forces was by no means a foregone conclusion. Indeed, as this brief chapter will show, analysis of many of the agreed intelligence indicators and warnings might well have predicted the opposite outcome. Yet the Allies lost the air battle at all levels of warfare: tactical, operational and strategic. At the strategic level, the aftermath of the air battle came as a shock to the politicians who had predicted rapid effect for strategic air power and led to deep mistrust and misgivings between Britain and France.[2] At the operational level, the paralysis of the air/land interface was profound and was to last for several years.[3] At the tactical level the results were mixed. The shortcomings of many Royal Air Force (RAF) aircraft, such as the Battle and the Blenheim, were tragically demonstrated by the enormous losses of valuable aircrew, but the Hurricane had performed well over France and the Spitfire very well at Dunkirk. More importantly, the RAF's tactical doctrine, techniques and procedures had been found wanting and many of them were changed – just in time for the Battle of Britain.

The psychological impact of the campaign upon the air leaders, staff officers, pilots and groundcrews on both sides was also profound. The aim of this chapter is therefore to demonstrate not just that air operations in France in 1940 represented a significant turning-point in the history of air warfare, but one that was eclipsed by subsequent campaigns. In 1940, Britain and France not only entered an air war with the equipment of the age but also, as we shall see, the attitudes, 'baggage' and arrogance of 1914–18. On the Allied side, experience was conditioned by friction between the key allies, Britain and France, both equally unready and unprepared for the type of high mobility warfare they were about to face. We would do well to remember that the predominant theme for the air forces of western Europe today is once again that of expeditionary intervention operations. Study of the air campaign in France therefore has deep contemporary relevance, which should help to inform the current debate and 'enthusiasms' regarding expeditionary coalition operations.

1940 AIR WARFARE IN CONTEXT

Many distinguished historians have argued convincingly that the period 1919–39 most clearly represents a long armistice.[4] During this period, the unfinished business of the First World War simmered in the stew of inter-war international relations, extreme political ideologies and military elites biding their time or rebuilding their strength. The Treaty of Versailles set the framework of blame and division; the Great Depression and global slump of the 1930s set the economic conditions; whilst the relative diplomatic order of the nineteenth century with its balances of power and 'great game' of international diplomacy had apparently been replaced by the disorder and confrontation of competing fascist and communist ideologies. In this geostrategic and political context, air power and air warfare apparently offered attractive highly technological alternatives to the mass slaughter of a generation as witnessed in 1914–18. Moreover, the war in the air had touched the popular mood, although this produced different implications and perceptions amongst the protagonists of the Second World War. In the air campaign over France in 1940, the principal protagonists were Britain, France and Germany, with valiant but largely ineffectual efforts at national defence by the smaller air forces of Belgium and Holland. This chapter will concentrate on the former group. The varying ideas, constructs, doctrines and theories developed by air power proponents in the inter-war years led to differing perceptions on how it would be used in the coming conflict. Thus, an analysis of the air campaign and any attempt to put it in the context of the time must first address how it was that the theories of the air power pundits and zealots came crashing to earth in France in 1940.[5]

THE DEVELOPMENT OF AIR POWER

It has long been a shibboleth amongst writers on air power that the *Luftwaffe* was a 'tactical air force led by soldiers first and airmen second who lacked a full commitment to air power'.[6] In fact, German military specialists in the inter-war years took a much broader view of air warfare than many of their former foes in Britain, France and the USA. The Germans had lost the First World War and those officers that remained in the military spent many years engaged in detailed analytical studies of the period 1914–18; they were also able to refine some of their analyses in tactical experimentation at Lippetsk in the Soviet Union. This meant that, when combined with the lessons of the Spanish Civil War, which the Germans used as a 'battlelab' for tactics and innovation, the *Luftwaffe* theorists and future leaders understood the operational level of war and the potential of air warfare when *combined* with land operations to achieve a decisive effect.

The implications of this mission analysis for the *Luftwaffe* were profound. The structure of the *Luftwaffe* was built around support for the Army – the 'Main Effort' in German Clausewitzian analysis of future warfare. As James Corum makes very clear, the leadership of the *Luftwaffe* in the 1930s understood the 'strategic effect' potential of strategic bombardment, but were constrained by the industrial base and technology available to them. Ernst Udet and others saw much more promise in developing the dive bomber in order to increase the accuracy and concentration of force delivered from the air in support of the ground campaign.[7] The structure of the German Air Fleets, or *Luftflotten*, combined all arms manoeuvre, with communications interoperability between spotter aircraft (sensor), the command post (decision-maker) deployed forward in an armoured vehicle on the same secure radio net, and the attack aircraft (shooter), and these epitomized *Blitzkrieg*. It was this combination together with shock effect, which became the dominant factor in deciding the outcome, but it was not the whole story. The commanders understood each other's scheme of manoeuvre in what we now term supported and supporting relationships. The *Luftwaffe* had invested heavily in three key elements which enhanced its performance: air transport for mobility; Flak for force protection; and interoperable communications for maximum flexibility.

By 1939, the *Luftwaffe* had the largest, most effective and most sophisticated air transport force in the world.[8] Similarly, the development of the *Luftwaffe* Flak forces as an integral part of the *Luftwaffe* but in direct support of the main campaign effort – especially around the Meuse bridgeheads – was to be a key feature of the Campaign.[9] The third element, equally understudied, was interoperable communications. Again this became critical in organizing the concentration of force at the vital moment in time and space. The *Luftwaffe* and the Panzer Corps, the main ingredients of the *Blitzkrieg*, had the same type of radio operating on a common radio net. This saw the Panzer, Spotter aircraft, Stuka, Messerschmidt, all linked to a Command Post co-located with the Army, to become a battle-winning combination.[10]

Thus, viewed from the perspective of a nation and an air force that had lost the earlier war, the German Air Force learned rather than ignored lessons. Technology was developed to work in combination. Air warfare was seen in Germany as a vital adjunct to any operational scheme of manoeuvre. When battle was joined, the effectiveness of German air power in a joint campaign proved itself but, as we will see, the seeds of later collapse were also sown. The question we may legitimately ask is why did the airmen at the Air Tactical School at Maxwell Alabama in the United States, at the RAF Staff College in the UK or the *Ecole de L'Armée de L'Air* not pursue and reach the same conclusions and put them into practice?

In the UK, the intellectual focus was very much upon the survival of the Royal Air Force as an independent service. The battleground was as much Whitehall as the far-flung imperial domains and mandates, which added to the burden facing the fledgling service in the 1920s.[11] When the spice of air policing across the Empire is added to the mix, the menu was indeed daunting to those former Naval and Army officers selected to make the RAF their chosen career. There were simply far more tasks, commitments and challenges than there were resources available. The RAF was pulled in many directions and, with Air Chief Marshal 'Boom' Trenchard at the helm, doctrine was shaped to achieve the art of the possible within the means available. Even if resources had been more plentiful, the intricacies of joint and combined warfare would have had to wait until the trouble spots of Empire had been quelled and the real battle with the British Army and Royal Navy won. Into this strategic melting pot, was poured the Trenchard doctrine of strategic bombing as a war-winning weapon. This doctrine, developed throughout the late 1920s and early 1930s, solidified the views of many early British air leaders. Although the tactical-level bombing results of the few UK-based bomber squadrons were poor, aspirations were high.[12]

Thus, in Britain air/land combined operations and expeditionary warfare were institutionally neglected at a time when the RAF was overstretched at every level of warfare. As the 1920s became the 1930s, the actions of the German government in ignoring Versailles, rearming generally, and building the *Luftwaffe* specifically, caused growing alarm within UK military circles. In consequence, the air defence of the UK became a top strategic priority. As if this was not enough for competing RAF priorities, still suffering from the effects of the ten-year rule, there were simply insufficient resources for the air defence of the UK. Despite the frantic efforts of industry and military procurement, the simultaneous expansion of air defence, the build up of a strategic bomber force, Royal Navy demands for investment in Coastal Command, and current operations across the Empire proved too much for the British defence 'system' to cope with.[13] In this context, and with the failure of the British Army's armoured force experimentation, the chances of resources being granted for the rapid development of tactical air power in support of armies were very slim.[14] Indeed, in 1938, the Chief of the Air Staff, Sir Cyril Newall, declared it the lowest priority for the Air Ministry, although we should note that at that time the government had planned to send only a very small expeditionary force to the Continent. If there was a sin, therefore, it was principally one of omission – there was simply too much to be done to permit focus upon British tactical air power in support of the Army.[15]

In France, there was a similar enormous gap between air-warfare aspirations and reality. Contrary to popular belief, French air leaders had followed the debate of the air power theorists closely and were probably closest to making Giulio Douhet's theories a reality with the creation of aircraft such as the Marcel Bloch MB 131 or Farman F222 as Bomber, Combat, Reconnaissance aircraft.[16] By 1940, however, these aircraft and most of the French front line could trace their lineage to the early 1930s and were outclassed. Similarly, French fighters lacked performance and, although many new aircraft, such as the Curtiss H75, had been ordered from the United States, the numbers were small and the majority of the front line were at least 50 mph slower than their *Luftwaffe* equivalents. The constant changes in the French government did not help, either politically or in terms of relations with industry. Between 1935 and 1939, there were no fewer than nine Ministers of Aviation.[17] Those, such as Pierre Cot, who knew what needed to be done were removed and their visionary programmes cancelled. But equipment and industrial capability were only part of the problem. As the battle developed, it was the structural weakness of the French Air Force, rigidly tied to the French Army with inflexible command and control, little freedom of action, and no ability to concentrate force in time and space that were to become battle-losing weakness.

GERMAN PREPARATION FOR WAR

In Germany, on the other hand, the late 1930s were busy years. The *Luftwaffe* used the Civil War in Spain as a means of testing the doctrinal concepts they had developed in the Soviet Union. During the campaign, the *Luftwaffe* harnessed doctrine with tactics and techniques to maximize the tactical capabilities of its equipment. It is probably an exaggeration to suggest that it was a mission rehearsal for the forthcoming wider war, but the impact of operations in Spain on all lines of development within the *Luftwaffe* and at all levels of warfare was profound. At the strategic level, with collocated commanders, the employment of air power in conjunction with ground forces to achieve a campaign effect was understood, particularly by those such as Wolfram von Richtofen, who would go on to command a *Luftflotte* in France a few years later. Equally, the activity of the *Luftwaffe* in Spain identified lessons for the campaign in Poland, which led to appropriate changes being made in time for the campaign in France.[18]

Another important lesson was the German insistence upon command dominance by German officers in coalition operations. This was to become ingrained during the Second World War, but has its roots in Spain. During the Spanish campaign the realities of 'coalition' friction in operations to ensure a German 'thread' of command were powerful negative factors.[19] The host-nation Spanish officers were simply ignored; in the German model of coalition operations there was no room for compromise and sentiment.[20] Similarly, the communications architecture worked, but only when commanders were collocated. At the operational level, many relatively new tenets of air warfare were exploited within the framework of combined operations. For example, the exploitation of air transport to aid mobility within the theatre of operations and, on occasion, to deliver airborne forces, became a key lesson identified which was to be fully exploited in France. *Luftwaffe* logistics had been severely strained by the Spanish campaign with higher than predicted consumption rates of weapons and spares, unreliable engines, radios and weapons. Again, lessons were learned and rectification work hastened. Another operational-level factor which was to have influence during the Battle of France, was the personal experience gained by senior commanders of the need to integrate forces with short command-and-control chains, good 'communications and attention to logistics – the essence of *Blitzkrieg*.

It was at the tactical level that lessons for 1940 were most significant. The *Luftwaffe* acquitted itself well and convinced the German Army of the need to take air power seriously. Of course mistakes were made or alleged – Allied war correspondents made good copy from accounts of German bombing at Guernica and elsewhere, information which was misconstrued by commentators in the UK and the United States as signs of German intent to conduct strategic-bombing operations. Both sides and their media pounced upon Guernica as a potential propaganda victory.[21] In fact, *Luftwaffe* sources were adamant that Guernica was a tactical target (a major road combination which represented a choke point for the assembly of ground forces).[22] Regardless of the historical controversy, the tactical lessons of operations in Spain were learned by the *Luftwaffe* and applied to subsequent doctrine and tactics. On the US and UK side, however, the lesson of Guernica was that strategic bombing worked. This reinforced the 'bomber will always get through' doctrine, and the allocation of scarce defence resources to the development of heavy bombers and weapons – not to tactical support aircraft – with consequences which would become all too clear in 1940.

The amended doctrine and tactics were soon put to the test in Poland in September 1939. Again the details of the campaign do not concern us. What does, rather, is the speed of the processing and subsequent application of the tactical and operational lessons learned. The Polish Air Force fought valiantly, but was outclassed technically and overwhelmed by shock action. German offensive counter-air attacks against Polish airfields were not as successful as they might have been, owing to the poor penetration capability and reliability of German bombs. Within a few days of the conclusion of the Polish campaign, German *Luftwaffe* operational analysis staffs swarmed over the targets of the previous days and weeks to make detailed assessments of weapon performance and damage mechanisms. As a result, 'tweaks' were applied to the production weapons, fuzes, tactics and doctrine to make ready for the coming campaign in France.

After the Allies declared war on Germany in September 1939, the autumn of 1939 was a time of consolidation for the *Luftwaffe*. Capability was steadily improved with the slight losses experienced in Poland rapidly replaced. Moreover, the *Luftwaffe* was operating on short interior lines of communication and held the strategic advantage of surprise. There were weaknesses. The *Luftwaffe* had failed to realize that aircrews could not be expected to operate permanently at a high tempo without respite. As we shall see, there were logistical weaknesses, especially with spares for newer aircraft and training difficulties as replacement crews were rushed into the front line with little flying experience. None the less, the *Luftwaffe* had now become battle-hardened and enjoyed extremely high morale, even swagger, from its success so far.[23] Thus, although plans kept changing with remarkable speed – 26 'be prepared to execute ...' orders for the invasion of France, Belgium and Holland were raised and cancelled between October 1939 and May 1940 – the *Luftwaffe* was ready.

ALLIED COALITION FRICTION

If the *Luftwaffe* was ready for the forthcoming conflict, the Allies were not. Muddle and confusion surrounded the deployment of the air elements of the British Air Forces in the summer of 1939 and the French Air Force was 'on the back foot' on all counts. The Chief of the French Air Force, General Vuillemin, was in no doubt that his force was inferior to the Germans – he had been completely taken in by what we would now call German 'Information Operations' following his visit to Germany in 1938. Furthermore, across all the lines of development which constitute capability: doctrine, equipment, people, training, logistics, command and control arrangements, morale of the force – the French Air Force was lacking. If there was a war looming, why was this the case? Alistair Horne[24] argues that just as the French Army was stuck in the malaise surrounding the Third Republic and the 'baggage' rather than the lessons of the First World War, so was the Air Force. Thus, the French Air Force struggled to establish itself and survive let alone thrive during the inter-war period. As shown above, the French Air Force front line was a *pot-pourri* of small fleets, each requiring separate and hollow logistics chains with command and control, communications, equipment, weapons and supplies all in the wrong place at the wrong time.

On the British side, as also shown above, the necessary focus upon Fighter Command, the domination of the 'bomber' doctrine with the 'cinderella' resources required for Coastal Command led to a neglect of tactical support for the Army. The then Wing Commander John Slessor, the Royal Air Force member of the Directing Staff at the Army Staff College Camberley had written on the dangers of this neglect in 1936. In his article 'Air Power and Armies', Slessor predicted with uncanny accuracy the difficulties the air/land interface would encounter in the coming war.[25] But, nothing was done. Instead by 1939, the British Air Commander, Air Marshal Arthur Barratt, was left with a force split between the squadrons assigned to direct support of Lord Gort's British Expeditionary Force (BEF) and the Allied Air Striking Force, which remained under the command and control of Bomber Command.[26] By January 1940, under French pressure following the Anglo/French air staff 'conversations', the unwieldy nature of this arrangement had been exposed. In consequence, Chamberlain's War Cabinet gave Lord Chatfield the job of adjudicating on the issue of air support for the BEF. Thus, in January 1940, Barratt became Commander-in-Chief British Air Forces in France. As Jackson and Bramall comment: 'this palliative soothed but did not cure the incipient ulcer that was starting to grow in Army/Air relations'.[27]

Even if the technology was up to the job, which in support of the

BEF it was not, a brief examination of the other lines of development, makes ever more gloomy reading. The deployment and location of the air component was driven by political not military factors. The French viewed the Maginot Line as invincible. They insisted that the British Battles and Blenheims of Number 1 Group (at this stage still subordinate to Bomber Command) were located close behind the forts. This was logical to the French Air Force, and although Barratt was unhappy his hands were tied. In consequence, what little resources were available for airfield construction were spent constructing airfields which were overrun in the first couple of days following the German invasion. Again, despite the efforts of Barratt and Blount,[28] the French authorities refused permission for the deployed British Forces to train in a meaningful way during the 'Phoney War', especially in terms of live or practice weapon-training and night-flying – both these omissions were to prove disastrous when the campaign began. Combined training with the French Air Force was non-existent. Sadly, it was a similar story with logistics. The excellent 'system' established by the Royal Flying Corps and Royal Air Force in France in 1918 was not set up in 1939. Instead, it was a hand-to-mouth existence for Barratt's squadrons, with many key elements in extreme logistics difficulty.[29] Thus, even a brief examination of capability as measured by force development shows distinct weakness waiting to be exploited by the enemy.

Nor were operational level Allied air command and control arrangements satisfactory. Barratt had spent months trying to bring a semblance of coherence to his command; coherence which proved elusive. Vuillemin was largely impotent as chief of the French Air Force. The real power lay with French Army Generals, notably Gamelin who simply ignored the Air Force. A gloomy man who had been 'chief' since 1938, Vuillemin's fear of the *Luftwaffe* spread to his subordinates. The French Air Force was very much the poor relation of the French Army. The dominant French Army, in its 'Instruction on the Tactical Employment of Major Units', stated that preparation for the attack was the job of the artillery, with troop concentrations on the march or in retreat the only fitting targets for air power.[30] Even de Gaulle's pamphlets on armoured warfare ignored air power. This was hardly *Blitzkrieg* in the making. Furthermore, even if the failures in command, doctrine and tactics could be worked around, the capability in terms of equipment and weapons was even more flimsy. Few lessons had been noted let alone learned from Spain or Poland. At the tactical level, however, uneasy French Air Force commanders hoped the Phoney War would continue. If not, the Maginot Line would protect. This was a completely false picture of the enemy – pointing to a failure in intelligence.

History has not been kind to Barratt, who remains relatively unknown to later generations.[31] He knew enough to agitate for more aggressive reconnaissance and combat patrols – without success because of the French fear of German retaliation if the border was crossed.[32] Several intelligence strands were wrongly misinterpreted (as is often the case with human intelligence), but it was the strategic prevention of aerial reconnaissance that failed to spot the Panzer Army massing in the Ardennes. Overall, therefore, in France the French Air Force and, due to the institutional subservience agreed in London, the Allied Air Forces, were locked into institutional subservience to the French Army. Lord Gort, as Commander-in-Chief of the British Expeditionary Force, could have challenged the French but, as Brian Bond makes clear in John Keegan's collection of essays *Churchill's Generals*, Gort was obsessed with small detail. In the run-up to the German invasion, Gort had administratively separated himself from his staff to be at his forward command post at Wahagnies near Lille; an unforced separation, which was to prove a disaster. This would have been bad enough, but it was made worse by the absolute reliance upon strict geographical boundaries aligned to a 'dirigiste' French Army peacetime garrison/conscription system with rigidly fixed lines of communication, rather than flexible radio communications.

Within the French Air Force, each 'Groupe' of squadrons was organized into zones with 'Zone Organization Aeriel Nord' (ZOAN) at the point of the German attack. In 1940, the commander of ZOAN, General D'Astier was highly competent and aware of the shortcomings inherent in such a rigid geographical organization, but he was locked into a system of compliance. In essence, the Allies were fixed on applying air power in 1940 in the strategic straitjacket of 1918 behind the glacis plate of the Maginot Line. Thus, before the Germans attacked, the Allied commanders' thinking was rooted in 1918, whereas the *Luftwaffe*'s was established firmly in 1940.

Allied interoperability was equally elusive. The BEF had no serviceable air/land communications. Although the BEF was equipped with a reconnaissance wing of Westland Lysanders with a primary role of supporting the BEF, radio communications were almost non-existent.[33] Moreover, the fixed lines of communication that the Allies relied upon had been penetrated by German signals intelligence capability – a capability that was to prove a critical addition to German targeting during the 'shock' of *Blitzkrieg*.[34] In addition, Allied force dispositions had been extensively and accurately mapped by German aerial reconnaissance, enabling vital intelligence preparation of the battlefield, fused with signals intelligence to identify headquarters and key logistic nodes. Furthermore, when German shock action was applied to this cumbersome and inflexible command-and-control system, it collapsed.

Thus, the paralysis at the operational level of the Allied air war can be explained by the operational circumstances.

Again, Barratt and Blount emerge as figures battling to deal with all these problems of command.[35] As Sir Edward Spears and other commentators testify, they tried hard to rectify the systemic command issues, whilst dealing with the myriad of force development issues which bedevilled any attempt to develop a combined force.[36] In sheer numbers, the combined Allied Air Forces were apparently equivalent to the German air forces facing them. Drawing from *Luftwaffe* archives, however, the 'absolute Staerke' (absolute strength) was 4,469 'allierte Bomber und Jaeger' (Allied bombers and fighters: Belgium 140, Holland 82, Britain 1,150 and France 3,097), compared with 3,578 German aircraft. When the intelligence preparation is added, however, the figures change. The amended figures are German 2,589 'davon einsatzbereit an der Front am 10 Mai 1940', or 'relative Staerke', facing 1,453 Allied aircraft (Belgium 118, Holland 72, Britain 879 and France 879).[37] This information, known to *Luftwaffe* commanders armed with surprise, short lines of communication and high morale explains the German confidence on the eve of the attack.

If Allied air-operational arrangements and capabilities before the battle were weak, what of the strategic level? Both London and Paris were extremely fearful of the consequences of retaliatory attacks for deep missions – even aerial reconnaissance. Thus, authority to cross the German border was not forthcoming, even when conclusive evidence of German massing of forces was provided. Even the official dispatches wryly observe that a British civilian, Sidney Cotton, 'loosely' working for the British security/intelligence authorities employing a specially modified Lockheed Electra, conducted the only meaningful Allied aerial reconnaissance. This imagery was useful, but could hardly offer Allied commanders a total picture of German intent. Although British frustration with Cotton's methods grew leading to the formation of 212 Squadron, still under Cotton's leadership, now as a wing commander, the results were useful but not startling.[38]

That said, air commanders at the tactical level did their best to identify, codify and allocate fixed targets for attack, but the estimate was based upon a postulated enemy course of action that the Germans would strike through Belgium – if at all. Thus, the Allied strategy of denial to prevent unnecessary retaliation provides a neat example of strategic cause and operational and tactical effect. As late as May 1940, the Allies were fundamentally blind to German intent. As with so many intelligence failures across history, the causes were many and the mitigation was plausible, but there was one tactical episode with strategic impact that had taken place as early as January 1940, during the Phoney War.

Between the start of the war and the invasion in May 1940, the German General Staff Planners worked overtime. In what became known as the 'Mechelen incident', on 9 January 1940, two German staff officers – an airborne forces Major Reinberger and Major Hoenemans, the pilot, a German First World War aviator – were flying to a top-secret conference at Second Air Fleet HQ in Cologne.[39] Reinberger was carrying the entire plan, 'Plan Gelb', for the German invasion. Unfortunately, when the pair set off from Munster, the weather was not as forecast and, as Hoenemans dodged the weather, they strayed off track to the west. Even more unfortunately, when the pilot realized his navigational error, the engine on the Messerschmidt failed due to icing and the hapless pair crash-landed at Mechelen in Belgium. Reinberger was horrified and immediately made off to burn the plans. Unfortunately, his matches would not light and although an obliging Belgian farmer helped him to light a small fire, Belgian troops alerted by the crash arrested the Germans, rescued the now slightly charred plans and escorted them to the Gendarmerie. During initial interrogation, Reinberger attempted to force the German campaign plan into the police's pot-bellied stove, but the Belgian Army captain rescued the – by now – somewhat more charred papers and sent them to Allied GHQ. The papers showed German intent to invade through Belgium and Holland into northern France in almost a re-run of the Schlieffen Plan of 1914.

The information threw the already confused Allied co-ordination efforts into disarray with French, Belgian and Dutch armies moving hither and thither over the next few days. The impact upon the German side was immediate. Hitler was furious. He had already, after countless arguments with his generals, authorized D-Day for 15 January at dawn, six days after the plans were lost. Reconnaissance reports of Belgian and Dutch mobilization, coupled with continued bad weather caused indefinite delay to Plan Gelb and the creation – by order of Hitler of a new plan based upon secrecy and surprise. The new plan, 'Sichelschnitt', was created by Manstein and was much more daring, with greater prominence being given to the Panzer/air combination that had proved so successful in Poland. Moreover, the retribution following the loss of the plans saw the rise of Kesselring to command of Second Air Fleet; a command decision that was to prove critical to the *Luftwaffe*. Although the machinations within the German General Staff need not be rehearsed, many senior generals were nervous over the prominence being given to air and panzers with a whole Panzer Corps (XIX) forming the main effort at Sedan. Indeed, many Army OKH (*OberKommando des Heer* or High Command of the Army in Berlin) generals were extremely nervous that the massing of forces in the

Ardennes in 'channelled' terrain would make a perfect target for Allied air power; a concern that was never to be exploited by the Allies.

In campaign-planning terms, there was one fundamental flaw in the German plan: the sequel planning for the breakout and subsequent operations was vague for the *Luftwaffe* and was to prove to be the 'Achilles heel'. As with the Allies' obsession with the Normandy landings rather than the following campaign in 1944, so it was that the Germans focused far too much on the initial attack across the Meuse and the Maginot Line and not enough on the breakout. Furthermore, if future operations included the invasion of Britain, the *Luftwaffe* were not carrying out the same granularity of intelligence preparation as had been conducted over north-east France in the winter of 1939/40 – an error that was to cost them dear in the summer of 1940.

A stocktake of the situation on the eve of the German invasion reveals at the strategic level a weak and demoralized French government. In Britain there was political disarray, since the British government had just fallen as a result of the disastrous campaign in Norway, and Churchill was literally in the process of assuming office as Prime Minister and Defence Minister. At the operational level, the Allies were not ready, prepared or even co-ordinated and at the tactical level, the brave men who were about to go to war in the air, were unready and technically and tactically ill equipped. Doctrinally, the Allies had ignored the obvious pointers of the German way in war. The tactical force multipliers that were to prove decisive in the coming days: leading echelons of dedicated *Luftwaffe*-commanded and controlled Flak, strong (almost 2,000) air transports to allow tactical resupply in a fluid battle, and collocated commanders with interoperable secure communications, were not readily available to the Allies.

'CONTACT'

Following the Mechelen incident and Hitler's strictures, German operational security was maintained. *Luftwaffe* crews were roused in the early hours of the morning on 10 May 1940 and did not even have time to shave. Every available German aircraft was employed in a bewildering array of roles and missions: offensive counter-air attacks against British and French airfields, accompanied by escorting fighters, German bombers carrying out maritime and land interdiction against transport targets and choke points to create confusion and blockages. Allied unpreparedness was exemplified by the Blenheims of 114 Squadron at Conde Vraux near Reims, which were neatly lined up on the airfield and, as a result, as dawn broke six were destroyed and the remainder damaged. Across the north-east of France, 50 airfields were attacked in the first wave. In an early tactical mistake with strategic impact, bleary-eyed *Luftwaffe* Dornier 17 crews mistook Freiburg im Breisgau in Germany for their target in France, killing 57 civilians. Goebbels immediately claimed this as an Allied attack, thereby allowing Hitler to authorize reprisal raids against Belgian and Dutch civilian targets.[40]

Attacks were most dense over Holland with the Dutch Air Force all but wiped out on the first day. In Belgium, the extraordinary and daring airborne raid on Eben Emael, the Belgian 'impregnable' fortress, was successful – to the amazement of the defenders. *Luftwaffe* defensive combat fighter patrols over the densely packed Panzers in the Ardennes were equally surprised at the lack of an Allied air response. General von Blumentritt, Rundstedt's Chief of Staff, remained concerned, alarmed even, at the 150-mile traffic jam of German military targets.[41] And yet still the Allies did not come. The French Air Force received no orders that morning. Barratt fumed; it was clear to him that this was the time to act immediately with maximum effort. Instead, he received the message at 0800 from Allied Headquarters: 'Air limited to reconnaissance and Fighters'. The first meaningful order arrived from General Georges at 1100: 'bomb enemy columns' and airfields, but ... 'at all costs avoid bombing built-up areas'. Barratt's impatience broke through his acquiescence and he independently ordered his Battles and Blenheims to attack into Luxembourg. They were the only Allied aircraft to engage German forces that day with 13 aircraft lost and 19 damaged.[42]

The only formal Allied air command and control action taken that day was that the war plan of the AASF (Advance Air Striking Force) should be activated with a large Allied air attack planned for the night of 10/11 May, with aircraft from Bomber Command in the UK joining in. General Georges vetoed the attack. Barratt was incandescent, but the Air Ministry in London ordered Barratt to obey French strictures. On the ground, chaos reigned. On the second day, the *Luftwaffe* continued to concentrate upon Holland with diversionary raids into France. Acting on Barratt's orders, not with French approval, the Battles targeted German columns in the Luxembourg border region. The ferocity and accuracy of German Flak surprised and shocked the crews. The Battle was particularly vulnerable with its slow speed, poor defensive armament, lack of armoured protection for the crews, small bombload and peculiar tactical characteristics. Inexplicably, the Battle's bombsight was connected to the Merlin Engine manifold, thus becoming white hot in flight preventing readjustment. Thus, Battle crews were constrained to level predictable attacks at 2,000 feet – easy targets for German Flak.[43] On the second day, the French Air Force was again stuck far to the rear waiting for orders and engaging only in sporadic and ineffective activity.

Barratt and Blount carried on grimly with losses mounting in the ZOAN sector, but worse was to come. Allied aerial reconnaissance had spotted the Germans massing in the Ardennes, but the French Intelligence Organization (the Deuxieme Bureau) had grossly underestimated the size of the German forces and failed to appreciate that the attacks in the north-east were a diversion; the main effort was about to be launched through the Ardennes with no action to 'warn' taken by the Allies. On the third day, the French Air Force finally swung into action, but logistical shortages – particularly of weapons – and almost zero mobility through a lack of lorries hampered the 'maximum' effort. Generals Gort and Billotte directed an air maximum effort against the Maastricht bridgehead – still not identified as a deception attack – with the French Air Force suffering similar losses to those of the RAF the previous day. It was on this day that the first RAF VC of the war was won in the suicidal attacks by British Battles of 12 Squadron against the Maastricht bridges. By now, the French ZOAN operational air commander, General D'Astier emphasized his serious concerns over the concentration of German forces in the Ardenenes with large amounts of bridging equipment identified by aerial photographs. Finally, at 1600 on 12 May, General Georges agreed to allocate new air priority to the Sedan area.

By many agreed military precepts, the German crossing of the Meuse in May 1940 was an audacious and extremely high-risk operation. The urgent tactical priority to establish a Flak cordon of dual role anti-air, anti-armour 88mm guns proved to be decisive in terms of its operational effect. Despite the tenuous foothold of the German forces, the efficiency of the *Luftwaffe* Flak and the complete lack of effective Allied co-ordination, saw mounting losses for no tangible gain and made this a terrible time for the Allied tactical air forces. The outstanding bravery of the crews against impossible odds remains unchallenged, but the effect of the Allied raids upon the Germans was slight. On the other hand, the *Luftwaffe* was enjoying the tactical fruits of several years of air/land co-operation which were about to reach new heights of integration and were rewarded with real campaign effect. For the *Luftwaffe*, the French campaign of 1940 represents the high-water mark of air/land co-operation in the Second World War and possibly in military aviation history. The concept had been devised and revised in Spain and Poland. Lessons had then been learned, not just identified, and applied to the tactical level. Furthermore, compared with the constipation and paralysis of command on the Allied side, the *Luftwaffe* generals were fully in the mind of the higher German Army commanders.

Turning to the other elements of force development, equipment, training, people and logistics: all had been honed to a fine pitch – at least for the initial part of the campaign. Although *Luftwaffe* equipment appears dated as the war progressed, in 1940 it was 'state of the art'. The Me 109 was a good day fighter, which had been developed since the Spanish Civil War into the 'F' version, which outflew and outgunned the Allies in May 1940. The medium bomber force of Junkers 88, Dornier 17 and Heinkel 111 outclassed French Leos and Potez and British Blenheims and Battles by a considerable margin. German Henschel 126 and Fiesler Storch had their French and British equivalents in the guise of Mureaux 115 observation aircraft and the Westland Lysander, but the Germans had secure communications with the ground and could immediately call fighters to their aid; the Allies could not.

Even had they had the equipment, the Allies did not have the tactical doctrine, training, or command and control system to exploit the information they observed; a weakness in intelligence which led to a complete failure of 'situational awareness' at the tactical level in the coming days and weeks.

Moreover, although the *Luftwaffe* personnel policy of leaving aircrew in the front line without respite was fundamentally flawed for a long war, in the short term it gave the *Luftwaffe* a distinct advantage. Many 'Gruppe' and 'Geschwader' commanders had learned to fly and fight in the Spanish Civil War and had been 'blooded' in Poland.[44] Few survived the war, but they made a difference in May 1940. If there was a flaw, it was in sustainability. *Luftwaffe* planners such as Milch and Udet fundamentally underestimated the 'wear and tear' and consumption rates on men and materiel once battle was joined. In terms of logistics, the historical parallel with today deserves further attention. Just as the actual consumption of munitions and the difficulties of resupply confounded the experts in the First World War,[45] so in the Second World War losses of aircraft, crews, munition supplies and trained ground crew became the key challenges.

For the *Luftwaffe*, the seeds of later fragility in the logistic system were already apparent in 1940, but in the short term, the experience gained from Poland and the investment made in transport aircraft and mobility paid off. Even so, Guderian's 'expanding torrent' and speed of advance confounded even the most optimistic *Luftwaffe* planner, and it was thus an exhausted *Luftwaffe* that arrived at the Channel coast. The strategic-level promise Goering made to Hitler before Dunkirk, that the *Luftwaffe* would wipe the Allies off the face of the Earth, foundered on the tactical reality of an exhausted *Luftwaffe*.[46]

A key question is the quality of the commanders themselves. In 1940, most *Luftwaffe* generals were junior army officers in the First World War who had been promoted following exceptional performances in Spain and Poland. All the *Fliegerkorps* commanders: Loerzer, Sperrle and (Wolfram) von Richtofen fell into this category. At the *Luftflotte* command level, Kesselring was firmly committed to air/land integration. This was not the case in Britain and France. The German air commanders were united in front of their staff in a way that was impossible with the inherent friction between Britain and France. If there was a nervousness on the German side unable to exploit success in France, it was in the High Command element, particularly von Runsdtedt, who could not place the speed of the German breakthrough into his military lexicon. He too was thinking in terms of 1918. Although the tactical commanders grumbled at the caution of the high command, they obeyed and lost an element of tempo – at the crucial time.

At the operational level, the *Luftwaffe Fliegerkorps* saw combined forces create an historic concentration of air power on a narrow front. This tactical action alone is arguably a turning point in air power history in its own right. In the execution phase, German air power was to have a strategic campaign impact. In addition to enabling the breakthrough, German air power protected Guderian's exposed flanks, requiring a degree of understanding, co-operation and integration impossible in the Allied air forces in 1940. This understanding was made possible through close co-operation between air and land commanders. A detailed planning conference had taken place between all the Corps Commanders, as the 'supported' element, and the 'supporting' *Luftflotte* commanders.[47] Furthermore, orders issued at Corps level by Guderian and his colleagues contained detailed annexes on co-operation with the 'air force' showing time lines, maps, sketches, recognition procedures and communications plans – a far cry from the 'armed reconnaissance of Sedan', which was the Allied equivalent.[48]

THE CONSEQUENCES OF THE CAMPAIGN

Once Allied aerial reconnaissance had revealed the massing of forces in the Ardennes as the German main effort it was too late. The attack had begun. Horne covers the struggle by the Germans to establish a bridgehead across the Meuse on 13 May 1940 in compelling detail.[49] But, he poses a question for air historians: 'the total failure of both Allied air forces at Sedan on 13 May 1940 is one of the more extraordinary, in some ways inexplicable, features of the whole battle'.[50] He goes on to posit the miasma of command and control of Allied air as a key factor in their defeat. As this chapter has shown, by not taking an holistic approach to force development, high command and interoperability, this operational and tactical-level paralysis was inevitable. After three days of tactical *Blitzkrieg*, the Allied air response was broken at every level, except for the reckless bravery of the Allied aircrews.

Even on 13 May, the French Army high commanders had failed to grasp the seriousness of the operational situation. General D'Astier's memoirs suggest that on 13 May, General Billotte tasked him to allot priority to air support to the 2nd Army in the 'next two or three days'.[51] Meanwhile at Sedan and Donchery, Rommel's and Guderian's forces continued to pour across the Meuse. French military education now takes centre stage. Opposing them was General Corap, a 'North African' general who was proud to have been mobilized against the British at the time of the Fashoda crisis. As Horne observes icily: 'his military education had ceased with 1918'. Similarly, the elegant General Huntziger, Commanding the French 2nd Army, was not prepared to mix air support with his beloved artillery. When his corps and divisional commanders requested air support from Allied fighters to keep the German air at bay, Huntziger observed that the men needed a 'baptism of fire' and denied the request.[52]

This is more than a failure in generalship, it is a failure to understand the nature of warfare in 1940. Even at the divisional level, the complex mix of a failure in education, doctrine, training and tactics proved a decisive weakness for the Allies – Horne refers to an instance where the French 2nd Army refused to sanction bombing of a target which was being engaged by artillery as this would only upset the observation of the artillery.[53] Here we see the conflation of all of Liddell Hart's dire warnings of the failure to heed combined air/land tactics in the 1920s and 1930s. If Barratt was fuming and railing on 12 May, he was consolidating and considering on 13 May. On 12 May, the Chief of the Air Staff, Air Chief Marshal Sir Cyril Newall had telegrammed Barratt: 'I am concerned at the heavy losses incurred by the medium bombers ... we cannot continue indefinitely at this rate of intensity. If we expend all our effort in the early stages of the battle, we shall not be ready to operate effectively when the really critical phase comes ...'.[54] By 13 May the critical phase had already arrived; yet the Blenheims stayed on the ground and the Battles launched just sorties to Holland. French air activity was sporadic and, such as it was, attracted heavy losses. Meanwhile, the *Luftwaffe* exploited the advantage of short lines of communication and the Stuka crews flew an average of seven sorties per crew that day. This was meant to be flying artillery in direct support of armoured thrusts across a vulnerable bridgehead, but it was fast becoming the exploitation of air power for strategic effect.

Horne has described what happened next at Sedan as the 'fatal moment', taking place as it was in Richard Holmes's 'fatal avenue'.[55] On 14 May the French High Command declared maximum effort. At the tactical level, the Allies responded with the most vivid and tremendous display of bravery. In desperate penny packets, Allied air power was pitted against the German bridgehead. The losses were terrible. Horne writes: 'for the RAF the Meuse that day was an unimaginable hell – a valley of death – from which few returned'.[56] The Official History, whilst more measured, is equally sobering: 'no higher rate of loss in an operation of comparable size has ever been experienced by the Royal Air Force'.[57] This sad record remains unchallenged.

On 15 May, the operational situation changed. At the tactical level, Allied air forces were paralysed, operational command and control was broken.[58] Too late, the High Command ordered 'main effort', but the Allied front line was a shadow. In order to preserve the remnants of his force following the appalling loss rates of 10–14 May, Barratt had, with the full blessing of the Air Ministry, relegated the Battle to a night role.[59] That night, however, the shackles came off the constraints on RAF bombing operations launched from the UK. Following the bombardment of Rotterdam by the *Luftwaffe*, the British War Cabinet authorized Bomber Command to 'unleash' its offensive against Germany. That night, 96 Wellington, Whitley and Hampden bombers were dispatched from the UK to the oil plants of the Ruhr rather than the target-rich but heavily defended area of the Meuse. The results of this operation were negligible, however, with only 24 aircraft claiming to have reached the target.

This pattern was to continue. Portal, as Commander-in-Chief Bomber Command, supported the BEF with night raids on the German rear area once the constraints had been lifted, but invariably 'kept a few sorties back for strategic targets'. Denis Richards, his biographer, concedes: 'even in the crisis of the Allied armies, the strategic tasks remained very much in his mind – and he could, of course offer good tactical reasons for spreading his attacks widely'.[60] The desks at Bomber Command's High Wycombe Headquarters were thick with revised Air Ministry Directives over the weeks that followed, but there was a common thread: preservation of the force and an extremely marked reluctance in the Air Ministry and in HQ Bomber Command at High Wycombe to abandon strategic bombing.

A second significant decision setting the conditions for the force estimation for the Battle of Britain, was the decision by the War Cabinet in London to take stock of the current operational situation in France. It was at this meeting on 15 May that Air Chief Marshal Sir Hugh Dowding made his famous intervention in order to preserve his forces for the defence of Great Britain. Specifically, Dowding invited the War Cabinet to refuse French Prime Minister Reynaud's desperate requests for more British fighters. Dowding carried the day. Meanwhile at the front, increasingly desperate attempts to defend the airfields positioned forward had failed. On the day of momentous decision in London, Barratt was forced at midnight to order the evacuation of

BEF/AASF combat units to the south and moved his own HQ from Chauny to rejoin the gloomy Vuillemin at Coulommiers.

In the confusion of the following few days, defeatism mounted whilst – incredibly – the strength of the French Air Force grew as replacement aircraft arrived in France, if not at the front line. Even more incredibly, the French Air Force required crews to detach from the front line to aircraft factories in the safe rear areas to collect aircraft and fly them back. These new aircraft were delivered without role equipment: weapons, radios or even weapon racks; they were all but useless to the Groupes engaged with the enemy.[61] For the British, the evacuation was hampered not just by a complete lack of the equivalent of the Ju-52 but also the lack of mechanical transport. The British air attaché in Paris came to the rescue through the commandeering of several hundred US lorries on a 'promise to return'. Nevertheless, despite superhuman efforts by aircrew and ground crew alike, the perception gathered in the French High Command that the RAF was 'running away'. In fact, the *Luftwaffe* now enjoyed air supremacy over France, launching large raids at individual targets and patrolling freely across the battlefield. As if further sacrificial evidence was needed, on 17 May, 82 Squadron (Blenheim) was wiped out, with 11 out of 12 aircraft shot down on a single mission. In addition to the obvious defeat of Allied air power, the perception of air supremacy by the Germans upon British and French units was to have lasting consequences on Army/Air relations.

PSYCHOLOGICAL EFFECT

Although the destruction meted out by the *Luftwaffe* to Allied defences was impressive, with Stuka attacks achieving very accurate bombing of French defences, it was the psychological impact of the attacks which mattered more as the campaign developed. Guderian's risk management in using air power for flank protection and as flying artillery had paid off. Stuka and Me 109 pilots flew up to seven times per day from dawn to dusk with medium bombers keeping up the pressure through the night. *Luftflotte* commanders realized the impact the conflation of the JU87 Stuka sirens, and the constant harassment attacks by Me 109 and Me 110 escort fighters had on a confused enemy. The Stuka in May 1940 represented the culmination of Udet's vision of highly accurate dive-bombing. Although they were slow and vulnerable if 'bounced' by Allied fighters, this campaign saw the effect of this aircraft and capability pay off.[62] Exhausted pilots were ordered back into the air, without loaded guns or bombs to fly mock attacks against the French positions. It worked. In the 55th Division sector, despite the efforts of

General Lafontaine to rally his men, the line broke. Horne describes this incident as a decisive point in the campaign.[63]

On the Allied side, crews flew with complete disregard for their safety or force protection in an attempt to stem the flood of Guderian's XIX Corps, which was fast becoming in practice the theoreticians' vision of an expanding torrent. But the correlation of forces was working against the Allies. Given the collapse of command and control and operational-level paralysis, the increasing penny packeting of Allied air power was making matters worse, with Allied losses rising and morale sinking for no tangible result on the enemy: perhaps with the notable exception of the Hurricanes of 1 and 73 Squadrons, which were giving a very good account of themselves. In particular, losses to the growing intensity of German layered air defences of anti-aircraft artillery and fighters were making continued Allied air operations untenable.[64] Horne describes the Meuse as a 'valley of death' for the Royal Air Force.[65] Allied air power would never again in the coming weeks be concentrated in anything more than flight/formation strength.

At the strategic level, the German bombing of Rotterdam on 14 May 1940 had caused mayhem in Paris and London. The panic in Rotterdam had quickly spread through the Dutch government. Grossly exaggerated casualty figures crossed the Channel, causing alarm in the British War Cabinet. The Dutch foreign minister quoted 30,000; post-war estimates suggest 3,000.[66] The British War Cabinet's rationale was that the German bombing of Rotterdam had changed the situation. Attacks by Bomber Command would relieve the pressure on the Allies in France through careful targeting of German industry – especially oil, which was estimated to be in short supply. We now know that this was pure fantasy. None the less, on the night of 15 May, a force of 58 Whitleys, Hampdens and Wellingtons set off from East Anglia and Lincolnshire for targets in north-east Germany. Terraine suggests that the only real damage inflicted was upon a warehouse in Bremen containing confiscated Jewish furniture. Here again, the psychological impact of the failure of Allied tactical air to stem the German tide has to be balanced against the need to preserve the forces for battles to come – and, at least, Bomber Command was taking the war to the enemy. At the time, the crews believed and reported that the night raids were having a major effect; it was subsequent analysis and the Butt Report of 1941 that were to revise this view.

The Allies' tactical air forces in France had expended their main effort to little avail and now needed rehabilitation and reconstitution. Meanwhile, at the tactical level, the *Luftwaffe* were 'on a roll'. That said, if the *Luftwaffe* Command looked hard enough there were many ominous signs: as Guderian's torrent expanded the short and internal lines of communication were becoming unsustainable, men and machines were already exhausted, weapon resupply was difficult, and the *Luftwaffe* had not yet been challenged in the air as they would be at Dunkirk.[67]

The days and weeks that followed were chaotic and confusing for Allied airmen in France. Allied air effort was largely a spent force.[68] Squadrons took off in flights and formations and recovered to their home bases to discover them occupied by the Germans. Equally, on 24 May near Arras, the *Luftwaffe* encountered French armour (forward elements of de Gaulle's 2nd Division) at the boundary of their 'new' airfield and took off hurriedly, with *Luftwaffe* groundcrew holding off French armour with Very Pistols. At the tactical level, the situation was confused. The Battle had been withdrawn to night operations – operations for which it was utterly unsuited.[69] At the operational level, command and control was broken; Barratt and Blount could not contact each other. Indeed, the command-and-control fracture was so deep that when Blount, as the Component Commander evacuated his Head-quarters codenamed 'Violet' at Premesques from France to Hawkinge in southern England to continue to attempt to operate from the UK, Barratt did not even know.[70]

At the strategic level, the Air Ministry was desperately concerned over the loss rate in France; an issue directly linked with Dowding's impassioned pleas for force preservation for the air defence of the UK. After the British counter-attack at Arras failed on 24/25 May, Gort realized that evacuation of the BEF was the only realistic option. The courage and determination that had won him nine Mentions in Dispatches, two Military Crosses, the Distinguished Service Order and the Victoria Cross in the First World War now came to the fore as he doggedly pursued this new and critical task. London, through Ironside as Chief of the Imperial General Staff (CIGS), did not understand the risk in the operational situation, and tried to move Gort to continue to support the French, but Gort would not be swayed from his course of action. For the air component, in the days that followed it was more of the same desperate struggles at the tactical level with one important difference. Now it was the *Luftwaffe*'s turn to stumble.

Despite the failure of the Allies' desperately unco-ordinated counter-attack at Arras and elsewhere, the German High Command was rattled. Confusion reigned as options were weighed and considered, culminating in the famous 'halt' decision in front of the Channel ports and Goering's bravura 'leave it to the *Luftwaffe*' claim. Goering had failed to understand just how tired his crews were – in campaign-planning terms, they had culminated and needed reconstitution. But, Goering's bluff and bravado held sway over Hitler's generals in the High Command, leading to Hitler's Directive: 'Dunkirk is to be left to the *Luftwaffe*. Should the capture of Calais prove difficult, this port too is to be left to the *Luftwaffe*.'[71] Now, Gort's dogged preparations and determination to rescue the BEF were given an unexpected window of opportunity. For British Air Forces in France (BAFF), the situation was desperate. Blount was attempting in vain to command and control the air element of the BEF from Hawkinge with sketchy information gleaned from the Air Ministry and virtually no idea of the situation on the ground in France. Even the successful tactical innovation of the combined Army/RAF reconnaissance mission had ceased to operate on 27 May.[72]

In the skies over Dunkirk during the withdrawal, the balance in the air switched to the RAF and its Spitfires. Again the perception differed from the reality. Dill, the newly appointed CIGS, defended the RAF stating that the squadrons had gone 'all out'. Ramsay, the Naval component commander, was less supportive. The Air Officer Commanding 11 Group, Air Vice-Marshal Keith Park, in his combat assessment reported 'total ascendancy' over the German bombers.[73] Furthermore, the remnants of Barratt's BAFF squadrons were attacking German interdiction targets in the rear of the battle area and, when they could be co-ordinated, providing direct support to British forces. Above all, the fog of war in northern France was intense. Land/air co-ordination was rare; 'blue-on-blue' engagements occurred, with Spitfires attacking Hurricanes over Dunkirk on more than one occasion.[74] To an extent that lingered, the shock effect of German air power against the BEF and French forces as they evacuated was the lasting perception.

Environmental factors were also seldom absent from interfering with military operations. Unseasonably poor weather intervened on several occasions to prevent German attacks. The evacuation was suspended on 4 June and, as the Official History recorded, despite the perception, the balance of advantage lay with the *Luftwaffe*, only on 27 May and 1 June.[75] The RAF had established local (albeit impermanent) air superiority. The German Army supported by a much-depleted *Luftwaffe* broke out to the south of the Channel coast in an offensive which began on 5 June. The RAF elements remaining in France did all that was possible in the days that followed to assist the Allied forces in a retreat fast becoming a rout. Vuillemin and the other French air generals pleaded with Barratt for more fighter squadrons and, even as late as 7 June, 17 and 242 Hurricane Squadrons were transferred to the AASF.

In a further twist, Mussolini (ever the opportunist) declared war on France and ordered his forces to invade the south of France. Authorized by the British War Council, 71 Wing of AASF formed the nucleus of a force named 'Haddock' to attack targets in Italy. The French authorities did not share British enthusiasm to take the war to Italy and on 11 June the situation descended into military farce when

British Wellington bombers at Salon preparing to bomb the Fiat works in Turin were blocked from take-off by French military lorries. The inherent friction within a military coalition now outweighed the military advantage. After six days of unsuccessful efforts, eight Wellingtons of 99 and 149 Squadrons attacked Genoa. One aircraft claimed to have found its target. The next day the French armistice ended the short life of Haddock force.[76]

Air Vice-Marshal Sholto Douglas, the Deputy Chief of Air Staff in London wrote to Barratt on 14 June, suggesting he should be prepared to evacuate. Failing to find sufficient suitable airfields in France, Barratt ordered the bomber elements of the AASF to evacuate to England on 15 June. By 17 June, Barratt was trying to cover seven evacuation ports with five fighter squadrons. This he did with the same grit and determination he had demonstrated since assuming command of BAFF as Commander-in-Chief in January 1940. But his war was over; he left for England the next day.[77] He was rewarded with a knighthood, promotion to Air Chief Marshal and command of the newly formed RAF Army Co-operation Command, but this was too starved of resources to make much progress in air/land cooperation.[78] In a twist of fate, Blount was killed in an aircraft crash in transit from RAF Northolt to RAF Aldergrove to act as the air component commander on an Army/RAF co-ordination exercise in October 1940. That said, Group Captains Woodall and Wann produced the Wann–Woodall Report, which clearly identified the need to improve land/air co-operation; a system that Barratt saw finally vindicated in 1944.[79]

THE RECKONING

The tempo of operations and the desperate situation for Britain in June 1940 prevented lengthy reflection by those who had triumphed, survived or had been humiliated. Both sides, however, had cause to reflect. By the end of June 1940, the French Air Force had more aircraft than at the start of the German attack in the west on the 10 May. Elements escaped to North Africa to continue to fight on. Large amounts of materiel were captured by the Germans and employed on several fronts throughout the war.[80] Of course this is largely explained by French production making good the losses and by deliveries from the United States. But it was largely irrelevant, because the fact is that the French Air Force system collapsed on all fronts under the shock of *Blitzkrieg*. The rigid command and control of air forces tied to land zones of responsibility broke down, severing effective communication. French aircraft proved largely inferior to the German aircraft, particularly in fighter versus fighter combat, and French crews, although they flew bravely, had not been schooled in aerial warfare, nor did they have the combat experience of the *Luftwaffe*. Moreover, the French air logistic system failed on all counts that mattered. Overall, therefore, the French Air Force failed in the test of battle; a battle for the survival of the nation. Vuillemin claimed at a meeting of the French War Cabinet on 25 May that the British had only 65 fighters in France and deliberately kept 650 aircraft in Britain. In fact, the majority of the RAF's fighter strength took part in the Battle in one way or another, with only three operational fighter squadrons out of 53 in total taking no part in the fighting.[81] French air generalship (with the exception of D'Astier) failed to exploit either the tenets of air power or the tactics and techniques of air warfare. Their career-long subservience to the Army mattered when moral courage was the order of the day.

The profit-and-loss account for the RAF was mixed. In addition to the squadrons in France, large elements of Fighter, Bomber and Coastal Command were continuously engaged in the struggle from 10 May to 17 June. The RAF hierarchy in the Air Ministry were only too aware of the fragility of the force they controlled. Barratt fully appreciated the strengths and weaknesses of the force he commanded.[82] The commanders did their best; Barratt and Blount emerge as leaders who understood the limits of the men and machines under their command. For example, Barratt took the bold step of limiting the Battle to night operations after three days, and ordered fighter protection for the Blenheim aircraft, whilst the Hurricane acquitted itself well. Tactics were changed after contact with the enemy, tactics that had a significant impact in the Battle of Britain. But Barratt and Blount were fighting with one hand tied behind their back, since Allied command-and-control arrangements were beset with peacetime compromises, which came apart under the shock of war. The disposition of the Force was made again for political rather than military rational. Sustaining the force from the UK proved problematic with weapons and fuel constantly in short supply. Indeed, for an expeditionary force, BAFF lacked internal mobility and flexible communications. Even if the efforts of the RAF made no difference to the outcome of the campaign, they made a difference to the service that was to go from strength to strength and become a force of over a million men. The *Luftwaffe* sustained losses of 1,284 aircraft and the core elements of the BAFF survived to fight again, now blooded in battle. Despite the perception born of tactical-level memoirs, the RAF made a significant contribution to the evacuation at Dunkirk.[83] The commanders of the BEF appreciated the efforts made to support them and the abiding heroism of the crews is testimony to their efforts.

For the *Luftwaffe*, the heady scent of victory was accompanied for a few commanders by doubts. The combination of the campaigns in

Poland, Denmark, Norway, Holland, Belgium and France had left it beyond the limits of sustainability. The German aircraft industry was not yet on a war footing; replacement aircraft were slow to arrive and the experience level of the replacement crews was a fraction of their forebears. The short lines of communication from within Germany in May had given way to stretched and broken lines of communication in June. It took months for the German forces simply to catalogue the sheer volume of matériel they had captured. Tactically, the exceptional levels of co-ordination achieved by the *Luftwaffe* during the Meuse crossing at Sedan had begun to break down by Dunkirk. The Stuka had proved to be easy prey for the Spitfires. Furthermore, the *Luftwaffe* had not prepared for maritime attack and, with violent evasive manoeuvre, Allied shipping had managed to avoid the fate of the French Army at Sedan.[84] On the people front, the seeds of destruction had been sown. The lack of a system of respite for squadrons and crews was to have dire long-term consequences. Morale was understandably high, but this led to complacency and swagger. The same level of intelligence preparation for the invasion of France had not taken place for the forthcoming, if putative, invasion of Britain. *Luftwaffe* generals Milch, Sperrle and Kesselring became Field Marshals; but the successful generalship which had carried the day at the Meuse would falter at the Medway.

CONTEMPORARY RELEVANCE

All campaigns must be placed in context. The context of 1940 will not be repeated. But that is not to say that this campaign does not have contemporary relevance. Following the end of the Cold War, coalition warfare has been in vogue with intervention expeditionary operations as the means of execution. Air components were established in the Gulf War of 1990, the Balkan Wars of the 1990s and the coalition operations against Afghanistan in 2001. History does not repeat itself but contemporary commanders will find much sympathy with the difficulties Barratt and Blount found in establishing and sustaining their forces. Allied command and control arrangements remain beset by compromise and, potentially, confusion. Local command remains reliant upon good, secure, interoperable communications even in the information age. A deep understanding of the enemy's intent, rather than counting his assets remains critical. Technology remains an enabler in warfare that offers crucial advantages, but it is the moral component that wins wars and the human qualities of leaders acting with determination and moral courage can prevail. For airmen of today, the critical nature of the air/land interface to sustain and support land manoeuvre is as true now as it was in 1940, and it remains as fragile.

The air campaign of 1940 has much to offer contemporary students of military history in general and the history of air warfare in particular. Airmen on all sides fought, won and lost with singular bravery. Few perhaps realized that they were participating in a turning point of air power history; that they were is not in dispute. This chapter is dedicated to them.

NOTES

1. Quoted in Richard P. Hallion, *Strike from the Sky* (Smithsonian Press, Washington, DC, 1989), p. 148.
2. Throughout the inter-war period British politicians who had taken an interest in aerial warfare predicted the 'bomber will always get through' (British Prime Minister Baldwin speaking in 1935).
3. After the Battle for France was over, the French Air Force became a rump force in North Africa with enormous amounts of air matériel in France falling into German hands. The looming defensive Battle of Britain rightly, distracted the Royal Air Force, Bomber Command was taking the war haphazardly to the enemy and Coastal Command struggling to contain the German submarine threat. Thus, air/land tactical co-operation continued to be neglected – with lasting consequences.
4. See, for example, Phillip Bell, *The Origins of the Second World War in Europe* (Longman, London, 1985), Ch. 2, or J. A. S. Grenville, *A History of the World in the Twentieth Century* (Belknap Press, Cambridge, MA, 1994), Ch. 25, p. 232.
5. See Phillip S. Meilinger, *The Paths of Heaven: The Evolution of Airpower Theory* (Air University Press, Maxwell, AL, 1997), Chs 1, 2 and 5 for an overview of the various air power theorists' views in the period 1918–39.
6. See Alan Stephens, 'The True Believers', in Stephens (ed.), *The War in the Air* (RAAF Air Power Studies Centre, Fairbairn, Australia, 1994), p. 70.
7. See James Corum, *The Luftwaffe: Creating the Operational Air War 1918–1940* (Kansas University Press, Lawrence, KS, 1997), Chs 4 and 5.
8. The neglect of air transport for air force mobility – a key enabler for operational level manoeuvre – by the Royal Air Force and the French Air Force remains undisputed. With the exception of a handful of obsolete bombers such as Handley Page Harrows and Dragon Rapides, the RAF and French Air Force relied upon mechanical transport – also in short supply. The French equivalent, the Potez 65 was not used until after the collapse of France in June 1940. Thus the mobility of Allied Air Forces was seriously inferior to that of the *Luftwaffe*. See Bill Gunston (ed.), *Jane's Fighting Aircraft of World War II, 1939–1945* (Studio Editions, London, 1999), p. 119.
9. This structural difference between the *Luftwaffe* and other air forces can trace its origin to 1917. The status, equipment and priority given to *Luftwaffe* Flak forces was a critical element in *Luftwaffe* success until 1943. Ground to air defence remains a much higher priority for the *Luftwaffe* than the USAF or the RAF to this day.
10. See Cajus Bekker, *The Luftwaffe War Diaries* (Macdonald, London, 1964), pp. 113–20.
11. See General Sir William Jackson and Field Marshal Lord (Edwin) Bramall, *The Chiefs* (Brassey's, London, 1985), p. 136 for the 'fun and games' surrounding the allocation of resources for defence in the 1920s and 1930s.

12. Unpublished history IX (Bomber) Squadron, RAF.
13. The 10-year rule enforced by the British Treasury postulated that Britain would have 10 years to prepare for war. The difficulty was in defining when the 10 years would begin.
14. See Kenneth Macksey on Hobart in John Keegan (ed.), *Churchill's Generals* (Warner, London, 1991), p. 250.
15. See B. H. Liddell Hart, *History of the Second World War* (Cassell, London, 1970), p. 19.
16. See André Van Haute, *Pictorial History of the French Air Force* (Ian Allan, London, 1974).
17. See Alfred Cobban, *A History of Modern France*, Vol. 3 (Penguin, London, 1965), p. 169.
18. See Shelford Bidwell on Kesselring in Corelli Barnett (ed.), *Hitler's Generals* (Phoenix, London, 1989), p. 270.
19. See Corum, *Luftwaffe*, p. 214.
20. Clausewitz, who always believed cohesion is the centre of gravity of any coalition, would have approved. As a sop, Wolfram von Richtofen took to wearing Spanish uniform!
21. See E. H. Carr, *Modern Spain* (Oxford University Press, Oxford, 1980), p. 150.
22. See Grenville, *History of the World*, p. 230; Corum, *Luftwaffe*, p. 222.
23. Some commentators ascribe a 'more Nazi' than the 'Imperial' German Navy or 'Weimar' Army, but at the tactical and operational level, the evidence is scant. See David Blackbourn (ed.), *Populists and Patricians: Essays in Modern German History* (Allen & Unwin, London, 1987), Ch. 3, p. 55, for a psychological interpretation.
24. See Alistair Horne, *To Lose a Battle, France 1940* (Macmillan, London, 1969), p. 123.
25. See Sir John Slessor, *The Great Deterrent* (Cassell, London, 1957).
26. The AASF represented the Bomber Command 'forward' element of No. 1 Group commanded by Air Vice-Marshal 'Pip' Playfair – ready to strike at Germany when the War Cabinet so decided. Bomber Command resisted all attempts to place AASF under Barratt. Orders issued by the Air Ministry settled the issue, but Barratt (understandably) relied more upon Blount than Playfair.
27. See Jackson and Bramall, *The Chiefs*, p. 187.
28. Following Barratt's elevation to become C-in-C BAFF in January 1940, Air Vice-Marshal Charles Blount became Lord Gort's Air Component Commander. See Victor Goddard, *Skies to Dunkirk* (Kimber, London, 1982), p. 97.
29. See Air Historical Branch Narrative, 'The Campaign in France'; pp. 114–24.
30. See Horne, *To Lose a Battle*, pp. 78–80, 155–6.
31. For a brief assessment of Barratt's part in the campaign and the difficulties he faced see Major L. F. Ellis, *The War in France and Flanders 1939–1940* (HMSO, London, 1953), pp. 324–5.
32. See John Terraine, *The Right of the Line* (Hodder, London, 1985), pp. 118–36. Terraine covers the difficulties facing Barratt once battle was joined. This chapter has highlighted the difficulties Barratt faced before 10 May 1940.
33. The Lysanders did their best, but there was no Allied equivalent of the *Blitzkrieg* system with its critical reliance upon secure radio communication over a single air/land radio net. See unpublished Squadron Histories of IV (AC) Squadron and XIII Squadron for the difficulties encountered by Lysander crews in France in 1940.
34. See Goddard, *Skies to Dunkirk*, p. 198 for the frustration felt by Blount and Goddard and senior British tactical commanders at the lack of operational security by their French colleagues.

35. See, Sir Edward Spears, *Assignment to Catastrophe* (Heinemann, London, 1956), p. 183 for a description of the exasperation experienced within the Allied Command Headquarters.
36. The summaries in the AHB Narrative make depressing reading.
37. Relative Air Strength 10 May 1940, German Archive Reference: DS3.
38. See Ursula Powys-Libbe, *The Eye of Intelligence* (Kimber, London, 1983), pp. 24–5 for the amateur nature of RAF photographic reconnaissance at this stage of the war. The AHB Narrative outlines the strength of 212 Squadron in May 1940 as 1 Ventura, 1 Electra, 1 Spitfire (p. 79).
39. For a more detailed account of the Mechelen Incident, see Philip Warner, *The Battle of France 1940* (Cassell, London, 1990), p. 37.
40. The myth was maintained until 1955, when the truth of the *Luftwaffe* mistake was revealed.
41. See Bekker, *Luftwaffe War Diaries*, p. 123.
42. For the action on the first day see Horne, *To Lose a Battle*, Ch. 9 *passim*.
43. The Battle was armed with a single rearward-facing Lewis gun – the same armament as First World War fighters!
44. Similarly the tactical-level experience gained by Barratt's crews during the Battle of France was to have a profound effect upon the Battle of Britain. Although not without friction or difficulty, the 'old sweats' from France were able to discredit the hallowed peacetime-derived tactical doctrine of Fighter Command – just in time.
45. See Jonathan Bailey, *The First World War and the Birth of Modern Warfare* (SCSI, Occasional Paper No. 22, Camberley, UK, 1996), for a vivid account of how First World War military planners under-estimated wartime consumption of shells by as much as 10:1.
46. Although accounts vary and give prominence to differing factors, all agree that Goering promised Hitler that the *Luftwaffe* could 'finish their job'. At 'Geschwader' level, the *Luftwaffe* was exhausted and the short and internal lines of supply, with which the campaign had commenced, had become long and fractured.
47. See Basil Liddell Hart, *The Other Side of the Hill* (Pan, London, 1978), p. 174, for an account of the detail of the conference and the 'vigorous' discussions between commanders.
48. See Heinz Guderian, *Panzer Leader* (Arrow, London, 1990), p. 481, for a description and layout of Corps-level German orders. See Goddard, *Skies to Dunkirk*, p. 147 for the British equivalent.
49. See Horne, *To Lose a Battle*, p. 320.
50. Ibid., p. 339.
51. Quoted in Ibid.
52. Ibid.
53. Ibid.
54. AHB Narrative, p. 207.
55. See Richard Holmes, *The Fatal Avenue* (Pimlico, London, 1996). Holmes's thesis is that this region of Europe has proved to be a continuous battleground for over 1,000 years; hence the 'Fatal Avenue'.
56. Horne, *To Lose a Battle*, p. 390.
57. Denis Richards, *The Royal Air Force 1939–1945*, Vol. 1 *The Fight at Odds* (HMSO, London, 1974), p. 126.
58. See Goddard, *Skies to Dunkirk*, p. 145 for an account of those desperate days.
59. Sadly, this did not end the misery for the Battle squadrons. The Battle was renowned to be a 'difficult' aircraft to fly at night largely because of the sparks and flames emanating from the exhaust of the Merlin engine, which blinded the pilot. This fact combined with desperate and rapid moves to new and unfamiliar airfields,

wartime blackout, poor weather and tired crews led to a loss rate from night operations approaching that of day – without interference from the enemy. Source: interview with veterans.

60. See Denis Richards, *Portal of Hungerford* (Heinemann, London, 1977), p. 154.
61. See Horne, *To Lose a Battle*, p. 543.
62. See Alfred Price, 'The Rise and Demise of the Stuka', *RAF Air Power Review*, Vol. 3, No. 4 (Autumn 2000), pp. 39–52.
63. See Horne, *To Lose a Battle*, p. 360.
64. The use of Flak as a tactical capability with operational effect was to be demonstrated time and again by the *Luftwaffe*. Flak troops were well equipped, well trained and motivated and in no way treated as a second-class elite within the *Luftwaffe*. Colonel von Hippel, Guderian's Flak commander was awarded the Ritterkreuz (German equivalent of the VC) for his supreme effort at Sedan. This focus upon air defence within the *Luftwaffe* survives to this day and is not replicated in doctrine or structures in British or US forces. See Stuart Peach, in Peter W. Gray (ed.), *Air Power 21* (The Stationery Office, London, 2000), p. 130, for the rationale behind this development which can be traced to 1916 and was to surface in Sicily and the Eastern Front.
65. Horne, *To Lose a Battle*, p. 390.
66. Despite the strategic impact of the bombing of Rotterdam, Kesselring insisted until his death that the bombing of Rotterdam was a tactical act against the port facilities and was in accordance with international law. See Barnett (ed.), *Hitler's Generals*, p. 252, for details.
67. For example, in the scale of events of 10–15 May, it was easy to overlook how successful the Hurricanes of 1 and 73 Squadrons had been in their early encounters with the Me 109. Tactics had been changed to 'spread' the harmonization of the eight machine guns, the Hurricanes had adopted German 'schwarm' tactics to excellent effect and replacement aircraft were fitted with the new metal propeller to enhance performance even more. For details, see unpublished History of 1 Squadron RAF.
68. See Basil Karslake, *The Last Act* (Leo Cooper, London, 1979), p. 252, for the administrative position of BAFF by 2 June 1940.
69. As the AHB Campaign narrative relates, several aircraft and valuable crews with battle experience were lost in accidents on landing because of the sheer difficulty of landing the Battle at night. Moreover, Wing and Squadron reports stated that the crews were simply bombing on estimated time of arrival since they had no means whatsoever to aid navigation at night. Barratt attempted to stamp out this practice; it continued but was not reported.
70. See Goddard, *Skies to Dunkirk*, p. 161.
71. Quoted in Laing (ed.), *Hitler's Diaries* (Cavendish, London, 1980), p. 123.
72. See Richards, *The Fight at Odds*, p. 131.
73. For the views of Dill, Ramsay and Park see ibid., pp. 131–3.
74. See ibid., p. 134.
75. Ibid., p. 141.
76. For a brief account of Haddock Force see ibid., pp. 145–7.
77. Ibid., pp. 147–9.
78. See Ian Gooderson, *Air Power at the Battlefront* (Cass, London, 1998) for details of the development of what, by 1944, had become close air support.
79. See ibid., p. 24.
80. See Neulen, *In the Skies of Europe* (Crowood, Munich, 2000), p. 219. The force comparisons on pp. 222–3 highlight the relative strengths between May and June 1940.

81. See Horne, *To Lose a Battle*, p. 627.
82. The AHB Narrative records Barratt's sober daily assessments despatched to the Air Ministry. It must have made grim reading for those charged with force preservation for the long war to come.
83. See Terraine, *Right of the Line*, pp. 155–7, Richards, *The Fight at Odds*, p. 133, for details which challenge the popular mythology of 'where was the RAF'.
84. See Richards, *The Fight at Odds*, p. 132, AHB Narrative, p. 330.

8

'Learning is Winning': Soviet Air Power Doctrine, 1935–41[1]

James Sterret

We are used to thinking that when Operation Barbarossa opened, the combat-experienced *Luftwaffe* met a combat-inexperienced VVS (*Voenno-vozdushniye sily*, the Soviet Air Force). Like most popular myths about the Soviet military, this is both true and false. While the VVS was woefully ill-prepared for combat, its pilots had seen combat in numerous locales in the previous five years.

Throughout almost its entire history, VVS officers would almost certainly have put forward two core principles for their actions: first, that their primary mission was to support the ground forces; and, second, that the means of doing this was to concentrate maximum force on the axis of the Army's main effort. This is an entirely logical attitude for a state with a large hostile land frontier. When war breaks out, the land war will be decisive because, as Lee Kennett puts it, 'when the infantry loses, everybody loses'.[2] Since the Soviet Union did not possess the strategic luxury of a large water barrier, the VVS accepted that strategic bombardment was a luxury. Furthermore, before the Second World War many were doubtful of its utility, on grounds of inaccuracy, technical limitations of the aircraft, and the realization that bombing cities and factories necessarily entailed bombing workers, whom many supposed would be the Soviet Union's natural allies in the expected revolutionary general war against the capitalist world.

How to accomplish that support mission, however, was not a topic of general agreement. Debate covered not only the value of close, near, and operational support, and the desirable level of subordination of VVS units to Army formations, but the expected nature of the upcoming air war itself. Until 1928, the central line of fracture in VVS debate ran between those who insisted on staying grounded in the reality of a 'small air force', such as the Soviet Union actually possessed, and proponents of a 'large air force', which the Soviet Union might, it was hoped, someday have the industrial power to possess.

The plans of the 'large air force' camp ranged from the plausible to the grandiose. The 'small air force' camp generally suggested that the VVS should engage in a strategy of force preservation, ruthlessly concentrating its forces to commit them on the most important axis at critical stages of the operation and thus seeking not to challenge the enemy air force overall, but only to wrest the ability to conduct missions for a limited time and space from a enemy expected to have numerical and technological superiority. Concentration of force on the decisive axis was the point of agreement between the small air force proponents, and the less outlandish of the large air force proposals.

However, beyond the general notions that the ground force should be supported, and that the air force should mass both to overcome aerial resistance and to ensure a sufficient density of fire on whatever targets were to be bombed, agreement on methods was often slight, and manuals generally vague, often simply presenting a laundry list of possible missions without suggesting one was necessarily more useful than another. In short, the Soviets knew what end result they desired, but were not certain how to obtain it.

With the unveiling of the first Five-Year Plan, the rational end of the large air force camp won that debate: the Plan placed great emphasis on creating the heavy industry necessary for the mass production of military machinery and on the subsequent production of that machinery. In addition, the Army was bringing forth its 'Deep Battle' and 'Deep Operations' theories, emphasizing the operational level of war. Both were intended to overcome the problems of warfare discovered in the First World War. Deep Battle concentrated on the need to suppress the enemy 'throughout the depths of his defence' in order to conduct a successful penetration attack, and assigned the Air Force missions at all stages of the battle: close support in the break-in, near support for the suppression of artillery and the tactical interdiction of reserves, and operational interdiction to isolate the entire area. Deep Operations considered the problem of what to do with a penetration once achieved, and, again, the VVS was expected to provide extensive support to the exploiting ground forces in overcoming enemy reserves, both through close support and through interdiction. This general concept fitted quite well with what the Air Force already thought it ought to be doing, though in fact the VVS tended to concentrate on tactical support rather than operational interdiction. One particular action the VVS considered its special province was the opening stage of a war, expected to occur before both sides had mobilized. The VVS intended, in theory, to conduct a highly active campaign to derail enemy mobilization and gain the upper hand over the enemy air force before the main ground forces had been mobilized and deployed – though it is unclear whether this oft-expressed intent was ever translated into concrete planning.

As did other states, the Soviet Union debated the sorts of aircraft it ought to build. This intertwined directly with debates over how air superiority ought to be gained and kept: which is more important, aerial combat or bombing airbases? Should fighters be single-seat and single-engined, or multi-engined? Were fighters useless in the face of the power of turret-mounted armaments? In the mid-1930s, Soviet opinion increasingly tended towards favouring strikes on airbases as the principal means of gaining air superiority. Most of the time, this was assumed to be a combined affair, with fighters, bombers and close-attack aircraft cooperating. However, in 1936, the Italian air strategist Giulio Douhet, who had hitherto routinely come in for criticism, suddenly came into vogue for reasons that are entirely unclear. Suddenly, nearly every commentator in the Soviet military press – though not their official manuals – became convinced of the overwhelming superiority of bombers through their ability to overfly all AAA (Anti-Aircraft Artillery), overcome all fighter opposition with their turret-mounted armament, and to gain air superiority through the destruction of enemy airbases. By the summer of 1936, the sole vocal heretic was A. N. Lapchinskii,[3] who doggedly continued to support his pet project, the Universal Aircraft (a fighter-bomber).

Beginning in late 1936, the VVS was presented with a series of opportunities to realistically appraise its situation: in Spain, in Finland and in three different wars in China. The Soviets were interested in learning lessons from these conflicts, and had in place mechanisms to do so: the Intelligence Directorate prepared and published reports, and various aspects of the wars were debated in Soviet military journals.[4] Of these five conflicts, two appear to have had relatively little impact on Soviet thinking.

In 1938, they faced no aerial opposition at Lake Khasan, because the Japanese government forbade the Japanese Air Force from becoming involved in the hope of keeping the conflict – which was initiated by the Japanese Army without government sanction – limited. Thus, the VVS was able to drop bombs at Japanese troops without interference – 'at' not on, because accuracy was quite poor, in part due to political insistence on bombing when the target was covered in fog. The other part of the problem was poor training, but notice of this appears to have fallen in with the routinely made and ignored complaints that aircrew training, as seen in manoeuvres and exercises, was not up to par.[5]

It is harder to understand why the Chinese war was largely ignored by Soviet analysts. Despite the fact that the Soviets sent 985 aircraft to China (648 were sent to Spain),[6] the war in China received little attention – to the extent that writers at the time would back arguments by saying 'Experience in Spain and China shows that ...' and then use examples exclusively from Spain. Spain may have been seen as a better example than China because both sides were European, but this is not entirely clear. In any event, the earlier half of the Spanish Civil War was carefully studied, as were the upcoming conflicts at Khalkin-Gol (May–September 1939) and Finland (December 1939–March 1940). However, study and generalization must be followed up with implementation. Examining the lessons the Soviets thought they had learned yields a picture of a force that examined its conflicts, but internalized the lessons in a very idiosyncratic manner, as a result of which lessons were discerned, but often had to be rediscovered in the next conflict.

Sometimes, the system worked even when the lesson ran counter to prevailing opinion. For example, when the VVS entered the war in Spain, Soviet fighters provided to the Spanish government began to oppose rebel bomber raids on Madrid. Never mind that the bombers were lightly armed: with 'Our Heroes' defending Right and Justice while flying single-seat fighters, it must have been both politically and patriotically difficult to continue to doubt the utility and effectiveness of the single-seat fighter. Few continued to hold that opinion, and almost overnight the right of fighter aircraft to exist was confirmed and not challenged again.[7] Equally, sometimes experience confirmed previously held opinions. The Soviets felt that the 1937 Battle of Guadalajara, where air power played a decisive role in shattering a rebel offensive, vindicated theories on the potential effectiveness of close air support, though most analyses of the operation were careful to point out its numerous special features and the equally significant contributions of other arms.[8]

Similarly, after suffering heavy losses going toe-to-toe with the Japanese Air Force in China at Wuhan, the Soviets adopted force-preservation strategies, developed for their expected small air force of the 1920s, to good effect. These entailed basing aircraft in the deep rear, ceding most of the airspace to the Japanese, but enabling their aircraft to escape Japanese raids. However, from these rearward bases they could move forward, briefly refuel at forward airbases, and then embark on concentrated raids, thereby creating a measure of surprise and also, they hoped, temporary local superiority over the Japanese. However, the Soviets took only limited note, since they no longer expected to be facing the same strategic situation themselves.[9]

Other lessons, however, were rather less clearly taken on board. A lesson that appears to have been completely missed was the new 'finger-four' tactics pioneered by the Germans in Spain. Whether this is because not enough Soviet pilots were still in Spain at the time of their introduction, or because the Soviets felt their own triplet-based tactics were sufficiently effective, is unclear – but hardly a whisper of these tactics showed up in the official analyses and Soviet military journals.

Before the Spanish Civil War, Soviet theorists had been quite taken with the notion of strikes on enemy airbases as a means of gaining the upper hand in an air war. A 1937 analysis of the Spanish War noted that bombing airbases was, 'a much more difficult matter than had been anticipated in peacetime'.[10] While some initial strikes by both sides met with a fair degree of success, both sides also quickly learnt that frequent basing changes, a good warning system, careful camouflage and false airbases made it difficult to discover enemy airbases, arrive with suffi-cient surprise to catch enemy aircraft on the ground, and bomb or strafe them with enough accuracy to do any damage. Despite the near-complete lack of success with such strikes in Spain once both sides had dispersed and camouflaged their airbases, most Soviet theorists were convinced that improved co-ordination between reconnaissance units and strike units, the use of low-altitude approaches, and repeated systematic strikes would ensure airbase attack remained an important technique in the air war.

In Spain, lessons regarding airbase communications, dispersal and *maskirovka* (operational deception) were learnt. These were learnt afresh in China. At Khalkhin-Gol, they had to be relearnt from scratch once more. The upper echelons of the VVS became increasingly doubt-ful of the utility of these strikes, as evidenced by the heated argument on the issue at the December 1940 General Staff Conference, the result of which was that many thought strikes on airbases could only succeed under special circumstances – such as the outbreak of war – given conditions of proper warning, dispersal and *maskirovka*. What is strange, however, is that having learnt of the importance of these methods in preventing losses at their own airbases in Spain, the Soviets did not implement measures to protect themselves before fighting broke out at Khalkhin-Gol – or in the western Soviet Union before Barbarossa.

The VVS finally engaged another air force in its own right, instead of through assistance programmes, in May 1939, when combat broke out in Mongolia near Khalkin-Gol. In the process, it demonstrated not only that it had completely failed to implement the lessons learnt in earlier conflicts, but also a distinct talent for learning quickly once combat had been joined: a pattern that would be repeated in Finland and in the war with Germany.

The VVS had two regiments stationed in Mongolia at the outbreak of the war, and their initial performance was dismal. Green pilots and poor states of repair led the Soviets to lose, by their own account, 15 Soviet aircraft for every Japanese aircraft shot down – a rate of loss sustained only through immediate reinforcement of the combat zone. After a disastrous attempt to attack a Japanese airbase on 27 May 1939, in which 13 I-15 fighters sortied, but only one returned, the Soviets stopped flying for nearly a month in order to try to sort out their problems.[11]

Marshal Zhukov summoned a group of 48 pilots and engineers, most of whom had combat experience in Spain and China. The group was headed by Iakov V. Smushkevich,[12] who was then the representative of the Chief of the Air Force Directorate and a decorated veteran pilot of the Spanish War. Debrief and analysis discerned numerous tactical flaws, including a near-complete lack of co-operation among aircraft, a consistent failure to attempt to gain altitude or positional advantages before entering combat, a dearth of experienced pilots, and Japanese use of radio communications. Three weeks of intensive training followed before the Soviets took to the air again.[13]

The VVS next entered combat on 22 June 1939. The training showed; both Japanese and Soviets agree the Soviet performance was much improved. The Japanese, in order to try to retain superiority, struck at the Soviet airbases on 27 June, destroying at least 16 aircraft. Smushkevich's team – which had already been there for several weeks – identified and corrected weaknesses in the early-warning systems, tightened up airbase defence, and instituted dispersal and *maskirovka* of the aircraft and bases. (The Chinese lesson of deep basing was not utilized because the Soviets aimed for air superiority, not force preservation, at Khalkin-Gol.) The Soviets claim not to have lost aircraft on their airbases after this.[14] Yet we must wonder why they were caught napping in the first place, since lessons on dispersal and camouflage had been repeatedly noted in both Spain and China and should have been corrected earlier.

Despite hard fighting in the air on both sides, the Soviets continued to improve, helping to blunt the Japanese offensive in July, and then preventing Japanese aerial reconnaissance from detecting the Red Army's deployments for Zhukov's shattering attack in August. Air commanders were attached to ground staffs to improve ground support, as had been done in China and Spain, and all aircrew worked on improving co-ordination in the air. All told, the Soviets engaged on a crash course in making their doctrine actually work; this crash course was reasonably successful.[15]

Several lessons learned at Khalkin-Gol were acted on. The importance of radios for organized group combat by fighters became clear enough that an official requirement for a light, reliable radio for all fighters resulted. The Soviets also learnt, as in Spain, that speed was a prime requirement for fighters. Thus, biplanes were proven to be ineffective, despite their better turning radius, and I-15 production was curtailed as the beginning of a belated process of phasing them out of service. Conversely, the development of new fighters and attack aircraft to replace the I-15, I-16 and SB, begun on the basis of the Spanish War, was accelerated, while development and production of more expensive heavy aircraft was greatly slowed. The aircraft resulting from those programmes began to roll off the assembly lines in 1940–41. Air-to-air and air-to-ground rockets were tested and the air-to-ground rockets found to be quite effective.[16]

A few incorrect lessons were also drawn: because machine-gun armed fighters got more kills against unarmoured Japanese aircraft, cannon armament was underrated, and though the development of heavier aircraft armament continued, some of their designs from this period have been criticized for lack of firepower. Flaws in the conduct of group battle, navigation and aerial combat appeared but were not addressed beyond the confines of the battle area. Some commanders, notably G. P. Kravchenko and P. V. Rychagov, who had also seen combat in Spain and China, came away from the war convinced that strikes on enemy airbases were largely ineffective – given camouflage and dispersal. The Soviets may have decreased the attention paid to airbase defence as a result.[17]

One particularly important lesson seems to have been missed: that it was strange that any of these lessons needed to be learnt at all. The same lessons had been learnt in both Spain and China. They had been written up, published and presumably distributed to Air Force units. But the use of experience is a two-way street, not only must experience be gathered and analysed, it must also be disseminated, understood, taught and put into practice. The effectiveness of Smushkevich's group in turning around the air war at Khalkin-Gol is noteworthy, and in doing so he earned his second Hero of the Soviet Union. Yet in a sense the honour was undeserved, since the need for a crash programme shows that the Soviets were unsuccessful in actually making use of the lessons they were learning until they had already got a bloody nose.

A few months after the conclusion of hostilities at Khalkin-Gol, Soviet aviation found itself engaged in a much more public arena: Finland. The disastrous performance of the Red Army in the first month of the Winter War (1939–40) is well known, but we should not forget that the Red Army reformed and retrained for eventual painful success in Finland.[18] The Red Air Force went through a similar process, with an equally painful beginning and eventually a somewhat less painful conclusion.

Some of the initial problems were ostensibly not of their making – the weather was terrible. Temperatures ran, on average, from minus 25 degrees C to minus 45 degrees C and dipped down to minus 50 degrees C for a few days. In the course of three months and 13 days of combat, only 24 days were good flying weather, the rest involving some combination of visibility under 4 kilometres, storms, low clouds and fog.[19]

However, the problems caused by low temperatures should have been foreseen. It is widely known that winter is cold in northern Russia and Finland, and this should have been no more of a surprise to the Soviets in 1939–40 than it is claimed to have been to the Germans in 1941. Thus, reports of engines and machine-guns freezing up, and of poor facilities for pilots and crews against the cold, indicate poor preparation in both cases. Further evidence of poor preparation comes from the 'very low' standards of maintenance found by an inspection team during the war.[20]

Bad weather would seem to be a better excuse for poor performance, but the Soviets were unhappy with their results in this regard. To their dismay, programmes intended to train pilots to fly in night and bad weather had almost completely failed – indeed, even the trainers could not perform the tasks well. Training was a problem to the extent that many pilots had great difficulty flying in formation in clear daylight, let alone manoeuvring in formation. As a result, performing these tasks in anything other than clear daylight was almost impossible.[21]

On top of this, bomber pilots were often unable to hit their targets. Komkor R. S. Shelukhin, reporting to Defence Minister Voroshilov on the activity of Soviet bombers in the first month of the war, stated that:

> Hundreds of bombers are sent, thousands of bombs are dropped, and tens of aircraft are lost, in order to destroy some object ... [T]he accomplishment of this mission drags out for weeks and in the end loses its intended purpose, and the destruction itself does not lead to the intended goal. This leads to a great waste of resources and pointless loss of strength, as a single zveno [triad of aircraft] should be sufficient for the destruction of one of these objects, if it were well trained with dive bombers and could accomplish the mission on one sortie.[22]

Air units repeatedly used the same paths to targets, allowing the Finns to predict their courses and meet them with defences of increasing power.[23] Co-ordination problems between the Leningrad Military District's Air Force and the Baltic Fleet Air Force led to several friendly-fire incidents and the loss of at least three aircraft before special recognition marks were added.[24]

Shelukhin, heading up a special investigation a month into the war, placed the blame for this on the youth and inexperience of the Air Force commanders, some of whom, he wrote, were so inexperienced that they were unaware of their ignorance. Not only were they unfit to lead their units in combat, they were incapable of administering them in peacetime.[25] In previous conflicts, the numbers of aircraft had been small and the crews experienced, by dint of bringing in every experienced aircrew available if need be. The same recipes were failing with inexperienced crews, the supply of experienced crews being insufficient to the task. In

Finland, the inexperience was part of the reason that, 'our powerful aviation, with such colossal numerical superiority, could do almost nothing to the enemy in the course of a month'.[26] The Soviets were aware that despite their efforts, traffic moved freely on Finnish railroads and roads, Finnish command and control had remained untouched, and attempts to blockade Finland from outside supply had been a failure.[27]

The Leningrad Military District's Air Force staff had a number of problems, not least of which was a continual alteration of the intended missions. While the air staff worked hard to try to deal with the many and changing requirements, Shelukhin found the lack of operational focus distressing:[28] 'There is no purpose, there is no co-ordination of actions, no calculations, not one planned operation. And in this manner people hope to win easily.'[29] This lack of a central planning was worsened by the theories propounded by F. A. Arzhenukin, who was successful in convincing others in the Soviet military that a very limited number of bombs were sufficient to devastate all targets in a given area. This theory, however pretty on paper, was thoroughly disproven in practice when the Soviets had dropped thousands of bombs on some areas to no appreciable effect – and of this the Soviets did take note.[30]

Shelukhin recommended that all of the Air Force commands be centralized into one command, and provided with specific goals for focused operations. The recommended operational goals were the suppression of the Finnish Air Force, breaking the Finnish road and rail net, destroying Finnish command and control, isolating Finland from external sources of assistance, and tactical support of the ground troops.[31] However, this recommendation was not followed, and Soviet air units were divided among armies and corps in order to ensure prompt and effective tactical support. This reorganization had disastrous repercussions, which I shall discuss below.

Despite the identification of many problems, matters did not dramatically improve, unlike at Khalkin-Gol. Part of the problem was the unco-operative weather. However, the deeper roots lay in training problems. While these appear to have been overcome at Khalkin-Gol, where the weather was better, the force smaller, and target areas easier to differentiate, they were not so easily overcome in the Karelian winter and forests with more forces engaged.

For example, the 50th Rifle Corps, tasked with cracking the Mannerheim Line at Summa, noted a near total lack of air support until 30 January 1940. The first ten days of February brought better weather and some 653 sorties into the Corps' area – a frontage and depth of six kilometres. However, bad weather prevented aviation from supporting the actual artillery preparation and initial attack on 11 February, and support thereafter was sporadic at best. A success on 18 February, when the 50th Rifle Corps' AAR (After Action Report) claims an artillery reconnaissance aircraft called effective artillery fire on to approaching Finnish reserves near Raiakorpi, serves to highlight the dearth of any other reported employment of aviation.[32]

At the Finnish war's end, the Red Air Force had not notably succeeded in meeting any of its objectives. Tactical support improved but was generally absent. The Finnish road and rail network continued to function. Finnish command and control was affected but not critically impaired. Finnish industry and foreign supplies were not slowed. Soviet efforts at terror-bombing towns and villages produced no useful results and probably stiffened Finnish resistance, as the Soviets should have known from their reports on the Spanish War. Overall, the results obtained were in no way commensurate with the effort expended and some 600 aircraft lost.[33]

Thus, from 1936 through 1940, the Soviets engaged in a series of combats of increasing scale. In Spain, when their aircraft were the most modern and their pilots hand-picked, they enjoyed a fair degree of success. At Khalkin-Gol, the local air units were caught flat-footed, but an infusion of expertise and reinforcements rectified the situation. The last of these small wars, against Finland, was also the largest, leaving the Soviets with the least ability to compensate for their problems by bringing in expertise from beyond the combat zone. Coupled with the difficulties of the theatre, the war with Finland exposed both the weaknesses in the combat preparation of Soviet air units and the fact that aircraft which had been world-class a scant four years before, over Spain, were already sliding into obsolescence. While in smaller wars the Soviets were able to overcome their problems, the Finnish war was of sufficient scope to overwhelm the ad-hoc solutions that had worked elsewhere.

Looking back over the record of these small wars, we see that a repeatedly missed opportunity in Soviet aviation is radio. With hindsight, radio was the obvious solution to many of the problems the VVS was struggling to solve. The Soviets were well aware that the *Luftwaffe* used it to great effect in Spain, and the Japanese at Khalkin-Gol. Some Soviets were great fans of radio, aware of the developments in tactics that radio made possible.[34] Yet what seems obvious in hindsight was not entirely obvious at the time. Radio in the 1930s was in a state comparable to the efforts to digitize the battlefield today: a potentially powerful tool, but a new and not necessarily reliable or wieldy one. The Germans had cracked the problem of making a lightweight, easy-to-use radio for a pilot, and the Soviets had not. Aircraft in Spain were initially equipped with radios, but the radios were heavy and slowed the aircraft down, thus reducing their survivability in combat. Moreover, external antenna either broke or slowed the aircraft, while internal antennae had to be supported by hand in order to function – a difficult task when flying in combat. Because of these difficulties, Soviet military intelligence reported in 1937, 'The fighter aviation of the Republican Army, in conducting its combat sorties, never once used its radios in the air, as a result of which they were removed.'[35] It took Khalkin-Gol to generate an official requirement for a lightweight, easy-to-use radio for all Soviet combat aircraft. Delays in the development of such a radio would be easier to understand if an official push to develop one had been begun earlier.

That delay links with a wider problem the Soviets faced. Despite repeated observations on the critical importance of good communications, consistent drastic underinvestment in signals ensured that Soviet communications were rarely up to scratch. This appeared not only in radios for aircraft, but also in communications gear for headquarters units. The latter deficits became starkly apparent in Finland, where they were a key factor driving the Soviets to sacrifice operational flexibility on the altar of tactical effectiveness by subordinating air units directly to ground armies and corps instead of holding them at the Army Group level. The sacrifice was not entirely successful. Worse, when extended throughout their force structure, it assigned 60 per cent of all aviation to armies, ensuring that the Soviets could not concentrate the VVS on the main axis in 1941. Thus, the inadequacy of their signals drove the Soviets to measures that ran directly counter to their thinking and intent for the employment of their forces. Overturning this force structure in 1942, by subordinating some aviation to *fronts* (army groups) and most of it as High Command Reserve, was perhaps the most important single step in improving the ability of the VVS to take on the *Luftwaffe*.

Moreover, some Soviets were aware that downward subordination was a poor expedient. Smushkevich highlighted the organizational and signals problems, alongside other dismal assessments of readiness, at the 1940 Conference. However, the VVS signals budget for 1941 only paid for 18 per cent of required equipment. As a result, regardless of an air unit commander's views on, say, the defensive value of dispersal over multiple airbases, greater dispersal than was practised in the spring of 1941 would have left air units cut off from the chain of command. The Soviets chose to retain the possibility of communications, and concentrated at far fewer airbases than they possessed. However, the consistent shortage of signals assets, which was present in the Army as well as the Air Force, and which extended to paper Table of Organization & Equipment (TOE) levels of signals equipment which were inadequate to the tasks intended, even if they had been met, suggests that the Soviet military systematically undervalued signals, and for this it paid a very heavy price.[36]

Experience in Finland made it impossible to continue to ignore the poor state of officer and pilot training, which had been repeatedly observed in exercises and was apparent in the early stages of Khalkin-Gol, but about which little appears to have been done. The Finnish War proved a sufficiently public humiliation that the Soviets took notice and moved to try to correct their faults. These efforts were still ongoing when the Soviets were plunged into their sixth war in as many years.

Thus, the Achilles' heel of the VVS learning process was peacetime implementation. The Soviets placed a premium on the 'analysis and generalization' of war experience. None the less, despite extensive analysis, the VVS demonstrated a consistent pattern of failing to learn from its previous errors, even when those errors had been identified and practical solutions tested in combat. Units at Khalkin-Gol seem to have been initially oblivious of experience from Spain and China, and those in Finland unaware of lessons from Khalkin-Gol. Why this occurred is not entirely clear.

We can suppose that the lessons learnt might have been considered too embarrassing for public discussion. However, failings in manoeuvres were discussed in the open military press before Finland. Possibly the RU analyses were not distributed to units, but their print runs were large enough to have made that possible, and the lessons were discussed in the open press. More likely is a confluence of problems in education and the stifling effects of the purges.

The 6,000 officers lost to the purges combined with a massive expansion of the force structure – from 1.5 million in the Red Army and Air Force in 1938, to 5 million in June 1941 – to create a deficit of some 60,000 officers in 1941, despite an equally gigantic expansion in the number of flight schools, from 12 in 1937 to 83 in June 1941. However, these schools lacked half of their aircraft and instructors, and over half of their allotted fuel. Moreover, the flight-training regimen was shortened seven times in 1939 and 1940, bringing the peacetime training programme to the ten-hour span used in wartime. Moreover, they filled out the ranks of instructors by taking the most promising students and placing them immediately into the role of instructor (and we should note that when the war broke out, the Soviets stripped instructors from the schools for front-line replacements). This deficit of officers and rapid attrition in the highest ranks produced extraordinarily rapid promotion. Most officers had held their posts for under a year, and some officers, such as Smushkevich, went from pilot to Head of the Air Force in five or six years. This combined with accelerated training to produce many officers who had been promoted well beyond their level of incompetence.[37]

That was, unfortunately, a poor structure upon which to build Timoshenko's crash reforms of 1940–41, as many units would be unable to absorb the lessons being taught.

Worse, the purges probably reduced an officer's willingness to rectify problems, because bringing to light the existence of problems might lead to arrest. Western societies tend to assume that 'the squeaky wheel gets the grease', the equivalent Russian proverb ran: 'the tallest nail gets hammered'.[38] Reporting one's command as being at less than perfect combat readiness, regardless of its actual state, might have been a short route to becoming a tall nail and thereby attracting the hammer of the NKVD (secret police). Thus, while the purges only accounted for 10 per cent of the total deficit of VVS officers, they cast a long and pernicious shadow by encouraging officers to hide problems in their units, hoping that rapid promotion rates would move them away before the problems were discovered. While the political climate became friendlier to effective reform after Finland, with General Timoshenko's emphasis on realistic training for combat, the pace of expansion also increased, creating a counter-balancing deficit of trained personnel. It should not be forgotten that Smushkevich wound up in very hot water indeed for daring to report that the VVS was unfit to counter the *Luftwaffe*, this being one of the factors that led to his being arrested in early 1941 and eventually shot. Equally, however, this factor should not be overestimated: while the purges made the penalty potentially quite extreme, every society contains come measure of censure for those who blow whistles.

None the less, after Finland the atmosphere was such that faults – and poor progress towards rectifying them – were openly discussed and improvement, however slow, was underway. Smushkevich summed up the difficulties facing the Soviet Air Force thus in December 1940:

> ... our problems stem from the fact that we do not bring into life that which we know; troubles / because we do not teach our VVS / how to carry out the forms of combat employment of the VVS / which we know.[39]

Yet under these troubles lay a lack of certainty on how to translate mission guidelines into action, as noted by S. K. Timoshenko[40] at the same conference in the section of his summary speech on the Air Force:

> ... the leadership of the VVS does not have a unity of views on such questions as the nature and conduct of an operation, assessing the enemy, methods of conducting aerial warfare and bending the opponent to our will, choice of target, etc. We must bring order to this area, and the sooner, the better.[41]

NOTES

1. As quoted in Daniel Bolger, *The Battle for Hunger Hill* (Novato, CA: Presidio, 1997), p. 39.
2. Lee Kennett, 'Retrospective', in R. Cargill Hall (ed.), *Case Studies in Strategic Bombardment* (Washington, DC: US Government Printing Office, 1998), pp. 623–32.
3. Aleksandr Nikolaevich Lapchinskii, 1887–1938, was a Tsarist artillery officer and observer-navigator, then a Soviet Air Force officer, and taught at the Zhukovskii Academy for many years; he was a prolific and lucid writer on the Air Force.
4. Key for this study were *Vestnik Vozdushnogo flota* (Air Force Herald), the journal of the VVS, and *Voennaia Misl'* (Military Thought), the journal of the General Staff.
5. Reina Pennington, 'From Chaos to the Great Patriotic War', in Robin Higham *et al.* (eds), *Russian Aviation and Air Power in the Twentieth Century* (London: Frank Cass, 1998), p. 49; Alvin Coox, *Nomonhan: Japan against Russia, 1939* (Stanford, CA: Stanford University Press, 1990), Ch. 10; B. M. Teplinskii, 'Boevaia aviatsiia vo vzaimodeistvii s nazemnimi voiskami', *Vestnik vozdushnogo flota*, 8 (1938), pp. 26–32.
6. G. F. Krivosheev (ed.), *Soviet Casualties and Combat Losses in the Twentieth Century* (London: Greenhill, 1997), pp. 46–7.
7. This change was noted at the time as well. See B. Ageev, 'Protivovozdushnaia oborona Madrida', *Pravda*, 29 Dec. 1936 (No. 318), quoted in I. Kovalev, 'Rol' i zadachi sovremennoi istrebitel'noi aviatsii', *Voennaia Misl'*, Nos 5–6 (1937), p. 102.
8. S. Liubarskii, 'Nekotorie vivodi iz opita voini v Ispanii. Nastuplenie', *Voennaia mysl'*, 10 (1938), pp. 12–31; *Voina v Ispanii*, 3, *Boevie deistviia aviatsii* (Moscow: Gosvoenizdat, 1937); P. I. Samoilov, *Guadalakhara: Razgrom Italianskogo ekspeditionnogo korpusa* (Moscow: Gosvoenizdat, 1940).
9. A. Alimov, 'Operativnoe ispol'zovanie VVS na Voina v Kitae', *Vestnik vozdushnogo flota*, 7 (1938), pp. 18–24.
10. *Voina v Ispanii*, 3, *Boevie deistviia aviatsii* (Moscow: Gosvoenizdat, 1937), p. 13.
11. M. V. Novikov, *Boevie deistviia na Khalkhin-Gole v 1939 godu i ikh znachenie dlia razvitiia Sovetskogo voennogo iskusstva* (Dissertation: Institute of Military History of the Ministry of Defence of the USSR, Moscow, 1974), pp. 56–8. Coox, *Nomonhan*, pp. 241–2. Coox confirms a single Japanese loss as of 20 May 1939, but in most respects the two accounts (Novikov's and Coox's) are very difficult to correlate beyond the general course of the air war.
12. Iakov Vladimirovich Smushkevich, 1904–41; political officer in an aviation brigade in the Russian Civil War, completed flight school in 1931, flew in defence of Madrid in 1936, Chief of the Air Force in 1939. Arrested and shot in 1941.
13. Novikov, *Boevie deistviia na Khalkhin-Gole*, pp. 58–60.
14. Novikov, *Boevie deistviia na Khalkhin-Gole*, pp. 59–61, 66.
15. Novikov, *Boevie deistviia na Khalkhin-Gole*, pp. 115–30.
16. Novikov, *Boevie deistviia na Khalkhin-Gole*, pp. 159–60, 177–8.
17. Novikov, *Boevie deistviia na Khalkhin-Gole*, pp. 155–8, 162, 177–8.
18. Carl van Dyke, *The Soviet Invasion of Finland* (London: Frank Cass, 1997).
19. *Boevie deistviya VVS KBF v voine c belofinami (c 30 noyabrya 1939 g. Po 13 marta 1940 g.)* (Moscow: Godvoenmorizdat NKVMF SSSR, 1941), pp. 6–7, 139.
20. *Boevie deistviya VVS KBF* (Moscow: Godvoenmorizdat NKVMF SSSR, 1941), pp. 131–6; *Doklad Komkora R. S. Shelukhina k N.K.O. Marshalu Sovetskogo Souiuza tov. Voroshilovu. 13.1.40.* (F. 29, d 26, o. 202, ll. 83–7).
21. *Doklad Komkora R. S. Shelukhina* (F. 29, d 26, o. 202, ll. 77–8); *Boevie deistviya*

VVS KBF (Moscow: Godvoenmorizdat NKVMF SSSR, 1941), pp. 5–6, 136.

22. *Doklad Komkora R. S. Shelukhina* (F. 29, d 26, o. 202, l. 80.)
23. *Doklad Komkora R. S. Shelukhina* (F. 29, d 26, o. 202, ll. 82–4).
24. *Boevie deistviya VVS KBF* (Moscow: Gosvoenmorizdat NKVMF SSSR, 1941), pp. 19–20.
25. *Doklad Komkora R. S. Shelukhina* (F. 29, d 26, o. 202, ll. 87–8, quote on l. 88).
26. *Doklad Komkora R. S. Shelukhina* (F. 29, d 26, o. 202, l. 88).
27. *Doklad Komkora R. S. Shelukhina* (F. 29, d 26, o. 202, l. 88); van Dyke, *The Soviet Invasion of Finland* (London: Frank Cass, 1997), pp. 91–3.
28. *Doklad Komkora R. S. Shelukhina* (F. 29, d 26, o. 202, ll. 89–92).
29. *Doklad Komkora R. S. Shelukhina* (F. 29, d 26, o. 202, l. 92).
30. *Doklad Komkora R. S. Shelukhina* (F. 29, d 26, o. 202, ll. 92–3).
31. *Doklad Komkora R. S. Shelukhina* (F. 29, d 26, o. 202, l. 94).
32. Maj.-Gen. Korneev, Maj. Chernov, and Maj. Moroz, 'Boevye deistviya 50 SK po propyvu linii Mannergeima (s 11.2 po 13.3 1940 g.)' (Moscow, 1941, typescript), pp. 41–4, 107–18, 131–2, 234.
33. *Doklad Komkora R. S. Shelukhina* (F. 29, d 26, o. 202, l. 94, p. 88); van Dyke, *The Soviet Invasion of Finland*, ch. 4; Korneev *et al.*, 'Boevye deistviya 50 SK' po propyvu linii Mannergeima (s 11.2 po 13.3 1940 g.) (Moscow, 1941, typescript); Pavel Aptekar', 'Falcons or Kites? The Red Army Air Force in the Soviet–Finnish War', *Journal of Slavic Military Studies*, 12, 4 (December 1999) pp. 138–48.
34. Starikh [*sic*], 'Radio kak sredstvo upravleniia istrebitel'iami', *Vestnik vozdushnogo flota*, 10 (1938), pp. 26–30; V. I. Migulin, *Teoriya i praktitka primeneniya sovetskykh VVS v mezhvoennyi period (1921–1941 gg.) Uchebnoe posobie* (Moscow: Voenno-Politicheskaya Akademiya, kafedra istorii voennovo iskusstva, 1988), pp. 76–9.
35. RKKA (*Raboche-krest' yanskaya Armiya*, Red Workers' and Peasants' Army), *Voina v Ispanii: boevie deistviia aviatsii (s nachala miatezha po avgust 1937 g.)* (Moscow: Razvedivatel'noe upravlenie RKKA, 1938), pp. 109–10.
36. G. V. Ul'ianov, 'Organizatsiia sviazi i radiotekhnicheskogo obespecheniia boevikh deistvii aviatsionnikh soedinenii i chastei v predvoennii period (ianvar–21 iiunia 1941 g.) i v pervie mesiatsi Velikoi otechestvennoi voini (22 iiunia–sentiabr' 1941 g.)', in V. E. Pan'kin (ed.), *1941 god – opit planirovaniia I primeneniia voenno-vozdushnikh sil, uroki i vivodi (po materialam voenno-nauchnoi konferentsii rukovodiashchego sostava tsentral'nogo apparata VVS, posviasshchennoi 70-letiu Sovetskoi Armii I Voenno-Morskogo Flota).* (Moscow: MO SSSR Tsentr operativno-takticheskikh issledovanii VVS, 1989), pp. 93–104.
37. N. Fedorenko, 'Podgotovka letnykh kadrov v 1939–1941 gg', *Voenno-istoricheskii zhurnal*, 4 (1976), p. 101; F. B. Komal, 'Voennie kadri nakanunye voiny', *Voenno-Istoricheskii Zhurnal*, 1 (1990), pp. 21–8; *Doklad Komkora R. S. Shelukhina* (F. 29, d 26, o. 202, l. 88).
38. I owe thanks to Dr Vladimir Boiko for explaining this to me.
39. Ia. V. Smushkevich, in V. A. Zolotareva *et al.*, *Nakanune voini: Materiali soveshchaniia vishchego rukovodiashchego sostava RKKA 23–31 dekabria 1940 g. Russkii arkhiv: Velikaia Otechestvennaia, T. 12(1)* (Moscow: Terra, 1993), p. 196.
40. Semion Konstantinovich Timoshenko, 1897–1970, Marshal of the Soviet Union from 1940 and Defence Commissar at the time of the conference.
41. Timoshenko, in Zolotareva *et al.*, *Nakanune voini*, p. 357. *Materiali soveshchaniia vishchego rukovodiashchego sostava RKKA 23–31 dekabria 1940 g. Russkii arkhiv: Velikaia Otechestvennaia, T. 12(1)* (Moscow: Terra, 1993).

9

The Development of Tactical Air Doctrine in North Africa, 1940–43

Brad Gladman

In 1918, the Royal Air Force (RAF) and the United States Army Air Service (USAAS) practised a variety of air-support operations on the Western Front, but during the inter-war years most senior British and American air commanders purposely overlooked the value of this use of air power.[1] Moreover, attempts by both the British and US Armies to control aviation for their own purposes during the inter-war years precluded any official discussion of air support between army and air force officers. As a result, in the early campaigns of the Second World War neither the RAF nor the United States Army Air Forces (USAAF) was able to provide effective air support. Their understanding of how to conduct such operations had largely vanished. Some American and British airmen understood some of the elements of how to conduct air support, but the operational experience had disappeared and neither force had a fully developed doctrine.

During the inter-war period, the senior commanders of both the RAF and the United States Army Air Corps (USAAC) refused to accept the value of tactical air power of any kind, and although both forces maintained small groups of aircraft to be used in support of ground forces, the equipment and training of these forces was wholly inadequate. Instead, both forces focused much of their attention on strategic bombing as the only acceptable use of offensive air power. Indeed, Hugh Trenchard once referred to strategic bombing as 'the Air Force Faith'.[2] The desire of both air forces for independent status from the other services in the context of stringent defence budgets made the focus on strategic bombing a means to an end. Given the geopolitical situation of the United States, strategic bombing made some sense, but the British were more likely to face a situation in which air support would have been an advantage. Despite this, the climate of hostility that existed between the RAF and the British Army for much of the inter-war period precluded any serious consideration of the problem; the same was true of the USAAC and the US Army. However, the preoccupation of many historians with the strategic bombing doctrine of both the RAF and the USAAC ignores the existence of some serious discussion by some influential members of both air forces about the importance of developing a doctrine for the application of tactical air power.

In the case of the RAF, however, a distinction must be drawn between the conditions in Britain as compared with those on the fringes of the Empire. The spirit of disunity fostered by the disagreements in Britain was not typical of the British armed forces in Africa, north-west India, Iraq or Palestine. Operational requirements forced much closer relations, and even at their worst relations were certainly much better than those between the Air Ministry and War Office in Britain. The difference in relations between the different areas was important, because although elements of effective air support were worked out in the frontier wars and in training in Egypt, the hostility between the Chief of the Imperial General Staff (CIGS) and the Chief of the Air Staff (CAS), and the increasing amount of distaste shown to such operations by air officers, prevented it from being adopted as a general doctrine for the whole RAF.

Egypt was the site of some very useful training schemes during the inter-war period. These training exercises 'led to the development of a close co-operation by bomber squadrons with the various Army Formations within the command', and saw an 'increased number of schemes in which bomber squadrons provided all forms of reconnaissance, practised the dropping of supplies by parachute and added message picking up and dropping to their normal inter-communication methods'.[3] Moreover, the attitude towards inter-service co-operation was completely different from that in Britain. The General Officer Commanding the British troops in Egypt during the early 1930s, was General Sir Jock Burnett-Stuart. He was one of the Army voices in the wilderness in favour of close relations with the RAF, and he thought that Air Force officers were the only ones with the skills to know how best to employ aircraft in support of the ground formations. For example, in 1937, Burnett-Stuart wrote a scathing condemnation of the Army's *Employment of Air Forces with the Army in the Field* manual, in which he denounced the practice of using the Air Officer Commanding RAF units 'purely in an advisory capacity so far as operating is concerned, a procedure that is contrary to all army principles, and likely sooner or later to break down in war'.[4]

Burnett-Stuart clarified the method in which both Army Co-operation squadrons and independent bomber and fighter squadrons should be employed in support of the Army in a 1931 training memorandum. He noted that although 208 Army Co-operation squadron was 'at our disposal', the rest of the RAF was always ready to assist, provided specific missions were requested.[5] He emphasized that it was important to give airmen as much help as possible, including what the intentions of the ground forces were, and what assistance air power could provide.[6]

This spirit of co-operation was typical not only of Egypt, but in other Air Control operations and small wars on the fringes of the Empire. In these areas close co-operation between the two services was an operational requirement, and the operational and command experience gained by men like Field Marshal Sir Claude Auchinleck, Marshal of the Royal Air Force Sir John Slessor, Air Marshal Sir Arthur Coningham and Marshal of the Royal Air Force Sir Arthur Tedder would prove to be important when the time came to evolve a system of close air support to meet the test of battle.

Wing Commander Slessor had the opportunity to put into practice his theories about air power when he returned to India in command of No. 3 (Indian) Wing in 1936. In particular, 20 Squadron at Peshawar organized a system of attack known as the VBL (Vickers–Bomb–Lewis), in which aircraft dived at its target and used its forward Vickers machine-guns to keep down enemy fire. Once over the target, the bombs were released and the rear-gunner sprayed the target with its Lewis guns to suppress anti-aircraft fire during the egress. Although the equipment and tactics used during these operations differed enormously from those that would be used in the Second World War, the important aspect is the genuine attempts to find workable methods of offering air support, as well as the understanding of the requirements for such support. The lessons learned during operations were incorporated into a *Manual of Frontier Operations* and a brochure entitled *Close Support Tactics – Provisional*, and, said Slessor, 'may be recognized as bearing at least a close resemblance to some of the principles of land/air warfare which crystallised in the Desert fighting of 1942 and 1943 and served us so well in the great campaigns in Italy, France, and Germany'.[7]

After the end of the First World War, Tedder was given command of 274 (later 207) Squadron. In 1921 he took 207 to Turkey as part of the British Expeditionary Force (BEF) deployed during the Chanak Incident – when Turkey and Britain came near to war over the presence of British forces on the shores of the Dardanelles – gaining him valuable experience of working closely with the Army. Moreover, Tedder continued his close association with Slessor throughout the inter-war period, and received copies of Slessor's writings relating to air operations in conjunction with the Army.[8] These ideas, combined with

Tedder's experience and personality would enable him to function smoothly with Army figures. Tedder understood not only the value of combined operations, but also the requirements for their success.[9] To this end, when he took command of the RAF in the Middle East in May of 1941, he moved his headquarters so that it was situated adjacent to that of the Army. When the time came to implement methods of delivering air support to the army, Tedder's beliefs, experience and personality served the British and their allies well.

Similarly, Coningham had gained valuable experience in the skirmishes with the Turks on the northern border with Iraq in 1922. Coningham and his fellow squadron members 'co-operated closely with ground forces by dropping supplies and keeping them informed about enemy strength and movements', but they also bombed and machine-gunned Turkish invaders.[10] Coningham came to share Air Marshal Salmond's (a future Chief of the Air Staff, CAS) beliefs concerning the importance of the experience gained in these operations. Salmond reported to the Air Ministry in 1924 that aircraft can aid 'in direct attack on ground targets by providing covering or supporting machine-gun fire; they disperse hostile forces and, when necessary, impede the escape of those forces by attacking bridges, fords or mountain defiles'.[11] Coningham came to believe that without intelligence, communications, supplies and close relations with the Army Commander this type of air support was not possible. The evolution of these beliefs, combined with the operational experience Coningham had gained in operations in Iraq, made it easier to develop a system for the application of air support in the Western Desert.

Taken as a whole, the experience of the operations on the frontier of the British Empire was important when the necessity of providing air support appeared after the Battle of France in 1940, but in most cases these operations were of a limited nature against poorly armed defenders. Although many important lessons were learned, the hostility against this type of operation prevented it from spreading to the whole air force. It is evident that the Air Ministry had no intention of diverting aircraft away from other purposes to answer calls for support, and ignored all arguments in favour of it. In 1939, the CIGS, General Ironside, wrote that he was disgusted 'with the way in which the RAF treat[ed] the co-operation of the Air Force with the army'.[12] That such statements were being made at the outset of the Second World War indicates the extent of the schism between the RAF and the Army in Britain.

Following the defeat of the French Army and the BEF in France in 1940, the need for the RAF to be able to deliver effective and rapid tactical air power became obvious. A series of trials was undertaken in late 1940 to develop a system to do just that, and the results of these trials were embodied in a joint report prepared by Group Captain Wann and Lieutenant Colonel Woodall. This report was submitted to the Air Ministry and the War Office in November 1940, and is commonly referred to as the Wann–Woodall report.[13] This system saw the control of tactical air power in most instances divested to the Corps level. The Army Air Support Controls were to be located at this command level, and, although the operational control was vested in an air officer, the result was a rather inefficient system in which each Corps possessed a piece of the available air power. The Allied forces engaged in operation 'Torch' brought a version of this system with them, and it failed to function effectively. Combat experience in the desert had shown the flaws of this system, and changes had been made. Unfortunately, for the Allied forces engaged in Tunisia, the Middle East system for the control and direction of tactical air power was not adopted until combat experience again showed the limitations to the existing system.

In contrast to the system employed during operation 'Torch', throughout the campaigns in the Western Desert, tactical air power was controlled at a senior command level. After late 1941, with the establishment of the Eighth Army, it was typical for operational control to reside with the Air Officer Commanding Advanced Air Headquarters, Western Desert at a combined headquarters with the Eighth Army. Initially, the reason for controlling aircraft at this command level was that there were too few aircraft available, and too many demands on them. However, it was soon discovered that because this command level had access to all available intelligence, aircraft could be directed against the best of available targets. Coningham explained the value of controlling tactical air power at such a senior command level when he described a situation where a

> front formation reports a concentration of 200 MT [motorised transport] and accompanying arms. Its request [for air support] is turned down. Fifteen or twenty miles away, however, there is a concentration of 2,000 or more, indicating an armoured division or even larger forces. This concentration we know from experience will probably affect the whole battle area perhaps 10, 18, or 24 hours later. It is this concentration which is receiving all the weight of air attack and that is why the comparatively little target on the front is ignored.[14]

Without centralized control, where access to intelligence was greater, the available air power may have been thrown at the smaller concentration to the detriment of overall efficiency. It was this pattern of operations that characterized the early stages of the Tunisian campaign.

Controlling aircraft at a command level with access to all available intelligence allowed for the cost-effective and flexible employment of tactical air power in the Western Desert. Strategic intelligence through such sources as signals intelligence, captured enemy documents, and prisoner of war interrogation allowed the RAF to focus its operational intelligence-gathering efforts, the most important being tactical, strategic and photographic reconnaissance, once certain prerequisites were in place. The first of these was sufficient familiarity with the various intelligence sources to avoid the pit-falls inherent in them. Second was an efficient system of command, control and communications required to make use of intelligence rapidly enough to guide tactical air operations. Third, and equally important, was the supply of suitable types of aircraft to undertake tactical air operations, and effective tactics employed by trained aircrews. Until these problems were overcome, the potential of the system was not realized. It was not until mid-1942 that these prerequisites were in place. Once they were, however, the effectiveness of the system was substantially enhanced.[15]

This system for the flexible application of tactical air power paid its highest dividends at El Alamein in the summer and autumn of 1942. The changes to the air-support system, as well as improvements to the command, control, communications and intelligence (C3I) systems in general, combined with the static battlefield imposed at El Alamein. The 'Y' service was increasingly valuable in reconstructing the Axis order of battle and deployment. Moreover, Ultra was providing more consistent information on the strength, disposition, and supply state of the Axis armies and air forces than ever before. This allowed the RAF to focus its operational intelligence-gathering efforts in a very cost-effective fashion.

The result of this was an marked improvement in the ability of the RAF to provide close air support and interdiction against supply convoys moving supplies to the front. In the context of a static battlefield, aircraft were easily able to operate over the front. Indeed, sorties routinely arrived over the target within 30–40 minutes of the time of request, as opposed to an average of three hours during the 'Crusader' operation of late 1941.[16]

Thus, the Eighth Army was finally in a position that could not easily be outflanked, and its overwhelming air superiority neutralized the Axis forces' main advantage – its ability to manoeuvre and rapidly deploy. Moreover, attacking by both day and night, air power eroded the morale of the Axis forces, something which interdiction against Axis supply columns on the way to the front made worse. Indeed, air power was quickly making Rommel's position untenable. Also, the Germans found that concentrated formations of troops and vehicles quickly drew attack from the air. In response to the threat from the air, Rommel was forced to deploy the 15th and 21st Panzer Divisions (the bulk of the *Afrika Korps*) at opposite ends of the line. Air power thus removed mobility as an Axis trump card.

It is no exaggeration to say that tactical air power played an important role in the victories at Alam Halfa and El Alamein in the summer
and fall of 1942. In roughly 18 months the RAF had designed an
admirably effective weapon that struck directly at the weaknesses of
the Axis forces. Close air support and interdiction, the two types of
operations that had initially competed for available air power, com-
plemented each other once C3I systems allowed. Interdiction took
away the strengths of the German forces, reduced their equipment and
rations to a deplorable state, and affected both morale and fighting
ability.[17] Close air support continued this attack by both day and night,
and the effect of these attacks was made worse by the poor morale of
German and Italian forces – a situation which interdiction operations
helped to create. The overall effect of air power was to remove the Axis
forces' advantages, and to turn them into an eggshell awaiting the
hammer blow.

> Once the Battle of El Alamein had been won, senior Army and RAF
> commanders were able to express their ideas about the relationship that
> had existed between the British Army and the RAF for much of the
> desert campaigns. It was understood that the soldier commands the land
> forces, the airman the air forces; both commanders work together and
> operate their respective forces in accordance with a combined Army/Air
> plan, the whole operations being directed by the Army Commander.[18]

> As a result of lessons learned during operations, it was stressed as vital
> that the commander of an Army in the field should have an air
> headquarters with him which will have direct control and command of
> such squadrons as may be allotted for operations in support of his Army.
> Such air resources will be in support of his Army and not under his
> command.[19]

This understanding prevented the dissipation of air resources into
penny-packets, 'with each packet working on its own plan', which had
been demanded by the British and US Armies during the inter-war
years and until 1943.[20] By keeping the air assets united, they could be
used with maximum efficiency, sometimes being directed quickly at
fleeting targets of opportunity, or alternatively being used in one overwhelming blow. The alternative was a degradation of air strength.
Since lower levels of command were not privy to all intelligence regarding enemy movements and intentions, and were understandably concerned with what was happening in front of them, they would tend to
use their aircraft to deal with immediate threats at the expense of
overall efficiency. Keeping the air assets united, and controlled from a
headquarters that received all the available intelligence in real time,
allowed aircraft to be used in the most effective way possible. Indeed,

in no other way could effective close air support or interdiction have been possible, nor could intelligence have helped them much, if at all.

Despite the success of the Middle East system for the employment of tactical air power, neither the rest of the RAF nor the USAAF had absorbed it. The result was an inability of either the RAF or USAAF to apply tactical air power with any effect in the opening stages of the Tunisian campaign. Although the CAS, Sir Charles Portal, understood the value of the Middle East system, the repeated failures of the British forces in the Middle East as late as two months before the planning for 'Torch' began hid the effectiveness of this system from many. The most notable opponent to the adoption of the Middle East system was the CIGS, General Alan Brooke, who thought the RAF was engaged in fighting its own separate war and that 'Air Staff policy conspired against meeting the Army's legitimate needs'.[21] Brooke wanted the Army to possess its own specialized aircraft under its operational control, with Army support as their primary role.[22]

Thus, although the Air Staff was convinced the Middle East system of air support worked, opposition from the CIGS and others prevented its adoption as a doctrine. It was not until 14 November 1942 that the old system, favoured by Brooke, of having an army 'component' supported by an RAF 'contingent' was abandoned in favour of Coningham and Tedder's system of a unified air force under the command of an air officer working in conjunction with the ground forces.[23] Still, it took time to work out an appropriate organization of the existing Allied air forces.

Rather than organizing the available air forces under a unified commander who had access to all the available intelligence and could thus focus his air strength against the most appropriate target, the RAF and USAAF components were essentially fighting separate wars. For example, an instance occurred in early 1943 where American ground commanders refused to allow the aircraft of XII Air Support Command (ASC) to respond to calls for close air support from the French XIX Corps, which had come under heavy Axis attack, because of a lack of interest in committing what was considered their own personal resources.[24] It was not until combat experience showed the flaws in the Allied system for employing tactical air power that the doctrine developed in the desert was adopted. The failure to do so added to the already considerable problems associated with fighting in the Tunisian theatre, and these problems together with a lack of understanding amongst the Allied ground forces of the proper organization and use of tactical air power, combined to render Allied air strength largely irrelevant.

This began to change on 19 February 1943 as a result of decisions made at the Casablanca Conference; the Mediterranean Air Command

(MAC) was formed under the command of Air Chief Marshal Tedder.[25] Beneath MAC headquarters was the new Northwest African Air Force (NWAAF), composed of three separate combat elements, including the North West African Tactical Air Force (NWATAF), commanded by Coningham, who brought with him his unequalled experience in tactical air operations. His command consisted of fighter, fighter/bomber, light bomber and reconnaissance squadrons from 242 Group RAF, USAAF XII ASC and the Western Desert Air Force (WDAF).[26]

This more rational command structure was based on experience gained in the desert, and many key officers from the WDAF and Eighth Army were brought in to ensure a smooth transition. Where previous air efforts were uncoordinated and largely ineffective, now there was at least a streamlined command structure that enabled intelligence and orders to flow with a minimum of delay. This allowed for the flexible use of aircraft against the best possible target revealed by Allied intelligence. Although the NWATAF's primary mission was the close support of ground forces, when not engaged in such operations Coningham was able to direct his tactical air force against Axis supply.

Reflecting experience gained in the desert fighting, combined army/air headquarters were established for the major ground formations. First Army formed a combined headquarters with 242 Group RAF; II US Corps had a combined headquarters with XII ASC; the Western Desert Air Force continued its association with the Eighth Army.[27] At each of these combined headquarters was an Army Air Support Control (AASC).

Thus, individual ground formations had quick access to close-support aircraft when necessary, but although this may seem no different from the system used during operastion 'Torch', there had been some important changes. Recognizing that even Army commanders had access neither to the total picture nor to all the available intelligence, and would likely use aircraft for their own purposes at the expense of overall efficiency, Coningham formed a main air support net at the combined 18th Army Group/NWATAF headquarters.[28] The purpose of this system was to connect all three AASCs with all available intelligence by a reliable communications network. Thus all three AASCs and the main air support control were in constant touch, and Coningham knew which targets were being attacked, the strength and time of the attacks, and the results. The ability to keep in touch with the system, combined with improvements to the intelligence system, enabled HQ 18th Army Group/NWATAF to redirect fighters and fighter/bombers, to 'apply the Tactical Bomber Force where most vital, and if necessary to call in the additional weight of the Strategic Bomber Force'.[29]

With the sweeping improvements to the C3I system, the ability to apply close air support quickly and effectively was substantially enhanced, as was apparent during Montgomery's attack on the Mareth line (codenamed 'Pugilist'), which began on the night of 20 March 1943.[30] As part of the battle plan, Coningham had directed Major-General Paul Williams, commanding XII ASC, and Air Commodore Cross, a desert veteran commanding 242 Group, to mount attacks against the *Luftwaffe*'s airfields by both day and night to distract their fighters and allow the Western Desert Air Force to concentrate on close air support.[31]

The main offensive against the Mareth line made little progress initially, and in response Montgomery directed the New Zealand Corps (consisting of 2 NZ Division and the 8 Armoured Brigade) on a long outflanking manoeuvre along a route mapped out by the Long Range Desert Group.[32] The New Zealand Division was stopped at the Tebaga Gap, some 20 miles south west of El Hamma, when the Axis detected the move and reinforced the area. Montgomery, in turn, sent X Corps and the 1st Armoured Division to reinforce the New Zealanders, and to aid in breaking through the Tebaga gap. This attack was aided by intense close air support from 16 squadrons of the WDAF flying low-level attacks.[33]

Similar to the pattern of operations at El Alamein, heavy and continual air attack was conducted against concentrations of vehicles and troops of 15th and 21st Panzer Divisions. These attacks damaged equipment, deprived the Axis forces of mobility, and their troops of sleep. During the two nights before the attack on the Tebaga gap, all available heavy, medium and light bombers attacked targets located by Allied intelligence.[34] Some 6,000 prisoners taken during this operation reported the tremendous moral and material effect of these close air support operations.[35]

The ground operation against the Tebaga gap began on 26 March, and was timed to coincide with 'light bomber, fighter bombers and strafing efforts in direct support of 2 New Zealand Division and the 8 Armoured Brigade'.[36] The air attack operated just ahead of the creeping artillery barrage that formed a nearly perfect bomb-line. Air Marshal Harry Broadhurst, the air officer commanding the WDAF, designed an air programme that made use of five fighter Wings, three light bomber Wings, and one Tank Buster Squadron.

A total of 514,000 pounds of bombs were dropped in close support of the ground forces on 21 March 1943 alone, and this weight of attack continued throughout the operation.[37] After the battle, Montgomery praised the close air support efforts of the WDAF by writing to Coningham and Broadhurst, saying that such 'intimate and close support has never to my knowledge been achieved before and it has been an inspiration to all the troops'.[38] According to Montgomery, the 'outstanding feature of the battle ... was the air action in co-operation with the outflanking forces'.[39]

Although the new arrangements required army commanders to relinquish their control of aircraft, the result more than made up for the loss. Coningham had created a system by which tactical air power could be controlled at the command level that had access to all available intelligence, but only exercised such control in order to direct aircraft where they were most needed. In general, the relationship between, for example, the First Army and 242 Group remained close, but Coningham's headquarters could redirect aircraft from 242 Group or other formations to areas requiring more air support. In order to be able to do so, intelligence systems were reorganized and integrated as they had been in the Western Desert. Thus, very quickly a system was established that made effective use of Allied air power.

The result was a dramatic increase in the ability of the Allied air forces to deliver close air support or interdiction in response to a specific plan designed by Army and Air Force commanders. Unthinkable before the reorganization in February 1943, aircraft could now be switched from one target to another, and aircraft from other areas in the theatre could be focused on air support without delay. The success of this system was noted by senior commanders in both air forces, who, near the end of the Tunisian campaign, sent observers to learn the important aspects of the doctrine for use in later campaigns.

For example, a visit from Air Marshal Sir Trafford Leigh-Mallory in late March 1943 was important to the adoption of this doctrine for the coming cross-Channel invasion.[40] Leigh-Mallory was particularly impressed with the liaison between air and ground personnel 'where the Military and Air Commanders and staffs [were] working side by side in the closest harmony, and each fully appreciative not only of the importance which air operations have on the land battle, but also of the effect of land action on the successful operation of air forces'.[41] Indeed, for the remainder of the war this became, with few exceptions, the foundation for the command relationship between the Army and tactical Air Forces of both the RAF and USAAF.[42]

Leigh-Mallory also noted the importance of aerial reconnaissance, and felt it was essential that a reconnaissance wing be attached to each Composite Group.[43] This was due to his observation that the vast majority of air operations were arranged 'as part of a pre-arranged plan worked out some time in advance', and therefore good intelligence was essential to the effective application of air power.[44] It was only occasional operations that were not part of the pre-arranged plan, and these only occurred when a favourable fleeting target was located by intelligence.[45]

The interest of several USAAF officers was instrumental in ensuring the adoption of this doctrine by their air force. The interest began in 1942 with the attachment of a USAAF contingent to the WDAF. The commanding officer of this contingent, Major-General Brereton, sent summaries of the WDAF method of operation. More important, however, was the way in which Coningham's doctrine had impressed Brigadier-General Howard Craig, the Chief of Staff of the Mediterranean Air Command. Craig was very impressed with Coningham's ideas, and circulated them amongst his own air force.[46] This prompted a visit by three USAAF officers to the North African theatre in April 1943, where Brigadier-General Kuter explained the doctrine to them in detail. This provided the spark for a restructuring of American air-support doctrine. A similar situation occurred with the RAF, which, after Leigh-Mallory's report, reorganized and renamed the British Army Cooperation Command the 2nd Tactical Air Force, with Coningham's NWATAF being the first.[47]

In response to the lessons learned during the Tunisian campaign, and the visit by observers to the theatre, General Marshall ordered a new manual on the command and employment of tactical air power. A committee was established, which included Colonel Martin McKinnon, the Commandant of the Air Support Department of the School of Applied Tactics, Lieutenant-Colonel Orin Moore, Armoured Forces liaison officer at USAAF headquarters, and Colonel Ralph Stearley, the Commander of the I Air Support Command.[48] The manual outlined many of the key points in the doctrine developed in the Western Desert, and introduced to Tunisia.

In July 1943, the USAAF published this field manual FM 100-20 and at the same time the Air Ministry and War Office issued their Training Instruction No. 1, which were very similar.[49] From air forces so opposed to even the idea of close air support prior to the war, this represented a revolution in thinking. Both doctrinal manuals emphasized the equal but interdependent relationship of armies and air forces. Air forces assisted armies through the attainment and maintenance of air superiority, which allowed 'freedom of action for land forces and supporting air forces'.[50] However, air forces were dependent upon armies to capture and construct forward airfields, to ensure their security, and to provide daily requirements of fuel, food, spare parts, and other essential requirements.[51] Thus, the interrelated nature of ground and tactical air operations was finally spelled out in official doctrine, and reflected the reality of the day-to-day operations in the Western Desert and later in Tunisia.

Both manuals held 'that the inherent flexibility of air power [was] its greatest asset'.[52] This flexibility could be adequately exploited only if its control was exercised through the air force commander with access to all available intelligence. He would be able to 'employ the whole weight of the available air power against selected areas in turn: such concentrated use of the air striking force [was] a battle winning factor of the first importance'.[53] This important realization was less a declaration of independence, as some scholars have argued, and more an acknowledgement of reality as learned in combat.[54] As demonstrated during the early part of the Tunisian campaign, placing air units under the command of army formations prevented their concentration against vulnerable targets. It frequently resulted in aircraft being used in a diffuse and largely ineffective manner, inflicting little damage on enemy land or air forces. The Tunisian campaign had shown the value of concentrating overwhelming air power at the point of attack. In particular, close air support attacks in the form of co-ordinated fighter-bomber and bomber attacks to soften enemy resistance before the breakthrough, and later to support the advancing troops.

After the Tunisian campaign it became standard practice for both the USAAF and the RAF to have a tactical air force attached as an equal partner in 'a theatre of operations where ground forces [were] operating'.[55] The control of available air power was to be centralized and command was to be exercised through an air force commander if its 'inherent flexibility and ability to deliver a decisive blow [was] to be fully exploited'.[56] Thus, both forces officially discarded the commonly held belief amongst Corps commanders during the initial stages of the Tunisian campaign, that air forces were theirs to command. Although there were still instances where air units were closely associated with ground formations, such as the WDAF and Eighth Army, ground commanders could no longer count on this arrangement. Instead, air power could be used against the most profitable targets within range of the aircraft responding.

The priorities for the application of tactical air power ranged from the attainment of air superiority, to interdiction and finally to close air support. However, the assignment of third priority to close air support did not mean that air officers were unwilling to conduct close air support. The fact that close air support ranked third in listed priorities represented more an understanding that it was only called for when armies were attacking or being attacked, and that 'separate air operations normally preced[ed] surface operations', rather than a dismissal of the value of close air support.[57] However, it was acknowledged that operations where troops were closely engaged were the most difficult to conduct effectively, and were only profitable at critical times. Indeed, even *Luftwaffe* doctrine held that close air support against enemy forces in a good tactical position 'as a rule [was] unlikely to produce results commensurate with the effort expended, although such action might be required in special circumstances'.[58] In such circumstances good intelligence was even more vital to success, as the risk of striking friendly forces due to navigation or target designation errors was greater.[59]

The USAAF tactical air commands, as the air-support commands became known, developed different procedures and structures for the prosecution of air support missions, but these systems were broadly similar to those of the RAF. It was not until Field Manual 31-35 was re-issued in August 1946 that the variations in terminology and procedure within the various tactical air commands would be standardized.[60] However, this did not interfere with the ability of the tactical air commands to provide swift and often effective close air support and interdiction operations. The close association of ground and air forces at Corps and Divisional levels was assured by the attachment of Tactical Air Party Officers to these headquarters to receive and transmit requests for support. Ground Liaison Officers, provided by the Army, were attached to all air headquarters down to the Group, as well as to photographic and tactical reconnaissance squadrons.[61] This new system was inaugurated in November 1943 in VIII Air Support Command, 'at which time selected air officers were attached to the Corps and Divisions then in training in the United Kingdom'.[62] The final procedures were worked out during these training exercises and from information brought back from observers who had visited the North African theatre during April 1943.[63]

At the end of the Tunisian campaign there was sufficient evidence that the doctrine developed in the Western Desert and Tunisia worked well. General Arnold moved to ensure this by ordering that every officer in the USAAF be given a copy of the new manual 'to read and study'.[64] Even before the manual was issued, its ideas were incorporated into the curriculum of the Infantry School at Fort Benning.[65] However, as might be expected, the speed with which this doctrine was adopted caused some controversy. In particular, it was adopted by the War Department without the consultation or approval of the commander of the Army Ground Forces, Lieutenant-General Lesley McNair. Ironically, McNair would later be killed by US heavy bombers operating in close support.[66] However, the way in which this doctrine was instituted did not represent an irreconcilable schism between ground and air forces.

For example, while commander of IX Tactical Air Command, Major-General Quesada, developed the Armoured Column Cover to provide armoured spearheads with instantaneous close air support. To deliver rapid air support, a flight of four P-47 Thunderbolts operated over the tank column, communicating by wireless with ground controllers in the lead tanks. The flights were relieved every 30 minutes, and if no close air support targets were available, they were frequently used to search the road ahead for German troops, guns or tanks.[67] While not the most cost-effective use of air power, this type of operation proved extremely effective during the 'Cobra' offensive, the American breakout from the Normandy area at the end of July 1944, and represented the degree to which air force officers were willing to work with ground forces to provide better support.[68]

Both air forces also adopted the methods of gathering and integrating intelligence that had been developed in the desert fighting. Indeed, this was of fundamental importance to being able to direct tactical air power at the best of available targets. The US armed forces had learned the value of signals intelligence in the Tunisian campaign, and had adopted British methods for exploiting it.[69] They had also learned the value of prisoner of war interrogation, and by 1945 felt it was 'the best measure of the effectiveness of air attack'.[70] Experience in the Tunisian campaign also showed that prisoner-of-war interrogation provided 'an abundant source of information respecting the effectiveness of air plans, tactics, techniques of attack, and the various weapons employed'.[71] The USAAF also adopted the British system of photographic interpretation and aerial reconnaissance.

In May 1943, Brigadier-General Kuter argued that the ineffectiveness of USAAF reconnaissance had been proven, and that the 'maximum effort should be made to elevate the position of our present observation aviation to a much higher level by the immediate formation of truly proficient tactical and strategical reconnaissance squadrons'.[72] He further recommended that reconnaissance squadrons should be equipped with high-performance aircraft, and their crews should receive special training.[73] Immediately following the end of the Tunisian campaign in May 1943, Kuter, Lieutenant-Colonel John Dyas, the commander of the 154th Observation Squadron, and Lieutenant-Colonel E. S. Biden, a South African Air Force staff officer with experience in the Western Desert and Tunisia, were invited to aid in working out an effective system of aerial reconnaissance. To this end, Dyas and Biden were sent to the USAAF Board at Orlando, Florida, where a reconnaissance sub-board had been established under the command of Colonel Minton W. Kaye on 9 June 1943.[74] The board adopted the British division of all reconnaissance into either strategic or tactical reconnaissance. Procedures for disseminating intelligence were similar to those developed in the Western Desert. General Arnold approved this system for aerial reconnaissance on 9 October 1943.[75]

The procedures for the collection and quick dissemination of photographic intelligence were identical to those developed in the Western Desert. First-phase reports, which dealt with a few 'important bits of intelligence upon which an operation may be waiting', were passed swiftly along to those who could use them since 'SPEED [was] their essence'.[76] This was considered vitally important to tactical air operations, which relied on reconnaissance for target location and bomb-damage assessment.[77]

Despite initial opposition by ground-force commanders, most found the results completely satisfactory. Indeed, with few exceptions, ground-force commanders were eminently pleased with the provision of close air support. In March 1945, the commander of First US Army, Lieutenant-General Courtney Hodges, wrote that the existing procedure for tactical and photographic reconnaissance had resulted from the long combat association of First US Army and IX Tactical Air Command and was 'an eminently satisfactory one ... The several Corps which have served with First Army have expressed complete satisfaction with the results achieved.'[78] Thus, the methods for gathering and employing intelligence, as well as controlling tactical air power, which were developed in the Western Desert, were adopted by both air forces with good effect.

The operational experience gained in the North African campaign taught the British and US forces a great many lessons, including methods for the effective application of tactical air power. The first of these lessons for tactical air operations was the importance of strategic intelligence for an understanding of enemy deployment and movements, and how this focused operational intelligence-gathering efforts in a very cost-effective manner. In order to make effective use of intelligence, the Allies realized the necessity of controlling tactical air power at an appropriate command level, one that had access to all available intelligence. Doing so enabled the Allied air forces to concentrate their air power against the best of available targets when necessary. For example, during the Battle of the Bulge in late 1944, Coningham added the weight of the Second Tactical Air Force to that of USAAF Brigadier General Quesada's IX Tactical Air Command to aid in the close support of the US forces that were in the path of the German advance. Quesada later recalled that Coningham's assistance 'helped tremendously'.[79] No system is ever perfect, or completely successful, but the system pioneered by the RAF in the Western Desert worked well, and formed the core of the doctrine for the application of tactical air power of both the RAF and the USAAF for the remainder of the war and beyond.

NOTES

1. Brereton Greenhous, 'Evolution of a Close-Support Role for Aircraft in World War I', *Military Affairs*, Vol. 39, No. 1 (February 1975), *passim.*
2. Public Record Office, Kew (hereafter cited as PRO), AIR 5/280, Memorandum to the Chief of the Imperial General Staff, 10 December, 1928.

3. PRO AIR 10/1914, Army Co-operation Training Memorandum, 1934, p. 6.
4. Liddell Hart Centre for Military Archives, King's College, London, (hereafter cited as LHCMA), Sir Jock Burnett-Stuart Papers, I/I, Southern Command Annual Report on Training of the Regular Army 1936/1937, Appendix 10 Air Co-operation, 1937.
5. LHCMA Sir Jock Burnett-Stuart Papers, I/I, Training Memorandum, 1931, p. 3.
6. Ibid.
7. Marshal of the Royal Air Force Sir John Slessor, *The Central Blue* (London: Cassell, 1956), pp. 124–8.
8. Tedder was included on the distribution list of many of Slessor's papers on air control. In particular, see AIR 75/27, Official Papers of MRAF Sir John Slessor, Air Control. The Other Point of View, 193, p. 2. In this paper, Slessor outlined the importance of ground troops in Air Control operations.
9. Royal Air Force Museum, Hendon (hereafter cited as RAFM) Tedder Papers, Lecture given to RAF Staff College, Andover entitled 'Air Aspects of Combined Operations', undated.
10. Vincent Orange, *Coningham* (London: Methuen, 1990), p. 39.
11. PRO AIR 23/542, Report by Air Marshal Salmond to the Air Ministry on his Command in Iraq, April 1924.
12. General Sir Edmund Ironside, *Time Unguarded: The Ironside Diaries 1937–1940*, ed. Roderick Macleod and Denis Kelly (Westport, CT: Greenwood Press, 1962), p. 140.
13. PRO WO 277 34 Army Air Support and Photographic Interpretation 1939–1945, p. 25.
14. PRO AIR 23/1299, Air Power in the Land Battle (Air Ministry, 1943).
15. Brad W. Gladman, 'Intelligence and Anglo-American Close Air Support in the Western Desert and Tunisia, 1939–1943', PhD thesis, University College London, 2001.
16. PRO WO 169/6638, War Diary of No. 2 Army Air Support Control, 28 August 1942.
17. Brad Gladman, 'Air Power and Intelligence in the Western Desert Campaign, 1940–1943', *Intelligence and National Security*, Vol. 13, No. 4 (Winter 1998), *passim*.
18. Quote from Air Marshal Coningham. PRO AIR 23/1299, Air Power in the Land Battle, 1943.
19. Quote from General Montgomery. Ibid.
20. PRO AIR 23/1299, Air Power in the Land Battle, 1943; Wesley Craven and James Cate (eds), *The Army Air Forces in World War II* (Chicago, IL: University of Chicago Press, 1948–51), Vol. I, *Plans and Early Operations January 1939 to August 1942*.
21. David Ian Hall, 'The Birth of the Tactical Air Force: British Theory and Practice of Air Support in the West, 1939–1943'. Oxford, DPhil. thesis, 1996, Ch. 8, p. 8.
22. Ibid.
23. PRO PREM 3/8, Organisation of Air Support for the Army in Continental Operations, 14 November 1942.
24. LC Papers of Carl Spaatz, I: Box 12, Memorandum on the Organization of American Air Forces by Brigadier-General L. S. Kuter, 12 May 1943.
25. PRO CAB 106/670, Commander in Chief's Dispatch North African Campaign 1942–1943, p. 37.
26. Ibid.
27. PRO WO 175/16, discussion of proposed amalgamation of 'J' and Phantom Units, Appendix 'A', 25 February 1943.

28. National Archives and Records Administration, College Park, Maryland (hereafter cited as NARA), RG 331 Entry 253 Box 5, MAAF Directorate of Operations and Intelligence, Operations Section, Army–Air Cooperation, 31 March 1943.
29. Ibid.
30. IWM Montgomery Papers BLM 31/4, Operation 'Pugilist' General Plan of Eighth Army.
31. Orange, *Coningham*, p. 143; Cross, Air Chief Marshal Sir Kenneth, with Professor V. Orange, *Straight and Level* (London: Bugg Street, 1993), p. 241.
32. PRO WO 214/11, Most Secret Cipher Message for Prime Minister copy to CIGS from General Alexander 8 March 1943; IWM Montgomery Papers, BLM 31/4 Operation 'Pugilist' General Plan of Eighth Army; LHCMA Papers of Brigadier General Sydney Divers 2/5, Account of the 'Left Hook' at Mareth.
33. PRO WO 214/11, Most Secret Cipher Message for PM and CIGS from General Alexander 29 March 1943.
34. PRO AIR 23/1708, Comment by AOC Tactical Air Force – The Eighth Army Break-Through at El Hamma, 26 March 1943.
35. Ibid; Orange, *Coningham*, p. 144.
36. PRO CAB 106/531, MT Instructional Circular No. 13, 28 April 1943, p. 3.
37. PRO AIR 41/50, The Middle East Campaigns Vol. IV, Operations in Libya, the Western Desert and Tunisia, p. 400.
38. PRO CAB 106/531, MT Instructional Circular No. 13, 28 April 1943, p. 3.
39. Denis Richards and Hilary St George Saunders, *The Royal Air Force, 1939–45*, Vol. II (London: HMSO, 1954), p. 266.
40. AIR 41/66, The Liberation of Northwest Europe, Vol. I, The Planning and Preparation of the Allied Expeditionary Air Force for the Landings in Normandy, p. 5.
41. AIR 20/6130, Report by Air Marshal Sir Trafford Leigh-Mallory on his visit to N. Africa March/April 1943.
42. PRO AIR 37/1057, Minutes of the Allied Air Commanders' Conference, 14 June 1944.
43. AIR 20/6130, Report by Air Marshal Sir Trafford Leigh-Mallory on his visit to N Africa March/April 1943. A Composite Group consisted of fighters, fighter/bombers, bombers of various types and reconnaissance aircraft.
44. Ibid.
45. Ibid.
46. LC, Spaatz Papers I: Box 9, Letter from Craig to Spaatz, 23 December 1942.
47. Orange, *Coningham*, p. 150.
48. B. F. Cooling (ed.), *Case Studies in the Development of Close Air Support* (Washington, DC: Office of Air Force History, 1990), p. 184.
49. NARA RG 337 Entry 55 Box 970, Field Manual 100–20, July 1943; NARA RG 331 Entry 272 Box 1, Mediterranean Allied Air Force Headquarters, Army Air Training Instruction No. 1, July 1943.
50. RG 331 Entry 272 Box 1, Mediterranean Allied Air Force Headquarters, Army Air Training Instruction No. 1, July 1943, p. 1.
51. Ibid.
52. NARA RG 337 Entry 55 Box 970, Field Manual 100–20, p. 1, RG 331 Entry 272 Box 1, Mediterranean Allied Air Force Headquarters, Army Air Training Instruction No. 1, July 1943, p. 4.
53. NARA RG 337 Entry 55 Box 970, Field Manual 100–20, p. 2.
54. Richard R. Muller 'Close Air Support, The German, British, and American Experiences, 1918–1941', in Williamson Murray and Allan R. Millett (eds), *Military Innovation in the Interwar Period* (Cambridge: Cambridge University

Press, 1996), p. 186. Muller is correct in his assertion that FM 100–20 dealt more with organization and control of air forces and less with the practicalities of delivering close air support. However, Army/Air Training Instruction No. 1 discussed practical methods for the employment of various types of aircraft in various roles. Also, organization and control are of critical importance to the success of close air support operations, and the significant practical experience gained by personnel in Tunisia provided the practicalities of delivering close air support.

55. NARA RG 337 Entry 55 Box 970, Field Manual 100–20, July 1943, p. 10.
56. Ibid., p. 2.
57. NARA RG 337 Entry 55 Box 970, Review of FM 100–20 (Advance Copy) July 1943. Ian Gooderson, in his book *Air Power at the Battlefront* (London: Frank Cass, 1998), p. 51, incorrectly focuses on the low ranking given to close air support as being a dismissal of its value rather than an acknowledgment of the infrequency of the need for it in relation to the more continuous attack on supply columns and enemy aircraft.
58. General der Flieger a. D. Paul Deichmann *et al.*, *German Air Force Operations in Support of the Army* (New York: Arno Press, 1962), p. 123.
59. NARA RG 337 Entry 55 Box 970, Field Manual 100–20, July 1943, p. 13.
60. Richard P. Hallion, *Strike from the Sky: The History of Battlefield Air Attack 1911–1945* (Shrewsbury: Airlife Publishing 1989), p. 174.
61. IWM Headquarters 9th Air Force Report on Tactical Air Co-operation, Organization, Methods, and Procedures, July 1945, p. 116.
62. Ibid.
63. Ibid.
64. LC, Arnold Papers, Box 42 9/23, File 'Employment of Air Forces' General H. H. Arnold to Commanding Generals, All Air Forces, All Independent Army Air Force Commands, Commandant Army Air Forces School of Applied Tactics, July 1943.
65. Hallion, *Strike from the Sky*, p. 174.
66. Ibid.; Thomas Hughes, *Overlord: General Pete Quesada and the Triumph of Tactical Air Power in World War II* (New York: Crown Press, 1995), p. 215.
67. PRO AIR 40/1131, General Bradley and the US 12 Army Group Air Effects Committee, Effects of Air Power on Military Operations, Western Europe, Wiesbaden, German: US 12 Army Group Air Branches, G-3 and G-2, 15 July 1945, pp. 41–2.
68. Martin Blumenson, *Breakout and Pursuit* (Washington, DC: Department of the Army, 1961), p. 309.
69. Lt-Col. John Hixson and B. F. Cooling, *Combined Operations in Peace and War* (Carlisle, PA: US Army Military History Institute, 1982), p. 111.
70. IWM Headquarters 9th Air Force Report on Tactical Air Cooperation, Organization, Methods, and Procedures, July 1945, p. 10.
71. Ibid.
72. LC, Spaatz Papers I: Box 12, Organization of American Air Forces, 12 May 1943.
73. Ibid.
74. R. Frank Futrell, *Command of Observation Aviation: A Study in the Control of Tactical Air Power* (Manhattan, KS: MA/AH Publishing, 1956), p. 25.
75. Ibid., p. 28.
76. IWM Photo Recon for MATAF and 15th Army Group by 3rd Photo Group, 1945, p. 1.
77. Ibid., p. 4.
78. Ibid.
79. Hughes, *Overlord*, pp. 281–2.

10

Logistics Doctrine and the Impact of War: The Royal Air Force's Experience in the Second World War

Peter Dye

Since it could be argued the Royal Air Force (RAF) has never had a formal logistics doctrine, any discussion on the subject seems destined to be brief. On the other hand, logistics is so fundamental to the effective delivery of air power that it is difficult, if not impossible, to separate out those many elements of RAF doctrine that bear directly on logistic issues.[1] It is perhaps ironic that this catholic view has its echoes in Hugh Trenchard's structure for the post-war RAF that envisaged an officer cadre – the General Duties (GD) Branch – that would exercise responsibility for all those activities bearing directly on the efficient and effective running of an air force, including maintenance, signals, armament and supply.[2] The increasing difficulties faced in sustaining this policy through the inter-war years offers some insight into how organizational arrangements may not only provide a physical realization of doctrine but also the subsequent battleground in any effort to achieve change. It is no exaggeration to claim that the debate over the introduction of a technical branch, which became increasingly vocal from 1934 onwards, struck at the heart of Trenchard's vision for the service – and was seen as such by many of the protagonists.

In this chapter I propose to consider the impact of the war, or the imminent prospect of war, on the RAF's logistic arrangements. It will inevitably embrace consideration of the First World War legacy and how the seeds were sown for the dispute over repair and maintenance that would polarize the Air Staff in the 1930s. Although many of the arguments over logistics were resolved on the eve of war, operational experience in 1940 inevitably revealed other shortcomings – notably during the campaign in France but also, to a lesser extent, during the Battle of Britain.

THE PERMANENT ORGANIZATION OF THE RAF

The Trenchard blueprint for the peacetime RAF, published as a memorandum in 1919, was in many ways a far-sighted and imaginative document that determined not just the size and shape of the service but its subsequent character and ethos. Some have compared it to a Victorian Infantry Regiment – with aeroplanes attached.[3] Like a regiment, every officer would be capable of doing any job with a minimum of specialist training. The intention being to 'avoid any danger of developing technical branches that were out of touch with flying and fighting arrangements and which would not co-operate properly with officers engaged in the conduct and control of operations'.[4] One can only speculate as to what incident may have been the father to this sentiment.

At the heart of the Trenchard system lay the squadron, self-contained as far as possible, its spirit sustained by its officers working closely with their men, on both the maintenance of aircraft and the other day-to-day activities that were the business of military life. Under this principle there was no place for career technical officers that might weaken the bond between officers and men. By the 1930s, almost a third of junior officers had specialist annotations – indicating completion of training in engineering, signals, armament or navigation, followed by at least one practical tour. Increasingly, however, questions were raised about the effectiveness of this policy – not least of all by the individuals themselves.

It is perhaps necessary at this stage to make some general comments. First, it would be misleading to suggest that the inter-war RAF organization was deeply flawed or that logistic issues were not taken seriously. There was an undoubted and unrelenting emphasis on technical standards, on professional training for officers and airmen, on the introduction of modern engineering practice, and on research and development. The system of providing selected officers, often ex-apprentices, with advanced engineering training, including sponsored university courses, provided a handsome return in the form of Whittle, Comper, Weedon and others. But, it is equally fair to point out that the peacetime RAF had also lost an immense body of technical skills and hard-earned practical experience through the decision to release all 5,000 of the technical officers serving at home and abroad at the time of the armistice. From this distance, it seems a great pity that one had to be sacrificed for the other.

The precise impact on the RAF is, of course, more difficult to determine. It certainly led to a service that lacked any significant body of logistic experience amongst its junior officers and, by extension, its future leaders. It also served to devalue engineering not only in the eyes of those not employed in technical duties but also those that were, but had only chosen specialist training as a means of enhancing their wider career prospects. Rarely can a policy have so evidently had the contrary effect to that intended. Lest this seem an unreasonably harsh judgement, I will quote from one of those trained under this scheme (who incidentally made a significant contribution to armament development during the Second World War):

> Nothing in my view, could have been more inept and unfortunate than the manner in which this matter was handled by the Air Ministry. They had obviously failed to envisage what was likely to be the cardinal need of the Air Force in the future. The shortage, among the officers on the air staff during the last war, of men with a sound and practical knowledge of engineering was distressingly evident only too often.[5]

A supporting view, but in a sense from the other camp, can be found in Sir Geoffrey Tuttle's recollections:

> I had joined the Royal Air Force to fly, but as I had not gone to Cranwell I needed a permanent commission. The only way to get one was to specialise in some subject, and for some extraordinary reason I chose engineering. I then spent the next two years at Henlow and managed to scrape through, thereby getting a Permanent Commission. I spent the rest of my career avoiding being an engineer and virtually managed to do so.[6]

In the immediate post-war period the likes of Sir Robert Brooke-Popham (who had presided over the most sophisticated and effective operational logistic system deployed by any air force on the Western Front) provided a valuable logistics input to high-level decision-making. But, as the years passed and the Second World War loomed, it is fair to say that logistics was neglected in favour of sustaining the largest possible front line. This gradual transition was greatly aided by the dogma of the 'knock-out blow' and a widespread belief that any future war would be short in duration.

A TECHNICAL BRANCH?

Concerns about the provision of engineer officers in the RAF were raised almost as soon as Trenchard's Memorandum had been published. As early as 1920, *The Aeroplane* commented that 'the shortage of good technical officers in the RAF is already a serious matter and must affect not only the efficiency but the actual effectiveness of the Air Force'.[7] It was readily acknowledged that, given financial stringency, any permanent technical organization would be only be a nucleus but it was still argued that staffs with deep technical knowledge were essential and that the proposed arrangements did not meet this requirement – or even recognize the need. 'The number of those who combine a wide and clear knowledge of the technique of aeronautical engineering, with any large practical experience of the use of aircraft is minute.'[8] The Air Ministry remained unmoved and there the matter lay for the next ten years; quiescent but unresolved.

Of course, matters did not totally stand still and there were some modest changes that recognized the need to employ full-time specialists in certain areas – notably the creation of a Stores Branch in 1922. In 1932, as a result of the growing difficulties that were being experienced in filling technical appointments, the Air Council decided to introduce commissioned technical Warrant Officers, mainly for employment in stations and maintenance units.[9] By 1936, there were 125 such technical officers, but the strain on the basic organization had not disappeared. In October of the previous year, an article had appeared in the *RAF Quarterly*, entitled 'An Engineering Branch for the Royal Air Force?' The anonymous author argued that with the increasing complexity of equipment, specialist engineers were required who could cope with the scope and intricacy of RAF engineering while also freeing GD officers to do what they did best, and had been trained for – to fly. Although there was a subsequent article rebutting this proposal, the debate continued both in the *Quarterly* and in the Staff College journal, *The Hawk*. All of this must have been deeply unwelcome by the air staffs who had observed, in 1933, that 'the frequent changes in personnel policy have led to a degree of discussion of the engineer question in the Service which is at least of doubtful advantage'.[10]

The service struggled on in the face of the inevitable until, in July 1939, the Air Council decided that the existing policy no longer met the needs of a modern air force. However, it would not be until April 1940 that a technical branch, with engineering, signals, armament and electrical sections was formed – the delay arising largely from Treasury concerns over the application of the same rates of pay and non-effective benefits as the GD Branch. Concerns that were only allayed by the promise of a review; once the war was over.

To be honest, the debate had never been about the self-evident need for engineering specialists. The problem was that the creation of a technical branch would undermine the credibility of the 'regimental' model bequeathed by Trenchard, as well as raising serious questions about the command role reserved solely for GD officers. In this respect, doctrine, dogma and organization were so entwined as to be indistinguishable. It is illuminating, therefore, to read the Air Ministry Order issued in 1942 on the Technical Branch to 'clarify uncertainties in the minds of officers'. Fully one-third of the document is given over to explaining the historical context and the rationale behind the decision to modify the broad principles laid down by Trenchard 20 years previously – such was the shadow he still cast.

EXPEDITIONARY LOGISTICS

As early as 1927, the Air Staffs had addressed the arrangements necessary to support an RAF Expeditionary Force and, in particular, the organization of maintenance during a mobile campaign.[11] It was believed, based on First World War experience, that the establishment of deployed squadrons should be kept as low as possible to enhance mobility. Squadrons would, therefore, be relieved of all repair work and hold only three days' supply of spares. Behind the squadrons, and within some 25 miles, would be a number of air stores parks carrying a month's supply of spares. Behind them, in turn, would be a non-mobile depot holding up to six months' supply of spares and undertaking all repairs. To cope with frequent squadron moves, advanced repair detachments would be provided located close to the squadrons. As time would show, this scheme was based on sound principles. It also looked uncannily like the system employed by Brooke-Popham in the latter months of 1918.

By 1932, however, there was opposition from some of the Air Staff – notably the Director of Organisation and Staff Duties – who felt that squadrons should be self-sufficient as far as possible. Salmond did not support these proposals, but in 1934 his successor as CAS, Sir Edward Ellington, was persuaded of their merit and agreed to the necessary changes to make squadrons self-supporting in the event of war. The implications of this decision would be all too clear in May 1940. Here again, one can detect an instinctive unwillingness to weaken the squadron – at least in conceptual terms – and thereby retreat from the fundamental building block of the Trenchard air force.

REARMAMENT

From 1933 to 1939, a succession of ambitious expansion schemes sought to achieve air parity with Germany and so to avoid war. In as much as deterrence was the primary aim of the exercise, it would be understandable if the allocation of resources favoured the front line – the shop window – at the expense of the support area (see Figure 10.1). What is less excusable is that the question of how the RAF would actually fight a modern, industrial war was largely ignored. It was not as if the Air Staffs had underestimated the likely scale of attrition. SD 78 (later to become SD 98 and first issued in 1933) made it clear that aircraft wastage as high as 100 per cent per month could be expected, but somewhat surprisingly ignored the question of spares, repair and salvage.[12] The prevalent attitude was neatly summed up in Ellington's famous remark 'In war, there will be no repair.'[13] It has been argued that this view was based on the belief that any war would be short and victory would be determined by the 'knock-out blow'. If so, then all previous experience attesting to the attritional nature of air warfare had been ignored.[14]

Figure 10.1: Increase in Air Force Annual Expenditure, 1933–38

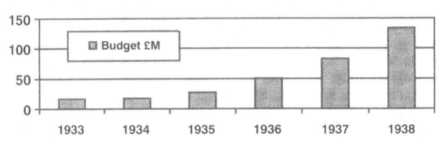

There were those that argued against this simplistic approach, notably Sir Cyril Newall and Sir Wilfrid Freeman – respectively Air Member for Supply and Organisation (AMSO) and Air Member for Research and Development (AMRD) – who insisted that war would bring a heavy and insistent demand for repair, and therefore compel the efficient use of scarce resources. Until 1938, however, Ellington's view prevailed.[15]

FORMATION OF MAINTENANCE COMMAND

Despite the lack of support, Newall and Freeman continued to develop plans for a service repair organization.[16] These bore fruit in September 1937, when Portal, as Director of Organisation, submitted proposals for the creation of a Maintenance Command to control and co-ordinate the RAF's support activities. The new organization was to be functionally based, comprising four groups: repair and salvage; ammunition and fuels; equipment; and storage. Although quickly endorsed by the Air Council, it would not be before the middle of 1938 that the new command's headquarters was in being and a start made on tackling the huge responsibilities it had been given.

REPAIR

The selection of Newall to be CAS in September 1937 transformed the debate. He was persuaded not only about the need for repair in wartime but also of providing adequate reserves. Wing Commander W. L. Welsh, his successor as AMSO, summed up the situation: 'We had been building up a frontline Air Force which was nothing but a façade. We had nothing by way of reserves or organization behind the frontline with which to maintain it.'[17] Unfortunately, matters would get worse before they got better. The AHB narrative is brutally clear as to the situation 'At the beginning of 1938 there was no RAF repair depot or properly planned system of repair.' The existing Home Repair Depot at Henlow had temporarily been turned into a technical training school to cope with the huge increase in manpower requirements (see Figure 10.2). Although new depots at St Athan and Sealand had been agreed, it would be another two years before they were in full operation.

Figure 10.2: Increase in RAF Manpower, 1933–41

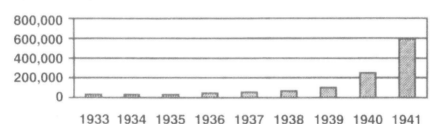

The scheme drawn up by the Air Staffs, primarily under AMSO's direction, for a wartime repair organization was undoubtedly ambitious. On the basis that industry would not have the capacity, the RAF would need to become self-sufficient in repair and maintenance. However, this also served to re-open an old debate with AMRD, and his successor – Air Member for Development and Production (AMDP) – as to who would actually control the repair organization.[18] While this question rumbled on, it soon became clear that the original plan to provide an entirely service-manned organization was unrealistic and civilian labour would have to be employed. In the event, even the provision of civilian-manned depots proved to be beyond the resources available. Moreover, these plans largely focused on aircraft rather than engine repair. As a result, when war broke out, the capacity was simply not available to cope with the increase in repairs arising – even before intensive rates of operation.

Events now moved rapidly. AMSO's desire to retain all repair activities within the service could not hide the deficiencies in the existing arrangements. In September 1937, Lord Nuffield had already been offered the task of running the new civilian repair depot at Burtonwood. He challenged the assumption that industry did not have the capacity to undertake repair and also the belief that the depots should concentrate on general rather than specialist repair. Nuffield then proposed that the main burden of repair be transferred to industry. Not surprisingly, both AMSO and AMDP disagreed but this merely forced the intervention of the Secretary of State for Air, who, at a meeting on 6 October 1939, stated that 'He believed in the necessity for a large-scale repair organization during the war. He could see the very precarious repair system then existing and the impossibility of meeting it from the resources of the RAF. He therefore considered it essential to take advantage of the Nuffield offer.' In this way the Civilian Repair Organisation (CRO) came into being. Initially part of the Air Ministry, with Nuffield as Director General of Maintenance and responsible to AMSO, the creation of the Ministry of Aircraft Production (MAP) under Beaverbrook in May 1940 saw the entire CRO, including the Service repair depots and salvage units, absorbed in the new organization – and thus outside the Air Ministry's control.[19]

Figure 10.3: CRO Output, 1940–45

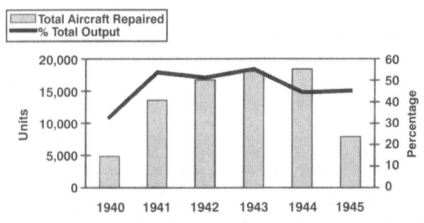

These developments did not resolve every policy issue, or end all the arguments. Suffice to say, events rapidly demonstrated the wisdom of using industry to expand repair capacity. Repaired Hurricanes and Spitfires made a vital contribution to the Battle of Britain, comprising over 40 per cent of all deliveries.[20] Throughout the war, over 79,000 airframes (48 per cent of the total number of aircraft issued to the Metropolitan Air Force) were provided by the CRO (see Figure 10.3). The creation of the CRO was a vital step in preparing the RAF to fight an attritional war and to conserve scarce resources for the wider war effort. For example, it was calculated that the matériel used between 1943 and 1945 to return 3,816 Lancasters to service would have only yielded 622 new airframes.[21]

The decision to hand control of all repair activities (other than overseas) to the CRO, and ultimately to the MAP, was hugely difficult for the Air Staffs to accept. However, the harsh reality of war and the urgent operational necessity of finding a solution to the problems of repair and maintenance forced their hand. The doctrine of self-sufficiency gave way to a higher imperative – the fight for national survival.

RESERVES

The provision of a significant repair capability had an important role in sustaining an adequate level of reserves, but the decision on the latter strategy was a separate and conscious change in policy with far-reaching implications. Slessor provides evidence that this change of heart was driven as much by the practical problems of over-rapid expansion – notably in personnel and training – as by concerns about the RAF's actual warfighting capability. Even so, the operational argument weighed heavily:

> If we constantly go on expanding in breadth, we shall never reach the stage when we can consolidate, put some depth behind the facade and put our force on a footing of readiness for war. The fact is we cannot be constantly expanding our nominal first line (which does not in any case represent our true war first line) and at the same time have a force fit to go to war.[22]

Slessor was properly concerned that the unremitting expansion in the number of squadrons – the 'façade policy' as he described it – would only serve to weaken the RAF's ability to fight.[23] In this view, he had the support of Newall and Freeman. While they were able to temper the expansion programme, to address key aspects such as reserves and repair and maintenance, the main emphasis continued to be on the increase in front-line strength. Given the political context, this was perhaps not unexpected.

To their credit, the Air Staffs had at least sought to tackle such issues, albeit late in the day, and had made them an integral part of the expansion programme. It is interesting to contrast this outcome with the very similar debate that occurred in Germany at much the same time. Unlike the RAF, the *Luftwaffe* made no specific arrangements for coping with the high attrition and wastage that war would bring. At a conference in January 1938, Erhard Milch as Under-Secretary of State for Air, announced that 'All campaigns will be short and German aircraft production so tremendous that during such periods of operation no major repairs will be necessary. Damaged planes will be repaired and salvaged at home after the campaigns are won.'[24] Ernst Udet, the *Luftwaffe*'s Chief of the Technical Office, had the temerity to question the wisdom of the existing policy only to be told that his remarks were 'outrageous'.[25] This was not an isolated incident but reflected a general lack of interest in logistics throughout the *Luftwaffe*. By and large, logistic concerns were seen by many commanders as a distraction if not an operational impediment.[26] It also seems likely that different lessons had been drawn from the First World War, during the course of which the German Air Services had generally experienced lower wastage levels than the RAF (see Figure 10.4). In fact, monthly aircraft wastage rates for the German Air Service had been closer to 30 per cent than the 50–55 per cent experienced by the RAF in 1917 and 1918.[27]

Figure 10.4: Overall Aircraft Wastage, 1914–18

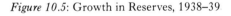

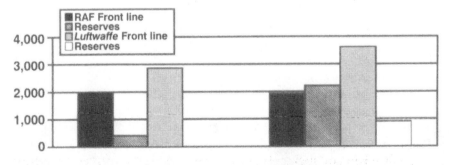

Figure 10.5: Growth in Reserves, 1938–39

The outcome of the policy changes made under Newall's tenure was to place the RAF in a better position than the *Luftwaffe* to fight an attritional war – notably in respect to reserves. Comparisons are always difficult, and there is a danger of including obsolescent types, but when war broke out the RAF possessed some 2,200 reserves, 115 per cent of its front-line strength, compared with the 900 held by the *Luftwaffe*, equivalent to just 24 per cent of its frontline – some sources have gone as far as arguing that the *Luftwaffe* effectively had no reserves (see Figure 10.5).[28] This deficiency would tell heavily against the *Luftwaffe*'s ability to sustain offensive operations during the Battle of Britain.

STORAGE

To cope with such large numbers of stored aircraft, special provision had to be made in the form of dedicated Aircraft Storage Units (ASU). The scale of this activity can be judged from the increase in overall holdings as the war progressed (see Figure 10.6). By October 1939, the ASUs held over 2,500 aircraft, a total that had grown to some 5,300 by August 1940. It would be misleading to suggest that these were all front-line aircraft, only 572 represented the Hurricanes and Spitfires so critical to Fighter Command. Nevertheless, the conscious decision to build up the level of reserves from 1938 onwards became the pattern for the remainder of the war, such that by the end of 1943, nearly 8,500 aircraft were held in reserve.

Figure 10.6: ASU Holdings, 1939–40

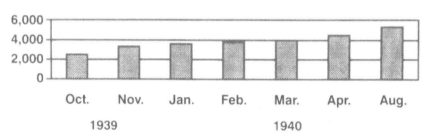

SPARES

The uncertainty over repair had its parallels in the confused approach to the provision of spares. During the war, MAP controlled all production programmes, including spares, but responsibility for forecasting requirements and for ordering spares remained with the Air Ministry. Unfortunately, both the RAF and industry viewed the manufacture of spares as a secondary activity to the production of new aircraft. Sir Alec Cairncross, who worked in MAP for most of the war, commented that 'the provisioning of spare components was one long muddle and the source of constant friction from the start'.[29]

Of course, the supply of spares was never going to be an easy business under wartime conditions. The multiplicity of aircraft and engine types, the urgent need to expand new production and the self-evident difficulty of predicting consumption rates in advance of any in-service experience presented huge challenges. However, the task was not made easier by the Air Staff's delay in recognizing the need to provide for repair and their unwillingness to allocate production capacity to the provision of spares. Until 1937, the Director of Equipment purchased spares on the basis of 27 months' peacetime maintenance rates, plus an additional four months' supply at estimated war-consumption rates. However, because of the serious difficulties that were being encountered in achieving these targets, spares were soon restricted to only a 15-month peacetime and four-month wartime supply. While this undoubtedly made it easier to meet new production demands, the provisioning cycle was really too short to allow adequate consumption data to be assembled before reordering commenced. More importantly, the real demand for spares had not fallen and thus spares shortages steadily got worse. For example, by September 1939 it was discovered that all the existing spares for the Hurricane had been consumed. There is little doubt that the over-riding emphasis on new production actually reduced availability. This was particularly true in the supply of engines. By late September 1939, there were 2,088 engines at manufacturers and another 157 with the RAF under repair – primarily awaiting spares.[30] Although the decision to restrict spares was rescinded in early 1939, it was not until August 1940 that the Air Ministry agreed to an actual increase in the capacity devoted to spares production. As a result, it would take some time before spares were no longer an operational issue (see Figure 10.7). Three years after the war had started, attempts were still going on to get factories to allocate 10 per cent of their floor space to the manufacture of spares.[31] Such problems were further exacerbated by the suspicion that many short-supply items existed but had been mislaid in the depots: 'The more ribald among us held that stock-taking

Figure 10.7: Percentage of Aircraft Awaiting Spares – RAF Home Commands, 1941–45

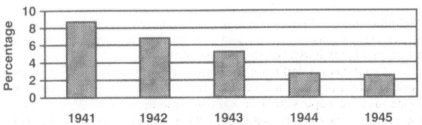

in the units was carried out by ex-ploughmen and dancers whose arithmetic was poor; and we nourished stories of storemen sitting on crates containing the very items whose existence they denied.'[32] Overall, it is difficult to avoid the conclusion that the preference for new production over the provision of spares was largely due to the instinctive prejudice in favour of front-line numbers that had dominated pre-war planning. As one observer put it, 'Spare parts had little dramatic appeal.'[33]

THE IMPACT OF WAR

The Battle of France

Just how high actual wastage would prove was demonstrated in the Battle of France. Nearly 1,000 aircraft were lost in a month, very close to the predicted losses for maximum-effort operations. The planned arrangements for repair and salvage were found to be totally inadequate. Thus, while only 66 out of the total of 452 Hurricanes sent to France returned, no fewer than 178 were abandoned or destroyed through lack of repairs.[34] In fact, only a relatively small number were lost in air combat (see Figure 10.8).

Figure 10.8: Hurricane Wastage, France 1940

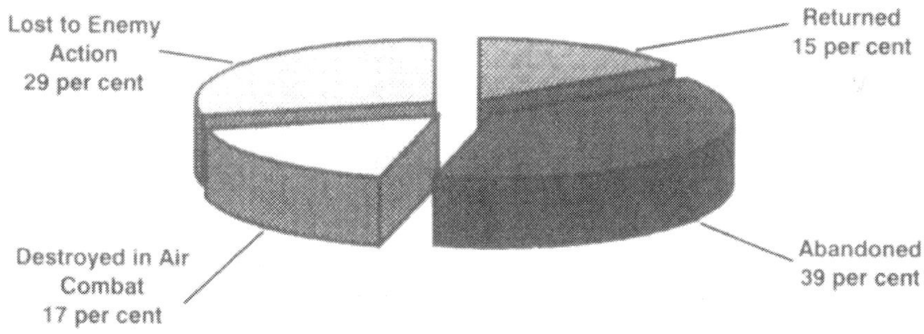

Lost to Enemy Action 29 per cent

Returned 15 per cent

Destroyed in Air Combat 17 per cent

Abandoned 39 per cent

Squadrons deployed to France found themselves desperately short of reserves, vehicles, spares, and repair and salvage capabilities. The latter deficiency had already been recognized and steps were taken late in 1939 to provide dedicated forward repair and salvage units – much as originally proposed in 1927. However, the resources available were inadequate to cope with the level of arisings (defects), or to handle the repair work that the squadrons were unable to tackle. The lack of vehicles and specialist equipment affected the parks and depots particularly badly. As a result, they rapidly became immobile and increasingly ineffective. In-theatre repair amounted initially to a mere two Hurricanes a week and had risen to only eight a week by June (and this after considerable effort). Almost no engine repairs had been completed owing to a shortage of tools.[35]

The Battle of Britain

With the expansion programme had come the realization that individual flights within squadrons could no longer continue to be self-sufficient in maintenance and repair. From 1936, therefore, a dedicated flight was created to undertake each squadron's major repair work and inspection.[36] This went some way towards coping with the increasing complexity of front-line aircraft and the higher flying rates that the expansion programme had introduced. Nevertheless, the focus remained very much on sustaining squadron self-sufficiency.

These arrangements remained in place for the first year of the war, but experience during the Battle of Britain showed that the mobility of squadrons was hampered by the static servicing organization. As the battle progressed, squadrons moved with increasing frequency and as a result it was not unusual to find the squadron's groundcrew spread over three stations – even when it proved practicable to move maintenance personnel by air. The problem was not helped by the need to leave repair parties behind to recover unserviceable aircraft. In December 1940, Trafford Leigh-Mallory proposed that the mobility of fighter squadrons be increased by creating a station maintenance party and reducing the squadron establishment to the personnel required to perform minor inspections and handling. A more radical proposal, to remove all ground personnel other than a small administrative staff, was rejected because it would 'destroy the body of the squadron owing to the absence of the squadron fighting spirit which depended not only on the skill and morale of the pilots but also on the efficiency and keenness of the ground staff'.[37]

One is tempted to describe this as the triumph of emotion over efficiency but, even as the revised arrangements were gradually introduced, it became clear that a more radical solution was needed. Accordingly, in 1943, it was decided that stations themselves should become mobile and squadrons relieved of their residual maintenance responsibilities. The new organization, developed with a view to the expeditionary needs of 2nd Tactical Air Force, comprised three mobile servicing elements: the advanced landing-ground area; the airfield area; and the base area. With some further refinements, this system remained in being until the end of the war.

CONCLUSIONS

We should not under-estimate the scale and depth of the changes that the RAF had to make in the period leading up to the outbreak of war. Change is difficult for any organization to embrace – even when faced with a pressing and visible threat. It was Basil Liddell Hart who said 'the only thing harder than getting a new idea into the military mind is to get an old one out'. However, in defence of the military mind, I would suggest that organizational change in any of the services is going to be difficult because of the doctrinal and cultural foundations that have to be shaken.

The development of an effective logistic system capable of sustaining the RAF in a modern, industrial war required policy changes that were contrary to much of the ethos inherited from Trenchard. It was also, of course, a very young legacy and one that had served the RAF extremely well through some difficult years, when even the continued existence of an independent air force was in doubt. In many ways, therefore, the fact that change – slow, painful and hesitant perhaps – did occur is a credit to the staffs involved, given the obstacles to be overcome. It is also, I believe, an indication of how influential corporate experience can be – in the form of the First World War – even if it is not provided with a clear, articulate voice. Much of the expansion programme, notably the provision for repair and reserves and the introduction of a technical branch was driven by the lessons identified in 1917 and 1918.

Criticism can certainly be made, however, of the thinking behind Trenchard's organizational model that appears to owe more to his personal prejudices than an open-minded assessment of how air power could be most effectively delivered. The failure to recognize the need for specialist officers, particularly those that would pursue a full career in the service, short-changed the RAF in its doctrinal development and, ultimately, weakened its ability to fight. This was not solely a question of logistics but extended, in particular, to navigation and armaments. These wider shortcomings became all too evident in the first years of the war.

In examining these issues, we do so with the benefit of hindsight. We need to guard against the luxury of elevating some individuals and pillorying others. It is certainly tempting to praise Newall and to criticize Ellington. What I feel is abundantly clear is that democracies tolerate, if not encourage, a level of debate that is intolerable in a totalitarian state. The point is not that some of the Air Staffs got it wrong and others right, but that individual voices were heard – that there was discussion – and that, ultimately, the right answers were found. The *Luftwaffe*'s fate shows exactly what can happen if debate is stifled and honesty sacrificed to dogma. Doctrine has to adapt and change if it is to be of value. An ability to tolerate criticism and to listen to different opinions, service and civilian, is the foundation of air power.

NOTES

1. See Peter Dye, 'Logistics and Air Power – A Failure in Doctrine?', *RAF Air Power Review*, Spring (1999).
2. According to the scheme for the permanent organization of the Royal Air Force published on 13 December 1919.
3. John James, 'The Branch Structure of the RAF', *The RAF Quarterly*, Vol. 18, No. 3 (Autumn 1978).
4. Report of a Committee on the Future of the Technical Branch, Air Ministry, 1945, PRO AIR 2/8518.
5. Air Commodore P. Huskinson, *Vision Ahead* (Werner Laurie, London, 1949), pp. 23–4.
6. Sir Geoffrey Tuttle, 'Fifty Years in Flying', *The RAF Quarterly*, Vol. 18, No. 2 (Summer 1978), pp. 140–51.
7. Hugh Trenchard, 'Aspects of Service Aviation', *The Aeroplane*, 27 October 1920.
8. Capt. W. H. Sayers, 'On the Future Technical Staff of the RAF', *The Aeroplane*, 1 December 1920, pp. 845–6.
9. See Memorandum on the Recruitment, Training and Qualifications of Engineer Specialist Officers, PRO AIR 2/1507.
10. Ibid.
11. *The Second World War, 1939–1945, Royal Air Force Maintenance* (Air Historical Branch, Air Ministry, 1954), pp. 54–5.
12. Air Staff Memorandum No. 50, PRO AIR 10/1522.
13. See The Repair and Maintenance of Aircraft, PRO AVIA 46/168.
14. Robin Higham, *Selected Aspects of RAF Concepts of and Planning for War, 1934–1941* (International Congress of Military History, Madrid, 1990), offers a variety of explanations – some more persuasive than others – such as: collective corporate amnesia; the belief that metal-framed machines would require less frequent repair and more frequent replacement; the incentive in peacetime to forego salvage in favour of obtaining new machines; the emphasis on the front line; and distractions caused by the expansion programme and, in particular, the increased training requirement.
15. Ibid.
16. It would appear that Newall was very much the driving force behind these proposals, although it has been claimed that Freeman was the inspiration. See Anthony Furse, *Wilfrid Freeman: The Genius behind Allied Air Supremacy* (Spellmount, Staplehurst, 2000), pp. 95–6.
17. *Development of RAF Maintenance*, pp. 4–5.
18. PRO AVIA 46/168.
19. This included the bulk of Maintenance Command.
20. See Peter Dye, 'Logistics and the Battle of Britain', *Air Power Review*, Winter (2000), pp. 15–36, for a wider discussion of the contribution of repair to the outcome.
21. M. M. Postan, *British War Production* (HMSO, London, 1952), pp. 316–22.
22. AVIA 46 1168, The Repair and Maintenance of Aircraft, 1935–1945, para. 22.

23. Sir John Slessor, *The Central Blue* (Cassell, London, 1956), pp. 170–1.
24. Horst Boog, 'Luftwaffe and Logistics in the Second World War', *Aerospace Historian*, June (1988), pp. 103–10.
25. Air Division, Control Commission for Germany, A Study of the Supply Organisation of the German Air Force 1935–1945, June 1946, p. 71.
26. Ibid.
27. German experience in the First World War indicated that a monthly attrition of some 30 per cent might be expected. In 1938 it was calculated that a front line of 2,307 would demand a monthly production of some 1,800 aircraft. On the outbreak of war, the *Luftwaffe*'s front-line strength was in excess of 3,600, but monthly production was fewer than 700 aircraft. Edward L. Homze, *Arming The Luftwaffe* (University of Nebraska Press, Lincoln, NB, 1976), pp. 182–3.
28. Karl Gundelach, 'The German Air Force', *Air Power Historian*, Vol. XVIII (1971), p. 25.
29. Sir Alec Cairncross, *Planning in Wartime: Aircraft Production in Britain, Germany and the USA* (St Martin's Press, New York, 1991), pp. 57–63.
30. Robin Higham, *Revolutionary Innovation and the Invisible Infrastructure: Innovation and the Development of Flight* (Texas A&M University Press, College Station, TX, 1999), pp. 235–62.
31. Robin Higham, 'Royal Air Force Spares Forecasting in World War II', *Air Force Journal of Logistics*, Spring (1996), pp. 23–6.
32. Cairncross, *Planning in Wartime*, p. 59.
33. PRO AVIA 46/228, *The Spares Problem*.
34. Norman Franks, *Royal Air Force Fighter Command Losses of the Second World War, 1939–1941* (Midland Publishing, Leicester, 1997), pp. 18–25.
35. PRO AIR 16/1023, Report on Operations of British Air Forces France.
36. *Royal Air Force Maintenance*, p. 179.
37. Ibid., p. 180.

11

Australia and the War in the Pacific, 1942–45

Ian MacFarling

The preparations for defending Australia during the period from federation in 1901 to the start of the war in the Pacific in 1942 are a sorry tale of wishful thinking, misplaced hope, and a failure to understand that Australia's geostrategic situation was vastly different to the one faced by Great Britain in Europe. The problem was that – being tied so closely to Britain's imperial apron strings – Australia tended to do as it was told,[1] and consequently made plans for wars that bore no resemblance to the strategic realities of home defence.

In essence, the Second World War was two separate wars. One was continental and fought in a relatively small area of Europe and the Middle East, while the other was maritime and fought in the vast, sparsely populated region of the Pacific, where there was little or no infrastructure. This essay sets out the tasks that Australia set for itself – or had set for it by bigger and more powerful nations – and discusses the problems faced by a nation when it subordinates itself to another's plans and then has to use equipment and processes that are totally inadequate to the vital task of defending itself against an attack that threatens its very survival.

THE GEOSTRATEGIC SETTING

The Pacific region is large. The map at Figure 11.1 gives the dimensions.

However, this does not provide a useful vehicle for the comparison needed here. Figure 11.2 shows the United Kingdom overlaid on the Australian continent. The square superimposed over the Darwin area is the approximate size of the area of operations during the Battle of Britain.

Figure 11.1: The Pacific Region

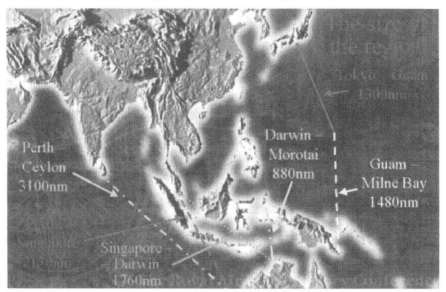

Figure 11.2: Comparing Australia and Britain

Australia has always been a sparsely populated country. The population data collected in the 1940 census is shown in Figure 11.3. The geostrategic issue associated with this population distribution was that few areas outside the towns and cities were developed in any way, and most of the development that was undertaken happened in the south of the continent. Darwin in 1940 was a small town of about 5,000 people, who were as isolated from the rest of Australia as if they had been on a coral atoll in the middle of the South Pacific Ocean.[2]

Figure 11.3: The Australian Population in 1940

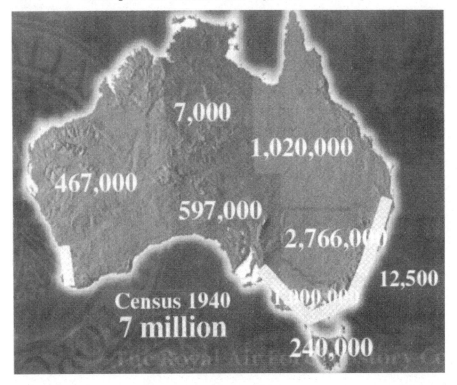

THREATS TO AUSTRALIA

The colonial governments that existed before federation in 1901 all saw the threats to Australia as coming from Asian expansion.[3] The gold rushes and development of the pearling industry in northern Australia during the mid-to-late nineteenth century brought Chinese and Japanese migrants to several of the colonies. In the manner of the time, successive colonial ministers grouped all Asians together and expressed racist views about the 'yellow menace'.[4] For those who were more discriminating in their racism, the Chinese were seen as the main threat to Australian security, while the Japanese, who dominated the pearling industry in the north-west of Australia, were grudgingly tolerated for commercial reasons. However, racism was brought to a head by the stunning Japanese victory over Russia at Tsushima in 1905.[5] Thereafter the Japanese were regularly declared to be the main threat to Australia.[6]

This policy preference had several difficulties. First, Japanese–Australian trade was significant but, more importantly, Britain and Japan had signed a treaty in 1902. Australian disquiet at Japan – a potential enemy – being involved with the 'mother country' increased further when the treaty was renewed for another ten years in 1911. The Australian Minister for Defence was particularly unhappy when, as a result of the treaty extension, Imperial Japanese Navy (IJN) warships were given primary responsibility for the protection of Australian convoys to the Middle East during the First World War.[7]

In the aftermath of the Versailles Treaty in 1919, Japan and Australia were given mandates over former German possessions in Asia and the Pacific. The Japanese acquisition of the Mariana and Caroline archipelagos in the western Pacific north of the Equator heightened Australian security concerns. The new territories moved Japan several hundred miles closer to Australia.[8] The consequence was that Australian defence plans, as early as 1919, included the concept of developing a force to meet a Japanese invasion force of 100,000 men.[9]

In 1918, Lord Jellicoe, the former British First Sea Lord, had been asked to provide a strategic plan for Australia's defence. The policy debate that resulted from his findings tended to support Australian worries about a Japanese attack. First, many commentators agreed with Jellicoe that 'the Pacific would be the main theatre of future operations'. Second, Britain moved to developing Singapore as the base for a Far Eastern fleet, and in 1923 the British Imperial Conference produced an understanding that Australian armed forces would be able to withstand an armed attack for six months before the British Royal Navy came to the rescue.[10]

The associated plans and force structure requirements did not achieve fruition for a variety of reasons, including the Great Depression and a war-weariness that tended to overshadow every other consideration. The consequences were far reaching. By 1932, when the Lyons government came to power Australia was defenceless. The Army that in 1920 had said it needed 180,000 men to defend against a Japanese attack had been reduced to 42,700 by 1927. The Royal Australian Navy was not capable of archipelagic operations, owing to the lack of numbers and the type of ships it operated, and the Royal Australian Air Force

(RAAF) had 68 aircraft and had been declared 'unfit to undertake war operations' in 1928.[11]

THE IMPORTANCE OF SINGAPORE TO AUSTRALIA

The British Imperial Conference of 1923 included the acknowledgment by those participating that each part of the Empire was responsible for its own defence. The minutes also include the comment that New Zealand, Australia and India 'took a deep interest in the development of the Singapore naval base'. The general plan was that Singapore would service the British main battle fleet and this would deter Japan from contemplating war.[12]

The strategy was based on several rather tenuous premises. These included the assumption that Singapore would be completed before another war occurred, that the British would actually send the main fleet, that it would be able to defeat the Japanese when it did arrive, and that Singapore would be able to defend itself until the fleet arrived. This strategy was based for the most part on wishful thinking.[13]

The consequence for Australia was that it was responsible for the protection of maritime trade on the Australia Station, became a contributor to the naval attack force based at Singapore, provided a secondary base at the rather primitive port of Darwin, and was required to develop an expeditionary force as well as forces for the continental defence of Australia.[14]

Australians continued to put significant resources into the Singapore plan, often at the expense of Australian home defence. There were still worries. The Japanese were told that Singapore did not represent a threat to Japanese interests in the north-west Pacific, which drew the remark from John Curtin, later the wartime Australian Prime Minister, that if Singapore was not a threat to the Japanese in the Yellow Sea, how could it be a source of support for Australian interests which were a thousand miles further away?[15] At the same time, Britain was making demands that took away resources from Australian defence. The focus of the demand was the building up of a large British air capability through the Empire Air Training Scheme (EATS).

THE EMPIRE AIR TRAINING SCHEME

When Hitler began the rapid expansion of the *Luftwaffe* in the mid-1930s it became clear that if Britain were to match the Germans in the air, then it would need help from its Dominions. A staff exercise conducted by the British Royal Air Force (RAF) in 1934 determined that in future wars the RAF could expect to lose 30 per cent of its aircrew each month, of which 60 per cent would be killed or missing. Large numbers of aircrew would be needed – figures of up to 20,000 pilots were suggested. This would require 90 flying schools and at the time Britain had just eight.

By 1939, after some particularly acrimonious debates, Australia agreed to supply 10,080 of the 28,000 aircrew drawn from the Dominions over a three-year period. This meant that, when the scheme was operating at maximum capacity, Australia would supply 432 pilots, 226 observers and 392 wireless operator/air gunners every four weeks.[16] Both the Australian Federal Government and the Australian Air Board saw this contribution as vital to Allied success in the European war.[17] The problem was that it did nothing for the defence of continental Australia.[18] By the end of 1940, Australian aircrew were going to Britain in large numbers – and being shabbily treated into the bargain – but none of the reciprocal supply of modern, effective combat aircraft was forthcoming from the British.[19]

The Australian federal government also showed its commitment to the Empire Air Training Scheme by appointing – in rather dubious circumstances – Air Chief-Marshal Sir Charles Burnett, an elderly RAF officer,[20] to be Chief of the Air Staff of the Royal Australian Air Force. It was in many ways a logical step to seek someone who could manage the extremely complex issues of EATS when the RAAF plainly did not have an officer who possessed such skills, but such was Burnett's commitment to the RAF that he neglected most other RAAF issues and angered many of his Australian subordinates with his continual dismissal of their concerns over Australia's security.[21]

THE OUTBREAK OF WAR IN THE PACIFIC

The demands of the war in Europe and the Middle East, the EATS and the chimera of Singapore's status as an impregnable fortress meant that Australia was not prepared for war in the Pacific. Despite the long-held view of Japan as the most likely threat to Australia, and the Australian plans for such hostilities, they did not have the equipment or the concrete activity that would have turned such plans into a successful defence. The wishful thinking that permeated everything was demonstrated at a conference held in Singapore in late October 1941, where, for ten days, the delegates 'examined evidence that was alarming in its revelation of the inadequacy of defence measures throughout the Far East'.[22]

The RAAF itself had little or nothing to meet the Japanese assault. In Australia, it had only 171 aircraft that it designated 'front-line', but this too was an overly optimistic assessment of their capabilities because 101 of them were Wirraways, 53 were Hudsons, and 12 were Catalinas.[23] The 306 'second-line' aircraft included Fairey Battles and Avro Ansons that had been sent to Australia as EATS training aircraft after their dismal performance in combat in Europe during 1940.[24] In Singapore and Malaya RAF Command had 164 front-line aircraft and 88 reserves. The majority comprised substandard, short-range cast-offs that had failed in Europe or had been rejected earlier in the war by the services that had ordered them. The RAAF forces allocated to the British forces in the Far East were two squadrons of Brewster Buffalos and two squadrons of Lockheed Hudsons. The arming of the Hudsons had been done at the expense of their sister units in Australia, and the Buffalos had been delivered directly to Singapore from the United States. This force did not offer much resistance to the invading Japanese, and most Australian aircraft were destroyed in the early fighting.[25]

The fall of Singapore and the attendant Allied military disaster throughout South-east Asia is outside the scope of this chapter. However, it does mark a turning-point in Australian policy. As Japanese pressure increased on Singapore, plans were discussed for abandoning it. This horrified the Australian government, which had set such store by its role in defending Australia, and hard words were said. The bitterest comment came in a cablegram from the Australian government to Winston Churchill on 23 January 1942, which included the following text:

> ... [We have been informed] the Defence Committee [in London] has been considering the evacuation of Singapore and Malaya. After all the assurances we have been given, the evacuation of Singapore would be regarded here and elsewhere as an inexcusable betrayal ...[26]

The consequences of this cablegram together with the disaster in south-east Asia were that Australian reliance on Britain diminished rapidly, though EATS continued after a brief halt in early 1942, and Australian squadrons still operated in Europe and the Middle East. Australia had decided to move rapidly to the American camp.

AUSTRALIA AND THE UNITED STATES IN THE SOUTH-WEST PACIFIC

It should be made clear at the outset that the United States did not come to Australia's aid from any altruistic motive, despite Australian urging.[27] Its aim was to return to its former dominion in the Philippines and it would have done this directly if that had been a viable alternative. However, the Japanese were aware of the policy and their drive to the south-east was in part a determination to ensure that the Americans could not disrupt their plans for a Greater East-Asian Co-prosperity Sphere in the former European colonies of South-east Asia. This meant that the United States had to use Australia as a stepping stone, or wait until its industrial might could produce sufficient forces to move directly to the Philippines. General MacArthur, who had left the Philippines in great haste, was made Commander South-West Pacific Area, and he brought with him commanders who would – after a short while – relegate the Australian forces under their command to secondary players. This did not mean, however, that Australian forces – particularly the RAAF – languished far from the battle or continued to be small and ineffective. There were several places where they were the decisive element in victory, and these are discussed briefly below.

The fact that the United States had joined in the Pacific War did not make the issues that beset Australia up until late 1941 go away. Even as late as July 1943 the Pacific theatre was seen as fifth in the order of priority set down by the Allies at their Casablanca Conference.[28] Australia continued to press for supplies. The general consensus expressed in the federal parliament by a Labour government minister, Arthur Calwell, was that Australia had a right to ask that sufficient aircraft should be sent for the defence of Australia.[29] However, requests such as these drew the comment that 'the tenacity and methodical comprehensiveness of the [Australian] campaign leaves Washington curious, baffled, and almost resentful'.[30] In the meantime, Australia felt that it was fighting for its survival and events such as those at Darwin supported this thesis.

THE DARWIN THEATRE OF OPERATIONS

The Japanese attacks through south-east Asia in early 1942 continued unabated and Allied resistance in the Dutch East Indies collapsed in a matter of days.[31] The result was that Darwin became the focus of attention for all sides in the war, because it represented either the most likely point through which the Japanese would invade Australia or, conversely, the base from which Allied operations would be launched in an effort to retake the Dutch East Indies. The Americans fell back towards it from Java, the Australians tried to develop the infrastructure with little or no equipment, and the Japanese decided to attack it.

On 19 February 1942, a force of 188 carrier-borne aircraft was launched from the same Imperial Japanese Navy carrier battle group that had attacked Pearl Harbor on 7 December 1941. The raid had been planned by the officer who had developed the Hawaiian raid, and the attacking force was commanded by the same pilot who had led that mission. Later the same day 54 land-based aircraft struck Darwin again from bases in Ambon and the Celebes. The raids were a complete success. The 11 USAAF P-40 Kittyhawk fighter aircraft that intercepted the first force were all shot down,[32] 23 of the 45 ships in the harbour were sunk, and numerous buildings were destroyed. Two hundred and forty-three people were killed and 350 injured. The seat of territory government moved to Alice Springs, 1,200 kilometres to the south, and Darwin became a military enclave. The Japanese attacking force lost five aircraft. These were the first two raids out of a total of 64 that were launched against Darwin up to 12 November 1943.[33]

The reason that the Japanese did not invade northern Australia had nothing to do with the strength – or potential strength – of the Allied defences. The Japanese Army did not agree with the Imperial Japanese Navy, which wanted to invade Australia as quickly as possible before any build-up of Allied forces. The Japanese Army thought the idea too risky and wanted to defend what they had already won in the territory they now called the Greater East-Asian Co-prosperity Sphere. They also realized that they had to develop Japanese warmaking potential and exploit the resources of the former European colonies they had conquered. Besides, the Japanese Army thought that Australia was too far south and calculated that it needed between 1.5 and 2 million tons of shipping to launch such an invasion, while it only had 2.1 million tons to meet all of its war needs.[34]

This respite provided Australia with the opportunity to recover. In concert with the Americans, it developed the northern part of the Northern Territory into a formidable defence base, though this always meant that it would continue to be a target while Japan had the wherewithal to attack it. Also, the Japanese could have attempted an invasion of the Darwin area to make the Allies cut back their forces in New Guinea – where they were driving the Japanese back – in order to counter the Japanese move against Darwin.

As the RAAF presence in the region grew, the service was given a set of five specific tasks:

- air defence of bases;
- reconnaissance to give at least a 36-hour warning of raids;
- protection of shipping;
- interdiction of Japanese shipping; and
- attacks on Japanese airfields.[35]

These tasks were undertaken with great commitment, though there were a number of problems. The first was that while Japanese activity was continual, it was not difficult to keep it in check. Thus boredom set in rapidly.[36] The second was the choice of aircraft for the theatre. It seems heresy to suggest that the Spitfire – one of the greatest aircraft ever built – was substandard. However, that would appear to be the case. The version sent to Australia was the Spitfire Mk Vc.[37] It had been 'tropicalized', which reduced its top speed and its maximum range, while increasing its maximum weight. This 'tropicalization' was not particularly successful. Atmospheric conditions resulted in engine and propeller failures, and the 20mm cannon frequently froze.[38] This meant that the aircraft tended to be used for defence rather than attack, and even this was fraught with mishaps.

A useful example of these worries occurred on the Allied worst day, 2 May 1943. Three squadrons of Spitfires intercepted a force of 21 Japanese bombers after their attack near Darwin.[39] Thirty-three Spit-fires had launched to engage the Japanese force, but five had to return early because of technical failures. The battle continued for some way out to sea. The defenders claimed seven enemy planes destroyed, four probably destroyed and seven damaged. Five Spitfires were lost or probably lost to enemy action. The claims reflect the over-enthusiasm of the inexperienced pilots, for, although seven G4M Betty bombers and seven A6M Zero fighters suffered some damage, all of the Japanese aircraft returned to their base.

In the aftermath of the battle, several Spitfire pilots had problems with their aircraft. Because of the need to use high throttle settings for long periods in combat, four Spitfires suffered engine or propeller CSU (Constant Speed Unit) failures. Five more ran out of fuel with one crashing into the sea and four making forced-landings. As a result of one engagement with Japanese forces, 14 Spitfires failed to return, and three pilots were listed as missing. Of the Spitfires that force-landed, one was later recovered intact, three were stripped for spare parts and one was written off.

This was not a good performance by any standard, but later General MacArthur's headquarters rubbed salt into the wound, by releasing an official communiqué stating that Spitfires had engaged Japanese bombers and their fighter escorts attacking Darwin, but suffered 'heavy casualties' in the process. The communiqué made headline news in Australian newspapers. Editorials spoke of 'a serious reverse', and some questioned whether the Spitfire was a match for the Japanese Zero in combat.[40]

The main factor was that European aircraft had been designed for European conditions. Consequently, machines that had been optimized for short-range operations in temperate climates did not perform well in the tropics, where they had to operate at the limits of their range. Furthermore, the lack of accurate weather forecasting and few accurate maps meant that all operations would be fraught with danger even if the enemy were not encountered.

The Japanese had made a decision that bombers would be escorted by fighters, so both types of aircraft were designed around the same premise. The Japanese machines were optimized for range and manoeuvrability. This meant that they could cover the vast distances between bases and targets in the Pacific and still be a formidable opponent in any combat. The optimization process and the Japanese warrior culture, however, brought weaknesses. The aircraft were very light and fragile with little protection for the pilot, so if weak spots were hit the aircraft would burst into flames or disintegrate.[41]

A comparison of aircraft is shown in Table 11.1. It shows how designers from different nations developed aircraft appropriate to the situation within their own nations rather than for a range of operating conditions. This meant that the much-vaunted concept of flexibility was in many ways designed out of European aircraft because of a narrow – or perhaps non-existent – view of the world and where aircraft would operate in it.

Table 11.1: Comparison of Fighter Aircraft Performance[43]

	Aircraft		
Feature	Supermarine Spitfire Mk Vc	Mitsubishi A6M3 Zero-Sen	Curtiss P40E Kittyhawk
Weight empty	6,420 lb	3,920 lb	6,550 lb
Range – internal tanks	410 nm	1,008 nm	695 nm
Range – external tanks	995 nm	1,680 nm	780 nm[42]
Service ceiling	37,000 ft	36,250 ft	33,000 ft
Maximum speed	325kt at 13,000 ft	293kt at 19,000 ft	304kt at 15,000 ft

The Darwin area then became the focus for offensive operations across the eastern half of the Dutch East Indies. The Allied air effort increased and a range of aircraft began operations from the Northern Territory. These included heavy bombers such as B-24 Liberators, attack aircraft such as Beaufighters, and long-range maritime patrol aircraft such as Catalinas. However, there was little to show for these activities and, apart for the comments about poor Spitfire performance, little was reported to the public about operations in the Darwin area. As Helson remarks, the war in this area was an air war and there were no invasions to report, no major sea battles, and after the last air attack on 12 November 1943, no aerial victories. Most people thought that the war had passed Darwin by.[44]

DEFENDING NEW GUINEA

While Darwin was being attacked, the Japanese continued their advance through the various archipelagos to the north of New Guinea. The aim was to form a barrier through which the Americans could not pass in their efforts to reinforce Australia.

Australia had no fighter aircraft that could offer resistance to any Japanese moves associated with putting a block between the United States and Australia, but had sought a number of different types in large numbers. These were promised but had not arrived. In the interim, a number of Curtis P40 Kittyhawk fighters were made available. Twenty-five aircraft were delivered in crates to Sydney in late February 1942. These were reassembled and flown north to Townsville and then to Port Moresby in Papua New Guinea. Operational training provided by RAAF pilots who had flown P40 variants with No. 3 Squadron in the Western Desert lasted nine days. When they arrived in Port Moresby with 17 aircraft only four of the 21 pilots in No. 75 Squadron had been in combat. They had some success, but within three days seven of the original 17 aircraft had been destroyed.[45] This, however, was not the main battle and Milne Bay on the eastern end of the island of New Guinea became the place where Australian legends were made.

MILNE BAY

Milne Bay was significant because of its location. Its retention in Allied hands blocked a Japanese line of advance to Port Moresby, which would have been much simpler than the one crossing the Owen Stanley mountain ranges that form the backbone of Papua New Guinea. It was also renowned for its bad weather, poor facilities, and tropical diseases.

In mid-August 1942, the Japanese made a further thrust southeastward and landed in force at the head of Milne Bay. In ten days of hard fighting the Australian force inflicted the first defeat on the Japanese, and cleared them from the south and south-eastern coast of Papua New Guinea. It was the first time that RAAF and Australian Army units had worked in a joint operation in the south-west Pacific, and it was a turning-point in Australian inter-service co-operation. This was not well received by General MacArthur and reflected his continued belittling of anything that Australian forces achieved throughout the campaign.[46] The general's curmudgeonly assessment of the Australian achievement does not reflect the result of the land battle, nor does it take into account the accomplishment of the air and ground crews. In atrocious conditions they maintained an average availability of 28 aircraft a day from a force of 35, fired 196,000 rounds and wore out 300 gun barrels in the course of the ten-day battle. From then on it became a slogging match, as the Japanese tried to beat the American forces in Guadalcanal and drive over the Owen-Stanley ranges from the north coast of New Guinea to Port Moresby. The RAAF's task was to prevent this by a variety of air operations, which included the interdiction of Japanese shipping moving men and supplies from Japanese-held territory in the Bismarck archipelago to the north coast of New Guinea. The most spectacular success was at the Battle of the Bismarck Sea.

THE BATTLE OF THE BISMARCK SEA

In late 1942 and early 1943, the Japanese still had the upper hand in New Guinea and the Solomon Islands. Allied land forces were holding up their advance but the issue was still undecided. Reinforcements on either would have tipped the balance. Allied air forces were still plagued by lack of equipment, and what was available was generally not good.[47] The Allied strategy still ensured that the highest priority was directed towards defeating the Axis powers in the Middle East and Europe. Also, there was a dearth of trained aircrew available for combat operations. To counteract this problem the Allied air commander, General Kenney decided to mix American and Australian aircrew where this provided more crews.[48] The composite crews were then trained in low-level anti-shipping operations because the only method of supply for the Japanese was by sea.

In late February 1943, the Japanese had control of the sea to the north of New Guinea. This meant that they could transport large numbers of troops to the front where Australian and American land forces were almost exhausted after the early campaigns on the south-west of the territory. The Japanese headquarters at Rabaul decided they would send two divisions as reinforcement prior to a move back towards Port Moresby. Allied signals intercepts showed that the forces would leave Rabaul on 1 March 1943.

The Allied air forces were tasked to intercept and destroy the convoy. They were fortunate that they had the time to prepare a thorough plan, which included attacks from medium level, attacks from very low level, and provision of fighter support from the Lockheed P38 Lightning squadrons that had recently arrived in theatre.

The battle was particularly one-sided. The use of mass was such that in five days the force of 14 or 15 vessels was routed. All eight transport ships were sunk and only four warships survived.[49] The Allies flew 93 bomber sorties and 117 fighter missions, they lost six aircraft and 31 others were damaged. They expended about 240,000 rounds of ammunition and dropped over 500 bombs. Forty-eight of the 70 direct hits were dropped at masthead height.[50]

These impressive statistics show that the Allied aircrews were dedicated professionals, a significant percentage of them were RAAF members. The communiqué from General MacArthur's headquarters described the action as 'perhaps the most devastating assault against naval surface forces during the entire war'. It did, however, fail to mention that Australians were involved in the operation.

For the first two years of the war in the south-west Pacific, Australian forces were on the back foot. They were forced to defend themselves against an enemy that enjoyed superiority in virtually all aspects of the war, including aircraft, weapons, logistics and morale. They learnt quickly and, despite some disparaging remarks from General MacArthur, were highly professional in the performance of their duties. As the war progressed, the RAAF increased dramatically in size and finished the war as the fourth-largest air force in the world. Why this happened and the consequences of the build-up for later RAAF activities form the last part of this chapter.

THE BUILD-UP OF THE RAAF

By August 1945, the RAAF had grown to a force of 54 squadrons, supported by a sophisticated infrastructure. It operated 3,187 aircraft, almost one per RAAF airmen in the service in 1939, with 1,100 front-line fighters, 439 attack aircraft and 256 heavy bombers. There were 154,511 RAAF personnel and another 16,584 WAAAF and RAAF Nursing Service members. This was vastly different from the pre-war Air Force, which, in trying to meet the principle of 'ubiquity of purpose', had sought to acquire aircraft that met the requirements of the other services as well as its own.[51] However, reaching this situation was difficult and only achieved because the larger powers had allowed it to happen.

Australia's policy was set for it by a foreign agreement that did not include Australian representation. In June 1942 the Commanding General of the USAAF, General H. A. Arnold, the Head of the United States Bureau of Naval Aeronautics, Admiral Jack Towers, and the British Chief of the Air Staff, Air Chief Marshal Sir Charles Portal, made an agreement that set out the policy governing Dominion air requirements. The two clauses that affected Australia stated that it was the duty of the United States Chiefs of Staff to define the strategic requirements of those Dominions falling within the United States' sphere of responsibility, and, once that had been defined, the United States would make the necessary allocations of aircraft, through the Combined Munitions Assignment Board.[52]

When the Australians sought more aircraft they were told bluntly that they were low on the priority list. Furthermore, when Arnold canvassed Portal's opinion on the type of aircraft that the RAAF should get, Portal was strident in his demands that the aircraft delivered would not take away Australian aircrew originally destined for RAF operations in north-west Europe. As one senior Australian noted, the RAAF was in the extraordinary position of competing with the RAF not only for aircraft but also for Australian aircrew.[53]

Given the control exercised over the RAAF by foreign powers, it is not surprising that only short-range fighters and attack aircraft were acquired until well into 1944. Many of these were produced in Australia, which had made remarkable strides in aircraft production in a few years.[54] What was missing was doctrine.[55] There was no attempt to develop a strategic level doctrine that would have supported the acquisition of a force that suited Australian geostrategic requirements. This is not surprising given the fact that, with the one exception of H. N. Wrigley,[56] Australia had not produced any thinkers on air power. The RAAF had been subordinated deliberately to the other services before World War II, and most of its officers had held junior rank and possessed a flying-club mentality, which did not encourage thought beyond the moment. Some RAAF officers had been sent to gather data on the Combined Bomber Offensive in Europe during 1943, but there is little evidence that their reports had any impact.[57]

In early 1944, some senior Australian officers were becoming sceptical about the future operational effectiveness of the RAAF in New Guinea. The problem was that the short-range aircraft with which the service was equipped meant that it 'could never hit the Japanese where they were in greatest strength'.[58] The Australians tried to acquire B-24 Liberators from the United States and, just when it seemed that their requests had been denied, these aircraft started to flow into Australia in large numbers.

RAAF commanders were happy with the result. They failed to realize that, yet again, they had been duped by their ally. General Kenney, the USAAF Commander in the South-West Pacific Area, had realized that the United States was producing a surplus of B-24 bombers. He realized that if he could replace USAAF squadrons in the Darwin region with RAAF bomber squadrons, then the American units would be available for the assault on mainland Japan while the RAAF mopped up the Japanese forces left behind in the region. Thus, the RAAF was left out of any real role, even though its leaders were deluding themselves that they could 'offer a substantial force in the final bombing of Japan'. As the former Chief of the Australian Defence Force Staff, Air Chief Marshal Sir Neville McNamara remarked, 'capability must be matched with ideas' because size does not denote power.[59] For the RAAF, in particular, the war in the South-West Pacific Area was ending with a whimper rather than a bang. Essentially, the RAAF did not have an airborne enemy only a ground one in jungle, where the effects achieved did not seem to justify the continuing losses. In the last nine months of the war, in several thousand sorties only five contacts were made with airborne enemy aircraft. Contact with enemy aircraft by Australian Spitfire fighters happened only three times.[60] The RAAF did play a major role in the Australian joint operations to recover the island of Borneo in early 1945. This was a great tactical success and showed that Australians were learning the lower-level lessons of war, but there seemed to be little thought about the independent development of doctrine for national air operations.[61] But with the subordinate role, limited targets and the lack of an air threat, the theoretical constructs of air power had been turned upside down. Australia in the end did not produce its own doctrine until the late 1980s and in the intervening period used RAF manuals for the education of its members.[62]

THE END OF THE WAR

At the end of the war the RAAF had 154,511 people serving in its ranks, 137,208 of these were serving in the South-West Pacific Area. The other 17,303 were serving with the RAF in Europe, predominantly in Bomber Command, where they had been used as individuals rather than collectively in Australian squadrons under Australian command. Few of those operating with the RAF had been given an opportunity to exercise command, because the British were determined that their men should not be commanded by Dominion officers. They were thus seasoned professionals who had exceptional tactical skills but were limited in other aspects of the control of air power.[63] They also took heavy casualties. EATS supplied 27,387 aircrew to the European theatre throughout the war. This was 3 per cent of the total Australians who enlisted during the Second World War – 6,612 were killed in operations in Europe.[64] This was just short of 30 per cent of the total Australians killed in action anywhere during the war. Their actions were not appreciated in Australia. Those who did return after a successful tour of duty in Europe were required to relinquish any acting rank that they may have been given,[65] and there were no campaign medals for the Combined Bomber Offensive.

In the South-West Pacific Area, the RAAF suffered 2,020 killed, 886 wounded, and 417 captured as prisoners of war. They had endured greater privation than their colleagues fighting in Europe, though it is difficult – if not impossible – to compare the two campaigns. They had been given a measure of independence, but this was always on the periphery of the theatre. They had thus developed some level of expertise at the operational level, while ensuring that their individual skills at the tactical level were first class. Their actions went largely unrewarded; there were few decorations handed out during the entire Pacific war, and they did not gain recognition, or even grudging thanks, from their allies.

Thus the war ended with Australia possessing the fourth-largest air force in the world, but it is difficult to find any domestic Australian policy that actually achieved this. Consequently, the RAAF had on the outside the appearance of a reasonably balanced force, while on the inside it was merely a gathering of tactical units being used for minor tasks, because the Americans had decided not to include Australia in the major actions. In part, this was Australia's fault. Its political leaders had no experience in air operations and they were given no professional advice from the RAAF because the service was wracked by inter-minable – and deplorable – wrangling among its leaders. Furthermore, it is difficult to see the politicians taking any notice of the airmen, because the civilians were in the thrall of General MacArthur, who was working to his own agenda and would brook no interference.

The conference at which this paper was originally presented was sub-titled 'Turning Points in Air Power History'. For Australia there were no such turning points. The issue that completely dominated its war was the decision to move from subordination to British to American control. Its air force reflected the complete lack of understanding about war policy and strategy among its leaders and, when the need for large scale was not there, the RAAF shrunk dramatically. By the Korean War in the early 1950s, the RAAF was a force of about 8,000 people with approximately 300 aircraft deployed in ten squadrons. The service was about to be commanded by another foreigner – though this one would be much better than his predecessor – and many of its units would be deployed overseas in Korea and the Middle East in activities that bore no relationship to Australia's own requirements for home defence. It had no indigenous air power doctrine and no clear thought on how aircraft should be used in defence of the nation. Clearly, not much had been learnt during the Second World War; certainly little that would have a marked influence on the way the RAAF conducted itself in subsequent years.

NOTES

1. David Day, *The Great Betrayal: Britain, Australia and the Onset of the Pacific War 1939–42* (Melbourne: Oxford University Press, 1988), particularly Ch. 1.
2. An example of how difficult the terrain is in northern Australia is given by an incident in May 1943 near Darwin. On 2 May 1943, Flight Sergeant Ross Stagg of No. 452 Squadron was posted missing after a disastrous engagement with a Japanese force. On 17 May 1943 he turned up at his airfield. During the action on

2 May 1943 his Spitfire aircraft had suffered a propellor CSU failure and he was
forced to bail out of his aircraft. He came down in the sea, boarded his dinghy and
paddled ashore at Fog Bay, which is about 75 kilometres south-west of Darwin at
the middle of the bay. But once on dry land he had to spend the next two weeks
trying to find a way out of the huge area of salt flats behind the shoreline. I am
grateful for the inputs of Alfred Price, the British air power historian, for his kind
permission to use the data on the operations over Darwin during May 1943. Private
Communication with Dr Price during July 2001.
3. There had been worries about Russian expansion at the end of the nineteenth
   century but this had diminished by the time the colonies formed federal Australia.
4. Henry P. Frei, *Japan's Southward Advance and Australia From the Sixteenth
   Century to World War II* (Melbourne: Melbourne University Press, 1991), especially Chs 5–7 inclusive.
5. Panic set in after the Battle of Tsushima on 27/28 May 1905. On that day 12
   Russian battleships, 15 cruisers and nine destroyers faced a Japanese fleet of four
   battleships, eight cruisers and assorted small vessels. Eight Russian battleships
   were sunk, the other four were captured. One Russian cruiser and two destroyers
   survived. The Japanese lost two cruisers, three torpedo-boats and had two
   battleships damaged. This was a turning-point for Australian foreign and defence
   policy. As the *Sydney Morning Herald* noted on 2 September 1905, 'the yellow man
   had taught the white races a lesson that Australians could neglect only at their
   peril'. There was no doubt in Australian minds that the Japanese had designs on
   the region. See John McCarthy in *Australia and the Threat of Japan*, ed. John
   McCarthy (Canberra: Australian Defence Studies Centre, 1992), p. 2.
6. See, for example, the Australian Prime Minister William M. Hughes's letter from
   London to his Cabinet colleagues in Melbourne, declaring his fears that 'Japan was
   most keenly interested in Australia', in Frei, *Japan's Southward Advance*, p. 93.
7. Vladislav Zhukov, 'Aftermath of War: Defence and Foreign Policy in the
   Washington Treaty Era', J. McCarthy (ed.), in *Australia and the Threat*, p. 9. See
   also Frei, *Japan's Southward Advance*, pp. 92–3, shore batteries in Fremantle to the
   south of Perth in Western Australia shot at the IJN vessels – but missed.
8. Zhukov, 'Aftermath', p. 13. This was despite the fact that the mandate included the
   stipulation that the territories should not be fortified.
9. David Horner, *High Command: Australia and Allied Strategy 1939–1945* (Sydney:
   Allen & Unwin Australia, 1982), pp. 1–2.
10. Zhukov, 'Aftermath', p.16.
11. Zhukov, 'Aftermath', pp. 18–19.
12. Horner, *High Command*, p. 2.
13. The Australian Prime Minister, Stanley Bruce, remarked at the conference, 'While
    I am not quite as clear as I should like to be as to how the protection of Singapore
    is to be assured, I am clear on this point, that apparently it can be done.' (Horner,
    High Command, p. 3.) Another aspect of this head-in-the-sand behaviour was the
    failure to take any notice of a British Army Staff College study that concluded that
    the Japanese could land a force of 100,000 men with three months' supplies in
    Australia long before the British fleet could arrive in Singapore. (Horner, *High
    Command*, p. 3.)
14. Horner, *High Command*, pp. 2–3.
15. Douglas Gillison, *Royal Australian Air Force 1939–1942* (Canberra: Australian
    War Memorial, 1962), p. 45.
16. John McCarthy, *A Last Call of Empire* (Canberra: Australian War Memorial,
    1988), p. 21.
17. The Minister for Civil Aviation, J. V. Fairbairn, described it November 1939 as

'the only activity we have undertaken which could lead to the winning or losing of the war by our success or failure in carrying out our undertaking is the Empire Air Training Scheme'. (McCarthy, *A Last Call*, p. 16.)

18. One of Australia's most distinguished airmen, Captain P. G. Taylor GC, noted in September 1941 that 'training for overseas service has completely overshadowed air defence'. (McCarthy, *Last Call*, p. 65.)

19. There was even a nasty dismissal of Dominion efforts to improve their own air defences by the British Secretary of State for Air, Sir Archibald Sinclair, when he wrote to Lord Beaverbrook, Minister for Aircraft Production, that 'we must see that these Dominions do not strip us of everything'. (McCarthy, *A Last Call*, p. 65.) They seemed to have forgotten that in the aftermath of Dunkirk, Australia immediately sent 30,000 Lee Enfield 0.303 rifles to Britain at a time when the total annual production of such weapons in Australia totalled 35,040. (I. D. Skinnerton, *The Lee Enfield Story* (Ashmore City, Queensland: private publication, 1993), pp. 308–10.)

20. Alan Stephens describes him as a 'rugged personality' who 'was unwanted by his own Service'. (Alan Stephens, *The Royal Australian Air Force* (Melbourne: Oxford University Press, 2001), p. 114.

21. Burnett's legacy can be judged by the comments of a senior RAF officer in 1951 when Australia yet again sought a CAS from the RAF. The Air Marshal said that the RAF was reluctant to oblige 'mainly because we felt that if we nominate[d] anyone, we must nominate one of our very best, and not repeat the follies of some years ago'. (McCarthy, *A Last Call*, p. 33.) See also Stephens, *The Royal Australian Air Force*, pp. 115–16, noting that as soon as Burnett returned to England in 1942 he was put on the retired list.

22. Gillison, *Royal Australian Air Force*, p. 143.

23. Peter Helson, an Australian aviation historian, has remarked: 'Aircraft were in short supply and so were guns to put in them. The Hudsons and Catalinas that were sent to Australia were unarmed. Photos of early RAAF Hudsons show some of them fitted with very primitive gun turrets (others have no turret at all). A former Catalina pilot told me that the RAAF had problems finding machine-guns for the PBYs and they were eventually fitted with Lewis guns left over from World War I. At that time the RAAF was not even being supplied with the .303 Vickers K machine gun that the RAF fitted to their Catalinas. I recall that both my father and a former Bomber Command gunner telling me that the Fairey Battles used for gunnery training at Sale [a base in Victoria Australia] were also "armed" with Lewis guns. One can assume that the capability of the front and second line aircraft was extremely poor.' (Personal communication.)

24. Gillison, *Royal Australian Air Force*, p. 238. Alan Stephens remarks that this was a case of 'the [Australian] Government's chickens returning to roost. For most of its existence the RAAF had been treated as a subordinate Service. It was poorly equipped and, in some cases, poorly trained. The Australian government, and through it the people, were arguably getting the kind of force they had paid for.' (Alan Stephens, *Power Plus Attitude* (Canberra: Australian Government Printing Service, 1992), p. 60.)

25. Gillison, *Royal Australian Air Force*, Ch. 9, particularly pp. 204–5.

26. Horner, *High Command*, p. 4. The return of Australian ground forces from the Middle East to Australia was also a source of much bitter debate and harsh words between Canberra and London, but that is outside the scope of this chapter.

27. The Australian Prime Minister, John Curtin, said in a broadcast on 27 December 1941, 'without any inhibitions of any kind, I make it quite clear that Australia looks to America, free of any pangs as to our traditional links or kinship with the United

Kingdom'. One Japanese long-term resident of Australia who was sent back to Japan in August 1941 described Australia as 'being isolated and slowly reduced to the wretched state of an orphan'. (Frei, *Japan's Southward Advance*, p. 199.)

28. The priorities were, in descending order: the defeat of the U-boat; help to the USSR; operations in the Mediterranean Sea; the build-up in Britain prior to the invasion of Normandy; and then operations in the Pacific and Far East. (George Odgers, *Air War Against Japan 1943–1945* (Canberra: Australian War Memorial, 1957), p. 4.)

29. Odgers, *Air War*, pp. 3–4.

30. Joseph Harsch, of the *Christian Science Monitor,* in Odgers, *Air War*, p. 4.

31. 'In March 1942 the Japanese 16th Army, 55,000 strong, occupied Java in ten days, capturing 80,000 Allied prisoners of war, losing 255 killed and 702 injured.' (Sadao Oba, 'Japanese Aspects', in Ian Nish (ed.), *Indonesian Experience: the Role of Japan and Britain 1943–1948* (London: London International Centre for Economic and Related Disciplines, 1980), p. 1.)

32. The Japanese crews were highly experienced from combat in China and in the preparation and execution of the Pearl Harbor raid. Most had between 600 and 800 hours' flying time. The American P40 pilots had less than 20 hours on type. (Bergerud, *Fire in the Sky*, p. 149.)

33. Peter Helson, 'The Forgotten Air Force: The Establishment and Employment of Australian Air Power of Australian Air Power in the North-Western Area 1941–1945', University of New South Wales, MA thesis, 1997, p. 73.

34. Frei, *Japan's Southward Advance*, pp. 162–5.

35. Helson, *The Forgotten Air Force*, p. 149.

36. The 457 Squadron RAF Operations Record Book remarks: 'Evenings are difficult to fill in after a day of waiting for something to happen, and pilots are faced with the prospect of doing the same thing which they did during the day, and are unable to visit other squadrons because of transport shortages.' (Helson, *The Forgotten Air Force*, p. 182.) A similar report from No. 457 Squadron notes that the month of April 1943 had 'been a heavy strain on the patience of both air and ground crews. Lack of action and days of monotonous routine and hot weather to make the Squadron personnel a little restless ...'. (Odgers, *Air War*, pp. 45–6.)

37. It must be noted that the Australian government was offered more Kittyhawks, but this was turned down by the Foreign Minister, Dr H. V. Evatt, on the grounds that even 'three Spitfire squadrons would have a tremendous effect on Australia'. (Helson, *The Forgotten Air Force*, p. 103.) There were some grounds for this comment. In late 1942, No. 77 Squadron RAAF had modified two P40Es, making them lighter and faster than usual, but they still could not catch the Japanese reconnaissance aircraft whose appearance generally heralded an attack. (Helson, *The Forgotten Air Force*, p. 100.)

38. Temperate climates have cool temperatures on the ground and at low altitude, but relatively warm temperatures at altitude. In northern Australia the ground temperatures are very hot, the conditions particularly in the dry season are very dusty, and at altitude it is very cold and moist. The source for this is the author's personal experience of flying for 20+ years in the Tropics.

39. Helson, *The Forgotten Air Force*, pp. 177–8.

40. The statement attributed some of the losses on adverse winds, which were said to have carried the Spitfires out to sea and this received prominence, though it was untrue. The weather report for the area on that day gives the wind at 15,000 feet from the east-north-east at about 20 mph – if anything, it would have helped the defenders during their return flights. (Personnel communication with Dr Alfred Price during July 2001. See also Odgers, *Air War*, pp. 46–50.)

41. Eric M. Bergerud, *Fire in the Sky* (Boulder, CO: Westview Press, 2000), Ch. 3. Also Odgers, *Air War*, p. 8.
42. Gillison, *Royal Australian Air Force*, Appendix 4.
43. Stewart Wilson, *The Spitfire, Mustang and Kittyhawk in Australian Service* (Sydney: Aerospace Publications 1988), pp. 18 and 138.
44. Helson, *The Forgotten Air Force*, p. 157. A sad note written in one report in the aftermath of the war included the words 'our role has been an unspectacular but worthy one'. (Helson, *The Forgotten Air Force*, p. 213.)
45. Gillison, *Royal Australian Air Force*, pp. 458–62.
46. Gillison, *Royal Australian Air Force*, pp. 603–17. MacArthur was singularly ungenerous in his letter to General George C. Marshall noting that 'the enemy's defeat at Milne Bay must not be accepted as a measure of the relative fighting capacity of the troops involved'.
47. Bergerud, *Fire in the Sky*, Ch. 4.
48. Lex McAulay, *Battle of the Bismarck Sea* (New York: St Martin's Press, 1991), pp. 24–6.
49. Vessels in the convoy ranged from 950 tons to 8,000 tons. The barges and boats they carried were also sunk. (McAulay, *Battle of the Bismarck Sea*, p. 177.)
50. McAulay, *Battle of the Bismarck Sea*, pp. 192–3.
51. Stephens, *Power Plus*, pp. 72–3.
52. Stephens, *Power Plus*, pp. 75–6.
53. Stephens, *Power Plus*, p. 76.
54. In six years Australian industry had developed the capability to produce Mustang, Mosquito, Beaufighter and Lancaster/Lincoln aircraft, as well as design sophisticated prototypes of its own. Australian factories produced 3,500 aircraft of nine different types, and 3,000 aircraft engines of three different types. (Stephens, *Power Plus*, p. 78.)
55. If one accepts the concept that doctrine is closely aligned to education, then the RAAF was certainly at a disadvantage. The RAAF's War Staff Courses were an attempt to bridge the gap. However, as several senior RAAF officers noted at the time, many of the relatively experienced, middle-ranking students had a poor standard of education and this was not helped by a serious lack of background reading material. There were few if any graduates of these courses who had studied the history of warfare in depth. (Stephens, *Power Plus*, p. 83.)
56. Air Vice-Marshal H. N. Wrigley CBE, DFC, AFC RAAF (1892–1987). See Alan Stephens and Brendan O'Loghlin (eds), *The Decisive Factor, Air Power Doctrine by Air Vice-Marshal H. N. Wrigley* (Canberra: Australian Government Publishing Service, 1990).
57. Some senior RAAF officers were sent to the UK on exchange and gained some command experience, such as A. T. Cole and F. M. Bladin. When J. P. J. McCauley was sent to the UK, Defence Secretary Shedden sent a confidential letter to the Australian High Commissioner in the UK, S. M. Bruce, asking that he use his influence to ensure that McCauley was placed in a position in which he would gain high-level operational experience. Late in the war Shedden noted that it was a pity that RAAF officers had to be sent to Europe in order to gain such experience. (Personal communication with Peter Helson, August 2001.)
58. Stephens, *Power Plus*, p. 80.
59. Stephens, *Power Plus*, p. 82.
60. Odgers, *Air War*, pp. 498–9.
61. Gary Waters, *Oboe: Air Operations over Borneo 1945* (Canberra: Air Power Studies Centre, 1995), particularly Ch. 6.
62. The ties with RAF were strengthened through officer education. During the 1920s

and 1930s RAAF officers attended the RAF staff college at Andover. Usually, two officers per year attended. They went to the UK for two years – the first was spent at the college, the second was on secondment to various RAF units. Senior Australian Defence officers (military and civilian) were able to attend the Imperial Defence College in London, pre- and post-Second World War. (Personal communication with Peter Helson.)

63. The author remembers a very senior officer of New Zealand origin in the RAF visiting 14 Squadron RNZAF on one of its deployments to Singapore in the late 1960s. He astonished his young audience with the comment that Australia and New Zealand had the best middle-ranking officers in the world – and the most abject generals. Given what has come to light about the unpleasant rivalry at the top of the RAAF in the Second World War, he now appears to be a shrewd observer of events.

64. In Europe, the RAAF also had 1,374 wounded in action and 1,459 captured as prisoners of war. (Odgers, *Air War*, p. 498, n8.)

65. Gillison, *Royal Australian Air Force*, p. 605.

PART III:

THE GULF WAR
1991

12

Planning the Air Campaign: The Washington Perspective

Diane Putney

The DESERT STORM air campaign consisted of four phases, reflecting the phasing of the DESERT STORM war plan. In 1991, the images of the air war seen globally on television screens depicted mostly Phase I strategic targets on the receiving end of laser-guided bombs. Two-thirds of the sorties of the air war, however, were flown against Phase III targets to prepare the battlefield.[1] This chapter will examine the phasing of the war plan and air campaign, and conclude with a discussion of Phase III in terms of doctrine and requirements levied on air.

On 25 August 1990, 23 days after Iraq invaded Kuwait, General H. Norman Schwarzkopf, the Commander-in-Chief (CINC) of the US Central Command, flew from his headquarters at MacDill Air Force Base (AFB) in Florida, to Washington, DC, to brief the Chairman of the Joint Chiefs of Staff, General Colin Powell, and the Secretary of Defense, Dick Cheney. In the Chairman's office in the Pentagon, Schwarzkopf presented his offensive war plan, which he had already named DESERT STORM. The CINC's offensive plan had four phases: Phase I, Strategic Air Campaign; Phase II, Kuwait Air Campaign; Phase III, Ground Combat Power Attrition; and Phase IV, Ground Attack.[2]

These phases formed the framework, the broad concept of operations for the offensive actions executed in January and February 1991. Phase I was the most developed of the phases, because the Air Staff had worked on it intensely since 8 August. The CINC's J-5 planning staff in Florida had produced the DESERT STORM briefing and discussed objectives, Iraqi and US strengths and weaknesses, deception and logistics. Phases II and III would undergo name changes over the next four months, but the phasing of the war plan would retain the basic structure as briefed on 25 August.

General Schwarzkopf's vision of using air power in support of ground forces influenced his thinking about the war plan. He retained for himself the role of Joint Force Land Component Commander (JFLCC) and always thought a ground war was necessary to liberate Kuwait.[3] From his perspective as CINC and JFLCC, the war would culminate with a ground offensive; therefore, the phase immediately preceding the ground offensive, Phase III, had to reduce Iraqi ground-force capability and neutralize the Republican Guard forces. Schwarzkopf expected vulnerable helicopters and B-52s to participate in Phase III attrition of the enemy forces, so in Phase II, he wanted airmen to achieve air superiority over Kuwait to make the skies safe for the Apache helicopter and Buffs (B-52s). The Phase I strategic air campaign would double as his retaliation plan if needed and start DESERT STORM by attacking leadership, destroying command and control, and eliminating Iraq's ability to reinforce troops in Kuwait and southern Iraq.

On 25 August in Saudi Arabia, Lieutenant-General Charles A. Horner was the US Central Command (CENTCOM) Forward commander, and he would hold that responsibility for just one more day, because Schwarzkopf would fly to Riyadh on 26 August and allow Horner to return to his jobs as the commander of Central Command Air Forces (CENTAF) and the Joint Force Air Component Commander (JFACC). Horner learned of the CINC's DESERT STORM phasing shortly after the CINC briefed Cheney and Powell. Horner cringed when he saw the sequence of the phases. He disliked seeing a discussion of air superiority in a 'Phase II'. Airmen would give the Coalition air superiority in Phase I. Air doctrine and experience mandated that achieving air superiority was the essential first step, enabling all subsequent military action to succeed. Horner felt far more at ease with describing the air operations as a shifting level of effort rather than as a series of distinct phases. Brigadier-General Buster C. Glosson, Horner's chief planner for offensive operations, often tried to merge Phases I and II when he briefed the CINC, but Schwarzkopf would always object and insist on seeing 'Air Superiority in the KTO [Kuwaiti Theater of Operations]' as a separate Phase II.[4]

Colonel John A. Warden III, the deputy director for warfighting concepts on the Air Staff, had given the CINC two briefings on 10 and 17 August extolling the value of strategic air strikes against Iraq, and presenting Schwarzkopf with what Warden considered an offensive, stand-alone, war-winning strategic air campaign which would induce the Iraqis to leave Kuwait. The CINC had called the Air Staff on 8 August, after calling the Joint Staff, for a strategic air campaign to serve as a retaliation option in case Saddam Hussein committed some heinous act, such as murdering hostages or dropping chemicals on Israel. General Horner's CENTAF staff at Shaw AFB in South Carolina had begun preparing the retaliatory option, the 'Punishment ATO [Air Tasking Order]', but once the DESERT SHIELD deployment started on 7 August, that small staff had to pack quickly, move to the theatre of operations, and assume enormous new responsibilities to receive incoming air assets and defend Saudi Arabia. Their hands were full, so the CINC called the Air Staff for help with the retaliatory air option.[5]

As Warden described the Air Staff's INSTANT THUNDER plan, it would theoretically achieve far more than the CINC had asked for, but Schwarzkopf liked it anyway and accepted it because it met his need for retaliation. Indeed, Colonel Warden inspired the CINC to think about the use of strategic air strikes in CENTCOM's offensive planning, which resulted in the CINC's decision to start the air war with a strategic air campaign as Phase I of DESERT STORM.

Schwarzkopf and Horner had travelled to Saudi Arabia on 5 August as part of the team led by Secretary Cheney to offer military assistance to King Fahd. When the King immediately accepted the offer, DESERT SHIELD swiftly commenced, and Schwarzkopf left Horner in the theatre to do the CINC's job as CENTCOM Forward commander. Schwarzkopf knew that Horner's staff would now be deploying, so he told the airman that he would call the Joint Staff for assistance with the air power option. Horner strongly objected to involving the Pentagon in such planning, saying it was the mistake of the Vietnam War all over again to allow targets to be picked in Washington DC and the planning to be done far from the theatre of operations. Schwarzkopf, also a veteran of the war in south-east Asia, empathized with his air boss and assured him that once the plan was formulated, he would send it to Horner to develop fully and finalize.[6]

True to his word, on 17 August the CINC told Colonel Warden to go to Riyadh to hand off the Air Staff's INSTANT THUNDER plan to Horner. In the meantime, Schwarzkopf and his J-5 staff continued to develop the four-phased DESERT STORM plan in great secrecy, unbeknownst to Warden and the Air Staff. The now legendary briefing Warden gave to Horner did not go well for the colonel and lost him the opportunity to remain in Riyadh to continue to develop INSTANT THUNDER.[7]

Horner called on General Glosson to turn INSTANT THUNDER into the CINC's retaliation option, with a fully developed air tasking order (ATO) ready to execute within days if needed. On 26 August, when Glosson briefed Horner on his revised version of INSTANT THUNDER, the JFACC told him about the CINC's four-phased war planning and told Glosson to drop the name INSTANT THUNDER and re-title his product 'Offensive Campaign Phase I'. By now the number of strategic targets had increased from 84 to 127. As the head of the Special Planning Group, the 'Black Hole', Glosson involved the wing commanders and operators in the planning effort to infuse the strategic plan with operational 'sanity checks'. He immediately sought out the CENTAF officers who knew how to produce an ATO and co-ordinate tanker and mission-refuelling requirements. Glosson's group quickly grew as he added representatives from the other services, the Royal Air Force, and experts in such vital functions as electronic war-fare, logistics and intelligence.[8]

On 6 October Chairman Powell telephoned Schwarzkopf in Riyadh and told him to send personnel to Washington to brief his phased war plan to the Joint Chiefs of Staff and the national command authorities. Schwarzkopf protested, saying he had no confidence in his Phase IV Ground Attack. Powell persisted and the disgruntled Schwarzkopf sent Glosson to brief the air portion of the DESERT STORM plan and the Army officer, Lieutenant-Colonel Joseph H. Purvis, and the CENTCOM Chief of Staff, the Marine officer Major-General Robert B. Johnston, to explain the land war.[9]

Glosson, Purvis and Johnston presented the war plan to the Joint Chiefs in the Pentagon on 10 October, and to the President, Vice-President, Secretary of Defense, Secretary of State, National Security Advisor, and others at the White House Situation Room on 11 October. While the air-dominated Phases I, II and III were judged to be basi-cally sound, the Phase IV land-attack portion was severely criticized for sending troops directly against Iraqi defensive ground strength. Secretary of State James Baker derided the CINC's Phase IV planning. 'We called it the Washington Monument plan: straight up the middle', he said. 'Our troops would have been ground up, and casualties would have been enormous.' The land campaign plan so disappointed Secretary Cheney that he established his own special unit in the Pentagon, headed by a retired Army-lieutenant general, to develop a ground-attack option through the western Iraqi desert. Cheney wanted to send the message to CENTCOM planners: 'Guys, get your act together and produce a plan because if you don't produce one that I'm comfortable with, I'll impose one.'[10]

Schwarzkopf hated Cheney's option and his intrusion into CENT-COM's war planning. When the CINC's staff evaluated the Secretary's product in November, they found many flaws. By then, Schwarzkopf had developed new, different ground-offensive concepts. By 15 October, he had instructed his planners to envision a wider sweep around the Iraqi forces in the Kuwaiti theatre and to plan for two scenarios, employing US Army one-corps and two-corps force structures.[11]

Although Glosson got off easier than Purvis and Johnston at the White House on 11 October, the leaders did ask the general about two dozen questions, most of which focused on Phase I. Glosson handled the questions well, and the leaders in Washington thought highly of the air campaign planning. Powell recalled, 'The air plan continued to impress.' The Chairman reported to the CINC in Riyadh, 'The White House is very comfortable with the air plan ...'.[12]

On 14 November in Dhahran, General Schwarzkopf breathed fire and for the first time unveiled his four-phased war plan to CENTCOM corps and division commanders. The phases were essentially the same as those the CINC had briefed on 25 August: Phase I, Strategic Air Campaign; Phase II, Air Superiority in the KTO; Phase III, Preparation of the Battlefield; and Phase IV, Ground Attack. The CINC envisioned the phases occurring in sequence, not simultaneously. The war plan now included the heavily armoured US Army VII Corps moving into position to do the great left hook attack against the Iraqi right flank to destroy the Republican Guard. Phase III required airmen to attrit the enemy fielded army to the 50 per cent level prior to the initiation of Phase IV. Airmen also had to isolate the battlefield with strikes against bridges to prevent the Iraqi Republican Guard from escaping and supplies and reinforcements moving into the theatre.[13]

During the coffee break after the CINC's presentation, Major-General J. H. Binford Peay III, commander of the 101st Airborne Division, asked his fellow Army officers an unanswered, intriguing, cynical question: 'If we can bomb them to 50 per cent in three weeks, why don't we take another three weeks and get the other 50 per cent for good measure?' A few weeks earlier in theatre, Secretary of the Air Force Donald Rice had provided an answer. He suggested to Schwarzkopf that if the air counter-land mission did not attrit the Iraqi Army in a few days, the Phase III attacks should continue for as long as it took to eliminate Saddam Hussein's military forces. He reasoned that as long as the air campaign achieved desired results, it ought to continue.[14]

The main CENTAF staff in Riyadh did the Phase IV air campaign planning to use air power in close, direct support of the ground attack. The staff worked outside of Glosson's Black Hole. They did not advertise what they were doing as DESERT STORM planning, but as the CENTAF 'Concept of Operations for Command and Control of TACAIR in Support of Land Forces'. They worked to ensure the effective operation of the tactical air-control system linking the tactical air-control centre, control and reporting centres, airborne elements, air-support operations centres and tactical air-control parties.[15]

On 20 December Horner and Schwarzkopf discussed the DESERT STORM planning with Cheney and Powell in Riyadh, and Phase III had two parts: Part One attacked the Republican Guard, and Part Two struck the regular army forces at the front lines. Cheney bluntly asked if air power could take down the Republican Guard to the 50 per cent level. Schwarzkopf said it could, but the attempt made his 'nervous' because it had 'never been done before'.[16]

In January, the Coalition issued its Operations Plan (OPLAN) for the Combined Operation DESERT STORM. Phase I, Strategic Air Campaign, would last six to nine days; Phase II, Air Supremacy in the KTO, would require one or two days; Phase III, Battlefield Preparation, would continue for eight days; and no time length was offered for Phase IV, Ground Offensive Operations. In addition to tactical air power, Special Operations Forces and naval gunfire would execute operations in Phase III.[17]

By the eve of the air war in mid-January 1991, the idea of distinct phases began to crumble. In November, President Bush had authorized doubling the size of US forces in theatre, and in December and early January the additional aircraft arriving in theatre allowed the air war planners to strike more targets simultaneously. Phases I, II and III began to merge.[18]

Looking at the structure of the four-phased war plan, which dictated the phasing of the air war, the question arises about which doctrine, if any, most influenced Schwarzkopf to envision the war unfolding in sequence according to the phasing he had briefed as early as 25 August. Was the DESERT STORM plan based on the US Army's Air Land Battle doctrine? Schwarzkopf was an Army officer and thoroughly familiar with Air Land Battle in the version of the document published in 1986 as Field Manual 100-5, Operations. Colonel Harry Summers, in his book, *On Strategy II: A Critical Analysis of the Gulf War*, asserted that the Air Land Battle doctrine served as the 'blueprint for Operation DESERT STORM' and the 'blueprint for victory in the Persian Gulf War'.[19]

This is not the case, however. The scenario assumed in Air Land Battle, with massive numbers of enemy troops and armour invading friendly territory and smashing into allied troops, does not reflect the situation the Coalition faced in Kuwait and Iraq. Phase I, the strategic air campaign, and Phase III, with its requirement that airmen attrit the enemy fielded forces to the 50 per cent level before friendly troops commenced their attack, did not emerge from Air Land Battle.

The phasing emerged early on from the sobering fact that the Coalition had to confront a million-man army. Although the entire Iraqi army did not deploy to the KTO, enough divisions were in place to persuade the CINC to rely on air power to change force ratios to favour the attackers over the defenders. When he briefed on 25 August, he had titled his Phase III, 'Ground Combat Power Attrition'. An early draft version of his plan had identified a phase titled 'preparation of the battlefield' with the objective to 'improve ground combat ratio adequate for the attack'. The CINC's pre-war planning, CENTCOM OPLAN 1002-90, had incorporated the scenario of air power attriting Iraqi divisions to change force ratios prior to a ground counter-offensive to retake Saudi territory lost to the Iraqis.[20]

The specific 50 per cent attrition requirement stemmed not from doctrine, but from computer simulations and calculations that the CENTCOM Combat Analysis Group (CAG) produced to answer two questions during DESERT SHIELD. Within days of the Iraqis invading Kuwait, CENTCOM planners asked Colonel Gary Ware, head of the CAG computer war gamers, 'If the Iraqis came across the border into Saudi Arabia, how effective does air power have to be to avoid "heavy casualties" or being driven off the Arabian Peninsula?' The answer required air power to attrit the enemy forces to the 50 per cent level, as measured against equipment – tanks, artillery and armoured personnel carriers (APCs). Shortly thereafter, when planners focused on the offensive, they asked Colonel Ware's group, 'How long should you let the air campaign run if your goal is to minimize casualties on the ground?' Again the answer showed destruction of 50 per cent of the tanks, artillery, and APCs.[21] The 50 per cent held even when the US forces doubled in size, starting in November 1990, because the Iraqis had also deployed more forces to the KTO. The 50 per cent attrition requirement was extraordinary, comparable to General Dwight Eisenhower telling the US Army Air Forces and the Royal Air Force in the Second World War that the D-Day invasion in Normandy could not proceed until the airmen had attrited the German fielded grounded forces in the European theatre to the 50 per cent level – in addition to achieving air superiority and waging strategic and interdiction air campaigns.

After the war, the Gulf War Air Power Survey team found that the allied airmen fell short of their 50 per cent goal. The pieces of Iraqi equipment destroyed before the ground war started were 1,388 tanks, or 40 per cent; 1,152 pieces of artillery, or 47 per cent; and 929 APCs, or 30 per cent.[22] None the less, enough Iraqi equipment and other targets were destroyed that the ground invasion could end in just one hundred hours. General Horner concluded that, even more important than destroying tanks and artillery, the airmen had destroyed Iraqi morale, which enabled the Coalition ground forces to defeat the Iraqi Army so quickly.[23]

Schwarzkopf always believed a land war was necessary to liberate Kuwait, and he identified air power as one of the Coalition's great strengths. His war plan determined the phasing of the air campaign, and he fully exploited the reach, versatility and lethality of the aerial weapon, in great part, to support ground operations. While the world watched television images of laser-guided bombs entering air shafts, the more numerous air missions to attrit the enemy army and isolate the battlefield to ensure the success of the ground war remained unseen.

NOTES

1. United States Department of Defense (DoD), Office of the Secretary of Defense, *Final Report to Congress on the Conduct of the Persian Gulf War* (Washington, DC: Government Printing Office (GPO), 1992), p. 101.
2. Ibid., pp. 66, 92; Colin L. Powell with Joseph E. Persico, *My American Journey* (New York: Random House, 1995), p. 472; Diane T Putney, 'From INSTANT THUNDER to DESERT STORM', *Air Power History*, 41 (Fall 1994), p. 44.
3. Notes of telephone conversation, General H. Norman Schwarzkopf with Diane T. Putney, 5 May 1992, Air Force History Support Office (AFHSO), Bolling AFB, DC.
4. Putney, 'THUNDER to STORM', p. 44; interview transcript, Maj.-Gen. Buster C. Glosson by Lt-Col. Richard Reynolds, Lt-Col. Suzanne Gehri, and Lt-Col. Edward Mann, 29 May 1991, pp. 52–3, CADRE, Air University (AU), Maxwell AFB, AL; interview tape, Buster C. Glosson by Diane T. Putney, 30 August 1993, AFHSO.
5. Putney, 'THUNDER to STORM', pp. 40–3; interview transcript, John A. Warden III by Lt-Col. Suzanne Gehri, 22 October 1991, CADRE, AU, 71; manuscript, Diane T. Putney, 'Airpower Advantage: Planning the Gulf War Air Campaign', Ch. 2, pp. 1–2; Alexander S. Cochran *et al.*, *Planning*, Vol. I, Part 1 of Gulf War Air Power Survey (GWAPS), under the auspices of the Department of the Air Force (Washington, DC: GPO, 1993), pp. 139–40.
6. Putney, 'THUNDER to STORM', p. 40; General H. Norman Schwarzkopf with Peter Petre, *The Autobiography: It Doesn't Take a Hero* (New York: Linda Grey Bantam Books, 1992), p. 320.
7. For accounts of the briefing on 20 August 1990, from Horner's perspective, see Tom Clancy with Chuck Horner, *Every Man a Tiger* (New York: G. P. Putnam's Sons, 1999), pp. 259–65, and from a Warden admirer's view, see Richard T. Reynolds, *Heart of the Storm: The Genesis of the Air Campaign against Iraq* (Maxwell AFB, AL: Air University Press, 1995), pp. 120–30.
8. Putney, 'THUNDER to STORM', pp. 44–5.
9. Schwarzkopf, *It Doesn't Take a Hero*, pp. 358–9; Powell, *American Journey*, pp. 483–4.
10. James A. Baker III and Thomas M. DeFrank, *The Politics of Diplomacy: Revolution, War, and Peace, 1989–1992* (New York: G. P. Putnam's Sons, 1995), p. 409 (Baker quote); DoD, *Conduct of the Persian Gulf War*, p. 67; Cheney, front line interview, http://www.pbs.org/wgbh/pages/frontline/gulf/oral, p. 6 of 11 (Cheney quote).
11. Schwarzkopf, *It Doesn't Take a Hero*, pp. 368–9.
12. Memo for record and slides, Brig.-Gen. Buster C. Glosson, 'Presidential Briefing Slides', folder 12, Deptula file, Checkmate, GWAPS, Air Force Historical Research Agency (AFHRA), Maxwell AFB, AL; Powell, *American Journey*, p. 485 (first quote); Schwarzkopf, *It Doesn't Take a Hero*, p. 361 (second quote).
13. Schwarzkopf, *It Doesn't Take a Hero*, pp. 380–4; Putney, 'THUNDER to STORM', p. 46.
14. Tom Donnelly, 'The Generals' War: How Commanders Fought the Iraqis', *Army Times*, Desert Storm After Action Review, 2 March 1992, p. 14 (Peay quote); Rice view on interview tape, Lt-Col. David A. Deptula by Diane T. Putney and Richard G. Davis, 12 December 1992, AFHSO.
15. Putney, 'THUNDER to STORM', p. 46.
16. Notes by Lt-Gen. Charles A. Horner, 'Mtg with SecDef & CJCS', 20 December 1990, DESERT STORM file, HQ 9 AF/CC (CINC comment as written by Horner).

17. Cochran *et al.*, *Planning*, Vol. I, Part 1, GWAPS, pp. 1–9.
18. DoD, *Conduct of the Persian Gulf War*, p. 101.
19. Harry G. Summers, Jr, *On Strategy II: A Critical Analysis of the Gulf War* (New York: Dell, 1992), pp. 157, 159.
20. Cochran *et al.*, *Planning*, Vol. I, Part 1, GWAPS, p. 29.
21. Notes of telephone conversation, Gary Ware and Barry Watts, 26 February 1992, GWAPS, AFHRA; notes of telephone conversation, Gary Ware and Diane Putney, 28 March 1994, AFHSO; DoD, *Conduct of the Persian Gulf War*, pp. 350–1; Report, Combat Analysis Group After Action Report, Col. Gary R. Ware, USAF, Chief, CAG, 4 frame 758, reel 27576, GWAPS, AFHRA.
22. Barry D. Watts *et al.*, *Effects and Effectiveness*, Vol. II, Part 2, GWAPS, 261. These are total figures; there was less destruction of Republican Guard equipment.
23. Clancy with Horner, *Every Man a Tiger*, p. 469.

13

The 1991 Bombing of Baghdad: Air Power Theory vs Iraqi Realities

John Andreas Olsen

In response to the Iraqi invasion of Kuwait on 2 August 1990, a small team of air power experts in the Pentagon, the so-called 'Checkmate office', proposed a conventional strategic air campaign to liberate Kuwait.[1] The team, which was under the guidance of Colonel John Ashley Warden III, sought to force Iraq's Army from Kuwait by applying air power directly against the sources of Iraqi national power. The concept, 'Iraqi Air Campaign Instant Thunder', called for focused and intense attacks on the Iraqi politico-military leadership and its associated command, control and communication systems. Rather than destroying the enemy heartland by devastating its people, industry or economy, this concept concentrated on concurrent and precise targeting of the regime itself.[2] The Instant Thunder proposal underwent several changes prior to the execution of the air war, but the original concept remained at the heart of what became the strategic air campaign – the initial phase of Operation Desert Storm.[3]

There is no doubt that a change in the Iraqi leadership was desirable as a consequence of the defeat of Iraq. Overthrowing or killing Saddam Hussein was never a declared objective, but it is fair to argue that some of the key air planners hoped and believed that concentrated air operations against the Iraqi regime's instruments of political control would facilitate Saddam Hussein's departure by either coup or popular revolt.[4] Although the White House never accepted the removal of Saddam Hussein as a stated objective, the Oval Office was briefed in considerable detail on the planned air campaign and there is no recorded instance of its either disputing stated military objectives or insisting upon changes to any proposed plan.[5]

The fact that the Iraqi leadership survived has led analysts such as Robert A. Pape, William M. Arkin and Jeffrey Record to conclude that the targeting of the Iraqi National Command Authority had little identifiable military or political effect.[6] The purpose of this chapter is to reassess the applicability of the (John A.) Warden approach to warfare by examining its theory against the inner workings of the Iraqi elite and the regime's political-power structure – the very instruments on which Saddam Hussein's rule depended.[7] It argues that the resilient and enduring nature of the regime prevented it from being overthrown, but the strategic air campaign, in the process of pursuing 'strategic paralysis', induced so much fog and friction into the Iraqi leadership that its decision-making capability was rendered largely ineffective. Consequently, rather than destroying the Iraqi leadership, the strategic air campaign contributed significantly to reducing the adversary's influence on strategic events.

THE FIVE RINGS SYSTEM

While a student at the National War College in 1985–86, John A. Warden wrote a paper entitled 'The Air Campaign: Planning for Combat', in which he focused on translating national political objectives into theatre campaign plans. Warden emphasized air power's potential contribution to the overall effort, the significance of 'distant interdiction' and the predominate role of air superiority.[8] He was inspired by the battles of Alexander the Great, the provocative ideas of William Mitchell, the thesis found in Haywood Hansell's *The Air Plan that Defeated Hitler*, and Liddell Hart's ideas on the 'Indirect Approach'.[9] Warden essentially sought to provide a conceptual framework for thinking about the practice of air power beyond the Cold War paradigm, and he seriously opposed the idea of air power being an adjunct to land forces. When assigned in 1988 to the directorate of warfighting concepts and developments (XOXW), the so-called 'Checkmate' office, he gradually developed into an air power theorist.[10] It was in this unconventional and innovative environment that he wrote an internal memorandum, 'Centers of Gravity – The Key to Success in War', in which he articulated a concept for describing the modern state as a 'system of systems'.[11] It was the genesis of the Five Rings Model, which became the theoretical foundation for the first phase of Operation Desert Storm.

Colonel Warden argued that one could analyse the enemy as a system by organizing the state and the society into five concentric circles. The centre circle was defined as the political decision-making apparatus and its ability to command, control and communicate. This was the state's national leadership, the collection of individuals with the power invested in them to initiate, sustain and terminate wars. It gave the state its strategic direction and helped it respond to external and internal changes. Warden equated the leadership of a state to the brain of a human body: it was the most important organ, generating and controlling all physical motions. Surrounding this core he identified the second circle as the state's energy facilities – oil, gas and electricity – the organic essentials with the function of converting energy from one form to another. The third circle contained the state's infrastructure, primarily industry and transportation links, such as roads, bridges and railways, the instruments that kept a society interconnected and enabled mobility and movement. The fourth circle was the population – the very citizens of the state. Unlike Giulio Douhet, Warden did not find it morally acceptable to target the citizens directly with anything but psychological means. The final ring was the state's fielded military force, the entity whose purpose was to protect the state and society from external aggression. Warden argued that traditionally the fifth ring had been at the centre of struggle, where huge armies fought against each other, moving towards the cumulative clash on the battlefield.

Moreover, in order to determine the accurate identification of the critical vulnerabilities within each ring, Warden proposed the further breakdown of each ring into five sub-rings based on the same structure, until the true centre of gravity was disclosed. When these targets were struck, the enemy system would be incapacitated through the rapid imposition of either total or partial paralysis. The intention was to create so much confusion and disorder in the enemy system at the strategic level that it would react inappropriately to activities that appeared simultaneously.

In Warden's mind the four outer rings should be attacked only as was necessary to expose the leadership ring to offensive action. The priority given to the 'inner ring' resulted in terms like 'inside-out warfare', 'bombing for (political) effect' (every bomb is a political bomb) and 'parallel warfare' (near-simultaneous attacks upon the strategic centres of gravity throughout the entire theatre of war).[12] By going for the leadership directly, attacking several target-sets in parallel, hard and fast from the opening moment of war, Warden argued that one could achieve strategic paralysis of the state's war making capabilities with decapitation as one possible outcome. Thus, he did not argue a 'decapitation strategy' *per se*, but a larger strategic air campaign in which 'decapitation' was but one element.[13] He stressed that the advent of stealth technology, long-range aircraft and precision targeting made it possible to translate this theory effectively into practice. He favoured carrying the war to the enemy's state organization (system warfare), rather than to the enemy's armed forces (military warfare), and the selection of targets would make sure that one rendered the enemy's strategy and decision-making irrelevant. In order to be successful, however, Warden emphasized that 'military objectives and campaign plans must be tied to political objectives *as seen through the enemy's eyes, not one's own*.[14] In effect, he argued that one could defeat a state without seeking to destroy its forces in the field. The occupying forces were therefore only a manifestation of the real problem, which resided with the leadership that ordered the occupation in the first place. Consequently, the purpose of war was not even to defeat the enemy's ground forces, but to force the decision-makers to do one's own will.

When Warden was assigned to run the XOXW, David A. Deptula was already leading its doctrine division. Warden asked Deptula to criticize *The Air Campaign*, write a paper on how best to use air power, and respond to an article that suggested air power should be controlled by the corps commander. The two worked closely together, exchanged ideas on how to improve air power capabilities and encouraged each other to develop innovative concepts. When Deptula left Checkmate at the end of 1988 to work for the policy group guided by Donald Rice, the Secretary of the Air Force, he took many of the new ideas with him. In the new position he became one of the key authors of the influential white paper 'Global Reach Global Power: Reshaping the Future', which was released shortly before the invasion of Kuwait.[15] The paper stressed that one should focus on 'airpower's inherent strengths – speed, range, flexibility, precision and lethality', and that should include, among other things, the ability to 'inflict strategic and operational paralysis on an adversary by striking key nodes in war-making potentials'.[16] The paper stood in stark contrast to the existing doctrines that equated 'strategic' with 'nuclear', and 'air power' with 'fire-support for the ground commander's scheme of manoeuvre'. It was, moreover, a counter-argument to an unpublished paper entitled 'A View of the Air Force Today', written by airmen in the autumn of 1989, essentially suggesting the abolition of the USAF as an independent institution.[17]

When Iraq invaded Kuwait, Deptula joined his former colleagues in the basement of the Pentagon. With the conceptual basis of the policy paper and the Five Rings model in mind, the Checkmate office developed an air plan that sought to liberate Kuwait without a ground campaign. Instant Thunder sought to incapacitate the Iraqi leadership's ability to command and control its population and military forces, with the intention of facilitating a subsequent change in the political leadership. The air planners did not have any particular knowledge of the Iraqi regime, but they believed that bombing for strategic effect was universally applicable.[18] When Warden briefed General Schwarzkopf on 17 August 1990 he opened by stating that it should be 'a focused, intense air campaign designed to incapacitate the Iraqi leadership and destroy key Iraqi military capability, in a short period of time'. It was importantly not 'a graduated, long-term campaign plan designed to provide escalation options'. The strategy elements were 'isolate Hussein; eliminate Iraqi offensive and defensive capability; incapacitate national leadership; reduce threat to friendly nations; and minimize damage to enhance rebuilding'. It was explicitly stated that Saddam Hussein's regime was 'the most important centre of gravity', and that it was an objective to 'rupture Hussein's links to people and military'.[19]

An alternative to Instant Thunder was developed by the Tactical Air Command (TAC), with an emphasis on demonstrating resolve, incremental escalation and concentrating air strikes on Iraqi ground forces in occupied Kuwait. The latter was in consonance with the Air Land Battle doctrine and the regional contingency plans, but the Warden–Deptula approach of strategic attacks against the entity of the Iraqi elite won the internal bureaucratic struggle in the Air Staff in mid-August 1990.[20]

Lieutenant-General Charles A. Horner, the air commander, was not too enthusiastic about the concept when it was presented to him on 20 August, but he chose to keep many of the ideas, asked Lieutenant-Colonel Deptula to stay in theatre to continue planning there, and established a 'Strategic Planning Cell' in Riyadh, later termed the 'Black Hole'. What was solely an air power *concept*, focusing predominantly on the Iraqi decision-making apparatus in Baghdad, was subsequently developed by the Black Hole under the guidance of Brigadier-General Buster C. Glosson and Lieutenant-Colonel Deptula over the next five months into a comprehensive strategic air campaign. The latter made sure that the essence of the strategic focus envisioned in Instant Thunder was upheld throughout the planning, while at the same time incorporating Horner's larger concerns into building the actual attack plans. Warden for his part made sure that Checkmate served as a think tank in support of the Black Hole planners. In summation, although the Instant Thunder concept had several shortcomings and was not operationally attainable as presented in August, the Checkmate team provided the military and political leadership with a strategic dimension to planning an air campaign that did not exist at the time. According to Deptula, 'the air campaign strategy capitalized on capabilities and highly adaptive attack plans designed to paralyse Saddam's control of forces', by neutralizing the enemy's capacity to fight, undermining its will to fight, and reducing its military production base and ability to build weapons of mass destruction.[21]

In order to evaluate the applicability of the Warden–Deptula philosophy, a closer look at the regime that the air campaign sought to incapacitate is required. While there can be no doubt that Saddam Hussein's authority and power were absolute, the state and societal institutions through which he exercised control of Iraqi society were far less tangible than the Air Force planners intuitively assumed.

THE IRAQI POLITICAL POWER STRUCTURE

In essence, Saddam Hussein ensured longevity and endurance by combining the instruments of power found in the Baath Party organization, the government structure, the military apparatus, the informal kinship system and the security and intelligence network.[22] As indicated in Figure 13.1, it was the combination of inter-connected elements of power that collectively provided for the Iraqi leader's unique personal power base. Saddam Hussein's authority provided the political cohesion that tied these various elements to a single cause.

Figure 13.1: Saddam Hussein's Instruments of Power

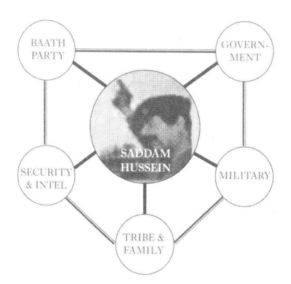

The first instrument of power was the pan-Arab Baath Party. Although not the only legal political organization in Iraq, it was, for all practical purposes, the state's official party and the only political party that offered ordinary Iraqis social or professional promotions. By expanding the number of Baath members and registered supporters from less than one thousand in 1968 to almost two million in 1990, the Iraqi leader managed to use the party to create his own personal power base.[23] By the late 1980s, Saddam Hussein had in effect succeeded in turning Iraq into a one-party state, which in principle reflected that depicted in George Orwell's *Nineteen Eighty-Four*, where truth was decreed by Big Brother, everyone felt watched and nobody could be trusted.[24] As for the subject of democracy in Iraq, Saddam Hussein stated on the eve of the Gulf War that 'nowhere in the region did the regime come to power by way of democracy and Iraq is no exception'.[25] It has become quite popular to demonize the Iraqi leader, but in that process one tends to overlook the fact that he created genuine Iraqi patriotism during the eight years of war with Iran.[26] In fact, when the air campaign started, the two major Kurdish opposition parties in northern Iraq declared that they would not use the opportunity to 'stab the [Iraqi] army in the back'.[27] Nevertheless, the Baath Party was essentially the means by which Saddam Hussein came to power and the only mass organization in Iraq. He had full control of the party's decision-making organ, the Regional Command, whose members he personally selected, and through systematic indoctrination he used the party's manifesto as an ideological framework for creating a broad-based popular support.

The second instrument of power was the government system. When the Baath Party came to power in 1968 a constitution was drafted with the Revolutionary Command Council (RCC) as 'the supreme institution of the state', with classic decision-making organs such as the National Assembly, the Council of Ministers and the Court of Cassation.[28] Within this government structure the Shia Arabs would find that they were provided with considerable representation. In theory, there was a government structure with a legislative, executive and judicial branch, wherein the Iraqi people found democratic representation, but in practice Saddam Hussein made sure that the Sunni-dominated elite of the Baath Party made all the important decisions. The Party's Military Bureau became more influential than the Ministry of Defence, the Foreign Relations Bureau became more influential than the Minister of Foreign Affairs, and in effect the whole government system was reduced to dealing with details rather than policy and its implementation.[29] Key individuals such as Defence Minster Abdel Jabber Shansal, Foreign Minister Tariq Aziz and the Chief of Staff for the Armed Forces Nizar Khasraji, actually heard about the invasion of Kuwait on the radio,[30] as did most of the military commanders, with the exception of a few in the Republican Guard, who were informed only hours in advance.[31] Arguably, by mid-July 1990, only three people were involved in the planning of the invasion besides Saddam Hussein himself: his son-in-law and nephew Hussein Kamil, his cousin Ali Hassan al-Majid, and the Commander of the Republican Guard, General Iyad al-Rawi. None of the members of the Revolutionary Command Council, according to the constitution the highest decision-making authority in Iraq, or the Regional Command, the highest decision-making authority of the Baath Party, was informed of the decision to occupy the whole of Kuwait. The point is that neither the party apparatus nor the government system was even informed of a decision that would ultimately bring the entire country into war. The Iraqi leader would typically give an order or an instruction to the Regional Command, and then the Revolutionary Command Council would release a statement based on the recommendation of the former. On occasions the Regional Command would release a statement in advance, and the Revolutionary Command Council would support it shortly after, to give the impression of wide-ranging consensus. Thus, the government system made sure that the Iraqi leader's personal preference was presented as a collective decision, and, accordingly, if the decision proved to be misguided he could blame the representatives. Saddam Hussein also made sure that individuals from the rural lower class replaced the typical urban middle class and that those in the most important party positions were from the region where he was born. In essence, by the late 1980s, Saddam Hussein had a government and party system that was tailor-made to strengthen his position as the sole leader of Iraq.

The third instrument of power was the military apparatus. Although Saddam Hussein did not have a military education, he was the supreme leader of the Iraqi armed forces, and on occasions he took direct command. The Republican Guard was the elite force and originally established as a loyal group that would serve as a counter-weight to the Iraqi Army, who had a proclivity for military coups. The Republican Guard was the force that conducted the invasion of Kuwait, and by 1991 it numbered eight divisions, but such was the system of personal rule that even this organization inspired its own checks. It was not allowed to operate within Baghdad, major movements of forces had to be sanctioned by appropriate individuals within the Military Bureau, the Ministry of Defence and the Military Intelligence,[32] and subsequently the Special Republican Guard was established. In terms of the personal security of Saddam Hussein, the Special Republican Guard was the counter-weight to the Republican Guard, which in turn was the counter-weight to the Iraqi Army. Herein lay the basis for one of the ironies of the 1991 campaign and the targeting policy of the US planners. The Special Republican Guard was not targeted, the Republican Guard was only partly targeted, while the least able force, the formations of the Iraqi conscripts, were comprehensively bombed.[33] It should be noted that although a strong military force was important to the Iraqi leader, it was at the same time a major concern, because the military itself was a potential threat to his personal power base. Traditionally, Army officers had played an important part in coups, and Saddam Hussein therefore made sure that civilian party officials replaced military officers in the most central positions within the Baath Party. Indeed, compared with other dictatorships, Iraq was surprisingly non-military when it came to who had influence in domestic and regional matters.

The fourth instrument of power was the tribal system. While

organizational charts may characterize a system, the real influence
resides in the individuals who actually run things on a daily basis. To
fill the ranks of the most important institutions and organizations,
Saddam Hussein drew largely from Sunni tribes, a small number of
Shia tribes, non-tribal elements and the most loyal Baathists. Those in
charge of the different institutions were carefully selected on the basis
of their tribe and birthplace, with the Dulaym area and the Jubburr and
Ubayd tribes being particularly favoured.[34] The whole ruling elite in
Iraq was closely linked by tribe, clan and family ties, and Saddam
Hussein systematically and intelligently applied the tribal structure as
an instrument of domestic power. The centre of political life in Iraq in
geographical terms was inside the so-called 'Sunni Triangle', which
was the fertile area between Baghdad, Ar-Ramadi and Sammarra. At
the heart of this triangle is the town of Tikrit and the village of Ouja –
the birthplace of Saddam Hussein. He belonged to the Albu Nassir
tribe, and therein the al-Majid family. It is a rather small tribe, but
Saddam Hussein relied on different factions of the tribe holding the
most important positions. There were also rival wings within the families,
and the Iraqi leader made sure that whenever one wing was in charge
of an agency the rival wing would have a deputy position, and vice-
versa. Sometimes, however, he would allow a Shia or a Christian, such
as Tariq Aziz, into a position of power in order to cut across all other
relations. The Sunni Triangle underpinned the Iraqi leader's power
base, but tribal structure permeated the whole of Iraqi society.

Rather than eliminate the tribal sheikhs as a socio-political power, as
decreed by the 1968 Baath Party manifesto, which saw tribalism as a
symbol of backwardness and a threat to the social elite, Saddam Hussein
managed to turn the sheikhs into instruments that served his regime.[35]
He allowed the sheikhs to govern rural regions, and in return they
would support him as their national leader. Families and relatives of the
sheikhs were given advantages in social life and education, officers from
the right tribal background were promoted most rapidly and Saddam
Hussein rewarded the villages of the tribes in which recruitment had
taken place with electricity, roads and water. The young men recruited
were proud to serve their leader, and, knowing that their tribe relied on
them, they provided Saddam Hussein with the most loyal force one
could imagine. In typical divide-and-rule fashion the Iraqi leader would
also distribute land areas among the tribes, so that the smaller were
strengthened at the expense of the larger, thereby maintaining a certain
local 'balance of power'. By the late 1980s, Saddam Hussein had been
successful in securing tribal support in the countryside, persuading
tribal chiefs to betray members of their own tribes who posed a threat
to his regime. Consequently, he relied on the tribal leaders themselves,
rather than his internal security forces, to police the tribes. The power

invested in these sheikhs provided the President with a certain leverage against the Baath Party becoming too strong. Saddam Hussein intuitively considered these tribal soldiers, of primarily rural Bedouin roots, to be more 'Arab', therefore placing a greater emphasis on honour and ferocity in war than non-tribal urban ones.[36] Using kinship relations as an instrument of personal power is truly an art, and the Iraqi leader had tuned this skill almost to perfection. Still, these were all manifestations of power that ultimately were conditioned by the Iraqi leader. While great power was invested in family connections they too were acting only on delegated authority, and their power was completely in the hands of Saddam Hussein.

While all these elements of force played an important part in keeping the Iraqi President in power, one could argue that the real crux of Saddam Hussein's stamina was the widely feared security and intelligence network. This network was the Iraqi leader's fifth instrument of power and it deserves considerable attention when analysing Saddam Hussein's ability to remain in power.

INSIDE THE IRAQI SECURITY NETWORK

Under the control of the Office of the Presidential Palace the network amounts to at least seven executive agencies: (1) the Special Security Service (Amn al-Khass); (2) the General Intelligence Directorate (Mukhabarat); (3) the Special Republican Guard; (4) the Secret Police (Amn al-Amm); (5) the Military Intelligence Agency (Estikhbatat al-Askariyya); (6) the Military Security Service (Amn al-Askariyya); and (7) the Hadi Project. Although Iraq's security apparatus was huge, Saddam Hussein controlled it closely, and the carefully selected employees realized that, despite officially working for the state and national interests, their jobs, privileges and even lives depended on complete loyalty to the Iraqi leader.

The sole objective of this elaborate security system was to keep Saddam Hussein in power, and the Iraqi President created it for that very purpose. The agencies, all run by highly trusted individuals, reported directly to Saddam Hussein's nerve centre, the Office of Presidential Palace, during Desert Storm. By design, their areas of responsibility overlapped, and to ensure that there was no internal dissent, each agency had a security branch that kept watch on its own members. Each agency would typically have three sub-divisions. M1, the political branch, collected and analysed information from all over the world and worked out possible scenarios affecting Iraq. M2, the administration branch, was pure administration of services such as cleaning, driving, payment and all supporting activities. M3, the political branch, was

Figure 13.2: The Iraqi Security and Intelligence Network[37]

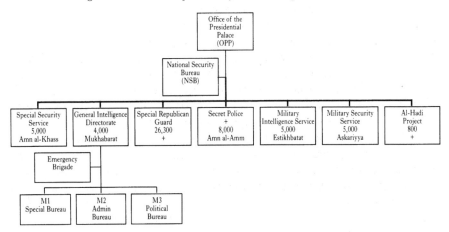

typically those who watched and kept control of the whereabouts of everybody else. In other words, they were watching the ones that were watching the ones that were watching the main institutions of power in Iraq. All members of the elite and their families were viewed with suspicion, and any criticism of the President was regarded as a national offence with severe consequences. Finally, most of the agencies included a rapid intervention force that was well armed with light and semi-heavy weapons.

The National Security Bureau (NSB) was tasked with co-ordinating the various activities of the seven main security agencies, and was afforded precedence over the Ministry of the Interior and Foreign Affairs Bureau. The agencies, or at least most of them, were represented within the NSB, the main office of which was co-located with the Office of the Presidential Palace in the main presidential quarters. It was not uncommon for the same task to be given to more than one agency, the activities of the NSB thereby being frustrated by all sorts of skulduggery and other nefarious activities on the part of agencies only too aware of the dangers of being seen to be second, or less effective, than rival organizations.

The first executive agency was the Special Security Service. Headed by the late Hussein Kamil, it provided the President and his immediate family with around-the-clock personal protection – a sort of extended bodyguard. This was the single most powerful agency, as it was responsible for detecting and neutralizing any threats to Saddam Hussein's personal security, and was considered to be very prestigious, because it had the right to investigate members of all the other security agencies. These people were trained in explosives, electronic personnel surveillance and detecting opposition. The inner circle of the Special Security Service was the Murafaqin, who were drawn exclusively from the al-Bu Nasir tribe and supposedly the only ones who were allowed unescorted and armed in the same room as the Iraqi leader. The members of the Special Security Service were carefully selected from Saddam Hussein's own district, and the agency played an important part in the suppression of the Shia and Kurdish rebellions that followed the Gulf War in 1991. The uprising, often referred to as the 'Intifada', would certainly have been more damaging to the Iraqi regime if the Special Security Service had been systematically targeted during the air war.

Unlike the Special Security Service, which was concerned with the personal protection of the Iraqi leader, the General Intelligence Directorate (Mukhabarat) was concerned with the security of the state. It was the main intelligence service in Iraq, and carried out operations, which included assassinations, both at home and abroad, against those considered a threat to the state. There was one office within the Mukhabarat, according to former instructor Major Harbi al-Jibouri, which ran a very popular six-week course on how to make letter and car bombs.[38] According to Scott Ritter, the directorate for special operations (M-21) educated terrorists.[39] To qualify for the agency, one normally had to be either from Tikrit or from the Albu Nassir tribe, but other members of the previously mentioned coalition tribes could also be accepted.

While the Special Security Service provided the inner protection of the ruling family of the regime, the Special Republican Guard served as a second shield, while the Republican Guard was the third. The Special Republican Guard protected strategic sites inside Baghdad, and its stated mission was fourfold: protect the President; conduct any other duty that may be ordered; protect presidential facilities; and prepare for combat duties.[40] For example, while the Special Security Service protected the families inside the palaces, the Special Republican Guard protected the gardens around the palaces, and the two agencies were not even allowed to communicate with each other.[41] There were some 200 palaces, including some luxurious villas, and at any given time these guards would not have known in which one Saddam Hussein was staying. Saddam had many doubles, and he certainly moved in mysterious ways.[42] He often arranged fake attacks on himself, or one of his doubles, in order to see who would sacrifice their lives for him,[43] continuously testing the loyalty of the Special Republican Guard and the Special Security Service.

The Secret Police was a special branch of the civilian police force. Originally, it reported to the Ministry of Interior, but during Desert Storm it reported directly to the Office of the Presidential Palace. In every police station in Iraq these officials were located on the second floor. They watched over the regular police forces and had in-depth knowledge of local areas and local groups.[44] They infiltrated organizations and operated under-cover in factories, universities and even elementary schools, as vividly explained by Kanan Makiya in *Republic of Fear*.[45] The Technical Directorate carried out sophisticated monitoring of Iraqi citizens, including cassette tapes of ordinary conversations recorded in homes, restaurants or cars, while the Investigations Department developed extensive files on informants: 'apparently everyone was willing to talk in depth about his or her neighbour'.[46] The thousands of middle-class citizens who fled from Baghdad during the opening days of the air war did not organize any action against the regime partly because of fear of the Secret Police. The Secret Police may have played only a limited role in protecting the regime during the air campaign, but, more importantly, it had contributed significantly to creating an environment prior to the war that deterred any organized opposition from establishing itself in the Iraqi heartland.[47]

The Military Intelligence Service evaluated military threats from both within Iraq and from abroad. It reported to the Ministry of Defence during the war with Iran, but during Desert Storm it reported directly to the Office of the Presidential Palace. The headquarters was a heavily guarded compound, which was fully sustained and independent from the rest of the armed forces. There were three regional headquarters outside Baghdad: the Kirkuk base handled information regarding the Kurdish region and north-east border with Iran; the Mosul base dealt with intelligence regarding Turkey and Syria; and the Basra base focused on the perceived threat of the Gulf states and the south-east border with Iran. The Military Intelligence Service was allegedly divided into 16 divisions in which the sixteenth was the most secret and powerful among them, as it was allowed to arrest virtually anyone at the highest levels of government.[48]

The penultimate agency was the Military Security Service, which was responsible for detecting and dealing with any dissent within the armed forces. It was an extended military police primarily focused inwards upon itself. One may question its efficiency in light of the high levels of desertion during the bombing, but on the other hand it may have played an important role in preventing organized resistance from within. The people in the south, rather than the soldiers, initiated the uprising, and although some conscripts and officers joined the Intifada it was done on an individual basis. The combination of the Secret Police, the Military Intelligence Service and the Military Security Service seems to have ensured that no organized revolt took place in Baghdad during the bombing.

The last agency that deserves to be mentioned is the so-called 'al-Hadi Project'. A group of 800 men operated 24 hours a day collecting information electronically about potential dissidents. The agency tapped telephone conversations and had an extensive database of people who were under suspicion. It also translated and unscrambled signal intelligence and sent the data to the relevant agency for action to be taken. Both its headquarters and part of the system were damaged during the Gulf War, but it became operational again shortly after the cease-fire.

All these agencies, which were manned by key personnel systematically selected for their loyalty to Saddam Hussein, together formed an elaborate network of organizations by which the dictatorship held down the population. There was massive redundancy within the system, an indication of the strength in depth of the regime, and the obvious point about the system as a whole was that there was no place for coherent, organized opposition within the country. By the 1980s, most organized opposition to the regime had to operate from places outside Iraq, such as Amman, Damascus and London, and there was no contact between the United States and the Iraqi opposition groups. Such contact had been prohibited in 1988 and the ban had not been rescinded, with obvious consequences. The US intelligence community had been predominantly concerned with the Soviet Union prior to the Iraqi invasion of Kuwait and had no real knowledge of the Iraqi state and system.[49] Consequently, the air planners had no inkling of the layer-upon-layer of Iraqi state, party, kinship and security organizations that held the Saddam Hussein regime in place. The last successful coup in Iraq had taken place in 1968, and over the next two decades Saddam Hussein systematically transformed the political institutions so that Iraq became one of the world's least 'coup-prone states'.[50]

Having examined the air power theory for incapacitating the Iraqi regime, and demonstrated the enduring nature of Saddam Hussein's leadership, this chapter now takes a closer look at what the strategic attacks against the 'inner ring' of Warden's Five Rings System accomplished.

THE BOMBING OF THE LEADERSHIP IN BAGHDAD

According to the Checkmate and Black Hole planners, the 'strategic core' of the air campaign contained the following eight categories: (1) leadership; (2) command, control and communications (C3); (3) nuclear, biological and chemical-warfare capabilities and storage facilities; (4) military support facilities; (5) ballistic missile launchers and their infrastructure; (6) electric power; (7) oil refineries; and (8) key bridges and railway facilities.[51]

The percentage of strikes against these target-sets, as shown in Table 13.1, was relatively small compared with the overall air campaign. For

Table 13.1: Coalition Strikes by Target Category for Desert Storm[52]

Target	Strikes	%
Leadership	260	0.7
Command, Control and Communications	580	1.7
Electrical Power	280	0.8
Oil	540	1.5
Nuclear, Biological and Chemical	990	2.8
Military Industry (production/storage)	970	2.8
Lines of Communication	1,170	3.3
Surface-to-Air missiles	1,370	3.9
Scuds	1,460	4.2
Iraqi Air Defence System (KARI)	630	1.8
Airfields	2,990	8.5
Naval Targets	370	1.1
Iraqi Ground Forces	23,430	66.9
Total	35,040	100.0

example, the first two counted for some 840 strikes, while the ground forces were subject to more than 23,000.[53] None the less, an estimated 30 per cent of the precision-guided bombs delivered during the air war were against the 'strategic core', and almost 60 per cent of the attacks against leadership and C3 were precision strikes.[54] There was therefore a disproportionate amount of attention focused on leadership targets in Baghdad – an otherwise statistically minor part of the overall air war. Over 90 per cent of the targets attacked in the first 72 hours fell into the original Instant Thunder categories, and the timing also remained largely faithful to the original concept.[55] Among the leadership targets that were eventually bombed were presidential palaces and bunkers, the Ministry of Defence and other government buildings, intelligence and security headquarters, the Baghdad conference centre and Baath Party command posts. Among the C3 targets were television towers, satellite communication stations, transmitters and receivers, microwave radio relays, fibre-optic and coaxial landlines. This was an unprecedented combination of stealth, precision and stand-off weapons, whose purpose was to disrupt the 'central nervous system' and weaken Iraq as a strategic entity. After the first night of operations, the Iraqi air-defence system was substantially degraded, the Iraqi aircraft did not challenge Coalition control of the skies, the national power grid was severely disrupted, Baghdad's ability to communicate with the outside world was reduced and there was relatively little collateral damage.[56] From the early moments of war, the Iraqis possessed *no effective* defence against attacks on their military and civil infrastructure. All the five rings with the exception of the fourth, the population, were systematically bombed.

In order to assess the effectiveness of the strategic air campaign, one must analyse all the target-sets that were attacked. One must also account for the interchanging effects of the other phases of the war, and the diplomatic and economic factors that played their part. This is an immensely complex task, including non-linear effects and intangibles open to multiple interpretations. It must be pointed out that this chapter focuses only on the Iraqi leadership and its instruments of communication.

Interviews with Iraqi officers suggest that the communications between Baghdad and the military forces occupying Kuwait were never completely severed.[57] Iraq had modern computerized equipment with high levels of redundancy, relying as it did on coaxial lines, multiple landlines, fibre-optic lines and microwave relays. The Iraqi leader furthermore relied on face-to-face meetings with his staff, couriers on motorcycles and pre-delegated orders.[58] Moreover, relevant equipment had been transferred, and many of the headquarters that were bombed were either relocated or evacuated prior to the air war. For example, the Ministry of Defence staff was moved to the Ministry of Youth building, parts of the Office of the Presidential Palace were moved to the Ministry of Central Planning, and files and computers were placed in schools and hospitals.[59]

Senior officers and officials also seemed to be safe. According to Robert A. Pape, 'all of the top forty-three Iraqi political and military leaders on 15 January 1991 were still alive after 1 March'.[60] The Iraqi leadership avoided meeting in bunkers and headquarters that were potential targets and Saddam Hussein himself operated mainly from residential houses and regional ad-hoc headquarters in the outskirts of Baghdad. He allegedly met his military and political leaders on a regular basis throughout the war in farmhouses or ordinary homes – places they knew would provide them with safety.[61] When the journalist Peter Arnett interviewed the Iraqi leader on 27 January 1991 they met in a modest residential house. The same was the case when the Russian premier Yevgeni Primakov came to the capital. Indeed, Saddam Hussein could never have been completely isolated from the outside world, because he relied on a network of unofficial channels of diplomacy with regional state leaders.[62] All this information, when accounted for separately, may lead to the conclusion that the air campaign's focus on the national authority facilities was a waste of sorties, but a different interpretation surfaces when accounting for the aggregated effect.

All these inconveniences ensured that the Iraqi leadership needed to spend a lot of time and energy on provisional and less-effective solutions. Secondary and tertiary command posts are less suited for crisis management than the primary facilities, by definition. The Iraqi elite was, for example, deterred from using cellular phones, depriving them of real-time and mobile communication. The bombing of a variety of communication links forced the Iraqi leadership to resort to far less secure means of communication, such as walkie-talkies, that could be monitored easily. While radio broadcasts continued throughout the war the transmission was on wavelengths that could not be received throughout the whole of Iraq. The reduced connectivity resulted in insecurity and passivity in the leadership, and distribution problems within the theatre of operations. Essentially, there was enough food and clothes in Kuwait to provide for the Iraqi forces, but they were not able to distribute them effectively. Relocation to secondary command posts made it more difficult for the Iraqi leader to keep track on key personnel, which in turn loosened his otherwise tight control of the regime. Saddam Hussein was also more vulnerable to attack, as he often travelled incognito and alone, rather than with large escorts of bodyguards. The secret police seemed to be more occupied with staying alive than protecting the regime, as some of its guards chose to abandon the jails and headquarters at night out of fear of being bombed.[63] Some even witnessed apathy by late January.[64] Witnesses claim that Baghdad was essentially a vacuum during the opening days of war, but, since there was no organized opposition group with a base in Baghdad, there was no serious thought on how to take advantage of the situation.[65] Saddam Hussein may well not have continuously feared for his life during the opening days of the war, but he had to take extraordinary measures to protect himself, and thus his ability to direct the war-effort was hampered.

The bombing certainly left parts of Baghdad with an impression of precision-targeting. Although there were collateral-damage incidents, large parts of the population who had evacuated Baghdad in the early days of the bombing returned to the city after a week or two.[66] Children and adults of all ages were constantly running to the rooftops to watch the bombing of military and political targets.[67] It has been claimed that the Battle of Britain and other strategic bombing campaigns strengthened the resolve of the people, but the opposite may have been the case for Baghdad. Many Iraqis applauded the bombing of regime targets, and an Iraqi Foreign Ministry official stated after the war that the pinpoint accuracy reduced the fear of bombing.[68] After years of suppression many would have welcomed a change, and when the bombing indicated that the regime rather than the people was the target one could argue that the Iraqi people accepted occasional collateral damage.[69] One should not conclude that this phenomenon is universally applicable, because in the Iraqi case there seems to have been a real discrepancy between the ambitions of the leader and the citizens. The bombing provided pressure from the air, but, again, without organized opposition on the ground, or any efforts from the Coalition's state departments to facilitate an overthrow, the one-sided pressure would be inadequate to change an entire leadership. Nevertheless, attacks on regime targets demonstrated that the leadership was unable to defend itself, and, as it was at the mercy of its adversary, there followed a certain loss of confidence in the leaders. The bombing of these targets showed determination on the Coalition's part, and sparing Baghdad would no doubt have increased Saddam Hussein's warmaking and warfighting capabilities. Not bombing regime targets when weapons allowed for precision attacks would definitely have indicated lack of resolve and commitment *per se* on the Coalition's part. Saddam Hussein lost considerable face during the war because of the Coalition's ability to bomb the Iraqi capital with impunity.

Communication on the tactical level was possible throughout the war, but the Iraqi leader was deprived of the strategic picture. According to Yevgeni Primakov, the Iraqi leader was genuinely surprised at how bad his situation was when he received the satellite imagery on 12 February.[70] One may ask, however, whether that was a result of reduced communication or whether Saddam Hussein's men chose not to present their leader with 'bad news'. Saddam Hussein was, after all, known to shoot the messenger, but this perception should not be taken too far. According to General Wafiq Samarrai, former Chief of the Military Intelligence, the Iraqi leader was more likely to execute somebody who proved to be withholding important information. Thus, if bad news was kept away from the Iraqi leader, and that information next proved important for timely decision-making, the official stood no chance at all.[71] The mere fact that Samarrai was not replaced during the war or in its immediate aftermath indicates in itself that Saddam Hussein did not blame his own intelligence service.

Another example of problems created by the bombing of communication facilities is found in the memoirs of the Iraqi Missile Commander, Lieutenant-General Hazim Abd al-Razzaq al-Ayyubi, who during the first three days of the air operations went without a single hour's sleep.[72] He argued that his Scud team had numerous technical problems because of reduced connectivity. Combined with the time and resources devoted to camouflage and concealment, the number of launches was far less than the Iraqi leader had requested. Saddam Hussein placed great emphasis on launching Scuds against Israel, but after the first week his team was unable to launch more than 20 missiles against its 'arch enemy'.[73] Given the fact that Saddam Hussein had predelegated orders for continued and massive strikes, one may observe that the reduction in Scud launches had more to do with the second-order effect of communication links being destroyed and the Scud hunt inducing stress than inadequate leadership *per se* on the Iraqi part.

As was the case for many other Iraqi generals, Al-Ayyubi received the information about the unconditional withdrawal via commercial radio rather than through the military command system.[74] This was also the case for the Iraqi representative to the UN Security Council, Abdelamir al-Anbari.[75] Both cases indicate a rather isolated elite without the ability to communicate with key diplomatic and military players, either inside or outside Iraq. It could of course be argued that the flip side of the coin is that if communication had been completely severed the Iraqi generals would have continued to fight after their leader had ordered a cease-fire. This raises a fundamental problem: if you manage to destroy the enemy leadership and its apparatus for command and control, with whom do you then discuss the terms of surrender? It is an interesting aspect that deserves attention, but suffice it here to suggest that with the multiple channels of information the chances of complete incapacitation are very small. In the pursuit of victory, the benefits of complete strategic paralysis seem to outweigh the potential disadvantages by a large margin.

According to General Wafiq Samarrai, the Coalition attacks on communications, combined with attacks on the electricity supply, substantially degraded efficiency within the Iraqi command system.[76] The bombing of Baghdad made rapid co-ordination of forces inside Iraq very difficult. The Department of Defense's report to Congress stated that the air strikes on the Iraqi leaders and national communication targets more or less paralysed Iraq's ability to direct battlefield operations,[77] and Saddam Hussein was genuinely surprised that air strikes could be so accurate and devastating.[78] Although the Iraqi leader was able to broadcast statements regularly on certain radio frequencies, he was deprived of using the television, his favourite media, to communicate with the Iraqi people. According to Saad al-Bazzaz, the author of the 'official' Iraqi account of 'the Mother of All Battles', Saddam Hussein believed that persistent and flattering television coverage played an important role in keeping him in power. By executive order, his name and image had to be incorporated into every programme on the non-religious channel, with the exception of late-night movies and cartoons.[79] During the Gulf War he was not able to use this media, and combined with Western radio broadcasts from Saudi Arabia, the effort undermined his power by sheer lack of presence. Some of the Iraqi officers who eventually took part in the uprising against their leader argued that they did so partly because they believed he had been unseated.[80] In war it is exceptionally important to have a leader who motivates, encourages and gives hope. In the Iraqi case the people and the military forces were left with no such comfort. Thus, the reduced communication between the Iraqi leader and the forces in Kuwait might well have played an important part in demotivating and demoralizing the Iraqi troops who chose to surrender before or immediately after the ground war started.

One is reminded of Sun Tzu's dictum that the most successful strategy is to attack the enemy's plans. The strategic bombing played its part in making it difficult for Iraq to adequately adapt to changing circumstances as it weakened and confused its management.[81] In a unique article, Saddam Hussein acknowledged that the Iraqi strategy anticipated a huge infantry battle, in which the United States' superiority in weapons and military technology would be made irrelevant.[82] Saddam Hussein stressed that the Iraqi strategy was one of prolonging the war 'to force them [the US-led Coalition] to fight us face to face and not just fire from a distance'. He argued that 'long-range firing' could not 'end a battle decisively'.[83] Several aspects of the air campaign ensured that a bloody ground battle did not become necessary, but the fact that Saddam Hussein started preparing for an occupation of al-Khafji only a few days into the strategic air campaign indicates that he became convinced that his strategy of merely sitting out the bombing was not working. The decision to invade was taken before the bombing of Iraqi forces in Kuwait had started in earnest, and the attempt to jump-start the ground war by moving into Saudi Arabia in late January was a clear indication of the Iraqi leadership becoming ever more desperate.

Deprived of decisive offensive action, the Iraqi leader was left with only the imperative of presenting himself as the victim. Rather than showing the action–reaction pattern that most wars witness, Iraqi decision-making was characterized by inaction. According to Philip Meilinger, 'air strikes against the Iraqi communications network, road and rail system, and electrical power grid made it extremely difficult, physically, for Saddam Hussein to control his military forces, but it also induced enormous confusion and uncertainty into his decision-making process. His OODA [Observation–Orientation–Decision–Action] loop was expanded dramatically and its cycle time was slowed accordingly.'[84] Borrowing from the thinking of John R. Boyd,[85] one could talk about progressive chaotic dislocation, wherein the offensive actions disrupted the capability of the Iraqi leadership to react and transmit relevant decisions. An example of a counter-factual argument that indicates second-order effect can be found in the Iraqi leader's appeal to several terrorist organizations for support during the bombing; but lack of dialogue made the effort futile. The Iraqis had detailed plans for kidnapping Coalition Generals Sir Peter de la Billiere and Norman Schwarzkopf, but the lack of outside support resulted in aborted operations.

The picture that emerges is one in which the Iraqi leader's *will* became irrelevant, because he was prevented from taking decisive action. Many elements of Saddam Hussein's government were essentially forced to relocate and shift to back-up communications, the Iraqi leader's ability to communicate with his own population and military forces was considerably reduced, and, to make matters worse, ordinary Iraqis started criticizing their leader openly.[86] The Baath Party was not able to prevent an unprecedented level of desertion and its grip on power was substantially weakened. One may disagree about what triggered the Intifada, but the reduced efficiency of the Baath Party made the uprising possible, and its officials became the focus of revenge.[87] The systematic and precise bombing of Baath institutions seems to have changed the Iraqi people's perception of the Party as infallible, and, as the Iraqis like to put it, *hajiz al-khawf inkasar* – 'the barrier of fear was broken'.[88] After the war 'Saddam castigated the senior and middle-level membership for their helplessness and isolation from the masses in the face of the insurrection.'[89] The cumulative functional disruption, confusion and disorientation at the strategic level of command certainly undermined the effectiveness of the Baath Party to collectively deter a spontaneous revolt. The actions taken by Saddam Hussein after the war make a case for the effectiveness of the bombing of leadership targets. The Iraqi leader went out of his way to strengthen the sheikh system at the expense of the Baath system, and the latter lost much of the prestige and power that it had enjoyed prior to the war. The party was blamed for its inability to act coherently during the air war and membership dropped substantially in the immediate aftermath. The failure of the Baath apparatus to prevent a popular and spontaneous uprising was nevertheless not sufficient to alter the regime. The previously mentioned sheikh system partly prevented the regime from having to spread its armed forces too thinly during the Intifada, and combined with the control of Baghdad through the security network, and repressive actions against the uprising, the regime managed to survive.

The strategic air campaign, in conclusion, contributed strongly in rendering the Iraqi leadership largely ineffective as a strategic entity. Together with the bombing of the Iraqi ground forces and the subsequent ground operations, it played an important part in achieving the stated military and political objectives. In sum, there is circumstantial evidence supporting the claim that the bombing of Baghdad weakened the regime, but there is little to support the idea that the strategic air campaign came close to actually changing the regime on its own. The strategic air campaign was not able to exceed the minimum level required for a coup or a revolt to succeed in changing the Iraqi regime, but it contributed to putting so much pressure on the leadership that it decided to withdraw from Kuwait. Well-informed sources argue that the strategic air campaign would have had more leverage if the

Special Republican Guard and the Special Security Service had been targeted. Additionally, one could have concentrated on Tikrit, which escaped bombing altogether, and a systematic targeting of the security network would surely have weakened the regime's grip on power even further. To suggest that a systematic air campaign against the *de facto* political power structure would have led to a replacement of the Iraqi leader would nevertheless be simplistic. The ability of human organizations to adapt to changing circumstances does not allow for such a direct cause–effect link to be made.

THE UTILITY OF THE FIVE RINGS SYSTEM

According to Casper W. Weinberger, 'A head of state and a head of government, by definition, can be assumed at least to be implicated in, if not responsible for, whatever actions his or her country undertakes which causes us to fight a war or pursue warlike reprisals.'[90] Saddam Hussein was the supreme commander of the Iraqi forces, and, as previously mentioned, was directly responsible for the occupation of Kuwait. Thus, the air planners saw every reason to attack the absolute leadership itself. Saddam Hussein, not the Iraqi people, was considered the problem, and he was the one that provided that strategic direction and co-ordination of combat. They argued that the higher the target, the more effective it had the potential to be, and if targeting the leaders could help end the war quickly, and thus spare the lives of hundreds of thousands of combatants and civilians, they found it morally unacceptable not to attempt to incapacitate Saddam Hussein. As it turned out, the air campaign failed to overthrow the Iraqi leader for several reasons, and it has been argued that the survivability of the Iraqi regime resided in a complex state, societal and security system which was able to survive because of its scale and redundancy. It has also been argued that the Iraqi leader sustained himself in power by creating a persuasive and seemingly omnipotent internal security and intelligence network, strengthened by the wider control of the republic through the Baath Party, government and military institutions. The resilience witnessed during the bombing was a result of two decades of systematic work by the Iraqi leadership.

In the end, there is only so much that air power can do without inside information, organized opposition on the ground, political will to see the job through and timely human intelligence. Most importantly, however, one has to understand how a regime works to be able to change it, and go into the difficult business of thinking about actual replacements for its leaders. The Iraqi people knew that action against their leader would result in revenge on their entire family, clan and tribe, and this in turn discouraged action altogether. Men may well act if their own lives are at stake, but not when the lives of their wives and children are on the line.

War is always characterized by confusion, and the Five Rings System provides a starting point for rationality and simplicity for planners who have limited knowledge of both air power theory and the nature of foreign countries. According to the theory, one seeks to change the opponent's energy level to make it compatible with one's own objectives. One seeks to change energy levels by looking at the opponent as a system and then affecting the centres of gravity necessary to produce the desired energy changes. The leadership will as such often if not always be an important centre of gravity that it is desirable to attack (see Figure 13.3). One must therefore focus first on the enemy as a system in the context of creating the better peace for which you have gone to war. In this way, the Five Rings System provides planners with a focus on the leadership that cannot be ignored. Its utility is evident in the high degree of fog and friction that was induced into the Iraqi system at the strategic level of command. Although the leadership was not overthrown, the Iraqi decision-making capability and strategy were rendered largely inappropriate and ineffective.

Figure 13.3: Analysing Centres of Gravity

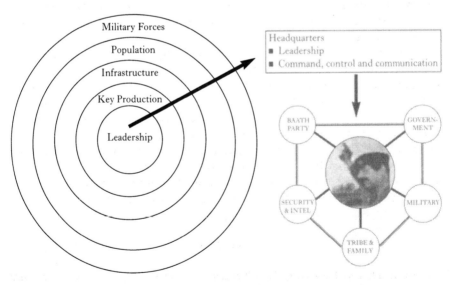

The Five Rings System can easily be challenged as rigid, schematic and formulaic, but so can any model whose purpose is to simplify the complexities of the real world. The model assumes that the centres of gravity are material, that they are subject to attack and that the enemy state is reasonably modernized; but the fact that the model is not universally applicable does not erase its utility as a conceptual framework. The model, when taken into the larger air power theory represented by Warden and Deptula, contains prospects for future planning, if used flexibly and with a comprehensive appreciation of the adversary's power structure. Further potential resides in dissecting the inner-ring target-sets in detail at the same time as looking beyond pure 'utility targeting' and moving into 'value targeting'.[91] When the target-group has been selected, one has to assess the adversary's vulnerabilities and values, and therein Maslow's study of the Hierarchy of Needs provides a framework for fundamental requirements of both individuals and societies.[92] In the words of Thomas Schelling, 'one needs to know what an adversary treasures and what scares him.'[93] It may be argued that the Warden–Deptula planning process should have been taken a step or two further.

Warfare represents a highly complex reality, and the best way to ensure success is to hold several models and strategies simultaneously in our minds, rather than relying on any single, inevitably simplistic, paradigm. One has to explore different scenarios, expanding the Warden–Deptula thesis by combining it with other air power concepts – into a synthesis on the one hand, and an analysis of the state's political construct on the other. In order to do so, one has to come together from different professional and academic disciplines and discuss how each part helps in achieving the post-war objectives. This is not a blueprint for success in war, because there is no such thing, but it is a framework for thinking about air power in a socio-cultural context. The model provides the planners with an option that might prove decisive in certain situations when combined with other elements of force. In an era of precision weapons of great quality, the challenge is to translate precise bombing into precise effects on the target regime, which one seeks to deter, compel or even change. The strategy for concurrent attacks by stealth and precision-guided weapons does not guarantee that an adversary will be defeated quickly and with a minimum of casualties, but a highly discriminate focus on its leadership provides an air campaign with an essential leverage in meeting political objectives.

NOTES

1. I would like to thank Dr H. P. Willmott and my colleagues at the Royal Norwegian Air Force Academy for their efforts to improve this chapter.
2. The phrase 'strategic air campaign' refers to the perception of those who planned and executed the air campaign. It focused, for all practical purposes, on attacking targets that were directly related to the Iraqi state and its sources of national power rather than the military forces that occupied Kuwait.

3. See, for example, Colin Powell with Joseph E. Persico, *My American Journey* (New York: Ballantine Books, 1995), p. 460; General H. Norman Schwarzkopf with Peter Petre, *It Doesn't Take a Hero* (New York: Bantam Books, 1992), pp. 369–71; Colonel Edward C. Mann, *Thunder and Lightning: Desert Storm and the Airpower Debates* (Maxwell Air Force Base, AL: Air University Press, 1995); and Colonel Richard T. Reynolds, *Heart of the Storm: The Genesis of the Air Campaign Against Iraq* (Maxwell Air Force Base, AL: Air University Press, 1995).

4. Eliot A. Cohen, *et al.*, *The Gulf War Air Power Survey: Volume II, Part II, Effects and Effectiveness* (Washington, DC: US Government Printing Office, 1993), p. 77; Richard G. Davis, *Decisive Force: Strategic Air Power in Desert Storm* (Washington, DC: Air Force History and Museums Program, 1996), p. 11; John A. Warden, 'Success in Modern War: A Response to Robert Pape's Bombing to Win', *Security Studies* 7, No. 2 (Winter 1997/98), p. 180; Schwarzkopf, *It Doesn't Take a Hero*, p. 319; Scott Ritter, *Endgame: Solving the Iraq Problem -- Once and For All* (New York: Simon & Schuster, 1999), p. 133; and Robert A. Pape, *Bombing to Win: Air Power and Coercion*, (Ithaca, NY: Cornell University Press), 1996, p. 221.

5. Cohen *et al.*, *The Gulf War Air Power Survey*, pp. 77–8.

6. Pape, *Bombing to Win*, pp. 316–29; William M. Arkin, 'Baghdad: The Urban Sanctuary in Desert Storm', *Airpower Journal*, XI, No. 1 (Spring 1997), pp. 4–20; Jeffrey Record, *Hollow Victory: A Contemporary View of the Gulf War* (New York: Brassey's, 1993), pp. 109–13. See also Caroline F. Ziemke, 'A New Covenant?: The Apostles of Douhet and the Persian Gulf War', in William Head and Earl H. Tilford Jr (eds), *The Eagle in the Desert* (Westport, CT: Praeger, 1996), pp. 290–310; Lieutenant-Colonel Jeffrey McAusland, 'The Gulf Conflict: A Military Analysis', *Adelphi Paper*, No. 282 (November 1993), pp. 63–4; and Grant T. Hammond, 'Myths of the Gulf War: Some "Lessons" Not to Learn', *Airpower Journal*, XII, No. 3 (Fall 1998), pp. 13–15.

7. For details and sources, see John Andreas Olsen, 'Operation Desert Storm: An Examination of the Strategic Air Campaign', PhD submitted at De Montfort University, March 2000.

8. Colonel John A. Warden III, *The Air Campaign: Planning for Combat* (Washington, DC: NDU Press, 1988).

9. Haywood S. Hansell, Jr, *The Air Plan That Defeated Hitler* (Atlanta, GA: Higgins-McArthur/Longino & Porter, 1972). See also Brigadier-General Mitchell's two most influential books: *Skyways: A Book on Modern Aeronautics* (Philadelphia, PA: J. B. Lippincott, 1930) and *Winged Defense: The Development and Possibilities of Modern Air Power Economic and Military* ([1988 reprint] New York: Dover Publications, 1925); and B. H. Liddell Hart, *Strategy* (London: Faber & Faber, 1967).

10. The XOXW contained five sub-divisions: the Air Force doctrine division (XOXWD), the strategy division (XOXWS), the war plans and mobility division (XOXWC), the long-range planning division (XOXWP) and the war-gaming and simulation division (XOXWX). The latter was originally referred to as the Checkmate office, but because of its size and layout it became the location for the actual planning. Thus, the whole planning team was referred to as simply the Checkmate office.

11. Colonel John A. Warden, 'Centers of Gravity – The Key to Success in War' (unpublished 1988 paper made available to the author). For an updated and published version, see Colonel John A. Warden, 'The Enemy as a System', *Airpower Journal*, IX, No. 1 (Spring 1995), pp. 40–55.

12. Colonel David A. Deptula, 'Parallel Warfare: What Is It? Where Did It Come From? Why Is it Important', in William Head and Earl H. Tilford Jr (eds), *The*

Eagle in the Desert, pp. 127–56. On the definition of parallel attacks, see David S. Fadok, 'John Boyd and John Warden: Airpower's Quest for Strategic Paralysis', in Phillip S. Meilinger (ed.), *The Paths of Heaven: The Evolution of Airpower Theory* (Maxwell AFB, AL: Air University Press, 1997), p. 374.

13. See Warden, 'Success in Modern War'.
14. Warden, *The Air Campaign*, p. 132.
15. Donald B. Rice, interview with author, tape-recording, Birmingham (England), 17 July 1999.
16. Donald B. Rice *et al.*, 'Global Reach Global; Power: Reshaping for the Future', *USAF White Paper*, published first in June 1990 and updated in September 1991.
17. See Carl H. Builder, *The Icarus Syndrome: The Role of Air Power Theory in the Evolution and Fate of the US Air Force* (London: Transaction Publishers, 1998).
18. Colonel John A. Warden, 'Planning to Win', in Shaun Clarke (ed.), *Testing the Limits* (Canberra: Air Power Studies Centre, 1998), p. 93.
19. Colonel John A. Warden to General Norman Schwarzkopf, 'Iraqi Air Campaign Instant Thunder', briefing, 10 August 1990 (the briefing slides have been made available to the author).
20. See, in particular, Reynolds, *Heart of the Storm*, and the 'Desert Storm Collection', which contains all the interviews conducted for the book. All the manuscripts are available on micro-film at the Historical Research Agency at Maxwell Air Force Base, Alabama.
21. Colonel David A. Deptula, *Firing for Effect: Change in the Nature of Warfare* (Defense and Airpower Series), (Arlington, VA: Aerospace Education Foundation, 1995), p. 3.
22. Ahmad Cheleby, Iraqi National Congress, interview with author, notes, London, 24 January 1999. Cheleby contends that the structure of the Iraqi security and intelligence network was known in 1990–91 by the opposition. See, for example, 'The House Saddam built', *The Economist*, 29 September 1990, pp. 73–4.
23. Faleh Abdul al-Jabbar, 'The State, Society, Clan, Party and Army in Iraq: A Totalitarian State in the Twilight of Totalitarianism', in Faleh A. Jabbar, Ahmad Shikara and Keiko Sakai, *From Storm to Thunder: Unfinished Showdown Between Iraq and the US* (Tokyo: Institute of Developing Economics, 1998), pp. 16 and 27.
24. George Orwell, *Nineteen Eighty-Four* ([1949] New York: Signet Classic, 1984 edn), pp. 5–18.
25. Saad al-Bazzaz, *The Ashes of Wars*, 1995, p. 53.
26. See, for example, Said K. Aburish, *Saddam Hussein: the Politics of Revenge* (New York: Bloomsbury, 2000).
27. Faleh al-Jabber, 'Why the Intifada Failed', in Fran Hazelton (ed.), *Iraq Since the Gulf War: Prospects for Democracy* (London: Zed Books, 1994), p. 105.
28. Helen Chapin Metz *et al.*, *Iraq: A Country Study* ([1990] 4th edn, Washington, DC: US Government Printing Office, 1993), p. 180.
29. Colonel Hassan Khafaji, interview with author, tape-recording, London, 3 August 1998.
30. Amatzia Baram, interview with author, tape-recording, Washington, DC, 19 February 1999. This is confirmed by Nabeel Musawi, Iraqi National Congress, telephone-interview with author, notes, 8 March 1999.
31. Saad al-Bazzaz, 'Saad al-Bazzaz: An Insider's View of Iraq', *Middle East Quarterly*, December (1995), p. 67; and Saad al-Bazaz, *The Ashes of Wars*, p. 8.
32. Colonel Hassan Khafaji, interview with author, tape-recording, London, 3 August 1998.
33. In total 5,646 sorties were flown against the Republican Guard, while the air strikes on surface forces amounted to 23,430. See Davis, *Decisive Force*, p. 38, and Cohen,

et al., *The Gulf War Air Power Survey*, p. 341.

34. For the first in-depth and methodical exploration, see Amazia Baram, 'Neo-Tribalism in Iraq: Saddam Hussein's Tribal Politics 1991–96', *International Journal Middle East Studies*, 29 (1997), pp. 1–31.

35. Baram, 'Neo-Tribalism in Iraq', pp. 1–2.

36. Baram, 'Neo-Tribalism in Iraq', p. 5.

37. The information in this section and the figure itself is to a large extent derived from various interviews with Iraqis and two articles written by Sean Boyne. See 'Inside Iraq's Security Network: Part One', *Jane's Intelligence Review*, 9, No. 7 (July 1997) and 'Inside Iraq's Security Network: Part Two', *Jane's Intelligence Review*, 9, No. 8 (August 1997). See also Fouad Ajami, 'Inside Saddam's Bunker', *US News and World Report*, 3 December 1990, p. 30.

38. Boyne, 'Inside Iraq's Security Network', p. 366.

39. Ritter, *Endgame*, p. 121.

40. Ritter, *Endgame*, pp. 124–5.

41. Colonel Hamed Salem al-Zyadi, interview with author, tape-recording, London, 25 January 1999; and Aras Habib, Iraqi National Congress, interview with author, tape-recording, London, 27 June 1998.

42. For two accounts on 'doubles', see Mikhael Ramadan, *In the Shadow of Saddam: Saddam Hussein's Former Double* (Auckland: GreeNZone, 1999), and Latif Yahia and Karl Wendel, *I Was Saddam's Son* (New York: Arcade Publishing, 1997).

43. Saad Salah Jabour, Free Iraqi Council, interview with author, notes, London, 14 July 2001.

44. Kanan Makiya, interview with author, tape-recording, London, 2 July 1998.

45. Kanan Makiya, *Republic of Fear: The Politics of Modern Iraq*, updated edition with a new introduction ([1989] Berkeley: University Press of California, 1998 edn); and Hussein Sumaida with Carole Jerome, *Circle of Fear: A Renegade's Journey from the Mossad to the Iraqi Secret Service* (Toronto: Stoddart, 1991).

46. Kanan Makiya provides an extensive account of this surveillance system, and the UNSCOM inspectors found documents that confirmed the overall theory. See Ritter, *Endgame*, pp. 122–5.

47. An Emergency Force (Quwat al-Tawari) was created in 1991 in response to the breakdown of law and order following the Gulf War.

48. Kanan Makiya, *Cruelty and Silence: War, Tyranny, Uprising, and the Arab World* (London: W. W. Norton, 1993), p. 339.

49. Kenneth Pollack, interview with author, tape-recording, Washington DC, 24 February 1999.

50. Pape, *Bombing to Win*, p. 233.

51. Thomas A. Keaney and Eliot A. Cohen, *Revolution in Warfare? Air Power in the Persian Gulf* (Annapolis, MD: Naval Institute Press, 1995), p. 55.

52. Cohen *et al.*, *The Gulf War Air Power Survey*, p. 148.

53. Keaney and Cohen, *Revolution in Warfare?*, p. 56.

54. Ibid., p. 60.

55. Cohen *et al.*, *The Gulf War Air Power Survey*, pp. 185–9.

56. Williamson Murray with Wayne Thompson, *Air War in the Persian Gulf* (Baltimore, MD: Nautical & Aviation Publishing Company of America, 1995), p. 109; Davis, *Decisive Force*, p. 39; and Ramadan, *In the Shadow of Saddam*, p. 221.

57. Colonel Muhammed Ali, interview with author, tape-recording, London, 23 August 1998; and General Wafiq Samarrai, interview with author, tape-recording, London, 28 October 1999.

58. See, for example, Staff Lieutenant-General Hazim Abd al-Razzaq al-Ayyubi,

Forty-Three Missiles on the Zionist Entity, first published in Amman al-Arab al-Yawn, translated by *Foreign Broadcast Information Service (FBIS)* (25 October 1998–12 November 1998).

59. Arkin, 'Baghdad', p. 17.
60. Pape, *Bombing to Win*, p. 230
61. General Wafiq Sammarai, interview with author, tape-recording, London, 28 October 1999; Tariq Aziz, interview with BBC Frontline Show (BBC 1), *No. 1407T* (part one), air date 28 January 1997, transcript, p. 17.
62. Saad al-Bazzaz, *The Ashes of Wars*, p. 28.
63. Lieutenant-Colonel William Brurner, interview with author, tape-recording, Washington DC, 18 February 1998.
64. Yahia and Wendel, *I Was Saddam's Son*, p. 225; Aras Habib, interview with author, tape-recording, London, 14 May 1998; Tashin Mualla, Iraqi National Accord, interview with author, tape-recording, London, 14 August 1998.
65. Nabeel Musawi, interview with author, notes, London, 13 July 2001; and Tahsin Mualla, interview with author, tape-recording, 14 August 1998.
66. Makiya, *Cruelty and Silence*, p. 77; and Aras Habib, interview with author, tape-recording, London, 14 May 1998.
67. Tashin Mualla, interview with author, tape-recording, London, 14 August 1998.
68. Arkin, 'Baghdad', p. 176.
69. Tashin Mualla, interview with author, tape-recording, London, 14 August 1998.
70. Yevgeni Primakov, interview with BBC Frontline Show (BBC 1), *No. 1407T* (part one), air date 28 January 1997, p. 3; and Ken Fireman, 'Hussein's Peace Feeler: Says He'll Co-operate with Soviets', *New York Newsday*, 13 February 1991.
71. General Wafiq Samarrai, interview with author, tape-recording, London, 28 October 1999.
72. Hazim Abd al-Razzaq al-Ayyubi, *Forty-Three Missiles on the Zionist Entity*.
73. Cohen *et al.*, *The Gulf War Air Power Survey*, p. 337.
74. Hazim Abd al-Razzaq al-Ayyubi, *Forty-Three Missiles on the Zionist Entity*.
75. Saad al-Bazzaz, *The Ashes of Wars*, p. 23.
76. General Wafiq Samarrai, interview with author, tape-recording, London, 28 October 1999.
77. United States Department of Defense, *Conduct of the Persian Gulf War: Final Report to Congress* (Washington, DC: Government Printing Office, 1992), p. 199.
78. Rick Francona, *Ally to Adversary: An Eyewitness Account of Iraq's Fall from Grace* (Annapolis, MD: Naval Institute Press, 1999), pp. 82–3.
79. Saad al-Bazzaz, 'Inside the Belly of the Beast', www.meforum.org/wires/bazzaz.html
80. Brigadier-General Tawfiq al-Yasiri, interview with author, tape-recording, London, 6 August 1998.
81. Saad al-Bazzaz, *The Ashes of Wars*, p. 8.
82. Associated Press, 'Hussein Recalls Gulf War Strategy', *Philadelphia Inquirer: International*, 27 July 1997.
83. 'Iraq: TV Carries Saddam Remarks on Gulf War', cited in *FBIS-NES-97-208*, 5 August 1997, p. 1; and Christopher Dickey, 'Rope-a-Dope in Baghdad', *Newsweek*, 4 February 1991, pp. 26–7.
84. Colonel Phillip S. Meilinger, 'Air Targeting Strategies: An Overview', in Richard P. Hallion (ed.), *Air Power Confronts an Unstable World* (London: Brassey's, 1997), p. 62.
85. See Grant T. Hammond, *The Mind of War: John Boyd and American Security* (Washington, DC: Smithsonian Institute Press, 2001).
86. Chris Hedges, 'After the War: Iraq in Growing Disarray, Iraqis Fight Iraqis', *New*

York Times, 10 March 1991, pp. 1 and 14.

87. Kanan Makiya, *Cruelty and Silence: War, Tyranny, Uprising, and the Arab World*, pp. 57–104.

88. Makiya, *Cruelty and Silence*, p. 62.

89. Amatzia Baram, *Policy Watch Sessions*, No. 218, pp. 3–5, the Washington Institute for Near East Policy.

90. Casper W. Weinberger, 'When Can We Target The Leaders', *Strategic Review*, Vol. XXIX, No. 2 (Spring 2001), pp. 21–4.

91. Richard Szafranski and Lieutenant-Colonel Peter W. W. Wijninga, 'Beyond Infrastructure Targeting: Toward Axiological Aerospace Operations', *Aerospace Journal*, XIV, No. 4 (Winter 2000), pp. 45–59.

92. A. P. N. Lambert, 'Air Power and Coercion', in John Andreas Olsen (ed.), *From Manoeuvre Warfare to Kosovo?* (Trondheim: Royal Norwegian Air Force Academy, 2001), p. 240.

93. Thomas Schelling, *Arms and Influence* (New Haven, CT: Yale University Press, 1966), p. 3.

14

The Gulf War and UK Air Power Doctrine and Practice

Sebastian Cox and Sebastian Ritchie

'Our task in peace is to train for war – and don't you forget it!'[1]

During the 1970s the above words were painted on a sign at the entrance to Royal Air Force Bruggen in Germany, home to one of the two Tornado GR1 wings in RAF Germany. Crews from the two Tornado bases in Germany, along with their colleagues from Marham in the UK were to form the core of the RAF's offensive capability during the Gulf War (known to the RAF as Operation Granby), with additional effort provided by a detachment of Jaguars from RAF Coltishall and Buccaneers from RAF Lossiemouth.

All these crews were to find, however, that in many respects the war they were to fight over Iraq and Kuwait was rather different from the war they had been trained to fight on NATO's Central Front in the heart of Europe. Training is rooted in doctrine, whether or not the latter is formally promulgated in doctrine manuals. By 1990, the Cold War in Europe had effectively come to an end with the reunification of Germany the previous year, but the doctrines by which the RAF trained had yet to take account of the fact. On one level this is hardly surprising. The concentration of intellectual effort at the time was largely focused, first, on trying to understand and adjust to the new political situation in Europe and its effect on the wider world, and, second, on attempting to preserve some viable and useful shape and capability for the forces in the face of the looming and inevitable cuts as politicians and Treasury civil servants rapidly identified a 'peace dividend' before anyone had established what form 'peace' might take. Indeed, the Iraqi invasion of Kuwait and the prospect of a war in the Gulf was itself clearly a harbinger of a new and more unstable world, which would require more flexible force structures.

At the time, however, such flexible forces were not in place: a good indicator of this being the fact that the RAF had no formal alert measures for undertaking operations outside the NATO area. Some parts of the RAF's military machine, including the Jaguar and Harrier squadrons, the support helicopter force, and various supporting units such as the Tactical Supply Wing and the Tactical Communications Wing, had an established deployment role, largely related to rapid reinforcement of NATO's flanks through the Allied Command Europe (ACE) mobile force. Others, notably the Tornado F3 and GR1 forces, did not. If flexibility was not built into large parts of the force, it would have to be improvised, and much of the RAF's performance in the war can be seen as a triumph of improvisation, albeit from a solid base.

At this point it will probably be helpful to give an appreciation of the state of RAF doctrine and concepts of operations at the time the crisis arose. It may come as a surprise to those familiar with the 'family' of British military doctrine publications available today,[2] to learn that there was no formal British air power doctrine manual available to the RAF at the time. The last formal iteration of RAF doctrine had been the final edition of Air Publication 1300, the original RAF 'War Manual', published as long ago as 1957, last amended in 1968 and withdrawn completely in 1970. Clearly, by 1990, the RAF was no longer working to a doctrinal manual written some 33 years earlier. In fact, it was not working to any formally published service doctrine in the sense we know it today. In so far as it worked to any formal doctrine it relied almost solely on NATO doctrine manuals such as *The NATO Tactical Air Doctrine Manual*. This tended to be the underpinning to RAF doctrine, and, although no formal RAF manual existed, there was some published writing available on the subject which provided guidance to those prepared to look. This largely took the form of a individual essays on the general theme of 'air power' in the RAF's magazine *Air Clues* – a publication more familiar to aircrews as being the forum for airing flight safety issues. These essays generally appeared as articles written by the RAF's Director of Defence Studies, or such senior officers or allies as he could persuade to contribute.

There were signs, however, that some within the RAF community (and particularly those who had held the relatively recently instituted Director of Defence Studies post) were increasingly committed to stimulating thinking on air power and to stirring what they had come to see as a somewhat moribund doctrine pot. Although by 1990 this had not progressed as far as the production of a new doctrine manual to replace the 1957 edition of AP1300, the then Director of Defence Studies (RAF), Group Captain (now Air Vice-Marshal) Andrew Vallance did produce a short volume of essays entitled *Air Power: Collected Essays on Doctrine*.[3] It is interesting to note the relative hierarchy in the title – 'Air Power' was quite literally writ large, and the word 'Doctrine' was very much less obvious. Of the eight contributors only three came from the RAF: Vallance himself, one of his predecessors the then Air Commodore Timothy Garden (now Air Marshal Sir Timothy Garden), and Squadron Leader Daulby who was serving at the USAF Academy at Colorado Springs. Daulby himself admitted that he had had only a 'hazy' idea of what doctrine was before he went to Colorado Springs, where he had to learn fast because he was required to teach a course on the subject.

Vallance's publication is revealing both for what it shows us of the generally accepted lines of doctrinal thinking in the RAF at the time, and for what can be gleaned regarding the attitude of the majority of officers in the service towards doctrine. We have already commented on the rather coy reference to doctrine in the title of the work, and this acknowledgement that doctrine was seen as something alien and strange by the RAF at large was present inside as well as outside the covers. The Foreword, written by Air Vice-Marshal 'Sandy' Hunter, the Commandant of the RAF Staff College – in a sense the keeper of the holy grail for the RAF – included the following slightly apologetic justification:

> Most practical officers tend to shy away form any publication which has a word like doctrine in its title. Any honest-to-God operator will regard anything with such a high-flown ring to it as someone else's problem: leave doctrine to the MOD and to the Staff Colleges and let the front line get on with winning the war! ... There are those who see little need for a statement of the basic principles that underpin the employment of air power ... to many, any attempt to set out an air power doctrine is irrelevant or even superfluous. Some see codifying a mixture of principle and practical experience as more likely to create a straitjacket than to make a platform for further evolution. To them, the effect will be to stifle imaginative development, or to restrict room for manoeuvre.

Air Vice-Marshal Hunter went on to argue that laying down doctrine provided the foundation for further thought and a datum by which to measure progress, and that 'far from inhibiting flexibility, air power's matchless characteristic, doctrine provides the springboard from which to enhance it'.[4]

Although it was published in 1990, the collection was compiled before the Gulf crisis erupted, and it therefore delineates and reveals much of the RAF's thinking on air power at the time the Service found itself faced with a potential war. Thus Vallance himself wrote: 'In the West, military doctrine – if it exists at all in a formal sense – usually consists of a set of loosely defined tactical guidelines and regulations, applicable only to a particular type of capability or weapon system.'[5] This was quite true, and, insofar as the RAF was concerned because it had, almost by default, allowed its doctrine to become synonymous with NATO tactical doctrine, it was wedded to concepts of air power which were almost entirely predicated on all out war on the Central Front. It was this mindset, perfectly reasonable in the Cold War context, which had produced aircraft and concepts of operations at the lower levels that were not always best suited to the situation that arose in the Middle East in 1990.

Thus the Tornado F3 had grown out of the requirement for an aircraft to counter long-range Soviet bombers, particularly Fencer and Backfire, penetrating domestic airspace from the north and east to threaten targets in the UK. The assessment was that an air defence variant of the Tornado interdictor-strike aircraft configured to undertake long-range interception duties would be capable of meeting this need, but that it would be outclassed by Warsaw Pact aircraft if it was required to fight in western Europe on the Central Front of NATO in the air-superiority fighter role. At the time such assessments were made the latter threat was seen as coming from the MiG-21 Flogger generation of Soviet aircraft.[6] By the time of the Gulf conflict the threat had moved on apace, and the Tornado F3 was even less capable of matching the latest Russian aircraft available in the Iraqi inventory such as the MiG-29. In particular, apart from its inherent lack of manoeuvrability, the F3 possessed only a limited self-defence capability, which restricted its capacity to operate in a hostile environment where there was a threat either from ground-based SAMs or from sophisticated airborne threats. In the Gulf this significant handicap persuaded the Air Commander that the F3 should not play a forward role in the air-superiority campaign. It was therefore relegated to the role of providing CAPs over the rear areas of Alliance territory, ensuring that any hostile aircraft which 'leaked' through the barrier of USAF and USN F-15s; F-18s and SAMs, would be dealt with effectively before it. That the first RAF aircraft to deploy to the Gulf should have been F3s, probably the aircraft least capable of fulfilling its mission, was in the circumstances more than somewhat ironic. That this was so was the result of two factors, one political and one accidental. The political factor was the need to show solidarity and support both for the threatened Gulf States and for the US, together with the feeling in the British government that the deployment of an obviously 'defensive' aircraft such as the F3 would send the necessary political signal to friends and enemies alike without being seen as unnecessarily provocative, in the way that the deployment of more overtly offensive aircraft might be. The second factor was the presence in Cyprus of two F3 squadrons. The squadrons were in Cyprus for an armament practice camp, and the fact that there were two squadrons was entirely due to the crisis erupting just at the point when the two Squadrons were due to change over, thus ensuring that two squadrons could be deployed rapidly and not one. Because they were already engaged in a long-planned deployment away from their home base, the two squadrons were in the unusual position for the F3 force of being in some measure in deployable mode, with engineering and logistic support available and in a reasonably readily transportable form.

The deployment of RAF Jaguars followed similar reasoning. As already mentioned, the Jaguar squadrons did have a formal commitment to deploy away from their home base at Coltishall in support of the ACE Mobile Force on the Northern Flank. This took the form of regular exercise deployments to Tirstrup Air Base in Denmark or Bardufoss in Norway. This meant not only that the Jaguar squadrons were practised in such deployments, but that they had basic provision to fulfil this role such as 'fly-away packs', that is, ready-prepared logistical pack-ups to support deployment. Even so, such exercise deployments were made to relatively well-found bases in NATO countries, not to the much more spartan airfield environment to be found in much of the Middle East. Nevertheless, the Jaguars were the first 'offensive' aircraft type deployed by the RAF during the crisis, and this was largely because at the time, with Iraqi forces thought to be poised on the Saudi border, deployment was 'timescale critical' which meant that reasonably rapid deployment capability was essential. In this situation, 'no other aircraft in the RAF's inventory was so well prepared for immediate deployment' as the Jaguar, and this was the main criteria behind its selection rather than through any 'detailed consideration of their potential military contribution'.[7] Indeed, the initial August 1990 decision to deploy the Jaguars to Oman was taken almost entirely on political rather than military grounds, as the Omanis needed reassurance and also operated the Jaguar. They would redeploy from Oman to Bahrain later in the autumn in order to reduce potential sortie times and improve operational efficiency.

Once the initial deployment of Tornado F3s and Jaguars to Saudi Arabia and Oman had taken place in response to the immediate threat, the senior leadership both in the Ministry of Defence (MoD) and in the chain of command began to consider what effective contribution the RAF could make to any coalition defensive effort designed to protect Saudi Arabia from further Iraqi aggression. By this time, after an early contretemps with the United States over rules of engagement, the Tornado F3s had settled into a routine of flying Combat Air Patrols, which was to continue almost unbroken until the end of hostilities. Once hostilities started in January, the F3s took the role of providing the rearward CAPs over Saudi designed to protect high value airborne assets, particularly the AWACs (Airborne Warning and Control System) and tankers, and to intercept any Iraqi attack aircraft which had penetrated the forward US F-115 and F-18 patrols operating inside

Iraqi airspace. Whilst the F3s' performance of this task was useful in freeing the more capable USAF assets to operate further forward it did not demonstrate a particularly effective or up to date capability to the world. Likewise, the small detachment of Jaguar aircraft did not significantly add to the massive ground attack capabilities available to the coalition. It was limited to daytime operation, and, as we shall see, its weapons options, at least at first, were fairly limited. As the USAF had many aircraft, such as the F-16s and A-10s, capable of performing such daytime roles as well as if not better than the Jaguar, the RAF's contribution did not, on paper at least, look particularly impressive, however professional the operators themselves might be.

The RAF was therefore looking to provide some more effective contribution to the coalition, and the RAF's in theatre commander, at the time Air Vice-Marshal 'Sandy' Wilson, was in discussion with the staff of the Joint Force Air Component Commander, General Horner, as to what that might be.[8] The capabilities which the massive US air forces in theatre most conspicuously lacked were any specialized capability for attacking airfields as part of an offensive counter-air (OCA) campaign, and tactical reconnaissance aircraft. At an early meeting with Horner's deputy, Brigadier-General Olsen, the Americans had indicated to Wilson that they would welcome further attack assets to support interdiction missions, a role specifically assigned to the GR1 in the context of NATO's Central Front. Wilson had also told Horner that Tornado GR1s carrying JP233 airfield-attack munitions could bring a significant enhancement in capability to the coalition, and it was not long before Horner took the hint and indicated back to Wilson that GR1s would be considered a very welcome addition to the force; a message which Wilson quickly relayed to London. At least to senior RAF circles such a message was neither unexpected nor unwelcome. Assessments prepared by the Air Staff as the crisis broke had rapidly concluded that the GR1 was the most capable aircraft in the RAF inventory, with an unmatched OCA night or day capability, and, not unimportantly, commonality with the Royal Saudi Air Force (RSAF), which also operated the aircraft. With regard to the latter, it was implicit that an RAF GR1 presence would bolster and improve RSAF performance.

The decision to deploy Tornado GR1s did not prove an easy one for the British government, despite the developing view in RAF circles that it was the aircraft most likely to make a significant contribution. Politically, at least early in the crisis, a GR1 deployment had distinct disadvantages. The Secretary of State for Defence had announced that the military deployments to the Gulf were 'purely defensive', and the despatch of such a capable offensive aircraft could appear to be at odds with such a line. In the Gulf the Saudi government had its own political presentational problems and was likewise stressing both the

Islamic contributions to the coalition and its defensive nature. The Chiefs of Staff recognized these presentational problems and in mid-August postponed any decision until after a visit to the Gulf by the Vice-Chief of Defence Staff (VCDS), General Sir Richard Vincent, and the Minister for Defence Procurement, Alan Clark. In the event the visit produced further strong support for deployment. Clark himself returned and immediately recommended it to Prime Minister Margaret Thatcher. He had been influenced by the views of senior British military and diplomatic figures in the Gulf who believed that unless Britain made a more substantial and effective military contribution UK representation in the senior counsels of the coalition would be severely limited. In Britain there was still political reluctance to deploy anything but 'defensive' aircraft, and there was some talk of compromises involving 'half-way' deployment of GR1s to RAF Akrotiri on Cyprus, with either an onward move to theatre if hostilities broke out, or the use of Akrotiri itself as an operating base. The military opposition to such half-heartedness was robust, and further pressure was applied when both the VCDS and the Joint Commander, Air Chief Marshal Hine, recommended deployment, and recorded strong endorsement from both USAF and RSAF circles in theatre.

Eventually, such concerted pressure overcame the remaining political opposition in London and the first deployment was ordered on 23 August 1990. It was to be followed by successive additions to the original deployment, the last taking place on the eve of war. The final deployment included an element of Tornado GR1As, which were equipped and trained for the reconnaissance role.

As the elder brother of the Tornado F3, the Tornado GR1 interdictor/strike aircraft was also a child of the Cold War. The original Tornado concept of operations called for an interdictor strike aircraft to replace the Vulcans, Buccaneers and Canberras in RAF service. It was expected that the aircraft would operate largely at night or in bad weather and that penetration of enemy territory, weapon delivery and escape would all take place at high speed and very low level using the aircraft's advanced terrain following radar to maintain mean operating heights below 100 feet by day and 200 feet by night. For weapon delivery the preferred methods were low-level laydown or loft attacks. Although dive attacks at an angle of 30 degrees were included in the original concept of operations, much greater stress was laid on low-level straight and level options for both visual and blind attacks. The original concept of operations was also quite specific in discussing the aircraft's role and tactics in the context of a major conventional war in Europe against the Warsaw Pact. The aircraft's primary task was seen as counter-air attacks at low level on Warsaw Pact airfields using JP233 munitions, together with interdiction of Warsaw Pact forces moving against NATO.[9] The JP233 munition had been specifically designed for use against Warsaw Pact airfields and this assumed low-level high-speed delivery to be essential.[10] The method of operation of the weapon therefore effectively precluded any means of delivery except low-level overflight of the target airfield. Two other important considerations in the concept of operations were that the aircraft would not normally operate from forward operating bases because of the requirement for dedicated engineering and logistical support, and that aircraft assigned to Supreme Allied Commander Europe (SACEUR) in the attack role would not normally be dependent on Air-to-Air Refuelling (AAR), which it was thought would be largely occupied supporting air defence and maritime attack forces. Both these considerations would impinge to some degree on Tornado operations in Op Granby. In the first place, because it meant that to a degree the logistical support of the aircraft had to be improvised, and in the second place because crews in RAF Germany, which provided a large contingent of GR1 aircrew, were not qualified in AAR Refuelling and had to qualify or renew their currency either before deploying or in their in-theatre work up.

This original concept of operations did not alter significantly before the Gulf War, and the RAF Tornado squadrons had trained as they expected to fight on the Central Front, almost exclusively at low level. Furthermore, with an unusual weapon such as JP233 there was no real opportunity for crews to drop live weapons, nor was any significant or widespread training undertaken before the crisis with dummy JP233 rounds, which in any case were in short supply.

The Tornado F3, Jaguar and GR1/1A were therefore the three principal combat aircraft types the RAF had in theatre by the time hostilities started on 17 January 1991. There were in addition maritime patrol aircraft, tankers, transport aircraft and helicopters, but their operations, although effective, are outside the scope of this chapter. As we have seen, the initial deployments were very largely the result of political factors, including the need to deploy aircraft into theatre quickly, and the desire to avoid presentational errors which could be interpreted or manipulated in provocative or escalatory ways. Once more serious consideration was given to the military use to which the aircraft might actually be put, the problems of deploying 'Cold War warriors' into a potential conventional hot war in a different environment from NATO's Central Front began to be revealed. We have already seen that the severe operational limitations of the Tornado F3, because of its original envisaged role in the Air Defence of the United Kingdom against long-range Soviet bombers, did not allow it to operate against the more modern air-superiority threat it would meet over Iraq. There were similar problems with the training, doctrine and equipment of the two attack aircraft types in theatre. In the cases of the Jaguar and the

Tornado, the principal question which emerged was whether or not to operate at very low level in accordance with accepted RAF doctrine and training.

The problem gained attention in the Jaguar force rather earlier than it did in the GR1 force.[11] The Jaguars were likely to be tasked with attack of ground targets including artillery sites and possibly armoured formations. The principal weapon types available were 1000-pound bombs, whether retarded, free-fall or laser-guided, and the BL-755 cluster munition. The latter was designed for purely low-level delivery, and the former normally delivered from low level, shallow (3 to 5 degree) dive passes or from loft manoeuvres. In October and November the staff in the Joint Headquarters in the UK were pointing to the abundance of Iraqi low-level anti-aircraft defences and the problem this posed for the Jaguars in delivering munitions by overflying targets at low level. There was concern that in these circumstances casualties to the Jaguars would prove heavy, whereas above 10,000 feet the risk from anti-aircraft artillery or infra-red SAMs was considered minimal. If, however, the aircraft went to medium level it immediately raised questions as to their effectiveness. Delivery of 1,000-pound bombs from medium level produced large aiming errors, which made the weapon unsuitable against the sort of dispersed or dug-in targets which the Jaguars may well be attacking. The use of laser-guided bombs was considered but ruled out because it would have necessitated the deployment of designating aircraft, namely Buccaneers. This had already been ruled out because it was felt that to deploy another, relatively old, aircraft type to theatre would create unacceptable logistical and maintenance problems, and also because there was believed to be a severe problem with ramp space on airfields in theatre, although this later proved not to be such a problem as had been imagined. Thoughts then turned to modifying or acquiring weapons for medium-level delivery – in the former case adapting BL-755, and in the latter acquiring Maverick anti-armour missiles. In the end both proved impracticable in the time available, which left the RAF with a dilemma in that Joint Headquarters still believed the threat to the Jaguars from Iraqi defences was unacceptably high, but equally had little confidence in the effectiveness of existing weapons from medium altitude. Planning and most, though not all, training therefore continued on the assumption that operations would be at low level. Attempts to obtain a suitable weapon in the form of US CBU-87 cluster bombs suitable for medium-level delivery fell victim to bureaucratic mix-ups, in part stemming from the gross overload of many of the desk officers in the organizations progressing them. These were only untangled at the last possible moment.

In the meantime with war now imminent the question of how the

Jaguars would fight could not be postponed any longer, and the decision was delegated to the Jaguar detachment commander in the Gulf. He opted for delivery from medium level, reasoning that, with the likely weapon configurations and fuel loads from Bahrain, the most likely operational area for the Jaguars would be Kuwait itself, where there were known to be very heaviest concentrations of anti-aircraft artillery (AAA) around the deployed Iraqi forces. By moving to medium level the threat from small arms, light AAA, and infra-red-guided surface-to-air missiles (SAMs) would be low, whilst the threat from larger radar-guided SAMs and Iraqi air defence aircraft could be countered by Allied assets such as Wild Weasel, EF111 Ravens and air superiority fighters.

However, the problems over the CBU-87's procurement meant that, although they were deployed operationally by Jaguars during the war, there were problems with software and carriage which limited the weapon's effectiveness. Similar problems affected the Jaguar detachment over another additional task and an associated new weapon which it was required to master, despite the novelty of the role and the weapons. The task was anti-shipping operations, specifically against the threat to coalition naval forces posed by Iraqi fast patrol boats inside the Gulf. The weapon was the Canadian produced CRV-7 rocket system. There were again delays and misunderstandings in the procurement of the weapon and problems concerning its integration with the aircraft's weapon aiming system, which meant it did not prove particularly successful on the occasions it was used against naval targets, but modifications to the software later in the campaign resulted in great improvements in accuracy, and it was subsequently used with great effect against Iraqi artillery positions in Kuwait.

There is little doubt that the Jaguar detachment performed very well during the course of the war, but they were not always best served by the chain of command or the bureaucracy, even though many of the failings in headquarters and the ministry can be traced to the frantic efforts of harassed individuals trying to rectify too many shortcomings simultaneously. The mere fact that the final decision over the way the war was to be fought was made by the detachment commander on the eve of war is indicative of this. There can be little doubt that he made the right decision – the Jaguar detachment operated throughout the war without losing a single aircraft. In part, the problems which followed from the move to medium level were due to the relative inflexibility of Cold War doctrine, and in particular the associated weapons with which the squadrons had trained. Attempts to procure suitable weapons, rush them into service, integrate them with the aircraft systems and give the crews on the job training were perhaps unsurprisingly not entirely successful, although the degree of success attained by the force later was undoubtedly higher than might have been the case had not the quality of the aircrews been so high. That is a tribute to the quality of both their flying training and their dedication, but the lesson is nevertheless that, although highly motivated and well-trained aircrew can overcome some shortcomings in doctrine and equipment, they can never be universally successful.

The GR1 force had the same low-level doctrine as the Jaguars, but its problems, although similar, were not exactly the same.[12] Whereas the Jaguars were going to be operating by day over Kuwait where the ground-based defences were heavily concentrated, it was thought the GR1s would be operating by day and at night, and, initially at least, over Iraq, where there may be heavy defences at the targets, mostly airfields, but where evasive routing and electronic counter-measures (ECM) support would give greater protection. In fact, if the RAF was to perform its expected role of offensive counter-air using JP233 against Iraqi airfields, which of course it had 'sold' heavily to the Joint Force Air Component Commander (JFACC), then it had no choice but to begin the campaign at low level, as JP233 required low-level overflight of the target. The option of medium-level bombing by night was simply a non-starter. Once the war started, two factors combined to persuade the RAF's air commander (Air Vice-Marshal Wratten), that the GR1s should move to medium level. The first was the poor response of the Iraqi Air Force, which largely ceased to fly after the first few days. There was little point in continuing a campaign designed to reduce the sortie generation rate of an opposing air force which showed little sign of generating significant activity. The second was the relatively heavy rate of loss suffered by the GR1s in the early days of the war. There was critical press comment at the time, to the effect that JP233 missions were proving too costly. As a matter of fact, only one aircraft carrying JP233 was lost, and that may have been to causes other than the defences. Nevertheless, the facts were that most US aircraft were flying at medium altitude, that there was almost no threat from Iraqi fighters, and that taking further losses in support of an OCA campaign which now appeared increasingly unnecessary, was insupportable. It is difficult to know whether the Iraqi Air Force (IAF) would have reacted with more vigour had their airfields been left unmolested. Those who argue that the JP233 attacks were a waste of time tend to ignore the fact that Iraqi reaction was unpredictable, and that even though the USAF's air-superiority fighters proved equal to the threat, it was still to their advantage to limit the rate at which the IAF could react to attacks. Air Vice-Marshal Wratten was certainly willing to alter his tactics when he thought it appropriate, as when he lost an aircraft in a daylight GR1 attack on the first morning and promptly decided that he would not for the time being operate the aircraft by day.

The problem over moving to medium level lay not in making the decision, which once the facts became clear was relatively easy. The problem lay, as with the Jaguar force, in the relative ineffectiveness of the GR1s when operating from medium level. The crews had not trained to drop 1,000-pound free-fall bombs in level flight from medium altitude, and aircraft systems were not optimized to do so and the bomb ballistics were not known to the force. The accuracy of such attacks in late January was therefore poor, and because of this the range of targets which could be attacked at all was fairly limited. This was where the early decision not to deploy a laser-designation capability in the form of the Buccaneers now came home to roost. As already indicated the reasoning behind this decision was to avoid deploying another aircraft type into theatre, with all the associated logistical and maintenance penalties. At the time the decision was taken there were not only concerns over ramp space on gulf airfields, but also the prevalent view that the Saudis were becoming anxious at the large numbers of Western military personnel flowing into the country. The Secretary of State himself had also expressed irritation at the ever spiralling numbers of military personnel being sent to theatre. Air Vice-Marshal Wilson had also obtained an assurance from General Horner that USAF F-15s would act as designators for RAF aircraft if necessary. In the event, this latter promise was undermined by the need to deploy the F-15s in the largely nugatory Scud-hunting campaign which unexpectedly absorbed so much USAF effort. While these concerns all seemed reasonable at the time they were taken, the early course of the war soon exposed them as mistaken. There followed some rapid action on the part of the RAF to rectify the situation and get a laser designation capability and associated weapons into theatre. This took the form of deploying Buccaneers, which arrived at the end of January, and also two experimental TIALD (Thermal Imaging and Laser Designator) pods and four TIALD capable Tornados which deployed on 6 February. After a short in-theatre work-up, both types commenced operational designating for the Tornado force. It was fortunate that the Assistant Chief of Air Staff had ruled in the late autumn that urgent development work to get the two TIALD pods operational should go ahead, despite the doubts of some in the MoD that they could be ready in time.

Whilst the Buccaneers and TIALD pods were in theatre and operational from February, in the interim the RAF was faced with the potential embarrassment of operating from medium level to no great effect. As the political background to the campaign within the MoD was an ongoing defence review designed to identify the cuts to be made in accordance with the expected 'peace dividend', there was accordingly some pressure from Whitehall because of concerns that, should the campaign come to an unexpectedly rapid close, the RAF would not have been seen to have performed effectively, with possible deleterious effects on future budgets. At least one senior officer suggested a return to low-level attacks, which was opposed by the Air Commander. Another senior representative from the RAF's Central Trials and Tactics Organisation visited the Gulf with a suggested profile for future attacks that involved making steep-angle dive attacks from medium altitude. At a meeting of detachment commanders this proposal received short shrift, and when one detachment commander flew the profile against the Iraqi defences he rapidly concluded that it was an unhealthy suggestion, as the pull out from the dive was made well within the envelope of the AAA and IR SAMs. Those back in the UK did not press the issue. It was effectively resolved when the laser designation capability arrived in theatre and became operational. In the latter part of the campaign the Tornado GR1 force again made an effective contribution with the inestimable assistance of the venerable Buccaneers, which despite their age, proved to have one of the best serviceability records of any aircraft in the conflict.

The conclusions we may reach on the Tornado force mirror those of the Jaguars, namely that training in peace as you intend to fight in war may sound sensible, but may not always prove enough when circumstances turn out differently from those anticipated. Leaving aside such problems as the lack of AAR currency in RAF Germany, there were other shortcomings in training which were rooted in attempts to keep training costs to a minimum. Thus, the majority of crews before they commenced their pre-war work up would never have flown their aircraft at the limits of performance whilst at the sorts of weights which a full weapon and fuel load imposed. Only trials crews had ever dropped JP233 in anger, and some crews were disconcerted to discover that as the weapon canisters unloaded over the Iraqi airfields the flash of the munitions rendered them extremely conspicuous for a number of seconds. It would be better to know such things in advance. In the case of the Tornado force, their performance like that of the Jaguars, proved mixed at first, but much improved later. As might be expected, the Buccaneer force, which was the one element of the attack force which had trained as it fought, proved themselves capable, professional and effective, despite the age of their aircraft. The use of the two development TIALD pods also proved far more effective than perhaps anyone should have expected for a system rushed into operation. The least effective of the RAF aircraft considered here were the F3s, and this was because the most serious shortcomings of the aircraft which limited its effectiveness were incapable of resolution in the timescale available. This did not prove the case with the GR1s or the Jaguars. Once war comes doctrinal flexibility, coupled with aircraft and weapons systems which allow some variation in approach, together with the overall professional flying skills of the crews are likely to prove essential.

One result of the Gulf War was to encourage the moves towards a new approach to doctrine which had begun to emerge from the office of the Director of Defence Studies in the late 1980s. Shortly after the war, the Director of Defence Studies (RAF) produced an entirely new doctrine manual for the first time in over 30 years, and it has been regularly updated in the years since.[13] Doctrine is now a more readily accepted part of RAF training, and although there will always be some officers who are suspicious of it, its importance in underpinning an officer's ability to understand and think about air power is now more widely understood than it was a decade ago.

NOTES

1. Quoted in Nigel Walpole, 'Battle Management in Operational Training', *Journal of the Royal Air Force Historical Society*, No. 20 (1999), p. 50.
2. British Defence Doctrine; British Air Power Doctrine; British Maritime Doctrine; and British Military Doctrine.
3. A. G. B. Vallance, *Air Power: Collected Essays on Doctrine* (HMSO, London, 1990) p. 18.
4. Ibid., pp. xi–xii.
5. Ibid., p. 108.
6. Air Force Board Standing Committee Paper (75)18, MRCA ADV – Air Defence Studies.
7. S. Ritchie, draft Air Historical Branch monograph on Operation Granby: Jaguar Operations, p. 2
8. The following paragraphs are largely based on S. Cox's draft Air Historical Branch monograph on Operation Granby: Tornado GR1 operations.
9. D/DDOPS(S)(RAF)7/18 Tornado GR1 Concept of Operations (Issue One, July 1977).
10. Air Force Board Standing Committee Paper (75)2, An Advanced Airfield Attack Weapon.
11. The following paragraph is based on S. Ritchie's AHB monograph on Jaguar operations and AHB oral history interviews with participants.
12. The following paragraphs are based on S. Cox's AHB monograph on Tornado operations and on AHB interviews with participants.
13. AP 3000. The current edition is the third, and is entitled British Air Power Doctrine.

PART IV:

AIR POWER IN
REGIONAL CONFLICT

15

Solidifying The Foundation: Vietnam's Impact on the Basic Doctrine of the US Air Force

Marc Clodfelter

In 1956, the US Air Force's Strategic Air Command (SAC) stood poised to unleash nuclear holocaust against the Soviet Union. General Curtis E. LeMay had moulded SAC into the world's most awesome aerial strike force, and he had no qualms about using that instrument to support a policy of 'massive retaliation'. 'The United States is committed to a policy of peace', he told his assembled commanders at Wright Patterson Air Force Base in January. 'That is, our military power will be utilized primarily to prevent aggression. However, if war cannot be prevented on terms acceptable to the United States, the Air Force must insure that we win – no matter how it starts or how hollow the victory might be.'[1]

Less than a year before, the Air Force had formally articulated this notion of victory through air power in its official doctrine. The new service had taken six years before publishing its first 'basic doctrine' manual in April 1953. The April 1955 update elaborated on air power's perceived decisiveness across the broad spectrum of conflict:

> Of the various types of military forces, those which conduct air operations are most capable of *decisive* results. This pre-eminence accrues to them because of their versatility – with or without armed conflict – and because their capabilities permit them to be employed wherever necessary. They provide the dominant military means of exercising the initiative and gaining decisions in *all* forms of international relations, including full peace, cold war, limited wars of *all* types, and total war.[2]

The Air Force supplemented its Basic Doctrine Manual with Manual 1-8, 'Strategic Air Operations', dated 1 May 1954. In that document, Air Force writers outlined *how* bombing would achieve national objectives. Harking back to the teachings of the Air Corps Tactical School and perceived lessons from the Second World War, Manual 1-8 gave scant attention to the recent example of the Korean War. It defined strategic air operations as attacks 'designed to disrupt an enemy nation to the extent that its will and capability to resist are broken', and noted that such operations would focus 'directly on the nation itself', not on its deployed armed forces. The authors of 1-8 also made a specific reference to the 'industrial web theory' that had guided pre-Second World War planning: 'Somewhere within the structure of the hostile nation exist sensitive elements, the destruction or neutralization of which will best create the breakdown and loss of the will of that nation to further resist ... The fabric of modern nations is such a complete interweaving of major single elements that the elimination of one of them would cause the collapse of the national structure insofar as integrated effort is concerned.' The Manual stated that the destruction of petroleum or transportation systems would be most likely to tear apart the 'fabric' of an enemy state.[3] The document remained current until its revision in December 1965.

By that time, the Rolling Thunder air offensive against North Vietnam had been ongoing for almost ten months. The thinking of the air chiefs regarding how best to attack the North was consistent with the doctrine espoused during the previous decade – and that thinking remained constant after the war. Despite the eight-year agony of the US military effort in Vietnam – which included the failure of the longest air campaign in US history – the US Air Force's basic doctrine that emerged from the war was virtually identical to that developed before the conflict – and those concepts still guide the service today. The emphasis remains on independently winning a war by bombing strategic centres, manifested most recently by Operation Allied Force in Serbia. The ossification of this belief owes much to perceptions that solidified as a result of Vietnam.

In the summer of 1965, shortly after retiring as Air Force Chief of Staff, Curt LeMay published his memoirs. In that volume, he offered his thoughts about how to handle the North Vietnamese in a phrase that has become a hallmark for the notion of unrestrained air power. 'My solution to the problem', he said, 'would be to tell them frankly that they've got to draw in their horns and stop their aggression, or we're going to bomb them back into the Stone Age.'[4] Despite the bluntness of its tenor, LeMay's plea was not a call for widespread civilian destruction. Instead, he aimed to afflict his enemy with exactly the conditions he had stated – the absence of the perceived technological essentials for modern life. He elaborated: 'The military task confronting us is to make it so expensive for the North Vietnamese that they will stop their aggression against South Viet Nam and Laos. If we make it too expensive for them, they *will* stop. They don't want to lose everything they have.'[5]

During his last year as Chief of Staff, LeMay had directed the development of a bombing plan for North Vietnam. The scheme consisted of 94 targets, including 82 fixed sites and 12 transportation lines, which LeMay and his planners considered the essential components of the North's war-making capability.[6] Realizing that the essence of the North's capacity to fight came from Soviet and Chinese sources, they recommended mining Haiphong harbour in addition to attacking oil-storage complexes and road and rail networks. Yet LeMay had no intention of letting the North's nascent industrial capability escape punishment. His planners slated the Thai Nguyen steel mill, the Hanoi machine tool plant, and three electric power plants for destruction. 'What you must do with those characters is convince them that if they continue their aggression, they will have to pay an economic penalty which they cannot afford', he reasoned.[7] LeMay aimed to make the North Vietnamese pay that penalty in short order. Through a 'severe' application of air power, he would destroy the 94 targets in 16 days.[8]

LeMay and his cohorts never got the chance to conduct a 'sudden, sharp knock' bombing effort against North Vietnam, but the Rolling Thunder air campaign that evolved during more than three years of Lyndon Johnson's presidency ultimately attacked all 94 targets – and more than 300 others. The categories of targets chosen – transportation, oil, electric power, industry – matched those recommended by Air Force doctrine. Mission directives continually stated that Rolling Thunder aimed to wreck North Vietnam's capability and will to support the Viet Cong insurgency in the South. Yet bombing's impact on the communist war effort was marginal. Air commanders attributed that lack of success to the incremental nature of the air campaign and President Johnson's extensive restrictions on it, rather than on faulty doctrinal underpinnings. 'We should lift these restrictions and then we would get results', LeMay's successor as Air Force Chief of Staff, General John McConnell, told President Johnson in 1966.[9]

To McConnell and other air leaders, unfettered Air Force doctrine offered the best guide for achieving victory. They knew the value of transportation and industry to their own nation's warfighting capability, plus they knew that the manufacture and distribution of goods were essential elements of American society. They assumed that any opponent would place a high premium on preserving what they perceived not only as necessary components for modern war but also as fundamental features of twentieth-century social order. In their eyes, the overall lack of technological sophistication only increased the value of the North's miniscule industry – and they could threaten Hanoi with the prospect of a rapid return to 'Stone Age' conditions. They contended that the destruction of transportation and industry would disrupt the Northern economy to such a degree that Hanoi could no longer support the Viet Cong. The Joint Chiefs argued in August 1965 to Secretary of Defense Robert McNamara: 'Stepped-up interdiction efforts against DRV [Democratic Republic of (North) Vietnam] target systems would significantly affect industrial and commercial activity in the DRV and place in serious jeopardy the viability of the non-agricultural sector of the North Vietnamese economy.'[10] Such logic persisted throughout Rolling Thunder.

Not until 1972 did air commanders see an application of air power that seemed to suit the Air Force's doctrinal tenets. President Richard Nixon's two 'Linebacker' bombing campaigns – the first from 8 May to 23 October, and the second from 18 to 29 December – severely damaged North Vietnam's Easter Offensive and spurred the US withdrawal from the war. Indeed, Linebacker II, the so-called 'Christmas bombings', was a predominantly B-52 offensive against key transportation links and storage facilities in Hanoi and Haiphong. The raids contributed to the resumption of negotiations in Paris between Henry Kissinger and Le Duc Tho, and those talks produced a settlement that ended US involvement in the conflict.

Many air chiefs looked at Linebacker II and the negotiated settlement as a cause-and-effect relationship – the peace accord occurred less than a month after the bombing campaign ended.[11] They thus viewed Linebacker II as a vindication of Air Force doctrine, and insisted that such an operation in the spring of 1965 would have ended the war then. When asked in July 1986 if the United States could have won in Vietnam, retired General LeMay was quick to answer: 'In any two-week period you want to mention.'[12]

This view of LeMay and others fails to acknowledge that the war's character and conduct were not constants – the type of conflict that the communist armies fought during the Rolling Thunder era was not the same as that waged during the Linebacker campaigns. The main enemy in the South from 1964 to the 1968 Tet Offensive was not the North Vietnamese but the Viet Cong, which totalled roughly 245,000 men in a 300,000-man enemy force five months before Tet (the remaining 55,000 troops were from the North Vietnamese Army).[13] The entire force waged an infrequent guerrilla war and fought an average of *one* day in *30*. Thus, its supply needs from sources outside of South Vietnam were minimal – only 34 tons a day, which equated to *seven* two-and-a-half-ton truckloads of supplies.[14] Unless it had a distinct advantage, the communist army simply refused to fight.

The situation had changed dramatically in 1972. By then, the 1968 Tet Offensive had decimated the leadership cadres of the Viet Cong, and the 12-division force that attacked South Vietnam in the Easter

Offensive consisted almost exclusively of North Vietnamese Army (NVA) troops. Large numbers of T-54 tanks and 130mm artillery backed that advance. The fast-paced, conventional offensive demanded enormous quantities of fuel and ammunition to sustain it, and made air power's attacks on lines of transportation and oil-storage areas enormously successful; mining Haiphong harbour also significantly damaged the North Vietnamese logistical effort. In addition, the concentrated attacks of fighter aircraft and B-52s in *South* Vietnam wreaked havoc upon the advancing echelons of North Vietnamese. By the time of Linebacker II in December, the continual pummelling of Northern forces, and the inability to resupply them, jeopardized the NVA's ability to fight at all. Northern General Tran Van Tra, the commander of communist troops in the southern half of South Vietnam, later recalled: 'Our cadres and men were fatigued, we had not had time to make up for our losses, all units were in disarray, there was a lack of manpower, and there were shortages of food and ammunition ... The troops were no longer capable of fighting.'[15]

In sum, Vietnam consisted of two very different types of conflicts fought at different times by different enemies, and air power's ability to achieve success varied in direct relation to the type of war being waged and who was doing the bulk of the fighting. However, many air leaders failed to see the distinctions, and deemed the doctrine that had guided the service through the conflict appropriate for the mission at hand. As a result, the fundamental aspects of that doctrine did not change following the war. To many Air Force generals in the aftermath of Vietnam, the 20-year-old proposition that strategic air power could achieve 'decisive results' as the 'dominant military means' in 'all forms of international relations' remained the word of truth.

Air leaders after Vietnam did, however, recognize that the service doctrine for providing air support to ground forces had been lacking. Poor co-ordination had plagued many of the joint efforts by Air Force and Army units in South Vietnam, partly as a result of a pre-war 'tactical' air doctrine that focused on the delivery of tactical nuclear weapons in the event of war with the Soviet Union. Accordingly, Air Force officers assigned to Tactical Air Command during the decade following Vietnam met with their counterparts from the US Army's Training and Doctrine Command and created 'Airland Battle' doctrine.[16] Like the earlier tactical doctrine, the focus of Airland Battle remained the potential Soviet enemy, poised for a thrust into western Europe. The key differences from the earlier model were twofold: first, the emphasis was on using air power to deliver *conventional* munitions; and second, the doctrine stressed coordination measures between air and ground commanders. The pre-Vietnam tactical doctrine did not elaborate on such procedures, because they were deemed largely superfluous in a war that would be decided by missiles and mega tonnage.

While an increased focus on tactical air operations occurred in the post-Vietnam Air Force, the belief that strategic air power was the key to military success continued to dominate service doctrine. Air Force Manual 1-1's 1979 edition contained 75 pages filled with cartoon-like graphics, quotations and illustrations of famous aircraft, as well as air power notions that might have appeared in a version from the 1950s. Dubbed a 'comic book' by critics,[17] the manual placed 'strategic aerospace offence' first in a list of service missions. The 1984 edition repeated that mantra. Titled 'Basic *Aerospace* Doctrine', the new term that blended the notions of air and space power, the 1984 manual removed the graphics and slimmed down to 43 pages. Harking back to its 30-year-old predecessor, the manual noted that 'aerospace forces may conduct strategic aerospace offence actions, *at all levels of conflict*, through the systematic application of force to a selected series of vital targets'.[18] Those targets included 'concentrations of uncommitted elements of enemy armed forces, strategic weapons systems, command centres, communication facilities, manufacturing systems, sources of raw material, critical material stockpiles, power systems, transportation systems, and key agricultural areas'.[19] Six of the ten categories were components of a nation's industrial apparatus, while three were components of its military establishment. The conviction that the manufacture and distribution of goods were the keys to warfighting capability and will remained firmly planted as a cornerstone of Air Force thinking.

The 1984 manual made few references to Vietnam. Colonel Thomas Fabyanic, who had directed the Air Force's new Aerospace Research Institute at Maxwell Air Force Base, reviewed the 1984 edition for the Air Force Assistant Vice Chief of Staff. Fabyanic remarked that 'this manual, like its predecessor, is written as if Vietnam never occurred'.[20] The references to the war that did appear were oblique. For instance, the manual quoted Italian Air Marshal Giulio Douhet on the need for unbridled air power as a key to its successful application: 'The employment of land, sea, and air forces in time of war should be directed towards one single aim: VICTORY ... The commander[s] of the Army, Navy, and Air Force should be given the greatest freedom of action in their respective spheres.'[21] Yet once again, the strategic air power that air leaders envisioned for a future conflict was of the nuclear variety, and in fact to many in the service the word 'strategic' equated to 'nuclear'. While that connection may not have disturbed most officers, it upset one in particular, and he determined to focus his efforts on planning for a strategic air campaign using conventional ordnance against an enemy other than the Soviet Union.

That individual was Air Force Colonel John Warden, a veteran of

211 missions in Vietnam as a forward air controller. In 1986, while a student at the National War College, Warden had written *The Air Campaign: Planning for Combat*, a guide for designing an air campaign based on historical examples and Clausewitzian logic. He concluded that the key to a successful air campaign was to target what Clausewitz called 'centres of gravity' – the essential components of an enemy state. Chief among those, Warden argued, was command. 'Command is a true centre of gravity and worth attack in any circumstance in which it can be reached', he observed.[22]

In elaborating on his idea, Warden revealed that his emphasis on targeting leadership related directly to the notion of 'vital centres' that had been the hallmark of Air Force doctrine since its inception. He contended that an enemy nation's centre of gravity consisted of five concentric, strategic rings. Warden placed leadership, which he deemed the essence of an enemy's war effort, in the centre ring. Surrounding this core was a second ring containing key production facilities, the most important of which were electricity and oil. Next came a third ring of infrastructure consisting primarily of the means of transportation and communication. The civilian populace comprised the fourth ring. While noting that air power should not be used to target an enemy population directly, Warden also insisted, 'It's important that people [in the enemy nation] understand that a war is going on, and they put some pressure on their leadership to stop the war.'[23] Surrounding the band of population was a fifth ring of fielded military forces. Warden maintained that fielded forces should not be the focal point of an air campaign, because those forces served only to shield the crux of an enemy's war effort, the internal rings, which contained the vital targets.[24] He noted: 'If a state's essential industries (or, if it has no industry of its own, its access to external sources) are destroyed, life itself becomes difficult, and the state becomes incapable of employing modern weapons and must make concessions.'[25] A member of the Air Corps Tactical School faculty speaking 60 years earlier would have provided exactly that rationale to explain the industrial web theory.

Warden's vision guided air-campaign planning for the first large-scale use of US air power since Vietnam, Operation Desert Storm. In the summer of 1990, he served as the deputy director of 'Checkmate', the air staff's Pentagon office devoted to countering a potential enemy threat. Until 1989, Checkmate had focused on thwarting potential Soviet aggression, but after the collapse of the Soviet Union Warden had nudged the office to turn its attention to fighting conventional war against non-nuclear opponents. As a result of his guidance, he received the nod to head an ad hoc joint staff working group that hammered out the concept for an air campaign against Iraq. His five-ring model became the basis for the 'Instant Thunder' air offensive designed – in direct contrast to its 'rolling' counterpart from Vietnam – to achieve success in short order.

Instant Thunder exuded the principles of Air Force doctrine. The main targets of the first phase of the campaign were transportation and communication facilities, electric-power transformers and generators, oil-production installations, and nuclear, chemical and biological warfare plants. Eliminating these targets, would, Warden believed, sever Saddam Hussein's ability to control the Iraqi war effort – much like the Second World War air commanders had thought that cutting Germany's 'industrial web' would wreck the Nazi capability to fight. Destroying those targets might also affect the will of the Iraqi populace to support Saddam. Air Force Lieutenant-General Charles Horner, who commanded the Instant Thunder assault, stated that he scheduled the middle-of-the-night raids against Baghdad targets to remind Iraqis that a war was being fought and that Saddam was incapable of containing it, as well as to destroy the command and control network of the Iraqi military.[26]

As in Vietnam, Desert Storm air commanders aimed to affect the enemy's popular support for the war indirectly rather than by bombing the civilian populace. Political restrictions prevented such targeting; furthermore, air leaders as well as Air Force doctrine maintained that direct attacks against Warden's 'fourth ring' were unnecessary to achieve success. The answer was the same as it had been for the Second World War – precision bombing – but now the Air Force could be truly precise. The United States had first employed 'smart' munitions in South-east Asia in 1967, but it was not until Linebacker I in 1972 that the ordnance achieved significant results.[27] By the time of Desert Storm, the accuracy of precision-guided munitions had improved dramatically. Modern laser, electro-optical and infrared targeting systems enabled Air Force pilots to bomb within one or two feet of a target, even at night. The combination of smart munitions with another technological wonder – the F-117A stealth fighter – made the dream of invulnerable precision bombing a reality. 'Desert Storm was … a vindication of the old concept of precision bombing', remarked former Air Force Chief of Staff General Michael Dugan. 'The technology finally caught up with the doctrine.'[28]

In much the same way that Vietnam-era air commanders had looked at Linebacker II as a vindication of Air Force doctrine from the 1950s and 1960s, Desert Storm air leaders saw Instant Thunder as proof that the fundamental principles of service doctrine remained sound. Moreover, they believed that they had exorcised many of the demons that had plagued the application of air power in Vietnam. Air chiefs pointed to the paucity of political restrictions placed on bombing Iraq, compared with the onerous controls that Lyndon Johnson and his advisors had levied on Rolling Thunder. Even though the Iraqi Army had not left Kuwait until the launching of an Allied ground offensive, many Air Force officers thought that the four-day ground thrust had simply collapsed an Iraqi military that unhampered air power had transformed into a house of cards. Air Force Chief of Staff General Merrill McPeak proclaimed at a Pentagon briefing shortly after the end of the war: 'This is the first time in history that a field army has been defeated by air power.'[29] The belief that air power was the dominant element of US military power permeated the service. In reality, the unique features of the 1991 Persian Gulf War – the combination of a fragmented, semi-industrialized Third World enemy, waging conventional war with Soviet equipment in a desert environment, and led by an international pariah who made all key decisions, had minimal amounts of intelligence data, and who gave the Allied coalition five-and-a-half months to refine planning and marshal forces – contributed enormously to the magnitude of air power's success.

When the new version of the US Air Force's Basic Doctrine Manual, which had been in draft form on the eve of the 1991 Persian Gulf War, appeared in print in March 1992, it highlighted air power's perceived dominance as a military instrument. The new Manual 1-1 did not, however, provide a completely uncritical assessment of air power's capabilities. Unlike previous doctrine manuals, the 1992 edition discussed air power's limitations and cited many examples from Vietnam. The edition was also unique in that it consisted of two volumes, with Volume I being a 'bare bones' quick reference guide in 20 pages, and Volume II providing 308 pages of 'evidence and supporting rationale'.[30] Yet much of the evidence supported such assertions as, 'With the appropriate degree of aerospace control, aerospace forces possess the versatility to deliver combat power on the enemy when and where needed to attain military objectives at *any* level of war.'[31] The manual also reflected Warden's impact on Air Force thinking. It stated: 'Strategic attacks are carried out against an enemy's centres of gravity including command elements, war production assets, and supporting infrastructure (for example, energy, transportation, and communication assets).'[32]

The 1992 edition also offered, for the first time, formal 'tenets of aerospace power', which included such aphorisms as 'centralized control/decentralized execution', 'flexibility/versatility', 'synergy' and 'persistence'.[33] Air Force Colonel Dennis Drew, who, along with a team of nine other officers at Air University's Centre for Aerospace Doctrine, Research, and Education (CADRE), wrote the two-volume manual, remarked that his group originally intended the tenets to serve as 'cautionary notes for airmen'.[34] Many air leaders viewed them differently. Drew stated that several Air Force generals saw the tenets as examples of air power's dominance in the aftermath of Desert Storm.

'What started as cautionary notes became a publicity bumper sticker', he recalled.[35]

The establishment of an Air Force Doctrine Centre at Maxwell Air Force Base in February 1997 spurred the development of a new basic doctrine manual. Published in September 1997 as Air Force Doctrine Document 1, the manual blended 1984's more streamlined format with pictures, graphics and quotations that beckoned to 1979. Much of the critical analysis in the 1992 edition disappeared in 1997; the new manual made two references to Vietnam in 73 pages.[36] It also discarded 1992's second volume of supporting essays – 'No one read them anyhow', Colonel Drew reasoned.[37] Yet the tenets of air power endured, now referred to as 'tenets of air and space power'. The manual also contained a detailed explanation of the Air Force's 'core competencies', followed by a discussion of Joint Vision 2010 – the combined services' view of how the United States would fight in the new millennium. Finally, the 1997 manual again stressed the Air Force's perceived ability to achieve success by strategic attack.

Some of the accent on strategic attack in the new manual was subtle. Of the six core competencies mentioned, two were directly related to strategic bombing – precision engagement and global attack. The manual's reference to Joint Vision 2010 further highlighted 'precision engagement', as well as 'dominant manoeuvre, focused logistics and full-dimensional protection' to achieve the ultimate goal of 'full spectrum dominance'.[38] Yet 'jointness' was not the new manual's overriding message. After a four-page analysis of how the Air Force would help accomplish Joint Vision 2010's objectives, this quote appeared from Giulio Douhet: 'Both the army and navy may well possess aerial means to aid their respective military and naval operations, but that does not preclude the possibility, the practicability, even the necessity, of having an air force capable of accomplishing war missions solely with its own means.'[39] Just in case the reader missed the point, the manual added the following comment after the quotation:

> Early air power advocates argued that airpower could be decisive and achieve strategic effects by itself. While this view of airpower was not proved during their lifetimes, *the more recent history of air and space power application, especially post-DESERT STORM,* **has proven** *that air and space power does now have the potential to be the dominant, and, at times, the decisive element* of combat in modern warfare.[40]

Curtis LeMay would no doubt have agreed.

Given the focus that the Air Force had placed on strategic bombing's perceived decisiveness, the 1999 Allied Force air campaign against Serbia over the ethnic cleansing in Kosovo likely appeared to many air chiefs as manna from heaven. The Deliberate Force air effort against the Bosnian Serbs four years before had seemingly demonstrated air power's prowess in a Balkan conflict, but some critics pointed to advances by the Croatian and Muslim Armies as the key factors behind the Dayton Accords. In Kosovo, President Bill Clinton eliminated the prospect of a ground offensive, leaving air power as the sole military instrument with which to force a Serb withdrawal and end the ethnic cleansing. Air power, however, did not equate to unrestrained bombing. NATO's 19-member coalition injected a large dose of gradualism into the air campaign that caused Air Force Lieutenant-General Michael Short, Allied Force's operational commander and a fighter pilot from Vietnam, to compare Kosovo's political restrictions with those that had hampered Rolling Thunder.[41] Short was also chafed by the military guidance provided by NATO's Supreme Allied Commander, Army General Wesley Clark. Clark argued that air attacks against Serb forces in Kosovo were the most likely to produce the desired effects, while Short maintained that attacks against 'strategic' targets in Belgrade would pay the most dividends.[42]

After more than five weeks of bombing with inconclusive results, in May 1999 Allied Force increased in intensity against electric-power and oil-production targets. One month later, Slobodan Milosevic accepted most of the Rambouillet terms and began withdrawing his forces from Kosovo.[43] Many Air Force officers saw a cause-and-effect relationship, much like their predecessors had seen almost 30 years before when the Paris Peace Accords followed less than a month after the end of Linebacker II. For many as well, the end of a conflict in which air power was the only type of military force used provided a final vindication for the promise stated in Air Force doctrine since its inception.

In all probability, that perception of air power as a war-winning instrument will appear in the revision to AF DD-1, currently underway and slated for publication in 2002. Indeed, a background paper at the Air Force Doctrine Centre recommends that the new edition 'shift from a war fighting emphasis to a theme that more accurately expounds upon the war winning nature of aerospace power and its unique global versatility'.[44] Doubtless the new manual will reference Kosovo, but it remains to be seen how much attention – if any – such factors as the threat of a ground invasion and Russian diplomacy receive in a discussion of why the conflict ended. It will be interesting as well to see if the new manual mentions Vietnam. If so, it is unlikely to give it much attention, and any criticisms of air power employment there are likely to be followed by assertions, similar to those found in the 1997 version, that the problems have been overcome.[45]

Since its first publication in 1953, the Air Force's basic doctrine has solidified the foundations established at the Air Corps Tactical School during the inter-war years. 'I think we have been consistent in our concepts since the formation of the GHQ [General Headquarters] Air Force in 1935', General Curtis LeMay stated as Chief of Staff in 1961. 'Our basic doctrine has remained generally unchanged since that time.'[46] His assessment remains true 40 years later. Even though the Air Force fought a bitter eight-year war in South-east Asia in which the United States' ally fell to the communist menace, the service emerged from the conflict with no reason to think it had been at fault for the loss. In fact, the view among the Air Force hierarchy was that its doctrine was sound, and, had air leaders been permitted to implement that doctrine earlier, the war's outcome would have been different. The belief that air power could independently achieve success in war has endured in the aftermath of Vietnam, spurred on by the persuasive powers of John Warden and the perceived success of Desert Storm and Allied Force. 'Air power is quintessentially an American form of war', Warden wrote following the 1991 conflict in the Persian Gulf. 'It uses our advantages of mobility and high technology to overwhelm an enemy without spilling too much blood, especially American blood.'[47] The appeal of that argument is likely to grow only stronger in the years ahead. The real test will be to assure that the notion of winning through air power does not result in hollow victories.

NOTES

1. 'Remarks by General Curtis E LeMay at Commander's Conference, Wright-Patterson AFB – January 1956', Folder B-51863, Box B205, Curtis E. LeMay Papers, Library of Congress.
2. Air Force Manual 1-2, 'United States Air Force Basic Doctrine', 1 April 1955, p. 10. Emphasis added.
3. Air Force Manual 1-8, 'Strategic Air Operations', 1 May 1954, p. 4.
4. Curtis E. LeMay with MacKinlay Kantor, *Mission with LeMay: My Story* (Garden City, NY: Doubleday, 1965), p. 565.
5. Ibid., p. 564.
6. JCS briefing text, 'Air Operations against North Vietnam and Laos', January 1967, Target Study – North Vietnam, Air Force Historical Research Agency (AFHRA), Maxwell AFB, Alabama, file number K178.2-34.
7. LeMay with Kantor, *Mission with LeMay*, p. 565.
8. US Congress, Senate, Committee on Armed Services, Preparedness Investigating Subcommittee, *Air War against North Vietnam*, 90th Cong., 1st sess., 22–23 August 1967, part 3, p. 212.
9. 'Summary Notes of the 556th National Security Council Meeting', 29 January 1966, National Security Files, NSC Meeting Notes File, Vols 3–5, Box 2, Johnson Presidential Library.
10. Appendix C to JCSM 613-65, memorandum, Chairman, JCS, to Secretary of Defense, 27 August 1965, National Security Files, Country File: Vietnam, Folder 2EE, Box 75, Johnson Presidential Library.
11. See Howard Silber, 'SAC Chief: B-52s Devastated Viet Defenses', *Omaha World Herald*, 25 February 1973; USAF Oral History interview of Lieutenant-General

Gerald W. Johnson by Charles K. Hopkins, 3 April 1973, Andersen AFB, Guam, AFHRA file number K239.0512–831, pp. 11–13; USAF Oral History interview of General John W. Vogt by Lieutenant-Colonel Arthur W. McCants, Jr and Dr James C. Hasdorff, 8–9 August 1978, AFHRA, file number K239.0512-1093, p. 69; U. S. Grant Sharp, *Strategy for Defeat: Vietnam in Retrospect* (San Rafael, CA: Presidio Press, 1978), pp. 252, 255, 272; and William W. Momyer, *Air Power in Three Wars* (Washington, DC: US Government Printing Office, 1978), p. 339.

12. Interview of Curtis LeMay by Mary-Ann Bendel, printed in *USA Today*, 23 July 1986, p. 9A.

13. 'Meeting with Foreign Policy Advisors on Vietnam', 18 August 1967, Meeting Notes File, Box 1, Johnson Presidential Library.

14. Headquarters USAF, *Analysis of Effectiveness of Interdiction in Southeast Asia, Second Progress Report*, May 1966, p. 7, AFHRA, file number K168.187-21; Senate Preparedness Subcommittee, *Air War Against North Vietnam*, 25 August 1967, part 4, p. 299; Annex A to JCSM 613–65, 27 August 1965, National Security Files, Country File: Vietnam, Folder 2EE, Box 75, Johnson Presidential Library.

15. Quoted in Gabriel Kolko, *Anatomy of a War: Vietnam, the United States, and the Modern Historical Experience* (New York: Pantheon Books, 1985), pp. 444–5.

16. For an analysis of the development of the 'Airland Battle' concept, and the Air Force's projected role in that doctrine, see John L. Rumjue, 'The Evolution of the AirLand Battle Concept', *Air University Review* 35, No. 4 (May–June 1984), pp. 4–15, and James A. Machos, 'TACAIR Support for Airland Battle', *Air University Review* 34, No. 4 (May–June 1984), pp. 16–24.

17. Andrew David Dembosky, 'Meeting the Enduring Challenge: United States Air Force Basic Doctrine through 1992', MA thesis, North Carolina State University, 1993, p. 28.

18. Air Force Manual 1-1, 'Basic Aerospace Doctrine', 16 March 1984, p. 3–2. Emphasis added.

19. Ibid.

20. Quoted in Dembosky, 'Meeting the Enduring Challenge', p. 57.

21. Air Force Manual 1-1, 16 March 1984, p. 2–1.

22. John A. Warden III, *The Air Campaign: Planning for Combat* (Washington, DC: National Defense University, 1988), p. 53.

23. John A. Warden III, 'Airpower Employment in the Future World', paper presented at 'Conference on the USAF', Tufts University, Boston, MA, 3 April 1991.

24. Ibid. In further developing his concept after the 1991 Persian Gulf War, Warden changed the label for his second ring from 'production facilities' to 'organic essentials'. Electricity and oil remained the main components of this ring, but Warden added food as a key source of energy, and also included money. See John A. Warden III, 'The Enemy as a System', *Airpower Journal* 9 (Spring 1995), pp. 40–55.

25. John A. Warden III, 'Employing Air Power in the Twenty-first Century', in Richard H. Schultz and Robert L. Pfaltzgraff, Jr (eds), *The Future of Air Power in the Aftermath of the Gulf War* (Maxwell AFB, AL: Air University Press, 1992), p. 66.

26. Julie Bird, 'Horner: Further AF Role in Gulf Not Needed', *Air Force Times* (18 March 1991), p. 8.

27. On 10 May 1972, 32 Air Force F-4 Phantoms dropped 29 electro-optically and laser-guided bombs on Hanoi's key span across the Red River, the Paul Doumer Bridge. The bridge collapsed the next day. On 12 May, Phantoms from the US Air Force's 8th Tactical Fighter Wing used smart bombs to wreck the defiant symbol of North Vietnam that had remained standing throughout the three-and-a-half

years of Rolling Thunder – the infamous 'Dragon's Jaw' bridge at Thanh Hoa. See HQ 7th AF, 7th *Air Force History of Linebacker Operations, 10 May–23 October 1972*, n.d., K740.04-24, pp. 7–10, USAFHRA.

28. Michael Dugan, 'First Lessons of Victory', *US News & World Report* (18 March 1991), p. 36.
29. Quoted in Julie Bird, 'McPeak: "Brilliant ... air deception", *Air Force Times* (25 March 1991), p. 8.
30. Air Force Manual 1-1, 'Basic Doctrine of the United States Air Force', March 1992, Vol. I, p. v.
31. Ibid., p. 11. Emphasis added.
32. Ibid.
33. Ibid., p. 8.
34. Telephone interview of Colonel Dennis Drew, USAF, Retired, with the author, 14 June 2001. While members of the Pentagon's Air Staff had drafted the previous basic doctrine manuals, a small group of air power experts at Maxwell drafted the 1992 version.
35. Ibid.
36. Those references are: 'During the initial engagements of World War II and through the entire Vietnam conflict, command of US airpower was fragmented and controlled by competing commanders. The results taught airpower leaders that **centralized control** *was the best way to effectively employ airpower*. The outcome of the Gulf War stands in stark contrast to that of Vietnam' (p. 23; original boldface and italics). 'We must not assume that things have not or will not change. It was a doctrinal disease called "dogma" that led hundreds of thousands of First World War soldiers on all sides to fall before the adversary's machine guns, that led thousands of unescorted bombers to challenge and almost lose to the first-rate fighters of the German Air Force in World War II, and that led to our lack of vision in applying air and space power in Southeast Asia. The shining success of air and space power in DESERT STORM and in the skies over Bosnia illuminates the ability of the Air Force to learn and apply its lessons' (pp. 73–4). See Air Force Doctrine Document 1, 'Air Force Basic Doctrine', September 1997.
37. Interview with Colonel Dennis Drew, 14 June 2001.
38. Air Force Doctrine Document 1, September 1997, pp. 36–40.
39. Ibid., p. 40.
40. Ibid., p. 41. Italics in the original; boldface added.
41. General Short stated that 'the major lesson we learned [from Vietnam] is if you're going to take the country to war, if the country is going to risk its young men and women, send them into harm's way, then you want to get it done as quickly as you can. You want to risk your young people, and your old people for that matter, to the minimum degree acceptable to get the job done. And you want to bring all the force to bear that you have at your command. You want to crush the enemy; you don't want to toy with them; you don't want to incrementalize; you don't want to stair-step, you don't want to try a little bit of this and a little bit of that to see how he likes it and then back off and see what the reaction was.' See 'PBS Interview with Lt Gen Short', undated text of interview for the PBS documentary, 'Frontline', p. 1. See also, 'Interview with Lieutenant General Michael Short Conducted by Colonel Mace Carpenter,' Washington, DC, 19 December 2000.
42. Ibid., p. 2. Short observed: 'I never believed that the [Yugoslav] Third Army in Kosovo was the center of gravity. I believe the center of gravity was Milosevic and the leadership cadre around him and they were in Belgrade.'
43. Two items from Rambouillet not included in the final agreement were transit rights for NATO forces throughout Yugoslavia, and a call for a referendum in

Kosovo to decide the region's political status.
44. 'Background Paper on AFDD 1 *Basic Doctrine* Spring 2001 Revision,' Air Force Doctrine Center, 30 May 2001, p. 1.
45. See the citations from AFDD 1 provided in note 36.
46. Quoted in Dembosky, 'Meeting the Enduring Challenge', p. 11.
47. Warden, 'Employing Air Power in the Twenty-first Century', p. 61.

16

Air Power Victorious?
Britain and NATO Strategy during
the Kosovo Conflict[1]

Sebastian Ritchie

This chapter provides a summary of the Air Historical Branch's research on strategic aspects of the Kosovo conflict of 1999. A strategic study represents something of a break from the traditions of AHB's past histories, which have tended to focus on the RAF's contribution to military actions at the command, operational and policy levels. But in the course of preparing a tactical-level narrative on Harrier and Tornado GR1 operations during the Kosovo conflict it became clear that something more was needed: that a tactical-level history would mean very little in this particular instance unless it could be placed in a strategic context. To do that it was first of all necessary to establish what, precisely, NATO's strategy was. Naturally there were limits to the extent to which the British archival sources could do justice to the history of a multi-national campaign, so what follows tends to reflect the British outlook on NATO's conduct of the Kosovo operation.

For NATO, the Kosovo conflict was essentially a coercive air operation, entitled 'Operation Allied Force', which ran from 24 March to 10 June 1999. The operation was NATO's response to the increasingly repressive measures taken by the Federal Republic of Yugoslavia (FRY) against the majority Albanian population of the province of Kosovo. At the strategic level the conflict can be examined under four headings: first, the origins of the war; second, the air campaign itself; third, the debate on whether to mount a ground campaign; fourth, the resolution of the conflict. Several basic questions soon emerge from this approach. Why did NATO favour an air campaign over other military media? What was the campaign expected to achieve? What problems were involved in its implementation and how, and to what extent, were they overcome? In considering the ground force issue it was important to establish to what extent NATO had accepted the need to plan for an opposed ground operation by the beginning of June 1999. Finally, on the resolution of the conflict, it was to be expected that the official records might shed new light on Milosevic's decision to withdraw from Kosovo and accept the presence of a NATO-led peacekeeping force there.

The long-term origins of the Kosovo crisis may be identified in many centuries of Balkan history and lie far beyond the scope of this essay. The key development in more recent years was Yugoslavia's progressive disintegration since the early 1990s, beginning with the cessation of Slovenia and Croatia in 1991, and then descending into civil war in Bosnia in 1992. Kosovo was the next in line and the potential for conflict there was recognized by the international community early in the decade. Previously an autonomous province of Serbia, Kosovo had been subject to sustained efforts from Belgrade to reassert direct Serbian government since the accession to power of Slobodan Milosevic in 1989. Belgrade's policies were deeply resented by the majority Albanian population. In the aftermath of the Bosnian war, the later 1990s witnessed a marked polarization between the Albanian and Serb communities in Kosovo. This was characterized by the emergence of the Kosovo Liberation Army (KLA) and its violent campaign against the FRY security forces, and by the employment of increasingly indiscriminate and disproportionate reprisals by the FRY troops and police against the Kosovo Albanian population as a whole. By 1998, the West believed that it was confronted by a second Bosnia and was deeply concerned over the potential for civil war in Kosovo to destabilize other Balkan countries. The so-called Contact Group of nations (France, Germany, Italy, Russia, Britain and the United States) therefore embarked on a diplomatic drive to resolve the crisis, and sponsored two United Nations Security Council Resolutions (UNSCRs), 1160 and 1199, calling for an end to violence and repression in Kosovo and the beginning of meaningful dialogue between the FRY and the Kosovo Albanians. But on the basis of past experience in Yugoslavia, it was considered that diplomacy would be ineffective unless it was supported by force.

Deliberations within NATO during the summer of 1998 revealed an overwhelming consensus in favour of the employment of air power for this purpose rather than ground forces, or an appropriate mix of air and ground forces. For this there were three reasons. First, air power could be deployed over Kosovo more quickly; a substantial NATO force was already present in southern Europe for operations over Bosnia, and could be enlarged rapidly. By contrast, the deployment of a sufficiently capable ground force would have taken months and could only have been achieved at vast expense. Second, a ground operation was likely to involve far heavier casualties. The prospect that significant Western casualties might result from a conflict over a relatively unknown Balkan province was anathema to most Western statesmen, and to the Americans in particular. And the United States was of course likely to be the major force provider. Third, there was a genuine belief that air power could be deployed coercively to produce a quick, clean, resolution to the crisis. This outlook was based on perceptions of what air power had achieved during the previous decade, partly in the Gulf but especially in Bosnia. In 1995, Operation Deliberate Force had apparently brought the Bosnian Serbs to the negotiating table after only two weeks without casualties or collateral damage. In 1999, Western military and political leaders hoped that air power would achieve identical results.

Did they have good grounds to do so? The answer is a matter of debate, but there is no general consensus that air power alone was decisive in 1995 in Bosnia. Some have argued that ground operations by Croat and Muslim forces were equally important; there was also a substantial UN military presence on the ground; and Serbia, under the pressure of UN sanctions, urged the Bosnian Serbs to seek terms. Deliberate Force was, furthermore, conducted in peculiarly favourable conditions; for example, it was mounted at the end of the summer, when the weather was clear; and the Bosnian Serbs lacked a capable integrated air-defence system. Such benign operational circumstances were not likely to prevail over southern Serbia in March 1999.

The British documents suggest a certain lack of clarity at the top level of government over the air strategy for Kosovo. There was general agreement on the desirability of a coercive air campaign if diplomacy failed, but no precise understanding of what this might involve. The NATO force assembled for the task did not boast a very large offensive capability, and its target list was confined to the FRY air-defence system and to military infrastructure targets in southern Serbia and Kosovo. Its capacity to coerce the FRY's political leadership in Belgrade was questionable. Nevertheless, expectations of the campaign were very optimistic; it was apparently believed that Milosevic would capitulate within a few days of the onset of hostilities. No alternative or contingency strategy was devised for implementation if Operation Allied Force failed to accomplish this formidable goal. Nor had much thought been given to the possibility that the FRY would respond to air strikes by launching an all-out assault on the Kosovo Albanians. By mid-March 1999, a considerable volume of information had in fact reached NATO leaders suggesting that this was precisely how Milosevic would react to air strikes. The British government did not entirely ignore this possibility, but merely concluded that air power might, in such circumstances, be employed to reduce the FRY's capacity to repress the Kosovo Albanians. It would not seem that the practical implications of such a strategy were considered in detail.

The prospect of outright hostilities over Kosovo diminished somewhat in the later months of 1998 after the US Special Envoy to the FRY, Richard Holbrooke, brokered an agreement under which an unarmed verification mission entered the province to monitor compliance with UNSCR 1199. But the situation deteriorated again in January 1999, and when 45 Kosovo Albanians were killed by FRY security forces at Racak there was general agreement within the Contact Group that a stronger line was essential. In so-called 'proximity talks' at Rambouillet, France, in February, the rival protagonists were issued with a series of demands, which were backed by the threat of force in the event of non-compliance. The Rambouillet Accords called for an immediate cease-fire, the withdrawal of nearly all Yugoslav security forces from Kosovo, the demilitarization of the KLA, the insertion of a NATO-led peace-implementation force, KFOR, into the province, and effective autonomy for Kosovo within the FRY. The Kosovo Albanians were eventually induced to sign the Accords, but the Yugoslav delegation refused even to discuss the deployment of an international peacekeeping force in Kosovo, and rejected a number of other terms on the grounds that they violated the FRY's sovereignty and territorial integrity. The NATO air campaign was launched on 24 March 1999 after the failure of last-ditch attempts to persuade Milosevic to reconsider his position.

The initial air strikes on the FRY's air-defence system and on military infrastructure targets in southern Serbia and Kosovo were heavily disrupted by poor weather, and Milosevic responded by launching a barbaric onslaught against the Kosovo Albanians. NATO found itself subjected to immediate pressure to protect them, and it therefore switched a substantial proportion of its limited offensive strength to operations against fielded FRY forces in the Kosovo Engagement Zone, (KEZ). Thus was NATO diverted from its original strategy within just three days. The campaign's orientation towards KEZ targets was then encouraged by three factors. First, the process of clearing other types of target proved long and convoluted, because it involved at least formal consultation with the entire NATO alliance; second, KEZ operations were favoured by political leaders because they were thought to involve less risk of collateral damage than attacks against other target sets; third, the Supreme Allied Commander Europe (SACEUR), General Wesley Clark, involved himself directly in the targeting process and (as he has since admitted in his memoirs) he insisted on attaching an overriding priority to KEZ strikes.

Unfortunately, KEZ operations proved very uneconomic. Operation Allied Force was largely conducted at medium altitude (at least 15,000 feet), a level from which it is very difficult to locate small ground-force targets even in ideal weather conditions; the weather over Kosovo was often overcast. Many of the aircraft involved were not optimized for

Close Air Support-type operations. The FRY forces proved adept in the art of passive air defence, employed decoys and camouflage to good effect, and made maximum use of the protection afforded by the weather. In the absence of a threat from NATO on the ground, they dispersed and concealed both troops and equipment. Finally, they apparently managed to secure ample intelligence on the timing and orientation of NATO attacks, and were able to tailor their dispersal and movement plans accordingly.

The air campaign's orientation towards KEZ operations unquestionably reduced its effectiveness during the first month of hostilities, but there were other problems too. At first, NATO's force was not sufficiently large to conduct sustained operations on a scale likely to coerce the FRY; consistently overcast weather led to the cancellation of many sorties, and concerns over force protection and collateral damage imposed further limitations on the effectiveness of attack missions. From a broader perspective, the campaign suffered under SACEUR's direction from a lack of strategic focus, from random target selection and from a failure to identify the FRY's 'centres of gravity'. The most prominent critic of the campaign's strategic direction was the Air Component Commander himself, NATO's COMAIRSOUTH (Commander Allied Air Forces Southern Europe), General Mike Short.

Where did Britain stand on the question of air campaign strategy? Among senior RAF officers there was some concern about the initial weakness of planning and tasking machinery, such as the Strategy/ Guidance, Apportionment, and Targeting (STRAT/GAT) cell in the Combined Air Operations Centre (CAOC), the headquarters responsible for the day-to-day management of the campaign at Vicenza. But British military leaders were otherwise largely supportive of General Short's position in the strategic debate on Kosovo. However, from an early stage in Operation Allied Force, British strategists were sceptical about the capacity of air power to achieve NATO's objectives independently, and fearful of the consequences for the Alliance if Allied Force failed. Increasingly, it was argued from a joint perspective that some form of ground intervention was necessary and that the correct use of air power should be to prepare the battlefield for this ground offensive. It was also maintained that clear time-lines should be drawn up governing the development of NATO strategy – from the existing air campaign, to battlefield preparation, to the insertion of a ground force. These arguments found some sympathy within NATO's high command; SACEUR himself favoured the concept of a joint air and ground campaign. But political leaders from other Alliance nations proved very much more cautious.

Several initiatives were taken to increase the effectiveness of Operation Allied Force. The enlargement of NATO's air component was particularly important. The force, which numbered fewer than 500 air-craft in March, was expanded to reach 900 aircraft in May, and the proportion of strike aircraft increased within this overall total. In late April, General Short produced a Strategy and Mission Statement, which envisaged increasing the bombing effort against military infrastructure and strategic targets in Serbia, while continuing with KEZ attacks. Within NATO, attempts were made to accelerate the target-clearance process, and in particular to ease clearance problems that had delayed attacks on the type of strategic targets that lay at the centre General Short's plans. There were also efforts to improve the strategic direction of the campaign. Better STRAT/GAT machinery was established at the CAOC, and efforts were made to persuade SACEUR that it was necessary to plan more methodically, and to identify and strike at the FRY's centres of gravity.

No dramatic improvement resulted. NATO's air component was enlarged, but for much of May poor weather continued to restrict the sortie rate and to hamper the task of target identification. General Short's Strategy and Mission Statement was implemented in theory but not in practice. Although some media and academic depictions of the air campaign have since suggested that Short ultimately got his way, the reality was very different. In fact, during the first half of May there was hardly any reduction in the campaign's emphasis on KEZ opera-tions. Some streamlining occurred in target-clearance procedures, and more strategic targets were approved for attack; but particular Alliance members continued to veto key targeting proposals. Finally, while there is some documentary evidence of more methodical planning during May, the CAOC continued to complain stridently about SACEUR's constant interventions. It was alleged that General Clark was attempt-ing to micro-manage the air campaign, that he was obsessed with striking KEZ targets, and that he had no clear strategy.

Only in the last week of May was General Clark finally persuaded that a major reorientation was necessary towards the strategic bombing of Serbia. Clark, with strong support from Washington, then approached the leading European powers. But he found them reluctant to accept his proposals, partly because they wished to confirm the legality of some of the targets independently, and partly because they feared that the pro-posed strikes would result in collateral damage and civilian casualties. The issue was unresolved when peace talks began at the beginning of June.

In other respects, though, there were at least some grounds for cautious optimism. The first clear evidence that the air campaign was causing serious alarm at the highest governmental and military levels in the FRY was detected at the beginning of May, when there was a sudden and very marked increase in ground-based air-defence activity.

Milosevic then began offering limited concessions, such as a partial troop withdrawal, if NATO would halt the bombing. Anti-war and anti-conscription demonstrations in southern Serbia were soon followed by overt criticisms of the war from certain provincial and civic leaders. And when the weather cleared during the final week of May, NATO was at last able to unleash all the offensive forces at its disposal. The result was a dramatic increase in the attack-sortie rate of over 90 per cent compared with the average rate recorded in the preceding three weeks, and most of these sorties located and bombed FRY targets. By the end of May, evidence was emerging to suggest the presence of a 'peace party' in Belgrade, although the 'war party' was considered to be stronger. Assessments of the air campaign's physical impact also became noticeably more upbeat, presenting an impressive record of widespread damage to the FRY's economic and military infrastructure, to its communications network and to its IADS. These assessments were only less optimistic in their appraisal of KEZ operations.

In Britain it was considered that the initial failure of the air campaign placed NATO's entire future in jeopardy. A high-level search began for an alternative strategy and Britain consequently became the leading advocate of a ground offensive, a so-called 'forced entry', into Kosovo. In the event, no such offensive actually occurred, but it has since been widely suggested that the threat of a ground assault played an important, if not decisive, part in persuading Milosevic to capitulate. According to this view, the air campaign was very much a secondary consideration for the FRY leader. AHB's research raised immediate and serious questions about the validity of this argument.

Once the British government had accepted the need to plan for a ground operation in Kosovo, its primary task lay in persuading close allies, particularly the United States, that such a strategy was necessary. If Britain could convert the United States, a combined British and US force might conduct the operation; if Britain could convert France and one or two other leading European powers, the United States might also be persuaded to contribute ground troops. However, Britain found itself confronted by steadfast opposition from both Washington and Paris. In both capitals the fundamental concern was of course that an opposed ground operation would result in high casualty levels, with disastrous political consequences. Britain argued that the FRY forces could be expelled from Kosovo by a NATO ground offensive without undue difficulty: many Serb troops were of low calibre and their capability would in any case have been severely degraded by months of bombing. But both the United States and France had far more respect for the FRY military. They also maintained that the ground-campaign issue would split NATO; divert attention and effort away from the air campaign; suggest to Milosevic that NATO had no faith in its own strategy, and might cause Russia to intervene on the FRY's side. The most that Washington would accept was an informal planning process within NATO.

Throughout April 1999, the British government achieved no notable success in persuading the other powers of the need to plan for an opposed ground operation. Nevertheless, within the Ministry of Defence (MOD) a number of outline plans were prepared, which envisaged several different ground options. Inevitably, these papers postulated deadline dates by which key decisions would have to be taken if ground operations were to be completed by the onset of the Kosovo winter. These deadlines in turn encouraged the government to increase the pressure on Britain's close allies. But, contrary to so many claims made since the end of the war, there is no evidence that either the United States or France altered their stance on the ground-force issue to any tangible extent. The French government remained implacably opposed to Britain's arguments, claiming that a forced entry would require an army of 500,000 troops; Germany followed France's line. Their position demonstrated to the United States that there was no general European support for a ground option, and on this basis the United States reaffirmed its faith in the capacity of the air campaign to achieve NATO's strategic objectives independently.

On 28 May 1999 it was agreed that the NATO peacekeeping force for Kosovo, KFOR, should be enlarged, but even the British Secretary of State for Defence declared publicly that this larger force, KFOR PLUS, was for peacekeeping only, rather than for a forced entry. In other words, there was not even an attempt to *threaten* Milosevic with a ground operation at this time. In any case, when the war ended both KFOR and KFOR PLUS existed on paper only. At the beginning of June 1999, KFOR numbered just 15,000 troops, a complement unlikely to have exerted much coercive effect on Milosevic. And the Ministry of Defence was arguing that it was too late to mount a ground offensive into Kosovo before the onset of winter. Thus, while it would be impossible to prove that Milosevic's capitulation at the beginning of June 1999 was not triggered by the prospect of a NATO ground assault, the proposal that this was his primary motivation is clearly based on conjecture rather than hard historical evidence. In fact the documents show that Britain was isolated on the ground force issue, that its closest allies remained unconvinced of the need for a ground offensive, and that such an offensive could not have been undertaken in 1999.

Why, then, did Milosevic finally accept the demands of the international community? There are several possible explanations. At the beginning of the conflict he almost certainly doubted NATO's resolve and preparedness to sustain a long campaign. He may also have hoped to divide the Alliance by unleashing the refugee crisis in Kosovo, thus demonstrating that air strikes were not merely futile but counter-productive. Yet it is important to remember that the refugee crisis was Milosevic's *final* military card; thereafter, he was left without any military options. Through the crisis he seized the initiative from NATO and held it for a time, but NATO gradually recovered it as the air campaign progressed. In the process the Alliance demonstrated a degree of unity that lay far beyond his expectations. By the second half of May 1999, Milosevic found himself facing an intensifying and insuperable assault, which was causing increasing military and economic damage, undermining the morale of both the military and the civilian population of the FRY, and weakening his own political power base. In these circumstances, it can plausibly be argued that his surrender was only a matter of time.

It is also important to consider the diplomatic efforts to resolve the crisis, the position of the FRY's only diplomatic ally, Russia, and the precise circumstances in which Milosevic capitulated. Russia's support was essential to the FRY; without it, Milosevic's regime would have been impossibly isolated. This was clearly recognized by Western diplomats, who therefore attempted to detach Moscow from Belgrade, and to align it more closely with their stance on Kosovo. Critically dependent on Western financial aid, Russia was very vulnerable to these pressures. Early in May 1999, Russia was persuaded to accept a G8 statement of principles for ending the Kosovo conflict, which was also broadly acceptable to NATO. In the following weeks, it was instrumental in turning this statement into a draft peace settlement. Yet it was only possible to bridge the gulf between Russia and NATO by couching this settlement in somewhat vague terms. This lack of clarity may have encouraged Milosevic to hope that he might obtain concessions during detailed peace negotiations.

It is popularly supposed that the peace terms finally accepted by Milosevic resulted from a joint diplomatic initiative undertaken by the EU envoy, Maarti Ahtisaari, and the Russian envoy, Viktor Chernomyrdin, at the beginning of June. But the documents show that Ahtisaari decided to visit Belgrade only *after* Milosevic had signified his willingness to accept the G8's principles for ending the conflict. By the end of May the FRY leader was, in fact, looking for a way out. When Ahtisaari presented him with the draft peace document Milosevic predictably sought a range of concessions, which were refused. But his military representatives afterwards tried to insist on a halt to NATO bombing before they withdrew their forces from Kosovo, and on an extension of the time-scale for implementing the agreement. Negotiations eventually broke down, but Milosevic's final act of brinkmanship came closer to success than is often recognized, as many NATO members sought the immediate suspension of Operation Allied Force. Had the air campaign been suspended, there would have been far less pressure on Milosevic to accept an agreement, and it might subsequently have been very difficult to persuade all Alliance members that offensive operations should be resumed. A senior NATO figure captured the very essence of NATO's dilemma at this time and simultaneously offered an eloquent tribute to the effectiveness of air power in resolving the Kosovo crisis:

> The problem lies, from a military point of view, in arriving at the delivery of the agreement while maintaining pressure. If we don't keep pressure on the Serbs we fear that we may arrive at a position where we cannot deliver the agreement ... We need to maintain the pressure of bombing ... until we have an agreement that can be delivered.

The air campaign was in fact moderated for a few days, but was then reintensified when the FRY refused to agree terms.

Subjected to further bombardment, Milosevic then signified his willingness to accept the peace terms on offer, if they were supported by a UNSCR. The SCR had to accommodate Russian and FRY political sensitivities by papering over certain remaining areas of dispute. Milosevic afterwards proclaimed publicly that it guaranteed the FRY's sovereignty and territorial integrity, and provided for the deployment of a peacekeeping force in Kosovo under UN auspices. The reality was very different. The SCR in fact proposed the establishment of 'an *interim* political framework' in Kosovo explicitly linked to the FRY's sovereignty and territorial integrity – in other words, a framework that might subsequently be altered. In this respect, from Belgrade's perspective, the SCR did not represent much of an improvement over Rambouillet. Indeed, the SCR went on to stress that the interim political framework was also to take 'full account of the Rambouillet Accords'.

Where the peacekeeping force was concerned, it is true that all reference to NATO was omitted from the main body of the SCR, which mentioned only the 'relevant international organisations to establish the international security presence in Kosovo'. It is also true that the SCR provided for a 'security presence' in Kosovo 'under United Nations auspices'. But this statement signified only the deployment of a peacekeeping force in Kosovo *sanctioned* by the UN – not directed by it. NATO had always desired UN approval for the deployment of KFOR, but had been unable to overcome Russian opposition in the Security Council. Crucially, Russia now agreed to the attachment of an annex to the SCR specifying 'substantial NATO participation' in the peacekeeping force which 'must be deployed under unified command and control'; in practice, this meant NATO command and control. Only the establishment of a new *civil* government in Kosovo was to be managed by the UN. Hence the SCR offered only cosmetic concessions to Milosevic and delivered absolute victory into NATO's hands. Its passage was swiftly followed by the signature of a Military Technical Agreement between the FRY and the Commander of KFOR, and by the suspension of Operation Allied Force.

Operation Allied Force was very far from being a model air campaign, if such a thing exists. It is probably not inaccurate to suggest that at the beginning of the operation NATO lacked the means, the will and the direction to exert a significant coercive impact on the FRY; nor had a realistic contingency strategy been developed for confronting Milosevic's ethnic cleansing of the Kosovo population. As a result the Alliance quickly lost the initiative in the conflict and subsequently encountered considerable difficulty in regaining it. A high proportion of the air campaign's effort was expended on uneconomic KEZ targets, and there were other serious flaws in its strategic management. These occurred primarily because of the political constraints within which it was conducted. Nevertheless, the conclusion here is that the air campaign was ultimately more effective than many commentators have claimed, and there is clear evidence in British appraisals and other documents to support this view. Moreover, united around the air campaign, NATO did ultimately regain the initiative in the conflict, leaving Milosevic without any military options. By late May 1999, the FRY could not sustain the damage being inflicted on its military infrastructure and economy; but it had no means of striking back at NATO. The only alternative was to accept the G8's terms for a settlement.

At the same time, the documents cast serious doubt on the proposition that Milosevic was coerced into surrender by the threat of a NATO ground offensive. By the beginning of June, the MOD's deadline for organizing such an operation had passed without any of Britain's close allies accepting that a forced ground entry was necessary. The coercive potential of a peacekeeping force barely half the size of KFOR and less than one-third of the size of KFOR PLUS seems extremely doubtful.

Yet it should not be supposed that air power alone brought victory in Kosovo. The air campaign was accompanied by sustained and ultimately successful Western efforts to divide the FRY from Russia in order to confront Milosevic's regime with the grim prospect of total diplomatic isolation. The general peace principles agreed between the West and Russia finally persuaded Milosevic that he might win concessions through detailed negotiations, and it was partly on this basis that he signified his willingness to come to terms. The interaction between air power and diplomacy was particularly evident during the last days of the conflict. When Milosevic's final gambit failed and talks broke down the air campaign was re-intensified and the FRY quickly agreed to resume negotiations. The final peace agreement represented an absolute capitulation by Milosevic, which was only superficially concealed by the accompanying UNSCR.

Although a key force contributor and a member of the all-important inner circle of close allies, Britain assumed a surprisingly independent posture in NATO's strategic debate on Kosovo for reasons that were both political and military. Its political priority was to safeguard the future of NATO, which might have been imperilled if air power had failed to defeat Milosevic. From a military standpoint, Britain's most senior airmen doubted that air power alone could protect the Kosovo Albanians and believed instead in the necessity of a joint campaign in which air power prepared the battlefield for a ground offensive. Their outlook was shared by the Chief of the Defence Staff, and was also adopted by the government after the initial failure of Operation Allied Force to achieve NATO's objectives. But the other allies rejected British proposals for a joint campaign, primarily out of unwillingness to consider an opposed ground operation in Kosovo and the casualties that were likely to result from it. Clearly, there are lessons to be drawn from Britain's experience on the potential for mounting future military operations that are both joint (multi-service) and combined (multi-national). The growing Western political concern with keeping casualties to the absolute minimum may well reduce the scope for deploying ground forces into non-permissive environments still further, unless the most vital interests are considered to be at stake. In any other scenario, it seems certain that air power will be cast in an even more prominent military role than it played between 24 March and 10 June 1999.

NOTE

1. This paper is an unclassified summary of the Air Historical Branch narrative on strategic aspects of the Kosovo conflict. Most of the sources on which it is based remain classified and therefore have regrettably had to be omitted.

17

The Balkans:
An Air Power Basket Case?

Peter W. Gray

'As soon as sufficient forces are available, and the weather situation permits, the Air Force is to destroy the City of Belgrade and the ground organisation of the Yugoslav Air Force by means of continuous day and night attacks.'

Adolf Hitler, 1941[1]

The extreme nature of the language, and the give-away attribution, clearly situate the opening quotation in the Second World War and the age of total war. And yet the sentiments, partly brought about by frustration, towards the Balkan conundrum are in reality very close to those expressed by NATO leaders in the context of Operation Allied Force – the air operations over Kosovo and Serbia in 1999. Although there were evident differences in priorities for Allied Force, and indeed likely duration of the conflict, the language used by all of the senior leaders was blunt, unmistakable in intent and uncompromising. SACEUR (Supreme Allied Commander, Europe), General Wesley Clark, stated in a NATO briefing on 25 March 1999 that:

We're going to systematically and progressively attack, disrupt, degrade, devastate, and ultimately – unless President Milosevic complies with the demand of the international community – we're going to destroy these forces and their facilities and support.[2]

Lieutenant-General Michael Short, who was the air commander (Joint Force Air Component Commander – JFACC) at the time, subsequently gave evidence to the US Senate (and in television interviews) admitting that there had been severe national differences over the targeting of Serbian centre(s) of gravity. Short nevertheless stated somewhat graphically that he would have preferred to have: 'Gone for the head of the snake on the first night.'[3]

Notwithstanding the degree of attention that Belgrade was likely to receive, the Yugoslav Air Force was undoubtedly as high on the agenda in the 1990s as it had been in 1941. Recourse to air power was also instinctive in both cases, as it has been in many others. This chapter will seek to examine the efficacy of air power in the Balkans, with the Second World War experience providing a suitable backdrop. It will then focus on the NATO operations of the 1990s with a comparison between Deliberate Force (in Bosnia in 1995) and Allied Force in Serbia in 1999. The chapter does not aim to study the tactics, techniques and weaponry in use as these are covered in great detail elsewhere. Rather, the military aspects will concentrate on the operational level of air war in the Balkans and what effect these had on the strategic-level processes – reaching diplomatic agreements and so forth.

AIR WARFARE IN THE BALKANS: THE SECOND WORLD WAR

The frustrations inherent in dealing with 'the Serbs' are all too evident in senior leaders' approach to the Balkans. Hitler thought that he had gained Yugoslav accession to the Axis pact on 25 March 1941, only to have his plans thwarted two days later by the military coup in Belgrade. This sense of overwhelming frustration is evident from the War Directive No. 25 cited above which, goes on to say that: 'Yugoslavia, even if it makes professions of loyalty, must be regarded as an enemy and beaten down as quickly as possible.' It is evident that Hitler's approach to operations in the Balkans went far beyond what was necessary for normal, or prudent, military utility.[4]

For the *Luftwaffe*, this excursion into the Balkans represented a return to operations after a relatively quiet spell from December 1940. Over 600 aircraft were deployed from Germany, supplemented by more than 400 from France.[5] Under the appropriately titled codeword 'Operation Punishment', the *Luftwaffe* was tasked with achieving air superiority followed by the destruction of Belgrade. Attacks on transportation targets and industrial plants were prohibited. Hitler did not intend this to be a grinding war of attrition and was determined to make full use of the infrastructure after a quick victory. The plan of attack for Belgrade was nothing if not thorough. A major bomber wave would attack the city over the morning using 75 per cent high explosives and the remainder incendiary ordnance. This would be followed after lunch with 40 per cent high explosives and 60 per cent incendiaries to capitalize on the devastation wrought earlier in the day and stoke up the fires ready to act as markers for the evening raid. This would be conducted with an equal mix of incendiaries and high explosives. The damage was, not surprisingly, very extensive and some 17,000 people were killed. It is highly ironic that these figures have been taken from David Irving's book, *The Rise and Fall of the Luftwaffe*,[6] and are very similar to his revised figures for Dresden.[7] Within less than a week, German mechanized divisions had taken possession of the smouldering ruins. Hitler had exacted some measure of physical revenge for the diplomatic frustrations inherent in any dealings with the Balkans.

Royal Air Force involvement in the Balkans started with Sunderlands of 230 Squadron providing the Royal Navy with detailed reconnaissance of the Italian fleet. This enabled Admiral Cunningham to force an engagement in which three enemy cruisers and two destroyers were sunk; a battleship was badly damaged.[8] Air power assets under the command of Air Vice-Marshal J. H. D'Albiac provided reconnaissance of the advancing Germans and sought to delay their progress. D'Albiac had, as the official historian puts it, been through the 'Staff College mill' and well understood the damage that could be inflicted from the air on concentrations of forces caught in narrow defiles.[9] He also launched bombing raids against the marshalling yards in Sofia (Bulgaria was an Axis partner). In a somewhat prophetic vein, Allied losses were light and bad weather (in April) baulked many efforts. Once Yugoslavia had been crushed, occupied and puppet organizations (such as the *Ustase* in Croatia) installed, Hitler withdrew the bulk of his forces to prepare for the 'main effort' – Operation Barbarossa and the invasion of Russia. The rapidity of his consolidation left sizeable numbers of troops roaming free through the mountains and hills with which the region is well endowed. These forces quickly settled down into guerrilla-style warfare that became the norm for the rest of the war. German formations, and local units friendly to the Nazis, were engaged in a constant struggle against these partisan groups. Internecine violence was frequent and extreme. In a speech to the House of Commons in February 1944, the Prime Minister Winston Churchill pointed out that 20 German and six Bulgarian divisions had been tied down by 250,000 partisans and air power.[10]

The Balkan Air Force was set up in June 1944 under the command of Air Vice-Marshal W. Elliot following the armistice with Italy. The scope for the utilization of air power in support of Marshal Tito's forces thereafter increased considerably. Tito requested, first and foremost, that Allied air be deployed to counter the *Luftwaffe* and wrest control of the air. He then asked for an increase in the support to partisan troops and finally for more casualty evacuation. Again somewhat prophetically, the Balkan Air Force also sought to attack shipping, ports, storage tanks, radio stations, oil dumps, gun emplacements and bridges to prevent reinforcements or concentrations of troops.[11] The marshalling yards at Sofia were again revisited. Arguably, the greatest impact of air power was in what modern doctrine terms Combat Support Air Operations.

Some 8,640 Special Duties sorties were flown with 16,469 tons of arms and ammunition delivered. Over 2,500 personnel were infiltrated and 19,000 evacuated by air.[12]

THE COLD WAR YEARS

For much of the period after the end of the Second World War, and particularly during Yugoslavia's years of isolation, the country had a fortress approach to its defence planning. The overall concept was that the Yugoslav People's Army (JNA) would inflict as much damage on its assailants (whether NATO or Warsaw Pact) as possible while falling back on pre-positioned stocks of matériel. A guerrilla, or partisan, campaign would then be fought aiming to tie down as many opposing troops as possible. Most of the Yugoslav Air Force was configured to support the JNA, supplemented by a comprehensive air-defence system.

THE DISSOLUTION OF YUGOSLAVIA

A detailed account of the break-up of Yugoslavia into its constituent republics, and arguably further given that Kosovo was (is) an autonomous province is beyond the scope of this chapter.[13] Nor is it feasible to look at even the military aspects in detail.[14] Rather, the chapter will concentrate on the two major operations for which air power advocates (and its detractors[15]) have made the more extravagant claims – Operations Deliberate and Allied Force.

In the early 1990s, warfare in the Balkans was essentially Hobbesian in nature – brutal, nasty and limited in scale. Towns and villages were shelled; populations were terrorized and expelled through systematic rape and torture; atrocities were perpetrated in revenge attacks, either for recent misdeeds or in recompense for earlier affronts with retribution for Second World War actions high on the list; and the norms of civilized society were consistently placed on hold. Much of the action was conducted by paramilitary groups, special police groups or local militia. Black marketeering became endemic over the whole region with a high premium of dealing in hard currencies (US dollars, Deutsche marks and Swiss francs). Lines of command and control were deliberately blurred or concealed. Regular war-fighting was the exception rather than the norm. Territorial weapons stocks and arsenals that Tito had established for defence of the homeland were ransacked – or more often their contents were distributed to whichever ethnic group was in the majority in the local area. Those in the international community who, for example, sought evidence of clandestine Serbian military

support for the Bosnian Serbs missed the point that there were probably more caches in Bosnia-Herzegovina than in Serbia itself, as part of
Tito's military planning legacy. In these circumstances, air power was
primarily used for local reinforcement with helicopters in frequent use.
The air defence was largely dormant, albeit with odd exceptions.[16] Fast
jet operations using Galeb and Jastreb aircraft were of limited utility
with more psychological effect than military impact. James Gow points
out that there were occasional attacks on towns such as Brcko and
Gradacac, but by mid-1993 these fixed wing sorties had largely stopped
following attempts to transfer aircraft to Serbia.[17] That said, each sortie
caused uproar, frustration and indignation in various segments of the
international community (especially the United States) and with those
involved in the negotiation process.[18] Not unnaturally, the Bosnian
Muslims exploited this pressure to the full.

The relatively small scale of the air operations did not, however,
prevent an increasing clamour for the imposition of a no-fly zone over
Bosnia. This stemmed in part from a wish to level the playing field
slightly, given the imbalance of weaponry (especially artillery and
heavy mortars) between the Bosnia-Herzegovina government forces
and those of the Bosnian Serbs,[19] who had inherited much of the JNA
equipment and command structure. Some also considered that robust
implementation of the no-fly zones would show resolve on the part of
the international community. Operation Deny Flight was instigated
following the passage of UNSCR (UN Security Council Resolution)
816 on 31 March 1993, and replaced the less aggressive Operation Sky
Watch that had been monitoring the airspace. It has been suggested
that the planning process for Deliberate Force was a natural follow on
to Deny Flight, involving, as it did, essentially the same staffs.[20]

It could be argued that Deny Flight did little more than assuage
consciences that 'something was indeed being done' and that the Muslims' disadvantage under the arms embargo was being partly redressed.
It certainly did little to stem the growing international concern over
events in Bosnia. Throughout the process there was considerable tension
between what United Nations commanders, and their civilian counterparts,[21] were trying to achieve in comparison with the far more gung-ho
approach of the Americans in Italy (who did not have troops on the
ground in UNPROFOR and were therefore not quite as restrained in how
they wished to see air power utilized). There was considerable concern
that a rash NATO air attack, possibly fuelled by high-level political
frustration, could seriously endanger the lives of the peacekeepers on
the ground.[22] This resulted in the so-called 'dual-key' approach, under
which a given target had to be approved at high level in both
organizations.[23] Ambivalence in Washington over the desired end-state
versus the art of the achievable was also evident.[24] Coalition air power

was used on occasions, such as the attack on Ubdina airfield in late 1994; NATO proudly announced that this had been the largest air raid in Europe since the Second World War – while US Special Envoy Richard Holbrooke described it in horror as being closer to 'pinpricks'.[25] General Sir Michael Rose defended similar actions as being 'textbook examples of the precise use of force in a peacekeeping mission'.[26] From these two viewpoints, it is evident that perceptions are all-important.

The probability of hostage-taking was always high on the agenda and the Bosnian Serb leadership was making full use of the fault lines. The UN's worst fears were realized in May 1995 when the Bosnian Serbs took 370 (largely French) peacekeepers hostage following NATO bombing of ammunition depots at Pale. Srebrenica fell to a brutal assault in mid-July, and the clamour within the international community for 'something to be done' rose to yet another peak. NATO planning within AFSOUTH (Allied Forces South) had by this time improved to the point whereby suitable Bosnian Serb targets had been identified throughout the theatre – including 'indirect' targets such as bridges and command facilities.[27] Attacks on other safe areas and continued ethnic violence led to a gradual hardening of attitudes along with new impetus towards a political settlement. The straw that broke the camel's back was the mortar attack on a crowded market place in Sarajevo on 28 August 1995. Deliberate Force was unleashed on 30 August and continued through to 14 September 1995. NATO air units flew 3,535 sorties, and dropped over 1,100 bombs with the loss of one aircraft.[28] For presentational purposes, the NATO attacks were carried out as part of the campaign to protect the safe areas – directly and indirectly. It is obvious from reading Holbrooke, however, that any coercion of the Bosnian Serbs towards a peace settlement would be beneficial.[29] Furthermore, the air campaign was materially assisting an ongoing Croatian Army[30]/Muslim ground offensive – much to the discomfort of the Bosnian Serb Army, who found that the concentrations of tanks and artillery necessary to counter this assault made excellent targets for air power. Holbrooke suggested to Milosevic that the air campaign was not co-ordinated with the ground offensive, but later in his account admits to having advised President Tudjman of Croatia as to which towns his troops should occupy to facilitate later negotiations.[31] The marked escalation in external military involvement resulted in a new momentum for the talks process.

Reaction has varied from restrained suggestions that air power achieved far more than could have been expected,[32] through confirmation that it was '*a* decisive element' in shaping the outcome (emphasis in the original),[33] to suggestions that the air campaign had delivered the Dayton peace accord. This was unequivocally challenged by General Sir Michael Rose, who commented that: 'Tragically, NATO came to believe its own rhetoric that it was the air campaign that had delivered the Dayton Peace Accord.'[34] Similar bold statements followed success in Allied Force, with exaggerated claims over what air power had achieved.[35]

Whatever the sceptics may say about either, or both, campaigns, the reality is that air power did make a major and significant contribution. Furthermore, for many governments, air power was the only game in town. There was an unmistakable reluctance, or inability, on the part of most governments to deploy serious numbers of troops on the ground with a genuine warfighting mandate. Even those countries that were willing had serious difficulties generating the necessary numbers across the range of specializations. The difficulties involved in separating small contingents of paramilitaries from harassed civilians made planners and politicians alike blanche at the prospect. The terrain, with the inevitabilities of partisan-style guerrilla fighting again invoked the ghosts – and not a few myths -- from the German experiences of the Second World War. The role of air power in contributing towards a settlement can, by definition, only be properly understood within the political, and economic, context of the international relations prevalent at the time. Implicit within this is the difficulty of judging a Balkan morass in terms of one's own values. Cross-cultural differences can be problematic, with areas such as the importance of perceived historical injustices being particularly difficult to grasp; the converse is also true when it comes to ascribing value to potential target sets.

Before looking at the similarities between the factors at work in both operations, it is worth noting one vital characteristic – scale. Deliberate Force figures have been detailed above. For Allied Force, the air operation commenced at 1900 GMT on 24 March 1999 and continued for 78 days. Some 38,004 sorties were flown, of which 10,484 were strike missions. The UK flew 1,618 sorties of which 1,008 were strike.[36] The air campaign began with a series of strikes on air defences across Serbia and Montenegro, and against a limited number of military targets in Kosovo and elsewhere in southern Serbia. Targeting policy was under political control in NATO and nationally. Fond hopes that Milosevic would collapse immediately were quickly shown to be wrong, as his special forces and para-military units set about an ethnic-cleansing operation of unprecedented brutality.[37]

DELIBERATE FORCE AND ALLIED FORCE

Similarity One: The Political Settlement on Offer Had changed

The demise of the Socialist Federal Republic of Yugoslavia caught the Western world with no real idea how such an eventuality could happen or be dealt with. The primacy of the sovereign state that is enshrined in the United Nations Charter did not cater for federal republics attempting to exercise their 'constitutional right' to secede from the federation, especially where the original document had essentially been a 'cut-and-paste' job from Soviet equivalents in which there was never an expectancy of realization. Expediency had always been evident in Tito's politics.[38] But as his creation began to unravel, this degree of realism was sadly missing from the outlook of the European Community and the United States. It was evident, although not politically correct to admit, that Bosnia-Herzegovina, like Humpty Dumpty, was not going to be put back together. The Serbs – in Bosnia and Serbia itself – were demanding that their secession from Bosnia be recognized. This was anathema in the United States and the Vance–Owen proposals consistently met blocks – especially with the advent of a new administration in Washington (and Ambassador to the UN) in 1993.[39] By the time the process had moved on to Dayton, there had been a significant change: Carl Bildt points out that, by this stage, the US administration was at last prepared actually to recognize politically the Bosnian Serb entity.[40] This subtle change made the Dayton Accords more acceptable to Milosevic and his Bosnian Serb colleagues.

The aftermath of the Dayton agreement traumatized the ethnic Albanians – particularly as Lord Owen's consistent calls for the plight of Kosovo to be included in the settlement were ignored. Their policy of non-violence had not worked. The subsequent (but unconnected) collapse into anarchy of Albania in 1997 resulted in an almost unlimited supply of weapons becoming available, and the scope for armed insurrection suddenly widened. The mounting frustration, along with a massive influx of light weaponry, resulted in the Kosovo Liberation Army (KLA) growing from a minor bunch of disillusioned expatriates into a serious threat to the Serbian authorities. The cycle of violence expanded with the inevitable counter-offensives through 1998. The spectre of massacres, ethnic cleansing and other atrocities prompted the international community into the Rambouillet talks process (6–23 February 1999).[41] Milosevic could not accept the terms on offer. Having come to, and maintained, power on the basis of rabid nationalism, he could not back down without some semblance of a fight. There was a clear risk of secession, and the detail of the agreement contained, from Belgrade's perspective, serious erosions of Serbia's sovereignty.[42] Acceptance would have been political suicide for Milosevic – not a trait for which he is renowned. Some of the specific terms, including those that allowed NATO untrammelled access through the whole of Serbia, were removed in June 1999, again allowing Milosevic at least to save face. The continuity between Deliberate and Allied Force is emphasized by the key factor in the political and diplomatic negotiation process, which was that the *dramatis personae* were largely the same for both – the personalities were known, as were weaknesses and inter-personal relation-ships. The remaining variable was domestic politics.

Similarity Two: The Russian Factor

Milosevic must have hoped, in both cases, that Russia would not tolerate an open attack on a fellow Slav sovereign state and would have anticipated a veto on Chapter VII action in the UN Security Council. Furthermore, he almost certainly hoped for matériel assistance, none of which appears to have been forthcoming (debate continues as to what, if any, intelligence support was given). In the event, Russia was not able to give little more than popular support – the forces of international economics proving stronger than pan-Slav nationalism. In reality, Russia was largely integrated into the political process during Dayton,[43] and could not afford to be marginalized during the Kosovo conflict.

Similarity Three: NATO and International Resolve

Up to 1995, the international community had given Milosevic every reason to believe that they would continue to dither indefinitely. How-ever, bombing during Deliberate Force showed that, once across the Rubicon, there was little likelihood of relief. The venue for the talks – Dayton, Ohio – was actually Wright-Paterson Air Force Base. The delegates arriving from the Balkans by air had to walk past ramps laden with operational aircraft, leaving the Serbs in no doubt as to the scale of air resources available to a US-led coalition. Richard Holbrooke tells of Milosevic's reaction to sitting under the wing of a B-2 bomber, and next to a Tomahawk missile, at a formal dinner in the USAF Museum.[44] He cannot have hoped for an early remission. By 1999, Milosevic was again gambling on lack of cohesion within NATO and a fundamental unwillingness to breach the sanctity of sovereign borders. In the event, Milosevic miscalculated. The West was quite clear that military action was justified as an exceptional measure to prevent an overwhelming humanitarian catastrophe.[45] Furthermore, after 78 days, there were few signs of NATO amending its demands or cohesion failing. It was a one-sided war of attrition and he was losing – despite the occasional unhelpful comment in the specialist press.[46]

Similarity Four: Air–Land Linkage

The Deliberate Force air campaign was materially assisting an ongoing Croatian Army[47]/Muslim ground offensive – much to the discomfort of the Bosnian Serb Army, who found that the concentrations of tanks and artillery necessary to counter this assault made excellent targets for air power. Despite Holbrooke's denials that the air campaign was not coordinated with the ground offensive, the marked escalation in external military involvement resulted in a new momentum for the talks process. As with the situation leading up to Dayton, Milosevic must have been concerned that NATO air power was at least being taken advantage of by the KLA.[48] Serbian military responses to KLA action brought troops and equipment out into the open for long enough for the NATO targeting cycle to respond. The scale of these operations was clearly different. But despite denials at the time, Milosevic will have been convinced that the United States was supporting the Bosnian Muslims with illegal arms supplies and probably surmised that the same would be true with the KLA.[49] Perceptions are often more important in the Balkans than reality.

Similarity Five: The West Bogged Down – Again

After Dayton, Milosevic had seen the West reluctantly commit sizeable numbers of troops to Bosnia, and he would have realized that this would inevitably be a long-term commitment. The same was true for Kosovo and – in best bridge-playing style of losing losers early – may have concluded that the international community would be even less willing to become involved 'the next time' (Macedonia or Montenegro).

Similarity Six: Milosevic's Centre of Gravity

After Dayton, Milosevic remained in power with Bosnia-Herzegovina divided into *de facto* ethnic areas as a direct result of the process. His political centre of gravity was largely intact. But the 78 days of the Allied Force air operations had ground down the Serbian economy and his real centre of gravity – his hold on power – was under real threat. He was probably unsettled by his indictment as a war criminal, not least because it left him, and his cronies, with neither an escape route to comfortable exile, nor access to their ill-gotten gains in frozen bank accounts. In the past, Milosevic had adeptly manipulated sanctions regimes and hyperinflation by allowing his cronies to profit from the constrictions in supply and demand. These had almost invariably worked in hard currencies, with black marketeers making huge profits on both the transaction and the rate of exchange. Ironically, in previous 'hard times', Kosovo, with its remunerations from the diaspora, had been a fertile source of Deutsche marks and Swiss francs. The continuing air campaign almost certainly was squeezing the Serbian economy to the point at which there were few profits to be made. Support from corrupt businessmen could only be taken for granted when they had something to gain; if Milosevic could not maintain the momentum of the gravy train, his erstwhile cronies could easily turn against him. This eventually saw the erosion of his support base and removal not only from power, but also to the Hague to face war crimes charges. His erstwhile cronies will doubtless turn and give evidence against him, hoping to benefit from international rebuilding aid packages and immunity from prosecution.

THE BALKANS AND THE CORE CAPABILITIES OF AIR POWER

The allusion to contemporary air power doctrine as enshrined in the third edition of AP3000 *British Air Power Doctrine*[50] invites a brief analytic comparison of air power used in the Second World War situation, and in Deliberate and Allied Force, measured against the modern core capabilities. The *Luftwaffe*, under direct orders from Hitler in War Directive No. 25, clearly attempted to use *air power for strategic effect* against Belgrade, where it was highly effective in bringing the unruly regime to heel. The inevitable difference was that the *Luftwaffe* were allowed free rein to obliterate Belgrade with overwhelming force. There was no specific attempt to target certain aspects of the regime, or its centre of gravity with any pretence of precision. The savagery of the attacks, with the certain knowledge that the German Army would follow on, must have had a clear impact on the decision-makers in Belgrade. This will have been exacerbated by the sure knowledge that factions within the country were ready to form puppet regimes in support of the Nazis. The use of air power for strategic effect therefore combined with the joint campaign under the influence of international politics.

At first sight, the targets selected for attack during Deliberate Force do not appear to be likely to have strategic effect; many were of a straightforward tactical nature. But successful attack of even tactical targets can have strategic effect when combined as part of a joint campaign in furtherance of international goals. The Serbs, and their brethren in Bosnia, were faced with a significant step change in international resolve. Their ground forces were under severe pressure from the Croatian Army (not just the Bosnian Croat forces) and they were losing much of the territory that they were ultimately prepared to cede at the negotiating table. Operation Deliberate Force was therefore a critical factor in the overall achievement of strategic effect. Likewise, in Allied Force, it could be argued that the cumulative effect of 78 days of air strikes had ground the Serbian economy down to the point that Milosevic had lost the vital support necessary to maintain his regime. International politics, and the lack of Russian support as a significant negative factor, played its own role. Despite the attempts to generate a significant ground threat, the absence of a comprehensive joint campaign from the outset almost certainly lengthened the whole campaign. At no stage is it suggested that air power 'did it alone': but it is certainly proposed that it was, at the very least, a vital factor in achieving success.

That *control of the air* was of vital concern to the *Luftwaffe* is evident from War Directive No. 25 and was obviously also high on Tito's list of priorities. The seamless transition from Deny Flight into Deliberate Force shows that the coalition understood the need for air superiority. In Allied Force, this control of the air had to be actively fought for, won and then constantly maintained. There was no question of the Yugoslav Air Force having ceded their airspace. Arguably, the need to operate above 15,000 feet suggests that the coalition had only achieved limited airspace control. The important factor is that sufficient control was attained for coalition operations to achieve their objectives.

It is evident that indirect and direct air operations played key roles in all of the operations discussed here. Direct air operations were again used by both sides in support of fielded forces and in the maritime environment. In the Second World War, the RAF used indirect air operations extensively against targets such as marshalling yards, troop concentrations and logistics areas. The coalitions in Deliberate and Allied Force used very similar target priorities. The reality that even very small numbers of guerrillas (or special forces) can force an enemy to concentrate its troops sufficiently to generate worthwhile air power targets should not be underestimated. This can be done as a pre-planned operation, or on an opportunity basis when collection platforms detect concentrations of forces.

Reconnaissance was vital throughout – particularly given the inaccessibility of the terrain, the nature of the troops deployed and the type of warfare. Air commanders in Deny Flight onwards relied heavily on AWACS (airborne warning and control system) support, and all forms of surveillance were utilized.

Finally, combat support air operations played a significant role in assisting the Partisans to combat the German divisions. Throughout the 1990s, these operations were constantly undertaken with special forces insertion an immediate similarity to 1941–45. The role of transport aircraft in delivering relief supplies and evacuating casualties was again evident throughout the period (the media made much of the evacuation of 'baby Irma' from Sarajevo, but this type of operation was conducted regularly). From the instigation of the 'air bridge' by President Mitterand in June 1992, this form of supply was of vital importance to Sarajevo; during the first five months of 1993, 16,235 tonnes of aid were flown in – more than reached the city by land convoy.[51]

CONCLUSION

It can be seen from this brief look at three major periods of air power employment in the Balkans that the core capabilities of air power have each had considerable utility. These have been most successful when they have been part of a truly joint campaign conducted in furtherance of achievable political aims. Air power cannot be seen as a panacea to the cries that something must be done. Nor should it be expected to 'do it alone'. This leads to the question of the 'basket case'. Hitler's anger over having to deal with Balkan temperament, politics, personalities and perversity provides much of the answer. Leaders during the Cold War suffered similar frustrations with the isolation of Tito's regime an ideal compromise. Richard Holbrooke, Lord Owen and Cyrus Vance are but a few of those who have wrestled with the sheer perversity of the region, the difficulties in coping with what seem to be irreconcilable viewpoints and the infinite range of interpretations that can be wrought from history. The scope for all sections of society to harbour perceived historical injustices, while living for two generations cheek by jowl, and then to allow them to surface with unfathomable ferocity is almost beyond belief. In short, it is the Balkans that are the basket case – not air power.

NOTES

1. Luftwaffe War Directive No. 25. Fuehrer Headquarters reference OKW/WFSt/ Abt.L (I Op) Nr 44379/41 gk Chefs dated 27 March 1941, classified as 'Top Secret' and signed by Hitler. (Translation held by author). For an Allied appreciation of the weather factor – unfortunately not replicated later in the century – see *The History of the Balkan Air Force*, HQ BAF, July 1945, p. 89.
2. Cited in 'What the World's Politicians Say', *Guardian*, 26 March 1999, p. 2.
3. Reported in Greg Seigle, 'USA Claims France Hindered Raids', *Jane's Defence Weekly*, 27 October 1999, p. 3.
4. Williamson Murray, *Strategy for Defeat: The Luftwaffe 1933–1945* (Air University Press, Maxwell AFB, AL, 1983), p. 75.
5. Murray, *Strategy for Defeat*, pp. 75 and 76.
6. David Irving, *The Rise and Fall of the Luftwaffe* (Kimber, London, 1963), p. 118.
7. See the discussion in Dudley Saward, *'Bomber' Harris* (Sphere Books, London, 1985), p. 392. In his book *The Destruction of Dresden*, Irving initially estimated the death toll as being between 35,000 and 220,000. In a letter to *The Times* on 7 July 1966, he revised these figure downwards to 18,375. These figures, and the controversy over them, fade into insignificance in comparison with the continuing acrimonious debate over the numbers killed in the internecine warfare. The Serbs estimate that 750,000 of their kin were killed by the Croatian *Ustase* (independent state of Croatia set up by Hitler); the Germans put the equivalent figure at 350,000. See Fred Singleton, *A Short History of the Yugoslav Peoples* (Cambridge University Press, Cambridge, 1985), p. 178.
8. RAF Official History – Denis Richards, *The Royal Air Force 1939–1945, Volume I,*

The Fight at Odds (HMSO, London, 1953), p. 292.

9. Ibid, p. 295.

10. Much was subsequently made of the scale of Axis forces deployed in Yugoslavia – especially when ground options for Kosovo were under consideration. The reality was that many of the divisions were seriously under strength. Furthermore, their role was not to occupy every square kilometre of Yugoslavia, but to keep open lines of communication through to Greece.

11. RAF Official History – Hilary St George Saunders, *The Royal Air Force 1939–1945, Volume III, The Fight is Won*, p. 234ff.

12. Ibid, p. 183.

13. The literature on the Balkans conflict has expanded considerably. Before the outbreak of hostilities, Singleton was one of few reliable sources and remains good value. See also Misha Glenny, *The Balkans, 1804–1999, Nationalism, War, and the Great Powers* (Granta, London, 1999); James Gow, *Triumph of the Lack of Will: International Diplomacy and the Yugoslav War* (Columbia University Press, New York, 1997). The early paucity of material led to some embarrassing incidents, with recommended reading often including blatant apologia for one side or another.

14. For an American view of Deliberate Force, see Colonel Robert C. Owen, *Deliberate Force: A Case Study in Effective Air Campaigning* (Air University Press, Maxwell AFB, AL, 2000).

15. John Keegan, 'So the Bomber Got Through to Milosevic After All', *Daily Telegraph*, 4 June 1999, p. 28. See also John Keegan, 'Yes, We Won this War: Let's Be Proud of It'. *Daily Telegraph*, 24 June 1999, p. 26. Contrast this with General Sir Michael Rose, 'Peacekeepers Fight a Better War than Bombers', *Sunday Times*, 20 June 1999, p. 26.

16. An exception was the use of Yugoslav Mig fighters, which intercepted, and turned back, Croatian special-forces helicopters in the Knin area in March 1991; see Karl Mueller, 'The Demise of Yugoslavia and the Destruction of Bosnia: Strategic Causes, Effects, and Responses', in Owen (ed.), *Deliberate Force*, p. 9.

17. Gow, *Triumph of Lack of Will*, pp. 132, 133.

18. See David Owen, *Balkan Odyssey* (Indigo, London, 1996), pp. 58–9.

19. Ibid, p. 54.

20. Colonel Robert C. Owen USAF, 'The Balkans Air Campaign Study', published in two parts in the *Airpower Journal*, Summer and Fall, 1997, pp. 11 and 13.

21. See Thomas Quiggin, 'Do Airstrikes Amount to an Effective Policy?', *RUSI Journal*, April/May 1999, p. 16. Quiggin was a staff officer with Mr Akashi, the UN Special Representative to the Secretary-General.

22. Richard Holbrooke, *To End a War* (New York, The Modern Library 1998), p. 63.

23. See, for example, General Sir Michael Rose, *Fighting for Peace* (London: Harvill 1998), p. 160.

24. See almost the whole of Owen, *Balkan Odyssey* and Richard Holbrooke, *To End a War* (New York: The Modern Library 1998), pp. 26–7.

25. Holbrooke, *To End a War*, p. 61.

26. Rose, *Fighting for Peace*, p. 161.

27. Owen, 'The Balkans Air Campaign Study', p. 20.

28. Lt-Col Mark J. Conversino, 'Executing Deliberate Force, 30 August–14 September 1995', in Owen (ed.), *Deliberate Force*, p. 131ff.

29. Holbrooke, *To End a War*, pp. 145–50.

30. Quiggin, 'Do Airstrikes Amount to an Effective Policy?, p. 17, is quite specific over the involvement of regular Croatian Army troops.

31. Holbrooke, *To End a War*, pp. 147 and 160.

32. Conversino, 'Executing Deliberate Force', p. 168.
33. Lieutenant-General Jay W. Kelley USAF, Preface to Owen (ed.), *Deliberate Force*, p. xii.
34. General Sir Michael Rose, in 'Lessons from Kosovo', *RUSI World Defence Systems 2000*, p. 1:8.
35. See, for the catchy title at least, Rebecca Grant, *The Kosovo Campaign: Aerospace Power Made it Work*, An Air Force Association Special Report, Arlington, VA, 1999.
36. Details taken from www.mod.uk/news/kosovo/account/nato.htm on 11 October 1999.
37. See, for example, Sue Cameron, 'Top Brass Brassed Off', *Spectator*, 17 April 1999, p. 14.
38. For a blow-by-blow account see the unpublished MPhil. thesis by the author: 'The Impact of the Dissolution of Yugoslavia on the International Law of Self-Determination', University of Cambridge, 1995.
39. Owen, *Balkan Odyssey*, p. 108.
40. Carl Bildt, 'Holbrooke's History', Review Essay, *Survival*, Vol. 40, No. 3, Autumn (1998), p. 187.
41. For a detailed discussion on the international legal aspects of these talks, see Marc Weller, 'The Rambouillet Conference on Kosovo', *International Affairs*, 75, 2 (1999), pp. 211–51. Weller has acted as counsel to the Bosnian Muslims and the Kosovo Albanians.
42. See John Pilger, 'Revealed: The Amazing NATO Plan, Tabled at Rambouillet, to Occupy Yugoslavia', *New Statesman*, 17 May 1999. Pilger contended that a full copy of the plan had been published in France but had been suppressed in the UK. His objection was that it allowed NATO unbridled access to any part of Yugoslavia and was therefore an excessive infringement of sovereignty.
43. Pauline Neville-Jones, 'Bosnia after IFOR', *Survival*, Vol. 38, No. 4, Winter (1996–97), pp. 45–65. This essay gives a UK perspective on the process to balance Holbrooke's somewhat Washington-centric view.
44. Holbrooke, *To End a War*, pp. 231, 244 and 245.
45. See the MOD justification on www.mod.uk/dicmt/kosovo/legal.htm. See also Catherine Guicherd, 'International Law and the War in Kosovo', *Survival*, Vol. 41, No. 2 (Summer 1999), pp. 19–34. AP3000 (see n.50 below) states correctly, on p. 1.1.10, that legal opinion is divided over this issue. In a less extreme case than Kosovo, intervention may be more hotly debated.
46. Greg Sample, 'US Cruise Missile Stocks Dwindling', *Jane's Defence Weekly*, 7 April 1999, p. 3.
47. Quiggin, 'Do Airstrikes Amount to an Effective Policy?', p. 17, is quite specific over the involvement of regular Croatian Army troops.
48. Bryan Bender, 'KLA Action Fuelled NATO Victory', *JDW*, 16 June 1999, p. 5.
49. Owen, *Balkan Odyssey*, p. 391.
50. AP3000, *British Air Power Doctrine*, HMSO, London, 1999.
51. See Gow, *Triumph of the Lack of Will*, p. 131.

Notes on Contributors

Tami Davis Biddle teaches diplomatic and military history at Duke University, NC, and is a core faculty member of the Duke–UNC Joint Program in Military History. She is the author of a number of scholarly articles on air power history, most recently 'Bombing by the Square Yard: Sir Arthur Harris at War, 1942–1945' in the September 1999 *International History Review*. She has also written articles on US foreign policy, and the history of the Cold War, including 'Handling the Soviet Threat: "Project Control" and the Debate on American Strategy in the Early Cold War Years', *Journal of Strategic Studies*, September 1989. Her book *Rhetoric and Reality in Air Warfare: The Evolution of British and American Ideas about Strategic Bombing, 1914–1945* was published in February 2002. She received her PhD in History from Yale, where she studied under Paul Kennedy and Gaddis Smith. She has held Harvard-MacArthur and SSRC-MacArthur fellowships, and was a fellow of the Smithsonian Institution. This year she is the Harold K. Johnson Visiting Professor of Military History at the US Army's Military History Institute.

John Buckley is Senior Lecturer in the Department of History and War Studies at the University of Wolverhampton. He has written widely on a variety of military-history topics, but particularly air power. He is the author of *The RAF and Trade Defence 1919–1945: Constant Endeavour* (1995) and *Air Power in the Age of Total War* (1999).

Mark Clodfelter is a Professor of Military History at the National War College in Washington, DC. A former Air Force officer, he served as a radar officer in South Carolina and Korea before beginning a career devoted largely to teaching. He twice taught history at the US Air Force Academy, and ultimately served as the Academy's director of military history. From 1991 to 1994, he taught at Air University's School of Advanced Airpower Studies (SAAS) as a Professor of Airpower History. He next became Professor of Aerospace Studies and Commander of the Air Force ROTC detachment at the University of North Carolina, where he also served as an adjunct professor of history. He began teaching at the National War College in 1997. He is the author of *The Limits of Air Power: The American Bombing of North Vietnam*, which the former Air Force Chief of Staff selected for his intermediate reading list.

James Corum graduated from Gonzaga University in 1975 with a BA in German and History, having passed the German University Sprachzertifikatprufung at Heidelburg University in the same year. He then attained an MA in History, from Brown University in 1976, and M.Litt in History from Oxford University in 1984, before completing his PhD in History at Queen's University, Canada, in 1990. A specialist in air power and military history, he taught history at Queen's University, Canada before taking up his post as Professor of Comparative Military Studies at the USAF School of Advanced Airpower Studies, Maxwell Air Force Base, Alabama in 1991. He has written numerous books and articles on the *Luftwaffe*, including: *The Roots of Blitzkrieg: Hans von Seeckt and German Military Reform* (1992); *The Luftwaffe: Creating the Operational Air War 1918–1940* (1997); and, with Richard Muller, *The Luftwaffe's Way of War* (1998). He spent six years on active duty as a US Army Officer (Intelligence Corps) and is a graduate of the US Army Command and General Staff course at Fort Leavenworth and the Air War College. Currently, he is a lieutenant colonel in the US Army Reserve.

Sebastian Cox graduated from the University of Warwick in 1977 with a BA in History, and from King's College London in 1979 with an MA in War Studies. He served in various posts at the Royal Air Force Museum, Hendon, and the Air Historical Branch (RAF), before assuming his current post as Head of Air Historical Branch and Chief Historian of the Royal Air Force in 1996. He has written widely on air power history and related topics, and currently edits two book series on air power subjects – Cass Studies in Air Power Series and the Whitehall History Group's RAF Official Histories. He serves on the editorial board of the *Royal Air Force Air Power Review* and the new *Defence Studies Journal*, and has lectured widely on air power history to Staff Colleges and military and academic audiences in the USA, Canada, New Zealand, Germany, France, and the Czech Republic.

Peter Dye attended Sevenoaks School and Imperial College of Science and Technology. He graduated from Royal Air Force College Cranwell in 1976 and has subsequently served in a wide variety of aircraft-related appointments including maintenance duties on the Victor, Vulcan, Canberra, Tornado and Jaguar. He was awarded the OBE for his work at Royal Air Force Coltishall during the Gulf War. He served as the

Personal Staff Officer to successive commanders-in-chief at Logistics Command before attending the Royal College of Defence Studies and the Higher Command and Staff Course. For the past two years he has been Chief of Operations and Deputy Chief Executive of the Defence Aviation and Repair Agency at Royal Air Force St Athan. He was the inaugural Slessor Fellow engaged in a study of the aviation aspects of the European Rapid Reaction Force under the auspices of the Centre for Defence Studies, King's College London. He is a regular contributor to the *RAF Air Power Review* and the *USAF Journal of Logistics*.

John Ferris received his PhD from King's College, London, and currently lectures in the Department of History at the University of Calgary. He is the author of: *Men, Money and Diplomacy: The Evolution of British Strategic Policy, 1919–1926* (1989); *The British Army and Signals Intelligence During the First World War* (1992); and of 40 published articles/chapters on British strategy, operations, diplomacy and intelligence

Brad Gladman was a pilot in the Canadian Armed Forces, as well as flight crew for two international charter airlines before embarking upon graduate school. He has recently completed his PhD at University College London under the supervision of David French, and is currently teaching military history at the University of Calgary.

Christina Goulter is a Senior Lecturer at King's College, University of London. She is head of Air Power Academic Studies at the Joint Services Command and Staff College. Between 1994 and 1997, she was Associate Professor of Strategy at the US Naval War College, Newport, Rhode Island. Her publications include: *A Forgotten Offensive: Royal Air Force Coastal Command's Anti-Shipping Campaign, 1940–1945*, and numerous articles on air power in the Second World War, maritime aviation, and intelligence, including a study of the Special Operations Executive. Her next book is on British strategy and economic warfare in the Second World War.

Peter Gray is Director of Defence Studies for the Royal Air Force. He has served operationally as an F4 Phantom navigator and, most recently, commanded 101 Squadron flying VC10K aircraft in the air-to-air refuelling role. Gray has also served as an analyst in the Cabinet Office and on the Central Staff of the Ministry of Defence. He is a graduate of the Joint Services Defence College and the Higher Command and Staff Course. Gray holds degrees from the Universities of Dundee (BSc.), London (LLB) and Cambridge (MPhil.). He edited *Air Power 21 – Challenges for the New Century* and has also published articles on air power in a wide range of journals.

Richard P. Hallion is the United States Air Force historian, and is responsible for directing its worldwide Air Force historical and museum programmes. He graduated with a BA in 1970, and a PhD in aviation history in 1975, both from the University of Maryland, College Park, and has extensive experience in museum development, historical research and management analysis. He served as a consultant to various professional organizations prior to assuming his current role in 1991. He teaches and lectures widely, is the author of more than 15 books relating to aerospace history and has received numerous awards for his writing.

Ian MacFarling joined the RAAF in March 1977 after serving as a navigator for 12 years in the Royal New Zealand Air Force (RNZAF). In the RAAF he flew as a tactical coordinator on P3B Orions, and his last flying duties were at RAAF's Aircraft Research & Development Unit. He has since served in a variety of RAAF defence and academic posts centred on the staff studies, politics and technology, and is currently the Director of the RAAF Aerospace Centre in Canberra where he is responsible for the production of strategic-level air and aerospace-power doctrine, supervision of the education of both RAAF and foreign fellows, and education in air power history and theory. He also participates regularly as the interpreter in bilateral Ministerial-level meetings between Australia and Indonesia. He was educated at Massey University in New Zealand, the University of Queensland, the Royal Melbourne Institute of Technology, and the University of New South Wales. His doctorate is in political science with a specific focus on civil–military relations in Indonesia. He is also a graduate of the RAAF School of Languages, the Indonesian Air Force Command and Staff College, the Asia Pacific Center for Security Studies in Honolulu, and the Royal Military College of Science, Shrivenham, England.

John Andreas Olsen entered the Royal Norwegian Air Force in 1987, and spent the period between 1989 and 1992 at CRC Sørreisa as a radar technician. Over the next three years he took an engineering degree in electronics in Trondheim and a masters degree in modern British politics at University of Warwick. He next served at the Material Command outside Oslo as a project officer between 1995 and 1997, whereupon he was given the opportunity to go to England to study for a Ph.D. He stayed at De Montfort University in Leicester for a period of 2½ years, where he completed his doctorate titled *Operation Desert Storm: An Examination of the Strategic Air Campaign*. He has recently completed the Royal Norwegian Air Force Staff College in Oslo and has for the last year or so been tutoring at the Royal Norwegian Air Force Academy in Trondheim. He is currently working on two books on the Gulf War.

Richard Overy was educated at the University of Cambridge. Professor of Modern History, King's College, London since 1992, Professor Overy is the author of 16 books, including: *The Air War 1939–1945*; *Goering: The Iron Man*; *Bomber Command 1939–1945*; *Why the Allies Won*; *Russia's War*; and *The Battle*. His most recent book is entitled *Interrogations: The Nazi Elite in Allied Hands 1945*. A Trustee of the RAF Museum, he is the winner of the Samuel Eliot Morison Prize of the Society of Military History, 2001, a Fellow of the Royal Historical Society and a Fellow of the British Academy.

Stuart Peach joined the Royal Air Force in 1977. A graduate of the universities of Sheffield and Cambridge, the Royal Air Force Staff College and the UK Higher Command and Staff Course and has lectured and written widely on air power and related subjects. He is the author of the current edition of AP3000, British Air Power Doctrine. He was Director of Defence Studies (Royal Air Force) from 1997 to 1999, the creator and first Managing Chairman of the Royal Air Force Air Power Review and editor of Perspectives on Air Power. He has completed six operational tours, four in the Middle East and two in the Balkans and has held operational command appointments in every RAF rank from Flight-Lieutenant to Air Commodore. He is a qualified weapons instructor and electronic warfare instructor and has 20 years fast jet-flying experience with a total of 2,750 flying hours. At the time of publication, he is serving as Commandant Air Warfare Centre, Air Officer for Doctrine and Collective Training, Headquarters Strike Command and UK Director of the Defence Electronic Warfare Centre, RAF Waddington.

Diane Putney is a historian with the Historical Office of the Office of the Secretary of Defense. From 1982 to 1983 she worked for the US Air Force and was assigned to the Military Airlift Command as the historian for the 1100th Air Base Wing at Bolling AFB. From 1983 to 1989, she served as the historian for the Office of the Assistant Chief of Staff, Intelligence and the Air Force Intelligence Agency. She next assumed responsibilities as the Assistant Deputy Chief Historian for Readiness and Field Programs, Office of the Air Force Historian. From 1992 until 2000 she was a historian with the Air Force History Support Office. Her doctorate degree in history is from Marquette University in Milwaukee, Wisconsin. She has written articles and book reviews, edited the book, *ULTRA and the Army Air Forces in World War II*, and wrote the volume currently undergoing policy review in the Pentagon, *Airpower Advantage: Planning the Gulf War Air Campaign*.

Sebastian Ritchie received his PhD from King's College, London, and subsequently held a lectureship in History at the University of Manchester. In 1996 he joined the Air Historical Branch (RAF) of the Ministry of Defence as an historian, with responsibility for preparing official narratives on recent RAF operations. He is the author of *Industry and Air Power: The Expansion of British Aircraft Production, 1935–1941* and of a number of scholarly articles on the RAF's inter-war and post-war history.

James Sterret graduated with a BA (History) from Haverford College and an MA ('Soviet South-Western Front Operations, June– September 1941') from the University of Calgary. He is currently working on a PhD at King's College London on Soviet Air Force theory from 1918 to 1945. He has worked as a teaching assistant at the University of Glasgow and has published an article in the *War Studies Journal* (on the trial of Admiral Keppel) and a review of David Glantz's *Kharkov 1942* in the 8 (3) 2001 issue of *War in History*; he presented a shorter version of this paper at the 2001 Society for Military History conference in Calgary.

Index